PUBLICATIONS OF RUSSELL SAGE FOUNDATION

Russell Sage Foundation was established in 1907 by Mrs. Russell Sage for the improvement of social and living conditions in the United States. In carrying out its purpose the Foundation conducts research under the direction of members of the staff or in close collaboration with other institutions, and supports programs designed to develop and demonstrate productive working relations between social scientists and other professional groups. As an integral part of its operations, the Foundation from time to time publishes books or pamphlets resulting from these activities. Publication under the imprint of the Foundation does not necessarily imply agreement by the Foundation, its Trustees, or its staff with the interpretations or conclusions of the authors.

GIRLS AT VOCATIONAL HIGH

AN EXPERIMENT IN SOCIAL WORK INTERVENTION

HENRY J. MEYER
EDGAR F. BORGATTA
WYATT C. JONES

In Collaboration With
ELIZABETH P. ANDERSON
HANNA GRUNWALD
DOROTHY HEADLEY

RUSSELL SAGE FOUNDATION
NEW YORK • 1965

© 1965
RUSSELL SAGE FOUNDATION
Printed in the United States
of America

*Library of Congress
Catalog Card Number: 65-16221*

WM. F. FELL CO., PRINTERS
PHILADELPHIA, PA.

Foreword

Is SOCIAL WORK on the wrong track?

This impolite question is neither asked nor answered in this book. The aim of the study reported here was much more modest and practical perhaps, namely, to determine: (1) whether or not potentially problematic subjects can be identified and involved in preventive programs before they present problems, and (2) the extent to which social casework is effective in prevention when applied to subjects so identified and so involved. But in answering their own questions, and they do this extremely well, the authors unavoidably raise the larger question.

Evaluation is a hazardous undertaking for all concerned. It is full of pitfalls for those who design and conduct the research. The institution or profession whose concepts and procedures are being tested risk the discovery of embarrassing discrepancies between claims and accomplishments. Not to be forgotten are the uncertainties confronting those who would interpret findings and draw implications for future policy and courses of action.

But if the risks are great, so are the rewards. Indeed it can be said that in any evaluation, negative findings may be just as important as and sometimes even more important than positive results. It may well be that the latter is true in the present instance.

In any case the study gave clear answers to the questions to which it was addressed. It is possible to identify potentially problematic adolescent girls and to involve them in relationships and activities that were designed to prevent their developing problematic behavior. The impact of the preventive effort, if any, was minor.

3

These results themselves make the study fully worth the investment of funds and painstaking effort. If nothing else, the findings will cause many to reexamine their assumptions, expectations, and requirements concerning activities variously designated as school social work, school psychology, counseling, and the like. But beyond this are products that make the project an especially valuable one.

In the first place, the effort to test the preventive effectiveness of casework technique led the agency to the discovery that a different technique was more effective at least for involving adolescent girls in the activities aimed at prevention. This technique may well be an important instrument for general therapeutic social work, also.

Second, the requirements of evaluative design revealed how extremely difficult it is to develop explicit descriptions of the complex processes that take place in casework. This finding will undoubtedly stimulate systematic and intensive efforts to make these processes more explicit and to relate them to practice theory.

Third, the study made clear the need both in social work and in social science for conceptualizations relevant to the processes and products of social interaction in types of situations dealt with in this project. Evaluative studies in social work, no matter how meticulously designed and executed, will continue to yield findings of very limited generalizability until more adequate hypotheses are articulated. More persistent and systematic collaboration of social work and social science theorists should emerge from such enterprises as the one here reported.

It is quite possible that the most important contribution of this study is its posing in a very concrete way the question stated at the beginning of this Foreword. Put in other words, the issue is whether or not the social work profession can continue to maintain that the individual casework, clinical approach is its central method for dealing with the kinds of problems presented by the population dealt with in this experiment. Without in the least denigrating the value and importance of clinical and casework approaches in appropriate settings, it is nevertheless proper to suggest that the profession must move rapidly to develop new technologies and skills for the diagnosis and management of environments in order to keep up with the growing demands for help in dealing with the massive problems of control and prevention of destructively deviant behavior.

A significant test of the value of a research project is the agenda it yields for further productive effort. By this test, the project here reported has more than paid its way.

LEONARD S. COTTRELL, JR.

January, 1965

Acknowledgments

THE NATURE of this project necessitated the close cooperation of a rather large group of collaborators representing a wide range of disciplines. Wellman J. Warner, Department of Sociology and Anthropology, New York University, introduced a research team from his department to Youth Consultation Service. The early phases of cooperative research were supported over a number of years by grants from the Vincent Astor Foundation. On the basis of a successful collaboration, the proposal for this project was presented to Russell Sage Foundation with a request for research funds and to The Grant Foundation with a request for support of the expanded service program required of Youth Consultation Service. We are grateful to these foundations for their generous support, both moral and financial. We are especially indebted to Donald Young, Leonard S. Cottrell, Jr., and Orville G. Brim, Jr., of Russell Sage Foundation, and to John G. Byler and Adele W. Morrison of The Grant Foundation.

We are pleased to give our warmest thanks to Youth Consultation Service. Our special appreciation is due Margaret Hoag, former director, whose prescience in the beginning and persistence in the end saw the project through to completion. The debt to our active collaborators, Elizabeth P. Anderson, director of casework services and now successor to Mrs. Hoag as director of the agency; Dorothy Headley, senior group therapist; and Hanna Grunwald, group therapy consultant, is everywhere evident in this report. In addition, we should like to thank the entire YCS staff who gave of themselves as well as their time and professional skills to the project. The supervisors were Helen Olson, Phoebe Rich, Mary Richards, and Adeline Strongin. The

7

caseworkers were Erline Collins, Grace Ford, Beatrice Hartley, Ida Lenihan, Caroline Oram, and Marilyn Voight. The group therapists, in addition to Miss Headley, were Evelyn Irby, Marianne Lothar, Greta Meyer, Nilde Molinary, Jean Rinaldi, Phyllis Slaughter, Mary W. Van Hyning, and two students, Suzanne Coral and Suzanne Salter. The casework consultants were William H. Cox, Morton S. Eisenberg, and Bernard Berkowitz. The group therapy program began under the direction of S. R. Slavson, consultant, and continued under Dr. Grunwald. The psychologist was Juliette C. Diller. The agency secretary and clerk, Madeline Carmichael, also served in the very special role of meeting the new referrals and introducing them to YCS. Mrs. Robert Winternitz, above and beyond the usual duties of an agency volunteer, served to interpret YCS to the project school personnel at all levels.

The Board of Education of the City of New York approved the research proposal and authorized cooperation of school personnel in the project. We wish to thank Nathan Brown, principal of the high school and now an assistant superintendent, not only for his help in initiating the project, but also for his sponsorship throughout. Leonore R. Miller, assistant principal of the high school, was the pivot about which the entire project turned. Her interest and enthusiasm, her skill and insight made the crucial difference between success and failure of the operating program. It was she who saw to it that the numerous impediments were overcome. The guidance she gave the girls to facilitate the service program was no more important to the success of the operation than the guidance she gave to the research operations and to the research staff members. The entire faculty and staff of the school accepted the demands of the experiment and contributed at many points to its successful operation. We would like especially to thank Theresa Fanelli, dean of girls; Mary Fuerst, chairman of the trade department; Murray Philips, admissions counselor; and Virginia Eckenrode, attendance teacher. The guidance counselors were the most important link between the agency and the school; we want especially to thank Pauline Bockian, Evelyn Chasan, Milton Dickman, Sophie Leiberman, and Esther

Schlanger. The availability of reports and records was crucial to the research program; we are indebted to Arthur Kaufman, assistant principal, and to Alice Metchik Gottlieb and Belle Binin for their help. Cleo Wassey and Sylvia Jaffee were helpful in ways that only secretaries to administrators can be. The school health staff were also very cooperative; we wish to thank Renée Imberman, school physician; Grace Lewis, school nurse; and Victoria Thumser, health counselor. The classroom teachers who suffered the frequent interruptions occasioned by our tests and the harassment of our numerous questions have also earned our warmest thanks.

The research staff itself, while small, was hard-working and loyal. We enjoyed a succession of research assistants—Nathaniel Seigel, John Stimson, and Martin Goldman—who deserve our special thanks. Most of the coding was done during the summer without benefit of air-conditioning; we want to thank Roberta Greene Ehre, Leah Glass, Tamara Obrebska, Ruth Moskowitz, Ann Higley, and Phyllis Esser Gunther for their perseverance. The sociometric tests were hand-scored by student volunteers from the sociology classes of Margaret Benz, New York University. We wish to thank them and her for help we probably could not have bought even if we had had the money. The Make A Sentence Tests were scored by Carola Mann, with some assistance by Ardith Stimson. Most of the early computer work was done by Jonathan Robbins and Joy Marie Hadden handled the later stages. The manuscript typing and retyping has fallen into the willing hands of Marian Iglesias. To these and others go our special and individual thanks.

H. J. M.
E. F. B.
W. C. J.

January, 1965

Contents

Tables

1. Objectives and Rationale for the Study

THIS BOOK describes a study of the consequences of providing social work services to high school girls whose record of earlier performance and behavior at school revealed them to be potentially deviant. Over the course of four years girls with potential problems who entered a vocational high school in New York City were identified from information available to the school. From this pool of students a random sample of cases was referred to an agency where they were offered casework or group counseling services by professional social workers. A control group was also selected at random from the same pool of potential problem cases in order that a comparison could be made between girls who received service and similar girls who did not. Since all these girls were identified as potential problem cases, they may be considered latent or early detected deviants. Services to them consisted in efforts to interrupt deviant careers.

Social work agencies and the professional social workers who staff them are dedicated to the achievement of constructive changes in their clients. They are constantly restive to know whether their efforts are successful, where they may be deficient, and how they might be improved. As their sense of professional security increases, social workers not only become more confident that their efforts are worthwhile, they also seek to test them against the hard, objective criteria of achievement.

There are those who contend that evaluation studies in social work are premature,[1] that attempts to assess effectiveness constitute attacks on the competence if not the integrity of the profession,[2] that dedicated effort is its own excuse for being. Others contend that evaluation studies are essential not only to justify

15

the considerable investment of effort and money in social agency operations and professional services but to provide guidelines for the development of practice principles in casework and in other helping efforts.[3] The research that is the basis of this monograph was undertaken in this spirit of constructive evaluation.

BACKGROUND FOR THE RESEARCH PROJECT

Two conditions constitute the background for the project described here. The first is that there are experimental social agencies that have sought to provide casework and group therapy services to adolescent girls with behavior and adjustment problems. The second is that such agencies have shown interest in rigorous scientific research that may have practical utility for the agencies and also contribute knowledge more generally to the field of social work.

Youth Consultation Service is a nonsectarian, voluntary social agency in New York City that for more than fifty years has specialized in offering services to adolescent girls. The characteristic problems that bring troubled girls and young women between the ages of twelve and twenty-five to YCS are: out-of-wedlock pregnancy, school behavior problems, chronic truancy, unmanageability at home, "immoral conduct," incorrigibility, and "runaway." At the time this research was undertaken, the agency served approximately two hundred clients each year, of whom about two-fifths were unmarried mothers. The urban offices of the agency, located in Manhattan and the Bronx, received relatively larger proportions of clients having general problems, whereas the suburban Westchester office in White Plains tended to serve primarily unmarried mothers.

The major service offered to clients of the agency is casework, but since 1952 it has conducted a supplementary group therapy program and has pioneered in group methods of treatment for unmarried mothers and adolescent girls with other behavior problems.[4] In addition to the regular complement of psychiatric consultants, group therapy consultants have been provided.

Youth Consultation Service has characteristically sought new approaches and methods. In fact, in recent years the agency has had a distinctly experimental attitude toward its role, seeking less to provide mass services than to represent a site for innovation and experimentation. In this spirit YCS embarked on a research program in the early 1950's and enlisted the services of sociologists and social psychologists to serve part-time as a research staff. A Research Committee of social workers and social scientists was constituted and met weekly to formulate concrete research plans. The widest latitude was given to the consideration of questions that had come out of the experiences of the agency and its staff. The only real limitations were that the research questions have direct import for the agency's program and that they be amenable to objective study.[5]

A persistent concern of the agency's staff has been its experience with adolescent girls identified through school difficulties and referred to the agency by the New York City Youth Board. Youth Consultation Service has had several contracts with the Youth Board to serve such clients which involved many complex problems. In the first place, it was frequently extremely difficult to make even initial contact with referred cases, a considerable proportion of whom never were seen or were seen only once or twice. Second, achieving involvement in casework was difficult or impossible, even when contact was made. The customary approaches to establishing relationships through regular casework interviews did not seem effective. Third, even when a casework contact was established, these clients often seemed to be in such severe stages of maladjustment and psychological pathology that it was felt that only sustaining and ameliorative goals could be set rather than more positive and constructive objectives. The caseworkers frequently felt that contact had been made *after* the optimum point for maximum help. They frequently were of the opinion that earlier intervention might have prevented an almost untreatable condition from developing or at least have permitted restorative treatment to be undertaken with more hope of success. Treatment was seen as having been attempted too late, both in the sense that the girls were older than the most promising ages for effective treatment and that their difficulties had become so severe as to make treatment problematical even as it accentuated the difficulties of establishing a casework relationship with these adolescent girls.

The Research Committee turned its attention periodically to this experience as various possible studies were proposed which might throw light on the problem of how to increase the agency's success with such cases. Hence an effort was made to conceive a research study of adolescent girls, similar to those that the Youth Board sought to reach, for whom treatment might be provided before severe difficulties developed.

It was clear that the caseworkers were willing to try new approaches for the purpose of research while maintaining professional responsibility in their treatment efforts. The staff of the agency were prepared to test their efforts in a research design that would permit arbitrary assignment of clients of a defined class of adolescent girls in need of help so that they could be compared with girls similar in situation and characteristics who would not receive service. It was recognized that studies confined to the existing caseload would be limited insofar as learning whether the efforts of the caseworkers were successful. A control-group experimental design was proposed which supplied new sources of arbitrary referral for a study of how to prevent adolescent girls from developing serious behavior problems. Thus a project took shape that was intended to study the effectiveness of social work for interrupting potential deviant careers.

Some General Considerations

What is meant by prevention? To prevent the culmination of processes that produce the problems of adolescent girls required, first, the *prior* identification of girls who, if untreated or unsuccessfully treated, subsequently would develop such problems. But to intervene before the problems are critically manifest means to detect general rather than specific tendencies, in the absence of sufficient knowledge about the etiologies of the problems to specify with certainty their preconditions. Nonspecific referrals were typical of the agency's adolescent girl clients. The usual agency caseload included clients coming from complex home situations and presenting a broad spectrum of problems.

It was the task of the caseworkers to make specific such general characteristics of their clients' situations by orderly and sensitive diagnoses so that appropriate treatment plans could be devised to fit the particular needs of each client.

Not only were diagnoses likely to be varied for adolescent clients, but treatment objectives as well were likely to be diverse. Hence successful treatment was likely to represent many different achievements, depending on the problems discovered and the goals set for each client. Unlike the examination of unitary treatment efforts directed toward specific and previously determined problems, preventive casework must apply a range of treatment efforts to a broad spectrum of potential problems. Only after problems can be resolved into diagnostic types for which symptomatic indicators are available can the specification of a particular treatment be appropriate.

What is meant by "treatment" for such an array of unspecified problems of adolescent girls? Casework and group therapy are not precise and limited methods of helping persons with problems. They are flexible approaches, adaptable to the varieties of situations in which clients find themselves. They take their specificity from certain underlying principles based on experience: that a professional person can help an individual in need if an appropriate relationship can be established; that this relationship involves confirmation through action of the willingness and ability of the helper to help; that such help can be provided through continuous interaction between helper and client in which the client is enabled to achieve further self-understanding, so that the components of her problem that arise from emotional conflicts, repressed experiences, and inadequate socialization can be dealt with effectively; that such reeducational processes can be achieved as will increase competence in the client and thereby enable her to meet the demands of her situation adequately and realistically. Such underlying principles as these, rather than specific prescribed actions, constitute the treatment approach of casework when the problems of clients are diffuse.

It is assumed that many of the problems of adolescent girls are amenable to a casework or group therapy approach. Furthermore, caseworkers are trained to be alert to those conditions of their clients that make casework inappropriate, for example, physical disabilities, severe psychological pathology, or extreme environmental circumstances. But, in the main, the kinds of adolescent girls who are referred to social agencies for help are thought to have problems for which casework and group therapy are treatment methods of choice. The screening process of the serving institutions of the community—medical, economic, educational—usually directs persons with specific problems elsewhere, leaving to the social agencies the task of dealing with the problems of behavior and maladjustment.

How can "effective treatment" be determined with so generalized a set of problems and so generalized a treatment approach? The problem of criteria is, of course, a difficult one. But just as it is necessary for prevention to discover clients prior to the emergence of specific problems for specific treatment, so it is necessary to examine a wide range of factors that may catch the evidences of desired change of behavior, reduction of undesirable behavior, or assumed improvement in functioning. Just as an array of behaviors and conditions can be taken to represent incipient problems for adolescent girls, so too can an array of behaviors and changes be taken to represent improvement or movement in the direction of less problematic, more "normal," acceptable conditions. For any one client, the criterion of improvement, of successful treatment, may be concrete and directly related to her particular problem and behavior. For each the criterion may be different, although it is to be expected that general types of problems and hence of changes will be discovered. But for adolescent girl clients as a whole, the criteria of success will be general. They will be reflected in the variety of different "improvements" and "changes" that occur. In the broadest sense, a group of clients should show "improvement" by being more "normal," more like those who do not appear to have problems. We may with some confidence assume that measures of normality will reflect the impact of successful treatment efforts if other factors are not responsible for the changes observed.

How can these "other factors" be taken into account? It is most difficult to determine when treatment rather than maturation, normal experiences, and other conditions are responsible for any changes observed. We must be able to say that clients who improve are not simply those who would improve anyway, that is, without systematic, deliberate treatment. To arrive at an accurate judgment, it is necessary to adopt some sort of comparison-group design so that treatment will constitute an experiment. Then we can discover whether untreated clients change as the treated ones do, whether the multifold processes of living, rather than the efforts of social workers, have achieved the effects we consider desirable. When we can see that adolescent girl clients who have received treatment differ from nontreated girls who were similar in their situations and characteristics before treatment, we can be reasonably sure that it has been the treatment effort that was effective.

Furthermore, through such an experimental design we can discover what aspects of treatment might have been effective, provided we can be specific in describing what constituted the treatment effort. If we can merely say that clients were provided with "casework and group therapy," then we must be content to attribute results to such general treatment efforts. If we can specify what such efforts are, we learn what produces a given result. However, even if we must be content with the general knowledge that "agency services" were provided, we will learn something that may be repeated because such services are identifiably different in some respects from the wide range of other experiences of adolescent girls, such as school, religious, recreational, and play experiences. And it is of value at least to ask whether the impact of "agency services" is visibly and constructively evident.

In short, such considerations as these, in view of the experiences of Youth Consultation Service with its adolescent girl clients and the research intentions of the social workers and researchers, constitute the background for the research project that began in the fall of 1955. It will be described in detail in the next chapter.

NOTES TO CHAPTER I

1. See Greenwood, Ernest, "Social Science and Social Work: A Theory of Their Relationship," *Social Service Review*, vol. 29, March, 1955, p. 31.

2. For discussions of some of the issues presented and positions taken by practitioners in the helping professions, see Blenkner, Margaret, "Obstacles to Evaluative Research in Casework," *Social Casework*, vol. 31, February–March, 1950, pp. 54–60, 97–105; Meyer, Henry J., and Edgar F. Borgatta, "Paradoxes in Evaluating Mental Health Programmes," *International Journal of Social Psychiatry*, vol. 5, Autumn, 1959, pp. 136–141.

3. See Eaton, Joseph W., "A Scientific Basis for Helping" in Kahn, Alfred J., editor, *Issues in American Social Work*, Columbia University Press, New York, 1959, pp. 270–292; Thomas, Edwin J., "Field Experiments and Demonstrations" in Polansky, Norman A., editor, *Social Work Research*, University of Chicago Press, Chicago, 1960, p. 295; French, David G., *An Approach to Measuring Results in Social Work*, Columbia University Press, New York, 1952, pp. 3–73; Herzog, Elizabeth, *Some Guide Lines for Evaluative Research*, U.S. Department of Health, Education, and Welfare, Social Security Administration, Children's Bureau, Washington, 1959, pp. 79–94.
   An extensive consideration of general and technical issues that must be faced in evaluative research is found in Hyman, Herbert H., Charles R. Wright, and Terence K. Hopkins, *Applications of Methods of Evaluation*, University of California Press, Berkeley, 1962, pp. 3–86.

4. MacLennan, Beryce W., and S. R. Slavson, *Group Therapy with Unmarried Mothers*. Youth Consultation Service, New York, 1956.

5. Completed research included: Meyer, Henry J., Wyatt C. Jones, and Edgar F. Borgatta, "The Decision by Unmarried Mothers to Keep or Surrender Their Babies," *Social Work*, vol. 1, April, 1956, pp. 103–109; Meyer, Henry J., Edgar F. Borgatta, and David Fanshel, "Unwed Mothers' Decisions About Their Babies: An Interim Replication Study," *Child Welfare*, vol. 38, February, 1959, pp. 1–6; Meyer, Henry J., Edgar F. Borgatta, and David Fanshel, "A Study of the Interview Process: The Caseworker-Client Relationship," *Genetic Psychology Monographs*, vol. 69, 1964, pp. 274–295; Pollock, Edmund, *An Investigation into Certain Personality Characteristics of Unmarried Mothers*, Ph.D. dissertation, New York University, 1957; Jones, Wyatt C., Henry J. Meyer, and Edgar F. Borgatta, "Social and Psychological Factors in Status Decisions of Unmarried Mothers," *Marriage and Family Living*, vol. 24, August, 1962, pp. 224–230; Jones, Wyatt C., "Correlates of Social Deviance: A Study of Unmarried Mothers." Unpublished manuscript.

II. The Plan for the Research Project and Its Implementation

AFTER A BRIEF DESCRIPTION of the research design, this chapter will present some of the conditions required for its implementation and the procedures instituted for its fulfillment. The purpose is to describe not only the structure of the research project but the operating context within the organizations—the agency and the school—in which it was conducted.

THE RESEARCH DESIGN[1]

The basic plan of the research was a simple experimental design requiring random assignment of adolescent girls with potential problems (1) as clients of Youth Consultation Service to constitute an *experimental* sample, that is, to receive treatment, and (2) as members of a group of *control* cases, with no treatment provided by YCS. The comparison of these two groups of cases after the former was exposed to the services of the agency will constitute a test of the effects of that service, since in other respects the two groups may be assumed to begin equally and to differ in experiences only to the extent that the control cases have not had the services of YCS. It is to be noted that these are assumptions and therefore require some empirical examination if they are to be accepted with confidence.

In order to check these assumptions, as well as to provide information additional to the experimental test, it was arranged that the total school population from which experimental and control cases were chosen would be tested *prior* to random assignment and periodically throughout the study so that equivalence could be examined and change differentials noted. Similarly, it was arranged that the total school population as well as the experimental and control cases would be observed at a determinate follow-up point according to criteria that reflected a range of objectives contemplated by YCS in its services to the experimental sample.

Through additional procedures, including clearance with the Social Service Exchange and direct inquiry from both experimental and control subjects, an effort would be made to estimate whether YCS service did, in fact, constitute the primary variation in experience of the two groups of cases, or whether, for example, similar or comparable services might have been provided elsewhere for the control cases. In the strictest sense, therefore, the experimental test was not one of provision of service vs. withholding of service, but rather the known provision of service vs. unknown experiences excluding these specific services. This is a severe test of the impact of such services. But it is also a powerful one and the sort of question that is, in effect, asked of social agencies: "Have your services benefited clients more than no services or services provided on a casual and haphazard basis?"

IMPLEMENTATION OF THE RESEARCH DESIGN

A number of conditions had to be met to implement the research design. These involved both the social agency and cooperating organizations.

Source of the Clients

The first question was the source of the adolescent girls who were to be clients of the agency and the subjects of the experiment. Since the objective was to examine whether fairly early intervention in a deviant career would be possible and effective (experience with Youth Board cases had been felt to be too late and ineffective), it was necessary to find subjects who were either younger than those who had been treated by the Youth Board, or whose problems were less developed. The function and experience of Youth Consultation Service were confined to girls of adolescent years, and hence it was decided that junior high and high school ages must be accepted as limits for the subject clients. They would be adolescent girls whose problems had not become acute or overtly severe.

Where were such clients to be found? And how were they to be obtained through random selection so that a control group similar in situation and characteristics could be compared with them? Obviously an outside source different from the usual voluntary and uncontrolled intake of the agency was required— a source willing to permit completely arbitrary selection of the experimental cases and completely arbitrary rejection of the control cases. The alternative of waiting for customary intake at the agency to provide the population that could be divided into experimental and control cases was clearly not feasible for several reasons. First of all, the flow of cases to the agency was too uncertain to provide the necessary numbers for the experiment within a reasonable time span. Second, experience had shown that most of the adolescent girl clients of the agency had already reached acute stages in their behavior problems. Furthermore, the ethical norms of social work operated to make it more difficult, or even impossible, to decide arbitrarily to serve or not to serve some clients rather than to make the decision on the basis of need and capacity to be helped by the agency.

The obvious source for the type of client to be served and studied was the school. A high school was sought that was large enough and varied enough in its composition to expect a reasonable number of adolescent girls with potential problems to be identified, and that was willing to cooperate by referring the selected sample of girls to YCS and by permitting the necessary testing and follow-up procedures. The school should not be one designated as primarily for students whose difficulties had already singled them out, such as the "600-schools" of New York City, because the study contemplated preventive rather than ameliorative services. But it also should not be one in which the student body was selected in the opposite manner, because of superior performance or outstanding behavior, or one in which families of higher economic and social class would be likely to provide alternative services to those of YCS for girls with potential problems.

Practical considerations also entered in the selection of the school to be used. It would be convenient as well as desirable to use a school in the neighborhood of the agency so that, if possible, transportation barriers would not make visits to the agency difficult, and so that contacts with YCS could be made during school hours without disruption of the usual school program of the students referred. Previous experience elsewhere with attempts to arrange systematic referrals from outside sources had emphasized the difficulty of getting referrals into contact with the agency.[2]

After some exploratory work, a nearby citywide vocational school, about two-thirds of whose student body were girls, was asked to cooperate in the project. The principal and the administrative assistant in charge of guidance readily agreed to participate. This school had an enrollment of about 1,800 students, with approximately 500 girls and 200 boys admitted each year from all over New York City. Although the school exercised some selection in its admission, the criteria for admission were stated largely in terms of capacity to learn the trades taught in the school. The administrative assistant has described it as follows:

> The high school is a vocational school with approximately 1,800 students, two-thirds of them girls, because the industry for which training is offered employs many women. Most students enter in the tenth grade for three years of study and training; a small number (mostly from parochial schools) enter in the ninth grade. The social composition of the student body reflects the changing population of the city's residents and hence includes various races and cultural and language backgrounds, natives and newcomers, and different socioeconomic levels. Teenagers from the *most* disorganized backgrounds are not heavily represented in the student population but the social class range is certainly wider than one would find in specialized academic high schools.[3]

Selection of Experimental and Control Cases

The cooperating school—here called Vocational High—agreed with the agency that the girls selected by the research staff for referral would be encouraged to accept the help of Youth Consultation Service and that the necessary home permission for the girls to go to the agency would be sought by the school in cooperation with YCS. Vocational High also agreed that the girls selected could fit into their schoolday schedules the required appointments with caseworkers at the agency and (as group procedures developed) the scheduled group meetings. The school also accepted the condition that the project would continue through four years in order that the requisite numbers could be referred and observed throughout their high school years, normally the time between entrance and graduation from the school (tenth, eleventh, and twelfth grades).[4]

Which girls were to be selected for referral and which for the comparison group? A number of possibilities presented themselves. On the assumption that all adolescent girls might benefit from the services of the agency, a random selection could have been made from the entire school. This is not an unreasonable assumption, since it is sometimes asserted that adolescence normally entails stresses that may be better met when the adolescents are helped to understand the problems of maturation and adjustment which they face. On the other hand, differential degrees of stress and deviant ways of responding to it characterize those adolescents who have been the primary target of agency services and who constitute the group of adolescents whose difficulties give general concern.

Generally, the schools and families and other social organizations that constitute the world of adolescents take the so-called "normal" problems of adolescence as part of the conditions with which they deal. Thus adolescent girls in high school are "normally" expected to have problems in their relationships with boys, with the redefinition of their status at home from childhood to adulthood, with their self-conceptions in this transition, with uncertainties about their future occupational and marital careers, and so forth. These, in addition to academic problems and some problems of social adjustment to high school, are accepted as normal conditions to be dealt with by the school in the course of carrying on its educational functions. It is, however, the extreme expression of such problems and the occurrence of more severe difficulties that extend beyond the limits of "normal" school responsibilities and interfere with the capacity of the school to perform its primary educational tasks. These are the situations for which specialized help might be most useful.

To meet some of the less extreme situations, schools have developed internal mechanisms, such as guidance and counseling services, disciplinary procedures, and so forth, but these are usually recognized as having limited capacity to deal with the more severe problems and hence frequently require auxiliary services. Further, much of the response to student needs is intended to maintain an acceptable level of behavior while the girls are at the school. Alert teachers and guidance departments are zealous to find resources for a more general and intensive response to student needs. Time and means permitting, they make use of available clinics, medical facilities, recreational and social work agencies on behalf of the students. To deal with some of the unacceptable student behavior directly affecting the school— such as truancy or academic failure—there are services that can be provided within the school system, for example, the services of attendance teachers and disciplinary officers. Measures such as suspension and transfer are also helpful. Rules about handling problems through these procedures are sometimes formal but usually they involve customary informal practices of the particular school.

Another way to select students for referral to a social agency, and one more in keeping with the concept of prevention, would be to make a systematic attempt to identify that segment of the school population that seemed more likely to have severe problems and to use this group as the source of clients. This assumes both that signs of future difficulties are identifiable and that intervention may have an effect on the course of their development. Both these assumptions are in keeping with a conception of social and psychological causation of the problems which YCS and Vocational High wished to prevent.

What indicators could be used to identify a portion of the entering girls at Vocational High who had potential problems and who might therefore benefit from the services of YCS? An elaborate diagnostic procedure might have been adopted, including psychological tests and psychiatric examination, but this was neither feasible nor in keeping with the usual routine of the school. Furthermore, with the focus on evaluating preventive effectiveness, it seemed desirable to use information that ordinarily would be available rather than some special body of information collected through procedures available only for this research. In addition, criteria for identifying those with potential problems would be more useful if they were of the kind that school teachers and guidance personnel could readily detect from the cumulative records that routinely accompany students throughout their school careers. It was, therefore, the information available to the school about entering students that was used to identify the potential problem population.

It was established school practice to examine each entering student's record not only to assess academic preparation and plan the student's program, but also to identify problems that might require special planning. Indications of language difficulties, for instance, among the Puerto Rican students whose native tongue is Spanish, were noted and they were assigned to special English classes. So, too, indicators of reading retardation were noted. An effort was made to identify health problems and handicaps, as well as special personal or family problems that might have been entered in the record. As a part of normal school operations, therefore, certain kinds of screening efforts were made and the special screening for purposes of the research project was a simple addition to this usual procedure.

Beginning with the class entering Vocational High in the fall term of 1955, the research staff examined the record of every girl in that class. The records contained a variety of information that could be interpreted as indicative of potential problems. Selection of a student as a potential problem case for the research project was a judgment based on combinations of factors evident from the school record. The primary objectives were to eliminate students for whom there were no or only minimal indicators of future difficulty and to include those for whom the constellation of indicators suggested future difficulties. Since the selection of clients and of the control sample was to be *from* this pool, it was decided to interpret indicators of potential difficulty liberally rather than by strict definitions, and hence to resolve doubts in favor of inclusion in the pool of potential problem cases.

The cumulative school record contains not only academic information (subjects studied and grades received, schools attended, and so forth), but also ancillary information about the student; for example, scores on intelligence, aptitude, and achievement tests; health information about accidents and operations, defects of sight, hearing, and speech, or exceptional physical conditions; and attendance and excused or unexcused absences. A variety of personal traits and work traits are rated by teachers for each year and notations made of co-curricular activities (clubs, teams, and the like) and special out-of-school activities (hobbies, special activities such as musical and athletic). Honors and other forms of school recognition are also indicated. Some information is also recorded about the family of the student, such as residential address, birthplace and occupation of parents, sex and birth order of siblings, and language spoken in the home. Occasionally, special personal or family problems are indicated. These are the types of information routinely available, and from them the selection criteria for the pool of potential problem cases were developed.

The records permitted judgments to be made about the school behavior of the student, about some of his personal characteristics, and about limited or unusual features of his home situation. With respect to *school behavior*, it was believed that such questions as the following might indicate potential problems for the girl entering high school:

> Do the elementary and junior high school records indicate unsatisfactory student-teacher relationships, such as classroom discipline problems?
> Is there evidence of difficulty in getting along with fellow students, such as fighting or arguing excessively with peers?
> Has there been formal disciplinary action taken, such as being sent to the principal or other disciplinary officer?
> Are there excessive or chronic absences without such reasonable explanations as illness, accident, and the like?
> Have there been unusual behaviors noted, such as extreme shyness or irritability?

Is there an obvious inconsistency between intelligence test scores and academic performance?

Are there unusual fluctuations in IQ test scores or in grades, indicating erratic performance, or unusual and marked decline?

Is there any indication of reading retardation?

Is truancy noted, or other formal violation of school regulations?

Such data in the earlier school record, especially in the more recent preceding years, were thought to indicate that the student had been observed by her teachers as behaving sufficiently beyond the normal to warrant inclusion in a pool of those more, rather than less, likely to have future difficulties.

Some of the school records provide additional information on *personal characteristics* similarly considered indicative of continuing or future difficulties, as suggested by the following questions:

Are there notations describing the girl as tense, overburdened, defiant, or anxious?

Has she been noted to have difficulties with regard to physical appearance, such as obesity or skin trouble?

Is she described as restless, depressed, likely to have temper tantrums, or be dishonest?

Are unusual mannerisms noted, or tics, stuttering, chronic crying, and the like?

Where teachers are required to rate personal traits on a scale from outstanding to unsatisfactory, are there frequent negative ratings on such characteristics as interest, self-control, dependability, industry?

It was considered probable that general negative indicators of personal characteristics would make the student more rather than less likely to have continuing or future difficulties and hence likely to benefit from the services of the agency.

Finally, do the school records indicate some unusual *family situation* that might suggest difficulties for the child? Have there been frequent changes of residence? Are one or both parents absent from the home? Are unusual circumstances noted for any family members, such as chronic illness, hospitalization, or difficulties with authorities? Is a special problem of language or acculturation noted? While less direct, these notations might also serve to forewarn of potential difficulties and hence, in combination with other indicators, qualify the girl as a potential problem case.

It is to be noted that the school records are not uniform in the extent to which all such indicators as the above are recorded. There are variations between the different junior high schools from which the students came, as well as variations in the extent to which different teachers might complete the records. As already noted, those students entering the ninth grade were usually from parochial or other private schools. The form of such records might differ; usually they contain less information than records of students entering the tenth grade from public junior high schools. Also, school records are said to underidentify withdrawn, excessively quiet, or "pathologically good" children and the selection criteria probably miss some such cases. On the other hand, it may be assumed that, in general, the behavior, characteristics, or situation of the student would have to be fairly noticeable and exceptional for such information to be recorded. Therefore, identification probably represented more than adventitious circumstances. It was not likely that the criteria would encourage selection of those students who were well adjusted and in no need of help.

A school teacher or other professional person who has some awareness of variations among adolescents could use criteria such as these to identify a portion of the class that appears likely to face difficulties in the coming school years. This is a deliberately naive procedure to identify potentially deviant persons but it makes use of the kind of information to which school teachers are sensitized and, often, the kind of information that is said to signal need for mental hygiene programs. If a syndrome of such characteristics was described to a social agency as the basis for bringing an adolescent girl there for help, it would generally be accepted as indicating at least the need for further diagnostic study and often the need for casework help of some kind. This identification procedure is nothing more than a formal recognition of the kinds of information to which guidance teachers and counselors, as well as others concerned with anticipating difficulties before they become acute, would give attention in school records. In a practical sense, the adolescent girls so identified constitute a meaningful population for preventive service and hence for the research purposes of the project.

To recapitulate, the records of four entering cohorts of girls at Vocational High were screened and potential problem cases identified for each. Only those entering in the fall term were included in order to provide as long a time for treatment as possible. Approximately one-fourth of the cohort was included in the potential problem cases and from this pool a random procedure was used to select those to be referred to YCS, the number depending on the capacity of the agency to accept additions to its caseload. At the same time, and by the same random procedure, the control group was selected from the potential problem cases. A total of 200 referred girls and 200 in the control sample was set as the goal and, over the course of four years, 189 referrals and 192 control cases were actually included in the experimental and control samples.

Referral from the School

It is one thing for researchers to screen school records to identify potential clients and another to convert a list of high school girls so selected into actual clients of a social agency. It was precisely at this point that much of the difficulty YCS had experienced with Youth Board referrals occurred. It is therefore worthwhile to examine the procedures and the requisite conditions for this aspect of the project.

When YCS indicated that it could accept a number of clients for the project, the names of those selected were drawn from the pool and given both to the school guidance department and to the agency. Neither the school nor the agency was given the names of other girls who had been selected as control cases, and they were not informed of the students who constituted the rest of the potential problem cases.

As already indicated, the girls selected for referral had to be approached with an explanation of the program and invited to accept help from YCS. They had to obtain parental permission to leave the school premises during school hours and arrange appointments with the agency within their school schedules. In addition, they had to be given some rationale for this unusual attention directed toward them. Furthermore, in keeping with the design of the research, the entire entering class of girls, including the potential problem cases, were given a series of tests and asked to fill out questionnaires so that uniform information would be available to describe the experimental and control samples. Data-gathering procedures are described later, but are mentioned here to indicate the range of adjustments Vocational High was called on to make. From the viewpoint of the school, referral of a few girls to YCS from time to time was only a part of the commitment to the project. The school's view of its adaptation to those requirements and its interest in cooperating have been described by the administrative assistant in charge of guidance as follows:[5]

> Those who teach or carry responsibility for guidance in a public school do not need to be reminded that it is often too late when an adolescent pupil announces, "I'm leaving school"; or when a student of average intelligence has failed in several subjects; or when a student becomes progressively disruptive so that he cannot be permitted to remain in school. But in the manifold operations of a large high school planned for the "normal" student, it is a complicated business to detect and communicate signs of trouble so that counselors and teachers may do something to prevent such difficulties. In a small community high school, the freshman counselor or guidance director may have watched his future counselees progress from the ABC's to algebra; he may know their parents as former classmates or neighbors. Not so in a large metropolitan, central school drawing its students from more than two hundred feeder schools throughout the many and varied neighborhoods of the city. The student appears first as an application form containing such information as results of group IQ tests, achievement test ratings, subject marks, recent attendance record, course preference, and cursory comments (intended usually to support the application for admission) on personal interests and qualifications. The student's total, cumulative folder, including health and confidential records, is not available until there is but little time to study it before the student arrives to begin classes. To the extent possible, counselors search these records to identify students who may need special attention so as to prepare lists of underachievers, home problems, emo-

tional and health problems, and the like. Then we take a deep breath and get ready for the "high priority" caseload for the fall.

In keeping with the purpose of the school, the staff includes teachers of both academic and vocational subjects with varying orientations toward the functions and services provided. The principal and administrative staff must balance multiple purposes and the program and services are structured accordingly, subject to requirements of the school system of which this school is a part. Despite awareness and concern for students for whom special attention is needed to bring them the full benefits of the school, innovation for such a purpose is difficult.

We were approached in the spring of 1955 by Youth Consultation Service to join in a study for the purpose of discovering criteria for predicting serious trouble for adolescent girls and evaluating methods of preventing trouble from occurring. The principal and the guidance staff agreed that such research would be valuable and would benefit our students as it proceeded. We felt, too, that it would give our staff a practical demonstration of ongoing research and an opportunity to participate in a program articulating the school and a community agency. Administrative approval set in motion the many requirements for implementation that commitment to the research and service project created.

The first requirement, minor though it may seem, was for physical facilities for the research operations. We discovered that research takes space! The guidance coordinator's office became headquarters and everybody moved over a little to make room for test forms, questionnaires, and researchers, who were given access to necessary records so that applications could be screened, data recorded, and operations planned. This was more than a spatial arrangement because it permitted research personnel quietly and tactfully to become accepted members of the office, even by the harassed secretary who stood as guardian. The important point is that the researchers and the research became a part of the school, different, to be sure, but not an operation from the outside.

The second—and continuing—requirement was for communication throughout the staff of the school to explain reasons for the adaptations necessitated by the extensive twice-a-year testing program. This meant scheduling about one and one-half hours for all girl students during their first month in school and again each spring throughout their high school years. At first, the girls were taken from vocational classes to larger rooms for large-group testing; subsequently, testing was arranged in the separate classes. Although testing and data gathering were done by researchers, teachers often volunteered their help.

When the experimental group was chosen, the time schedule for casework interviews had to be met. Appointments outside of school hours were impracticable because of the longer school day in vocational schools, the fact that many students had after-school jobs, and the travel time from school to home. We had again to seek understanding and cooperation from vocational chairman and teachers because appointments were more feasible during the longer trade classes rather than during academic-subject classes. There was some resistance at first about loss of school time: "What's the point of having a student fall behind in her work?" "I thought students came to school for instruction." "Mary is such a nice, clean, quiet girl, why does she need to talk to anyone about her problems?" The guidance department assumed responsibility for orientation of the teaching staff; individual cases were discussed with teachers.

In addition to informal and daily procedures, several formal presentations by agency and research representatives to the total faculty made informal communication easier. Social workers and teachers had not often met under such circumstances. They found the aims of the agency and those of the school not at all antagonistic. With regular and frequent visits of Youth Consultation Service staff to discuss cases with guidance personnel and teachers, mutual appreciation of the responsibilities and the sincere efforts of each increased, not without occasional misunderstandings and minor frictions.

School and agency collaboration was also required for external communication in the crucial task of informing and enlisting cooperation of students selected for referral to the agency and their parents. The agency director of casework services and school guidance personnel together drafted a letter acceptable under Board of Education rules to inform parents and solicit permission of students to leave the school premises during school hours. The guidance department took responsibility for following up on these letters, explaining to students and parents what was involved, and interpreting the service program to skeptical parents and students. The number of parental refusals was negligible. Student cooperation was enhanced by initial contact, first on an individual basis and later in groups, between social worker and students at the school, with school sanction but without the presence of school personnel. Subsequent treatment interviews and group meetings were held at the agency or in a nearby Y building.

Whatever the IBM machines may show about our project, we in the school are convinced of the practical values it has held for our students and for our staff. Procedures became almost routine over the life of the project; research and agency personnel "belong"; teachers now want to know how they can get Mary to Youth Consultation Service: "She's such a nice, clean, quiet girl. She deserves to be helped." Some students themselves have asked to be allowed to go to Youth Consultation Service. The highest compliment, I believe, came when the Teachers' Council sent a letter of thanks to the agency and made a plea that the project be extended and made permanent.

The specific act of referral was handled in various ways by the Guidance Department but, in general, it consisted in telling the girls individually that they had been selected because the school thought that they deserved the opportunity to have the extra assistance that YCS could give them with the problems usual for high school girls. They were told that such opportunity was available only to a few of the students and they were encouraged to take advantage of it. There is little doubt that the warm and friendly interest of the administrative assistant in charge of guidance was a factor in conveying a positive attitude toward referral even if, as the caseworkers subsequently reported, the girls were uncertain and confused about the basis of their selection and expressed the fear that they were thought "crazy" or otherwise invidiously identified. The school's interest was emphasized to them by its willingness to permit them to go to YCS on school time and this, also, undoubtedly entered into the success with which referral was achieved. Whatever doubts the referred girls entertained, they did, for the most part, make contact with the agency. As the project proceeded, the referral and first contact procedures were modified; these will be described later when the agency's efforts are described. It is to be noted at this point, however, that of the 189 girls who completed the intake procedure, only 3 per cent failed to have at least one further service contact with a social worker at YCS. The median number of casework interviews or group counseling services that the experimental group had with YCS workers was 16.

Acceptance at the Agency

Just as the school had no choice, under the design of the project, with respect to which students it could refer to YCS, so, too, the agency relinquished its freedom to decide by its own criteria which girls it wished to accept for treatment. Both accepted this restriction to protect the validity of the experimental results from unknown selective processes that would affect the equivalence of the experimental and control cases. In the interest of the preventive goal of the project, it is also to be noted that the agency agreed to accept clients without the overt presenting problems customary for its intake, which is a novel situation for a voluntary social agency. However, as will be indicated later when the treatment efforts as seen by the social workers and consultants are considered, it constituted not only a challenge but a fruitful professional experience.

From the standpoint of evaluative research, the requirement of arbitrary referral and acceptance created an experimental population that could be expected to differ in some ways from the usual clientele of the agency, but in what ways it was not possible to say. One might speculate that Vocational High students were less motivated to accept help than clients who came on their own initiative. However, adolescent girls were often seen by YCS under conditions not likely to encourage positive motivation. They frequently came with problems and difficulties that were serious and with attitudes resistant or even hostile to adult help. The arbitrary referrals from Vocational High might not have been as visibly in need of help as some of the usual clients of YCS. But, as previously indicated, the preventive objective of the project accepted this as the major question to examine. That is, could help given *before* problems were clearly visible prevent them from developing? It was not the effectiveness of the agency with its usual clientele that was in question but rather the effectiveness of its special effort with a determinate clientele that was to be examined through the experimental project.

The agency's procedures changed with experience as the adolescent girls referred through the school to the project continued throughout four years. The obligation to accept meant also the obligation to make contact and to try to offer appropriate services. These obligations were faithfully pursued and hence the caseworkers and group therapists took more than customary initiative to involve project clients. Again, such "aggressive casework" was in keeping with the objective of the agency when it undertook the project: to seek out clients with potential problems and treat them so that the potential would not be realized.

Administrative adaptations at YCS were also necessary. The most obvious consisted of increasing the staff. This entailed rearrangements of supervision and shifting of caseloads; it also entailed new arrangements with consultants. In a more subtle sense, it required reorientation of staff viewpoint with respect to approaches to clients, bases for determining treatment plans, and procedures of service. All these were modified as the project itself evolved; hence they represent not the customary activities of the agency but its special effort in a preventive project.

The most elusive aspect of the project, and the heart of the agency's effort, is the specification of what is meant by treatment. The analysis of what was attempted, the treatment philosophy and the procedures used, will be described later. In the initial plan for the project it was proposed that "treatment" be described more systematically than was the usual practice at YCS or other social agencies. The plan was described as follows in the research proposal:

> Services currently provided by YCS for adolescent girls include individual casework treatment and activity and interview group therapy. Appropriate treatment is determined on the basis of conferences between caseworker and supervisor (with psychiatric and/or psychological consultation where deemed necessary by the staff).
>
> Current procedure at YCS calls for the statement of casework goals in each case and the making of plans for casework or group therapy treatment. It is proposed to standardize this procedure so that the case record will be as explicit as possible as to the objectives and treatment intended.
>
> In addition, caseworkers will be asked to indicate for each case after each interview the nature of the activity which took place during the interview by means of a form (now under development) on which they can record, "How much attention and effort during the interview just completed was devoted to: . . . ," for example, establishing rapport or "transference," overcoming resistance, encouraging talk about problems, interpreting feelings, discussing practical problems, etc. Although this is a limited objectification of the casework process, it constitutes an advance over information now available about what caseworkers actually do for their clients.

Although the Casework Interview Checksheet was developed and used in a pilot study with other cases, and although it appeared to be a promising device for describing the interview process, it was not possible to carry out its routine use with the girls from Vocational High referred to the project. In the first place, the administrative problems of instituting and supervising the completion of this instrument after each interview could not be overcome. There was a limit to what could be reasonably expected of the caseworkers faced with so many other unfamiliar adaptations required by the project. Second, the treatment approach, after the first year and a half, shifted from individual casework to group and individual methods, especially for initial involvement and diagnostic purposes. The Casework Interview Checksheet was not adapted to group therapy.[6]

RESEARCH DATA OBTAINED FOR THE STUDY

With the focus of the research on evaluation of effectiveness by comparing referred and control samples, data on criteria of success and change were required. This section considers the kinds of information sought and the rationale for seeking them. Since the same sorts of data are also useful to provide knowledge about adolescents generally as well as about treatment efforts, some note will be taken of the potential use of the data for such purposes.

Criteria of Successful Preventive Treatment

The professional staff of Youth Consultation Service, the school officials, and the researchers were all well aware from the beginning of the project of the common difficulties of establishing criteria by which to test effectiveness of preventive efforts. Establishing such criteria, of course, is a central requirement for evaluative research. But criteria of success in social work, as in other helping and counseling professions, are often extremely vague and elusive. And in a preventive effort, with undifferentiated client problems and generalized treatment approaches, the problem of measuring success might be viewed as even more difficult.

The fact that the project had an experimental design imposed certain restrictions on the kinds of criteria that might be used. It was necessary that the criteria be applied with equal objectivity to the treated (experimental) and the untreated (control) samples. Therefore, judgments on the part of caseworkers of their own success, whatever other merits or deficiencies they may have as criteria, could not be directly used, since similar judgments would not be available for the control cases. It was theoretically possible to have clinical judgments of both samples made "blind" by outside social workers or clinicians but practically this was not possible with available resources. To rely on the judgments of teachers in the school as indications of success was also deemed unsatisfactory because of the possibility of biases. It was decided that caseworker assessments of the treated clients would be obtained and explored but not used as criteria. It was also decided that limited appraisals by school guidance personnel would be sought on all the girls in the cohorts included in the project. Although such judgments might contain biases (since girls referred to YCS would be known by the judges), they would provide uniform professional judgmental data on the total school population.

Another restriction on the type of criteria arose from the fact that the needs of the clients selected for preventive services were varied and of a general nature. The bases for selection of clients have been described earlier. It was not possible to match these general, perhaps almost intuitive, potential-problem indicators with their counterparts three years later. Since no clear diagnosis of disability or need was possible in a preventive effort, no measure of the absence or diminution of symptoms could be obtained. To use such a diagnosis as a baseline would, if it were possible at all, require extensive contact and observation of the control cases (as well as the treated cases), and this might in itself have an unknown effect.

In thinking of appropriate criteria, the key questions are: What sorts of behavior are we seeking to encourage or to prevent? What sorts of characteristics do we seek to develop in adolescent girls that will be more likely to promise a "normal," "healthy,"

or "nondeviant" future? Thus criteria were developed that would
reflect appropriate current behavior of adolescent girls on the one
hand, and "healthy" or "normal" personal characteristics on the
other hand.

Criteria of appropriate behavior of adolescent high school girls can,
at the least, be defined in the commonly expected performance of
main social tasks of such girls: to complete their education without interruption and with maximum achievement in keeping
with the school program; to conform adequately to school rules
and to the norms of proper behavior out of school; to maintain
suitable relationships with peers; to prepare for normal vocational and marital careers. Although these criteria can be stated
positively, they must be measured negatively, since "normal" is
usually a global range of behaviors the limits of which are known
primarily by deviant or abnormal behavior. In the negative
sense, "getting into trouble" is the general statement of failure
and "not getting into trouble" is the inclusive statement of
success.

Thus for experimental and control cases alike, information was
obtained about *school performance and behavior*. Did the student
finish school or drop out? Was she ever suspended or expelled
from school? Was she "truant" from school? Did she pursue the
vocational training program provided for her? Was her attendance at school good or poor? Was her school conduct satisfactory
or unsatisfactory? Did she receive honors, awards, and good
ratings for school service? Did teachers regard her as outstanding
or as presenting a serious problem to them?

Some *out-of-school behavior* also is indicative of getting into
trouble but this was more difficult to obtain without resources for
an extended field follow-up. Out-of-wedlock pregnancy, however, was one event that became known to the school and represented unsatisfactory behavior and it was included among the
criteria. Also, getting into trouble with police or becoming
known through delinquent acts was a relevant negative behavioral criterion, and an effort was made to obtain information
about this for experimental and control cases through use of the
Social Service Exchange, in which contact with juvenile authori-

ties as well as social agencies is recorded. In general, it might be expected that out-of-school serious trouble for a girl would result in her removal from school or impairment of her school record so that school continuity was considered a reflection at least in part of out-of-school situation.

It may be asked whether such behavioral and objective criteria as these can be expected to reflect the type of treatment offered by an agency such as YCS. From one point of view, the agency is not directing its primary effort to achieving school continuity and good behavior. It is more likely to see itself as seeking to achieve optimal functioning, healthy personalities, satisfactory interpersonal relations, and the like. It can certainly be argued, however, that the latter are not ends in themselves but are basic to "normal and appropriate" living and hence the more objective criteria are minimum secondary objectives of treatment.

It may be asserted that for some adolescent girls "misbe-havior," "acting out behavior," or even concrete acts such as truancy and dropping out of school are signs of growth and appropriate personality change under casework or other ther-apies. However, it can hardly be maintained that school dropout, truancy, out-of-wedlock pregnancy, and the like are desirable in general, and for a group of clients served by a social agency one would expect an effort to be made to achieve constructive psychological changes without such drastic intervening difficul-ties. At any rate, lack of educational success may be expected to have serious consequences for later life and increase in educa-tional success may reasonably be assumed to be beneficial. A group of high school students who had been helped by a social agency ought to show more satisfactory school records.

In addition to objective differences such as those just dis-cussed, adolescent girls who have been helped by social workers may be expected to differ in more personal ways from those who have not received help, if success is to be attributed to treatment. From the viewpoint of prevention, more positive attitudes toward the future, more confidence about meeting problems, more acceptance of social norms of behavior ought to be manifest. Likewise, indications of more balanced and less extreme personality characteristics might be expected to promise less difficulty in the future life of the girl. Therefore, a set of what might be called *clinical criteria of success* is useful in assessing the effects of preventive treatment.

We are on uncertain ground when we attempt to state the characteristics of "healthy personalities"; nevertheless, it cannot be denied that casework and similar counseling services are directed toward enhancing such psychological good health. Therefore, we must at least seek to examine changes that occur and interpret them in the light of available clinical concepts of normality, effective functioning, and personal competence. From this point of view, a number of measures were introduced that could be examined in relationship to treatment and judged in terms of criteria of success.

Our measures included a general personality inventory, a projective test, and self-report indicators of social adjustment and attitudes. On some of these measures we sought to detect trends, or changes through time, and on others we sought only to discover if the treated experimental group differed from the control group and from the rest of the school population.

Two direct measures of *personality change* were used, the Junior Personality Quiz[7] and the Make A Sentence Test.[8] The JPQ is a questionnaire containing items that have been selected through factor analysis to reflect twelve personality dimensions. This personality test was expressly developed for use with young adolescents between twelve and sixteen years of age. Its dimensions have meaningful relationship in content to the more fully developed 16 Personality Factor Test that has been widely used in studies of adult personality.

One of the common criticisms of measures on such "objective" personality tests as the JPQ is that they will not be sufficiently "sensitive" to reveal changes that therapists say they "see" in their clients. It is sometimes asserted, for example, that paper-and-pencil questionnaires of self-report personality items, or preference statements, or value orientations will be so general that only superficial verbal responses are tapped. These might be relatively impervious to demonstrations of change even when persons actually do change. Furthermore, such measures may, it is sometimes noted, have little relationship between personality and the behaviors on which the clinicians are focusing. Finally, it is sometimes held that socially expected responses are more readily given to questionnaire items than to projective test stimuli and hence systematically false presentations are provided, rather than valid representations of personality such as might be available with extended clinical interviewing.

With such considerations in mind, an alternative method of reflecting personality was sought. It appeared that the sentence-completion form had more advantages and fewer liabilities than other projective tests. Responses to sentence-completion test items are capable of content analysis by standardized techniques and such surface interpretation of content appears to be an important part of even the more subtle uses of projective tests. Other projective test approaches—the TAT and Rorschach, for example—appeared too demanding of language ability for group administration as well as prohibitive in individual administration. Therefore, the MAST was adopted after considerable developmental work. The scoring categories have been used reliably and have been shown to be correlated with apparently similar dimensions as measured by a number of objective personality tests.[9]

It may be argued that the type of treatment to which the adolescent girls referred to YCS were exposed cannot be expected to affect fundamental personality characteristics such as those presumably measured by these tests. Persons may not change basically from limited contact with social workers. This may very well be true but it is an open question and one on which light may be shed by examining these measures. Plausible differences to be expected from "healthier," "more normal," "less disturbed," "better functioning" persons may readily be hypothesized in terms of the categories of these tests and therefore they may suggest differences between treated and control cases that are in directions accepted as indicative of successful treatment.

It may also be argued that some changes in personality characteristics are normal concomitants of adolescent growth; that this is a period of maturation most likely to see such changes. One of the advantages of a control group design is that it permits examination of changes that might be attributable to the different experiences of the treated adolescent girls when they are compared to the nontreated control sample rather than to maturation, selection, or other factors. Furthermore, when successive measures of each girl are taken through the years of the study, it is possible to examine "normal" changes as well, especially since the entire cohort is observed by use of the same tests and other instruments.

A more superficial level of change for successfully treated adolescent girls might be expected to be reflected in *general attitudes* toward themselves and their situations. Particularly relevant attitudes might be those concerned with self-assessment of difficulties, of felt capacity to handle their own problems, and of attitudes toward accepting help with their problems. A short questionnaire was included to permit the girls to rate how they felt, whether they felt better "now" than in the recent past, how well they were getting along with friends, schoolmates, and family, whether they felt they were bothered by many problems, and whether they felt that they would be able to take care of these problems in the future.

Although it might be meaningful to hypothesize the type of differential responses of successfully treated girls compared to the control group, it would seem preferable to examine changes and make comparisons on an exploratory basis because we have no norms of "healthier" or "more appropriate" responses. Further, in studying attitudes one must be especially cautious because of variations in verbal meanings and, even when meanings are certain, because of tendencies of respondents to give socially desirable or conventional responses. Nevertheless, examination of attitude differences may contribute to assessment of effects on the clients referred by Vocational High to YCS.

Special attention has been given to *attitudes toward dynamics of behavior* and the use and *value of getting help from others* when one has problems. Casework, like most efforts to counsel, seeks to develop some insight into feelings and the psychological sources of a person's behavior. To succeed in doing this, caseworkers seek to establish a relationship with their clients and gradually to explore with them some of the less obvious aspects of their personalities. For adolescents, in particular, this would seem to be a crucial precondition of the kind of help YCS believed would be useful for girls with potential problems. It will be recalled that establishing contact and involvement in a relationship were most difficult with Youth Board referrals and hence a point of particular interest in this research. If girls who were clients of YCS expressed more self-understanding and more acceptance of efforts to help them, they might be considered benefited by the agency.

A questionnaire was constructed and administered to all girls in Vocational High during one year to detect such attitudes. Unlike the measures previously discussed, this questionnaire was used only once but at a time when the school population would contain the maximum number of YCS clients having contact with the agency. Thus comparisons could be made between experimental cases of varying periods of treatment and control cases and other high school girls.

A final inquiry into general attitudes, as well as future outlook by the girls, was made by having all senior girls complete a questionnaire about their plans, their confidence or worry about the future, and their judgment as to whether they had been helped outside of school in personal problems by designated "helpful persons," such as parents, friends, doctors, social workers, ministers, and the like. They were also asked about their employment plans and marital expectations. In addition, they were asked to assess their recent (last two or three years) troubles as compared to those of "most girls in school," and to write what they liked best and least about being in school.

Although it might be reasonable to expect girls who had been in contact with YCS for several years to give more positive responses to such questions, it was not hypothesized as to what differences, if any, between them and the control group might be found. It was thought preferable to interpret findings as they occurred. Nevertheless, it was assumed that the existence of even *some* differences in a positive direction might be taken as an indication of success in treatment.

In addition to the objective criteria and the more clinical criteria that have just been described, another behavioral measure was sought that might possibly have some relationship to changes induced by treatment and hence become available as an interpretable criterion of successful preventive treatment. This was a general *sociometric questionnaire* asking the student to list classmates who are "friends of yours, whom you pal around with." Several alternative hypotheses bearing on successful treatment experience might be investigated with such sociometric data. First, it might be hypothesized that casework treatment might reduce perception of social isolation at school or increase gregariousness. Second, it might be hypothesized that the healthier girls would be more often chosen than those with more manifest problems. Third, the hypothesis might be proposed that composition of the friendship circle might change for successfully treated girls toward greater association with those showing positive rather than negative characteristics. Thus successfully influenced clients might be expected to have fewer "bad associates." In particular, changes through the years in the type of choices made and received might reflect trends in positive or negative directions that could be indicative of beneficial influence from YCS.

For reasons mentioned earlier, the *judgments of the social workers* of their own clients could not be taken as criteria of success with them. Nevertheless, in order to examine such judgments against the criteria that were used, the social worker with primary responsibility for each of the referred clients was asked to make a series of judgments as to the need of the client for help, the type and degree of involvement developed, and the amount of change perceived, including estimates of movement based on the Hunt-Kogan Movement Scale.[10] Social workers were also asked to make certain prognostic ratings about the future for each client. In addition to serving as indirect criteria of perceived benefit, such ratings would permit a subjective differentiation among the experimental cases on the basis of judgments of success. Hence those clients seen most to benefit could be compared with those not thought to derive any good from it and with the control group. Such judgmental observations could also be compared with objective indicators of treatment, such as number of contacts with the agency.

Conclusion with Respect to Criteria of Successful Preventive Treatment

The viewpoint taken toward the crucial question of criteria of success is evident in the lengthy discussion of measures sought. To meet the lack of specificity in latent problems, the uncertainty as to definitive indicators of appropriate change and behavior, and the generalized treatment approach necessarily used, a wide range of objective, clinical, and behavioral criteria was used. It could not be expected that differences between the experimental group and the control group would be found for all, or even for many, of these varied criteria measures. But it was believed that at least some of them should detect the kind of effects that preventive efforts of social workers could produce.

OTHER DATA OBTAINED

It has been indicated that most data were collected in successive testing sessions for the entire school cohort. Specifically, the class of girls was tested (on all the research instruments) within the first month of their entry to Vocational High and subsequently during the last month of each school year that they remained in school. Thus for students entering the tenth grade and remaining through graduation in the twelfth grade, four sets of data were obtained. For students dropping out before their senior year, data were obtained for as many years as the time in the school permitted. Objective information from school records and from school personnel was obtained for all students who had entered, whether they completed the school years or not. Also, in the initial period of testing, certain information about all the students' family and home backgrounds was obtained.

NOTES TO CHAPTER II

1. A general description of the project, including the research design, appears in Meyer, Henry J., and Edgar F. Borgatta, "Social Agency and School as the Context for Studies of Mental Health: Research in Progress," *Social Work*, vol. 5, January, 1960, pp. 21–26.

2. See Meyer, Henry J., and Edgar F. Borgatta, *An Experiment in Mental Patient Rehabilitation*, Russell Sage Foundation, New York, 1959, pp. 34–45. As it turned out, the agency moved its location during the course of the present project but provision was made to meet referred clients in the neighborhood of the school.

3. From comments by Leonore R. Miller in a panel discussion (unpublished) on "Preventive Treatment for Adolescent Girls: A Pilot Project," at National Conference on Social Welfare, Atlantic City, June, 1960.

4. A few girls entering the ninth grade were also included, but the designated period of observation was three years.

5. Miller, Leonore R., *op. cit.*

6. A study of the casework interview process based on the use of the Casework Interview Checksheet was carried out in another social agency, which is reported in Meyer, Henry J., Edgar F. Borgatta, and David Fanshel, "A Study of the Interview Process: The Caseworker-Client Relationship," *Genetic Psychology Monographs*, vol. 69, 1964, pp. 247–295.

7. Test developed by R. B. Cattell, J. Beloff, D. Flint, and W. Gruen, Institute for Personality and Ability Testing, Champaign, Ill. For a description, see Cattell, R. B., and H. Beloff, "Research Origin and Construction of the I.P.A.T. Junior Personality Quiz: The J.P.Q.," *Journal of Consulting Psychology*, vol. 17, 1953, pp. 436–442.

8. Test developed by Edgar F. Borgatta and Henry J. Meyer. For description, see Borgatta, Edgar F., in collaboration with Henry J. Meyer, "Make A Sentence Test: An Approach to Objective Scoring of Sentence Completions," *Genetic Psychology Monographs*, vol. 63, 1961, pp. 3–65. Also Borgatta, Edgar F., and Henry J. Meyer, "The Reliability of an Objective Sentence Completion Scoring Technique," *Journal of Social Psychology*, vol. 58, 1962, pp. 163–166; Borgatta, Edgar F., "The Make A Sentence Test (MAST): A Replication Study," *Journal of General Psychology*, vol. 65, 1961, pp. 269–292.

9. Borgatta, Edgar F., in collaboration with Henry J. Meyer, *op. cit.*, pp. 27–46.

10. Hunt, J. McVicker, and Leonard S. Kogan, *Measuring Results in Social Casework: A Manual for Judging Movement*. Family Service Association of America, New York, 1950.

III. Social Characteristics of Potential Problem Girls Within the Total School Population

Since descriptive information about the social characteristics of high school students is not commonly available, this chapter will describe the characteristics of the total population of girls attending Vocational High. It also has three other objectives: (1) to compare the segment of the student population designated as "potential problem cases" with the students not deemed to be potential problems, termed "residual cases"; (2) to compare the potential problem cases that were referred to Youth Consultation Service (identified as "experimental cases") with the potential problem cases that were not referred (identified as "control cases"); and (3) to note any changes in the characteristics of the samples of residual cases and of potential problem cases that might appear as a result of selective effects during the course of their high school careers.

The comparison of potential problem and residual cases is necessary in order to test the intention of the project to identify girls especially in need of social work services so that a random sample of them might be referred for help. Therefore, we shall be looking for differences between potential problem and residual cases. On the other hand, the design of the research called for initially similar experimental and control cases to be drawn from the pool of potential problem cases. Random assignment was the procedure chosen to achieve such similarity. A comparison of experimental and control cases will be a test of whether this procedure did, in fact, achieve initial similarity on those variables for which measures are available.

As cohorts of students go through their high school years, certain students drop out and the composition of the remainder

51

of the cohort may be selectively altered. Although not a primary objective of this research, it will be of some interest to observe any differences between the social characteristics of the girls who began their high school careers but dropped out and those who graduated. Such information has obvious bearing on the question of which girls drop out and which girls stay to graduate.

The development of the inclusive sample of girls involved in the research occurred in stages over a period of four years. Four consecutive entering cohorts of girls were utilized (1955 to 1958), and from each a pool of potential problem cases was designated. Entering students in each of these cohorts completed questionnaires and tests during the first month of school, in the fall of the year (September). They were subsequently retested the following spring during the last month of the school year (May or June) and each spring thereafter until the cohort had completed the three years of high school to graduation or until the project terminated. The following chart summarizes the development of the inclusive sample.

	Cohorts Entering School in the Fall of Each Year:			
Test Period	1955	1956	1957	1958
1955–1956				
Fall	First test			
Spring	Second test			
1956–1957				
Fall		First test		
Spring	Third test	Second test		
1957–1958				
Fall			First test	
Spring	Fourth test	Third test	Second test	
1958–1959				
Fall				First test
Spring		Fourth test	Third test	Second test
1959–1960				
Fall				
Spring			Fourth test	Third test

The first cohort (1955), used for developmental or pilot experience, was particularly concerned with the potential problem group, the suitability of research instruments, and the administrative arrangements necessary for the experiment. Complete data collection was achieved for the potential problem cases of this cohort but certain background information was not obtained for the residual cases. The last cohort (1958) had completed only two of the three years of high school when the project terminated and, although data were obtained for the potential problem cases of this cohort that paralleled the other cohorts, this cohort differs from the earlier three cohorts in duration of the observation period in school. The second (1956) and third (1957) cohorts thus constitute the central sources of data to be described in this chapter, since these entire cohorts were tested at entrance and at each of the three subsequent end-of-year test periods. These cohorts represent two classes of students observed through all three years of high school. Information about the 1955 cohort will be utilized as a supplement when potential problem cases are compared with the residual cases from the two central cohorts. Data for residual cases in the 1958 cohort will not be used in this chapter since the full three-year period cannot be examined. In later chapters when experimental and control cases are compared, the potential problem cases from all four cohorts can be included.

BASIC COMPARISON OF POTENTIAL PROBLEM AND RESIDUAL CASES

The design of the experiment was predicated on the assumption that high school girls who constituted potential problem cases could be identified so that an experimental sample offered social work services could be compared with a control sample. In the sections of this chapter that follow, differences between the social characteristics of potential problem cases and those of the residual cases will be examined and comparisons made to support the basic assumption. However, there is one important criterion available to test whether this assumption was meaningful, namely, whether potential problem cases completed school to the same extent as the other girls in their cohorts. Using this criterion, it is dramatically clear that a smaller proportion of potential problem cases remained in school long enough to be present at the final test period at the end of their graduation year. Table 1 shows that 61 per cent of the residual cases as compared to 49 per cent of the potential problem cases were present at the final test period. The difference is statistically significant at the .05 level accepted for this study.

TABLE 1. POTENTIAL PROBLEM AND RESIDUAL CASES BY PRESENCE AT FINAL TEST

Presence at Final Test	Potential Problem Cases		Residual Cases	
	Number	Per cent	Number	Per cent
Present at final test	127	49	334	61
Not present at final test	134	51	212	39
Total	261	100	546	100

Thus the initial designation of potential problem cases may be viewed as a successful delineation of high school girls who are less likely to complete their high school careers and in this sense, at least, constitute girls for whom social work services would seem desirable. In other words, the girls identified as potential problems differed from the rest of the girls in their high school cohorts by dropping out of school in greater numbers, and hence can be said to constitute a special group.

The potential problem cases include both experimental and control cases but we will not discuss at this point any differences between them. It is to be noted, however, that if referral to YCS of the experimental cases had any effect on remaining in school until the final testing period, it is not sufficient to obliterate the difference implied in the initial division of girls into potential problem and residual cases.

ETHNIC COMPOSITION OF THE SCHOOL POPULATION

As previously indicated, the vocational school studied accepts students from all areas of the city but entrance is not necessarily representative of the ethnic composition of the city. Of more direct concern to our study is whether potential problem and residual cases differ in this respect. The relevant data are presented in Table 2.

TABLE 2. ETHNIC COMPOSITION OF POTENTIAL PROBLEM AND
RESIDUAL CASES PRESENT AT FIRST AND FINAL TESTS

Ethnic Group	Potential Problem Cases			Residual Cases
	Experimentals	Controls	Total	
	(Per cent)			(Per cent)
First test				
White	27	27	27	26
Negro	50	58	54	41
Puerto Rican	23	15	19	33
Total	100	100	100	100
Number of cases	129	132	261	546
Final test				
White	28	23	26	27
Negro	51	64	57	44
Puerto Rican	21	13	17	29
Total	100	100	100	100
Number of cases	67	60	127	334

Approximately one-fourth of both the potential problem and
the residual cases are white girls. Significant differences do occur,
however, between the proportions of Negro and Puerto Rican
girls in these two samples, with a greater proportion of Negroes
and a smaller proportion of Puerto Ricans appearing in the
potential problem group than in the residual group. The same
ethnic composition is maintained at the final test, as indicated in
the lower section of Table 2.

In the absence of further data, we may only speculate on the
reasons that Negro girls are overselected and Puerto Rican girls
are underselected among the potential problem cases. The population of the school as a whole, it should be noted, is disproportionately composed of nonwhite girls compared with the population of the city from which the students are drawn. Data from the
1960 census indicate that 14 per cent of the female population of
New York City, fifteen to nineteen years of age, were Negro and
21 per cent were Puerto Rican, whereas the proportions in the
total sample for the school are 32 per cent and 28 per cent,
respectively. Even when the ethnic composition of the school
sample is compared with the population of Manhattan—with its
greater concentration of Negro and Puerto Rican families—there

is still a disproportionate number of nonwhite girls in the school. Evidently, the labor force of the industry for which this school offers vocational training attracts nonwhite female workers. What is of particular interest, however, is the unequal number of Negroes and Puerto Ricans among the potential problem and the residual cases. The higher rate of Negroes identified as potential problems may reflect some tendency to direct troublesome Negro girls to the trade schools as a measure of social control of deviant behavior. On the other hand, Puerto Ricans may be channeled into the school more explicitly to learn the trades and hence the less troublesome are so directed. These interpretations are compatible with the data but should not be mistaken for knowledge of actual selective factors that produce the differences indicated in the data.

Within the potential problem group, as between the experimental and control cases, there are only minor differences. The random selection procedure apparently equalized ethnic composition. This composition was maintained at the time of the final test.

Despite the overrepresentation of Negroes among potential problem cases relative to Puerto Ricans, a significantly greater proportion of Negro girls than Puerto Ricans remained in school through their senior year. Dropout was relatively greatest for Puerto Ricans, least for Negroes, and intermediate for white girls. (See Table 3.) This difference may well reflect, however, higher residential mobility of Puerto Ricans in New York rather than factors more directly concerned with school work or behavior.

TABLE 3. ETHNIC COMPOSITION OF POTENTIAL PROBLEM AND RESIDUAL CASES PRESENT AT FINAL TEST

	Potential Problem Cases		Residual Cases	
Ethnic Group	Number at first test	Per cent at final test	Number at first test	Per cent at final test
White	71	47	141	62
Negro	140	51	226	65
Puerto Rican	50	44	178	55
Total	261	49	545[a]	61

[a] Excludes one case whose ethnic designation was "other."

As might be expected from the disproportionate number of Puerto Rican girls among the residual cases, a significantly higher percentage of potential problem cases than of residual cases (71 per cent compared to 53 per cent) report English as the only language spoken in their homes. Conversely, 32 per cent of the residual cases compared with 19 per cent of the potential problem cases indicated that Spanish was spoken at home.

CHARACTERISTICS OF FAMILIES

High school students who have school difficulties have often been found to come from home backgrounds revealing greater disorganization and lower economic status, and differing in other ways from students not having difficulties. We may compare the potential problem cases among the population of high school girls in this study with residual cases on a number of family characteristics.

Presence of Parents in Home

As shown in Table 4, the percentage of potential problem cases with both father and mother present (56 per cent) is somewhat less than the percentage found for residual cases (63 per

TABLE 4. PRESENCE OF PARENTS OF POTENTIAL PROBLEM AND RESIDUAL CASES AT FIRST AND FINAL TESTS

Presence of Parents	Potential Problem Cases			Residual Cases
	Experimentals	Controls	Total	
	(Per cent)			(Per cent)
First test				
Both father and mother	54	58	56	63
Only mother	40	36	38	28
Only other persons	6	6	6	9
Total	100	100	100	100
Number of cases	129	132	261	546
Final test				
Both father and mother	55	59	57	69
Only mother	37	38	38	25
Only other persons	8	3	5	6
Total	100	100	100	100
Number of cases	67	60	127	334

cent), but this difference is not statistically significant. However, the proportion of potential problem cases in which only the mother is present (38 per cent) is significantly greater than the proportion among residual cases (28 per cent). Thus girls whose school records caused them to be designated potential problems came disproportionately from broken homes.

Between first and final test periods, selective processes were at work that evidently intensified this difference in family composition. Because disproportionate numbers of residual cases from homes with both father and mother present remained in school, the residual group differed significantly at the final test from the potential problem group in percentages from homes with both parents present as well as from homes where only a mother was present. (See Table 4, lower section.) For residual cases, but not for potential problem cases, absence of both father and mother is positively related to leaving school. One may speculate that in the constellation of factors related to dropout, broken homes play a greater part when girls are not already visibly headed for trouble, whereas other factors have greater effects on girls identifiable as potential problems. It should be remembered, however, that the latter drop out disproportionately (see Table 1) despite the selective effect of broken homes on residual cases.

As would be expected from the random selection procedure, there are no significant differences at first or final test period between experimental and control cases with respect to the presence of parents in the home.

Family Extension

Girls designated as potential problem cases show a somewhat greater likelihood of coming exclusively from nuclear families, whereas residual cases come disproportionately from extended families. Although not a statistically significant difference, 79 per cent of the potential problem cases as compared to 73 per cent of the residual cases reported that they lived only with their nuclear families. This difference is worth noting in view of a common expectation that the nuclear family constitutes a superior setting for the type of parental supervision and control that is thought to be related to educational success. If the finding here were borne out in additional study, it would support the hypothesis that presence within the home of additional adults in the extended family may deter, rather than encourage, behavior likely to result in identification as potential problem. It might be suggested that the simple addition of adults adds weight to parental values, or that the structure of the extended-family home protects adolescents from influences leading toward potential problems.

There are negligible differences in family extension between first and last test periods, and between experimental and control cases.

Size of Household

The size of household, independent of family type involved, is approximately the same for potential problem and residual cases. The former reported an average size of 5.32 members present in the household and the latter reported an average size of 5.35. No differences of a systematic or meaningful nature were found in size of household between girls who stayed in school and those who dropped out, nor between experimental and control cases.

Sibling Structure

The average number of siblings living at home with potential problem cases was 2.51 and the average for residual cases was 2.31. This small difference is not statistically significant, although it is consistent with the suggestion that potential problem cases might be more likely to occur in families where available resources for supervision and control have to be spread over more children. No differences were found in number of siblings at home of girls who remained in school and those who dropped out before the final test period.

One finding became obvious in examination of the data on sibling structure. For both potential problem and residual cases, the number of younger siblings living with the family is significantly larger than the number of older siblings reported. The potential problem cases indicated an average of .86 older siblings and 1.65 younger siblings, and the residual cases reported .87 and 1.44, respectively.

Although it may be tempting to speculate that the effects of a different structural position predispose older children to attend vocational school, the explanation is more simple and direct. The question as asked creates an artifact of data collection, since older siblings are those not likely to be living at home and so were not enumerated.

Family Housing

On the single measure of housing for the samples in the study—number of rooms per person—there were no significant differences between potential problem and residual cases, between cases remaining in school and those dropping out before the final test period, or between experimental and control cases. Of the residual cases, 45 per cent reported one or more rooms per person compared to 43 per cent of the potential problem cases.

SOCIAL AND ECONOMIC LEVELS OF FAMILIES

We may examine first the employment and occupational characteristics of the families in the school samples of this study. Then we shall examine educational level.

Employment

Somewhat more of the residual cases than of the potential problem cases reported two or more employed persons in their households. There were 46 per cent of the former and 40 per cent of the latter, but the difference is not statistically significant. Almost equal proportions (16 per cent for residuals and 17 per cent for potential problem) reported no employed persons. Therefore, slightly more of the potential problem cases (43 per cent) than of the residual cases (38 per cent) had one employed person in the household. Thus the two major divisions of the school population do not appear to be greatly dissimilar in this respect.

With respect to employed persons in the household, however, a significant difference was found between the experimental and control cases within the potential problem group. The proportion of control cases was 49 per cent with two or more employed persons, whereas only 33 per cent of the experimental cases so reported. Proportionately fewer of the control cases came from households where there was only one or no employed person. Since selection of experimental and control cases was random, no explanation can be given for the difference between them other than random error. It is necessary, however, to note such differential characteristics when they occur.

Occupational Level

Table 5 shows the occupational levels of the samples in the study. It is apparent that only small (and statistically insignificant) differences occur between potential problem and residual

TABLE 5. OCCUPATIONAL LEVEL OF FAMILIES OF POTENTIAL PROBLEM AND RESIDUAL CASES AT FIRST TEST

Occupational Level	Potential Problem Cases			Residual Cases
	Experi- mentals	Con- trols	Total	
	(Per cent)			(Per cent)
Professionals, proprietors, managers, officials	1	4	3	5
Clerks, salesmen and kindred white collar workers	9	8	8	8
Skilled workers	12	13	13	15
Semi-skilled: factory workers	17	16	16	23
Semi-skilled other than factory workers	22	20	21	19
Unskilled, common labor	8	5	7	7
Domestic and personal service	9	7	8	2
Not employed	22	27	24	21
Total	100	100	100	100
Number of cases	129	132	261	496[a]

[a] Excludes 50 cases for whom occupation was unknown.

cases. What differences there are suggest that the level of potential problem cases is somewhat lower than that of residual cases. Thus higher proportions in the levels of semi-skilled factory workers and above tend to be associated with residual cases, whereas the lower levels appear slightly associated with potential problem cases.

As a whole, the population of the study is clearly from working-class occupational backgrounds, and probably more from less skilled and lower income occupations than skilled work. A little more than one-fifth of the heads of households were reported as not employed; in all probability these families depend on irregular employment or public sources of support. The occupational level is in keeping with what one would expect for the students of a vocational school.

Educational Level

The high school girls involved in this study had already attained higher educational levels than most of their parents, as might be expected with a working-class background and a high proportion of Negro and Puerto Rican families. Thus as Table 6 reveals, approximately one-third of both fathers and mothers had only elementary schooling, another third had some high school, and the remaining third are reported as having a high school

TABLE 6. EDUCATIONAL ATTAINMENT OF FATHERS AND MOTHERS OF POTENTIAL PROBLEM AND RESIDUAL CASES AT FIRST TEST

Educational Level Attained	Potential Problem Cases			Residual Cases
	Experimentals	Controls	Total	
		(Per cent)		(Per cent)
Mothers				
Elementary school only	38	42	41	30
Some high school	29	28	28	34
High school graduate or more	33	30	31	36
Total	100	100	100	100
Number of cases	129	132	261	463[a]
Fathers				
Elementary school only	39	45	42	34
Some high school	26	28	27	34
High school graduate or more	35	27	31	32
Total	100	100	100	100
Number of cases	129	132	261	405[b]

[a] Excludes 83 cases for whom educational attainment of mother was unknown.

[b] Excludes 141 cases for whom educational attainment of father was unknown.

education or more. This educational background for the high school students is by no means unusual in American society where the general trend has been for succeeding generations to receive more education than preceding ones. However, it may be noted that two-thirds of the parents did not finish high school and therefore represented models of educational attainment lower than that expected of the girls in the study, namely, that they complete their high school education.

The educational level of the parents of potential problem cases is somewhat lower than that of residual cases. The difference is most evident in the proportions reported as attaining only elementary school level where it is statistically significant for mothers but not quite significant for fathers. It is probably justifiable to say, therefore, that potential problem cases are drawn from somewhat lower educational backgrounds than residual cases.

No meaningful differences were found between parental educational backgrounds of girls who stayed in school through the final test period and those who dropped out.

Although control cases had somewhat lower parental educational backgrounds than experimental cases (see Table 6), the differences are not statistically significant.

So far as family members might represent educational models for the girls involved in this study, the educational attainment of older siblings is of interest. The girls were asked to indicate how much schooling their oldest sibling had completed, regardless of whether the oldest brother or sister was presently living in the household. As may be noted in Table 7, most of the girls (94 per cent of the potential problem cases and 92 per cent of the residual cases) reported that an older sibling—if they had one—had at least some high school education. About two-fifths (41 per cent of the potential problem cases and 45 per cent of the residual cases) reported that their oldest brother or sister had at least finished high school. The difference between potential problem and residual cases, favoring the latter, is not significant. The somewhat larger difference, favoring experimental cases (44 per cent high school graduates or more) over control cases (39 per cent),

TABLE 7. EDUCATIONAL ATTAINMENT OF OLDEST SIBLINGS OF POTENTIAL PROBLEM AND RESIDUAL CASES AT FIRST TEST

Educational Level Attained	Potential Problem Cases			Residual Cases
	Experimentals	Controls	Total	
	(Per cent)			*(Per cent)*
Elementary school only	*3*	*8*	*6*	*8*
Some high school	*53*	*53*	*53*	*47*
High school graduate or more	*44*	*39*	*41*	*45*
Total	*100*	*100*	*100*	*100*
Number with older siblings	61	89	150	287
Number with no older siblings	68	43[a]	111[a]	259[b]

[a] Includes 3 cases for whom information was not available.

[b] Includes 12 cases for whom information was not available.

indicates some selective effect within the potential problem group but the difference is not statistically significant. No significant differences were found with respect to educational attainment of oldest siblings of girls who remained in school and those who dropped out.

An indirect comparison may be made between the educational success of girls in this study and that achieved by their parents and oldest siblings. All of the girls in the study had entered high school and their success in finishing school can be compared to the success of parents and oldest siblings who at least entered high school. In this way both intergenerational and intragenerational models of educational achievement available in their nuclear families can be examined. Such comparisons are presented in Table 8.

Of the potential problem cases, approximately the same proportion of girls completed high school (remained through the final test period) as the proportion of their mothers who had some high school education but did not stay to graduate. A significantly larger percentage of potential problem girls than their fathers who had ever attended high school (49 per cent and 34 per cent, respectively) did finish. Furthermore, more of these girls than of their oldest siblings (49 per cent compared to 44 per cent) finished high school, but the difference is not statistically significant. Thus once having entered high school the potential

TABLE 8. SUCCESS IN ACHIEVING HIGH SCHOOL GRADUATION OF POTENTIAL PROBLEM AND RESIDUAL GIRLS, COMPARED TO THEIR MOTHERS, FATHERS, AND OLDEST SIBLINGS WHO HAD AT LEAST SOME HIGH SCHOOL EDUCATION

Educational Level Attained	Potential Problem Cases				Residual Cases			
	Girls	Mothers	Fathers	Oldest Siblings	Girls	Mothers	Fathers	Oldest Siblings
	(Per cent)				(Per cent)			
Some high school	51	48	66	56	39	49	52	51
High school graduate or more	49	52	34	44	61	51	48	49
Total	100	100	100	100	100	100	100	100
Number of cases	261	155	107	141	546	323	267	264

problem girls exceeded their fathers and oldest siblings and approximately equaled their mothers in achieving graduation.

The girls who constitute the residual cases, on the other hand, show significantly greater educational achievement than the other members of their families (mothers, fathers, and oldest siblings) who had ever entered high school. Approximately one-half of the other family members, compared to three-fifths of the girls, were reported as high school graduates or more.

The educational achievement of the girls in the samples when compared to their oldest siblings is probably somewhat understated in these data. Some of the oldest siblings may still have been in high school at the time their educational attainment was reported by their younger sisters. It is unlikely, however, that a substantial number of girls had older brothers or sisters still in high school when they entered. Since it is generally observed that boys drop out of high school in greater proportion than girls, one must only with caution conclude from the data that the proportion of girls in our samples who succeeded in finishing high school exceeded that of their older siblings. It is likely that they exceeded their oldest brothers and equaled their oldest sisters but our data do not allow us to examine this hypothesis directly. The difference between girls and oldest siblings among the residual cases is great enough to suggest that perhaps these girls do exceed both brothers and sisters. Since residual cases, by design of the research, exclude girls thought to have potential problems, such a difference would not be surprising.

When potential problem and residual cases are compared, the most noticeable difference (aside from that between the girls themselves) is between the percentage of fathers of residual cases and that of fathers of potential problem cases; 48 per cent of the former compared to 34 per cent of the latter are reported to be high school graduates or more, a statistically significant difference. The effect of this difference as an example of educational achievement set by their fathers would not seem to be substantial, however, since girls among the potential problem as well as the residual cases exceed their fathers to approximately the same extent.

The upward educational mobility of the girls among the residual cases is unmistakable but it must be remembered that this is a sample from which girls with potential problems have been removed. Upward educational mobility of girls among the potential problem cases is limited to their achievement in comparison with their fathers. They approximately duplicate the achievement of their mothers and probably of their oldest siblings as well. Except for the fathers, the educational models in the nuclear family represented in these data are approximately the same for potential problem and residual cases. Factors other than the example set by high school graduation of nuclear family members would seem to account for the lesser achievement of potential problem cases. Upward educational mobility is normally expected in American society. We may speculate that personal life histories and greater deprivations of other kinds, perhaps associated with greater proportions of Negroes among the potential problem cases, have inhibited such mobility. We cannot confirm such a speculation from our data. It is quite clear, however, that relative to the achievement of high school graduation by nuclear family members once they had entered high school, the potential problem cases achieve less than the residual cases.

We may summarize the available data on family characteristics by noting that potential problem cases, compared to residual cases, tend to come from Negro families but not from Puerto Rican families, from homes in which only the mother is present, from somewhat lower occupational and educational levels. No important differences appear with respect to these variables between girls who dropped out of school and those who remained through their senior year. Except for a greater proportion of families with two or more persons employed among the control cases, the experimental and control cases are essentially similar. Potential problem cases at least equaled their parents and oldest siblings in educational attainment, and residual cases exceeded them.

REPORTED HOME SITUATIONS AND FEELINGS ABOUT SELF OF POTENTIAL PROBLEM AND RESIDUAL CASES

The description of the backgrounds of the high school girls involved in the research in the preceding sections has utilized demographic and social characteristics found in many sociological studies to be related to various aspects of social and personal disorganization. Thus ethnic background, occupational level, family size and composition, and educational attainment are variables that usually differentiate segments of urban populations in which disproportionate incidence of school retardation and dropout, delinquency, poor mental health, dependency, and other social and personal problems are found. These variables, in one degree or another, constitute the indicators of what is often abbreviated by the designation "lower social class." It is assumed that such a position in the class structure of American society indicates limited attainment of styles of life deemed "normal" by middle-class standards and, hence, lower-class position exposes its members to the attention of official and unofficial agencies of social control and amelioration. It is not surprising, therefore, that the girls identified as potential problems should generally come from backgrounds that may be considered somewhat lower in socioeconomic status than the rest of their high school peers who constitute the residual cases. That the difference is not more evident is perhaps due to the fact that the entire population involved is primarily from working-class backgrounds.

Lower-class status is sometimes assumed, as well, to signify differential subcultures. In the context of socialization experiences these are assumed to result in different attitudes and personality characteristics. Under the further assumption that such differences are related to adequate personal and social functioning, social work agencies often seek to deal with them. Attitudinal and personality characteristics, seen as individualized in each person, are deemed to be not only crucial factors in the problems such clients present but they are usually considered to be accessible to the techniques of social work. It is therefore of interest to compare potential problem cases in this study with residual cases on such characteristics, to the extent that our data permit.

Girls' Perceptions of Aspects of Their Home Situations

At the time of their first test period, all girls were asked four questions about aspects of their home situations believed to be especially important for adolescents. These questions were necessarily general, subject to the limitations of the test situation, but they sought to reflect the girls' sense of affective cohesion of the home, their perception of the discipline they were subject to, and their feeling of independence.

Sense of Affective Cohesion. The girls were asked: "Do you think that people in your home feel very close to one another or does each one go his own way?" Responses of residual cases indicated a sense of somewhat closer feeling in the family than responses of potential problem cases, but the difference was not statistically significant. As Table 9 shows, 58 per cent of the residual cases compared to 53 per cent of the potential problem cases reported, "We are very closely tied together," the extreme response category available. Only 10 per cent of both groups indicated that family members "fairly often" or "always go their own way."

A more substantial difference, not quite statistically significant, appears between experimental and control cases. Forty-seven per cent of the former compared to 59 per cent of the latter reported people in their homes as "very closely tied together."

Perception of Discipline. When asked: "How does your family treat you at home about the things you are supposed to do?" the

TABLE 9. SENSE OF AFFECTIVE COHESION EXPRESSED BY POTEN-
TIAL PROBLEM AND RESIDUAL CASES AT FIRST TEST

"Do you think that people in your home feel very close to one another or does each one go his own way?"	Potential Problem Cases			Residual Cases
	Experi-mentals	Controls	Total	
		(Per cent)		(Per cent)
Very closely tied together	47	59	53	58
Fairly closely tied together	42	33	37	32
Each goes own way fairly often or always	11	8	10	10
Total	100	100	100	100
Number of cases	129	132	261	545[a]

[a] Excludes one case for whom information was not available.

potential problem cases saw themselves somewhat more "pushed" and "punished" but, once more, the difference was not quite statistically significant. Of the potential problem cases, 40 per cent compared to 34 per cent of the residual cases checked the categories, "They push me and punish me severely if I don't do them" or "They push me and punish me at first, but then let up." Thus the potential problem group reported that they were somewhat more often disciplined than the residual group. But for both groups, more than half reported that their families "remind me about (things I am supposed to do) but don't do much else."

When compared to the experimental cases, the control cases also reported they were more often disciplined but the difference between the two groups was not large.

Sense of Independence. Two questions were asked relating to a sense of independence in the family situation and on neither were the differences between the responses of potential problem and residual cases significant. To the question: "At home, does your family decide important things for you or do you make the important decisions that affect you by yourself?" 12 per cent of the potential problems and 11 per cent of the residuals reported: "My family decide these things." Most of the girls (61 per cent of the potential problems and 65 per cent of the residuals) reported "My family mostly decide but they talk to me about them."

The other question bearing on independence concerns sources of spending money. The same proportion of both potential problem and residual cases (59 per cent) reported that they got spending money "From my family when I need it." "Regular allowances" were reported for approximately the same proportions of potential problem and residual cases: 28 per cent of the former and 32 per cent of the latter. Relatively few of either group got their spending money by working or indicated that they "really don't have any spending money."

For neither of these questions were there statistically significant differences between experimental and control cases or between girls who stayed in school and those who dropped out.

At least insofar as these questions could detect them, the aspects of home life considered do not appear different for the potential problem and the residual cases. On the whole, both groups see their families as closely tied together, as exercising only mild discipline, and themselves as fairly dependent on the family for important decisions and for spending money. This is the situation that would reasonably be expected for girls of fourteen or fifteen years of age.

General Feelings About Self and Others

A series of questions asked how the girls felt, how they thought they were getting along with friends and family, whether they felt they had problems that were bothering them, and whether they felt they could take care of their problems in the future. These questions were not intended to probe deeply into the girls' perceptions of their own situations; the operational restrictions on the research precluded more extended inquiry. But it was considered useful to obtain a general sense of how the girls felt things were going so that any changes in such feelings could be noted as a result of treatment by social workers.

Approximately three-fifths of the potential problem and of the residual cases answered that they were getting along "very well" with their families and with their friends, people they work or go to school with, and other acquaintances. What slight differences there were showed residual cases less likely than potential problem cases to report that they were getting along "not too well" or "not well at all." Nine per cent of the potential problem group so reported as compared to 5 per cent of the residual group (not a statistically significant difference).

To the direct question: "Generally speaking, how do you feel?" almost exactly half of the potential problem and of the residual cases answered "excellent" or "very well." Once more, however, potential problem cases tended more than residual cases to report negatively even though the difference between the two samples did not achieve statistical significance. Thus 13 per cent of the potential problem cases compared to 8 per cent of the residual cases said they felt "not too well" or "not well at all." Similarly, the same difference was found in the negative responses of "a little bit worse," "worse," or "much worse" in reply to the question: "Do you feel better than you did about two months ago?" These replies were given to that question by 15 per cent of the potential problem compared to 10 per cent of the residual cases. Proportions were essentially equal (70 and 71 per cent, respectively) between these groups for those feeling "much better" or "better" now than about two months ago.

Potential problem and residual cases were almost identical in responses to the question: "Do you feel you are going to be able to take care of your problems all right in the future?" Approximately three-fifths of each sample said they would be able to take care of their problems "very well" or "satisfactorily" and about one-seventh said they would have "a little trouble" or "a lot of trouble." Nevertheless, a greater percentage of potential problem than of residual cases indicated that they had "a great many" or "quite a few" problems that were bothering them. This statistically significant difference is shown in Table 10.

Considering all these self-attitude questions together, we may conclude that potential problem cases tended to see themselves with respect to their feelings, associations, and sense of having problems somewhat more negatively but by no means dramatically so. One should perhaps not expect marked differences in replies to such direct, undisguised questions but the differences that did appear may indicate the utility of self-prognostic reports —particularly when they are at the negative extreme. In any

TABLE 10. SELF-REPORT ON PROBLEMS BOTHERING POTENTIAL PROBLEM AND RESIDUAL CASES AT FIRST TEST

"Do you have a lot of problems that are bothering you?"	Potential Problem Cases			Residual Cases
	Experi-mentals	Controls	Total	
	(Per cent)			(Per cent)
A great many problems	12	9	11	6
Quite a few problems	19	16	18	14
A few problems	37	38	37	40
Hardly any problems	32	37	34	40
Total	100	100	100	100
Number of cases	129	132	261	521[a]

[a] Excludes 25 cases for whom information was not available.

event, it appears that high school girls selected because their school records suggested potential problems confirm the selection in their self-appraisals. They tend to show a subjective counterpart to the lower socioeconomic level found to characterize their backgrounds.

Experimental and control cases did not differ significantly in their responses on any of these attitude questions, nor were any significant differences found between girls who remained in school through the fourth test period and those who dropped out.

PERSONALITY TEST MEASURES OF POTENTIAL PROBLEM AND RESIDUAL CASES

The major descriptive measure of personality used in the research is the IPAT Junior Personality Quiz (Cattell). The JPQ was administered both to potential problem and to residual cases at every test period. Therefore, it provides comparative data for these populations; in addition, it allows us to examine changes over a period of time. Here we shall be mainly concerned with significant or suggestive differences or trends rather than with consequences of the experimental intervention, although the latter will be noted when they appear in the data.

The JPQ was selected because it appeared to be the best available instrument developed for the age group involved, having some validation data and experience in its use reported in published form. The subtests of the instrument are based on factor analytic study and were especially developed for high school students. The subtests have been reported to be generally parallel in structure to factors in the IPAT 16 Personality Factor Test at the adult level. In addition, the manifest content of most of the factors appears to be particularly relevant for our study of a high school population.

In order to convey the nature of this test and our reasons for choosing it, we quote at some length from that section of the handbook on the JPQ entitled "What the Test Measures":[1]

> The need for an effective, penetrating measure of personality in the preadult, middle-childhood age range has always been very great. Notably, in clinical psychology, we need to know the personality resources of the child-in-a-quandary and to measure reliably his progress under therapy. Again, in modern education, we are concerned to analyze and predict progress with respect to more than is encompassed by measures of achievement or scholastic achievement alone. . . .
>
> However, unless the various measures used are concerned with what is psychologically real, functionally unitary, and practically important, the test is a mere toy. It is only recently that factor analytic research in personality has extended to the childhood range and produced tests systematically related to independent traits. The present questionnaire is, indeed, the first practicable, standardized, routine measuring tool resulting from basic research which has related questionnaire factors to rating factors and to objective test factors, in child personality.
>
> As a questionnaire it partakes of some of the weaknesses of the inventory method. . . . But it also has advantages: principally that it can be used in those frequent situations where shortage of time or professional help preclude the apparatus and time requirements of objective tests. Besides, when properly designed and validated a *factorized* questionnaire avoids most weaknesses of the older inventories. It does not take introspective answers at their face value, e.g., by assuming that when a child *says* he is shy he *is* shy, but treats them as behavioral responses to be validated by correlation with observed social behavior and objective test factors.
>
> As to the nature of the actual personality dimensions incorporated in this questionnaire . . . essentially they are those already familiar as the "primary personality factors" of Emotional Stability or Ego Strength, Dominance vs. Submissiveness, High Intelligence vs. Low Intelligence, Surgency vs. Desurgency (the principal factor in so-

called "extraversion"), Cyclothymia vs. Schizothymia, Will Control, Nervous Tension, and Emotional Sensitivity. The deliberately comprehensive sampling of personality responses in the original research has ensured that no important aspect of the total personality has been omitted in these factors. For the JPQ is meant to be an all-purpose analytical tool, dealing with the essentials of personality as they show themselves alike in guidance, education, clinical diagnosis, and clinical treatment.

Some overbusy psychologists may initially be disinclined to a test that requires the calculation of twelve separate subscores. But . . . research indicates that the real complexity of personality is such that most prediction situations require specially weighted scores of many different factors. . . . The psychologist does a better job by respecting this complexity than by indulging in the fool's paradise of oversimplification shown in much direct test-to-criterion "prediction."

The same form of the test was used at each test period even though there was some danger that students might remember some of their earlier responses. This danger seems minimal, however, when a test of this length is repeated with at least eight months and usually a year intervening. Scores utilized in analysis of the test data were standardized according to the instructions of the test manual and all comparisons and statistical operations have been carried out using the standardized scores. The meaning of each factor will be briefly described before findings concerning the factor are presented.

It is the assumption of the test and a premise of the approach of this research that all the components of personality measured by the subtests of the JPQ are relevant. Therefore, findings with respect to each factor will be considered here. Since we are primarily concerned, however, with differences between potential problem and residual cases, and with any selective or time changes evident in the data, we shall present first those factors in which differences are evident. Brief notice can then be taken of the remaining factors.

1. Emotional Sensitivity vs. Toughness

According to the test manual, when a person is high on this score he is ". . . sensitive, imaginative, timid, friendly, soft-hearted, kindly, preferring adventures in imagination to those in fact." The low score is associated with ". . . toughness, emotional hardness, practicality, independence, and lack of artistic feeling."

When we compare the scores of potential problem and residual cases, we find scores of 5.00 and 5.49, respectively. Thus potential problem cases are more associated with the "toughness" pole of this factor, and the difference is statistically significant. Apparently, the selection of potential problem cases from their school records also identified girls exhibiting "toughness," "emotional hardness" as personality concomitants of school behavior. Perhaps this characteristic is associated as well with the differential backgrounds from which the potential problem girls come.

No differences were observed between experimental and control cases at first or at last testing and no differences were found between girls who remained in school and those who dropped out.

The test manual notes that emotional sensitivity tends to decline with age and in our data such a trend is quite clear. For the 127 potential problem cases available for first and fourth tests there is a statistically significant decrease in this score between the two time periods covering three high school years. A smaller but not statistically significant decrease is also noted for residual cases, and the data are parallel when experimental and control cases are examined separately. Thus in every comparison, the decrease in score with increase in age is visible, suggesting that as the school population gets older its responses on this personality test become more associated with "toughness" and "practicality" and less associated with "sensitivity" and "timidity." From a common-sense viewpoint, this is a plausible change accompanying increasing experience during the high school years.

2. Impatient Dominance

According to the test manual, a person who scores high on this factor is ". . . impatient, quick to anger, slow to calm down, unable to tolerate differences of opinion with others. . . ." The manual indicates that the factor is not well defined and may be subject to refinement with further research, so that any interpretation of it should be provisional.

In our data, the potential problem cases score significantly higher on this factor than the residual cases (4.96 compared to 4.22). Insofar as we may legitimately interpret this finding with the reservation already noted, the association of the characteristics of the high scorer on this factor with girls who have been selected because their school records indicate potential problems is reasonable.

No time trends appear in the data on this factor, nor are differences found between experimental and control cases either initially or at the conclusion of the experiment.

3. Socialized Morale vs. Dislike of Education

The test manual states that "children *high* on this factor are fond of school and all that goes with it, quick to accept cultural standards, and attentive and friendly to their associates. . . . The *low* scoring individuals dislike learning, feel they are badly treated, and have a surly reaction to authority and to associates." The content suggested in the description makes it particularly relevant for the type of study we have undertaken. The manual also notes that there may be some decline in this factor on entering adolescence but the age reference of adolescence is not clear and therefore any time trends in our data must be interpreted cautiously.

Residual cases are significantly higher in scores on this factor than potential problem cases (4.75 compared to 4.03). Since the selection procedures were designed to divide the school population into those more and those less successful in school, this difference between the two groups is not unexpected. Girls noted as likely to get into trouble at school would reasonably be expected to exhibit the negative orientations characterizing the lower scores of the factor.

The only other finding of note on this factor relates to the difference between girls who remain in school and those who drop out. When the initial score of those among the potential problem cases who drop out before a second testing (N = 30) are compared with those who were present for at least a second test (N = 231), the latter are significantly higher on this factor (3.07 and 4.16, respectively). Other differences in the same direction, though not statistically significant, are found when other comparisons are made between "dropouts" and "successes." The data also suggest that the scores on this factor tend to decline with increasing age but differences are relatively small.

Thus the findings on this personality variable appear to correspond generally to expectations, although not at a level of statistical significance in every instance. Persons who drop out of school seem to exhibit more dislike for learning and surly reactions to school than those who remain, and there appears to be a slight decline in such an orientation as time passes. It should be noted that this time trend does not occur among the residual cases; their somewhat higher scores—indicating more fondness for school—remain relatively constant.

4. Energetic Conformity vs. Quiet Eccentricity

According to the test manual, the person who scores high on this factor ". . . is lively, goes along with the group, is a good mixer, has 'cheap' interests, and does not think much for himself. The low scorer is eccentric, likes to think on his own, has more thoughtful tastes, and reports fatigue and slowness in action." This appears to be a somewhat complicated variable and neither end of the dimension can be taken on face value as necessarily a more favorable personality characteristic in terms of the interests of this study.

However, potential problem cases are significantly higher (4.52) than residual cases (4.08) in scores on this factor. The implication is that the former are more likely to respond to others rather than determine their own behavior, and this is not an unlikely characteristic of girls who may be headed for difficulties.

One time trend that appears in the data is the statistically significant difference among the residual cases between scores at first and last tests, with the latter being higher. Since a similar shift is not found for potential problem cases, interpretation is uncertain. The manual notes "a slight but significant rise at adolescence" for this factor. It is possible that potential problem cases are somewhat more precocious than residual cases and the time trend of the latter may represent a reduction in the lag between the two groups.

5. Will Control vs. Relaxed Casualness

"The high scoring child," according to the test manual, "is self-controlled, orderly, inhibited, persistent, and punctual. . . . [The factor] is presumably associated with more parental attention to behavior standards and character training."

The scores for residual cases are slightly higher than those of potential problem cases on this factor, but the difference is not statistically significant.

Time changes are more evident in the data. There are statistically significant shifts for residual cases (N = 334) and for experimental cases (N = 67), but not for control cases (N = 60), between the first and the fourth tests. (At the first and fourth tests, the scores for residual cases are 4.95 and 5.72, respectively; for experimental cases, 4.63 and 5.24.) It would appear that, during their high school years, the girls selected as potential problems but not provided with therapeutic services (control cases) do not gain more self-control, persistence, and the other characteristics of this factor, whereas similar girls who had access to the therapeutic program do acquire more. Before interpreting this finding as an effect of therapeutic intervention, however, we must note that a similar effect is observed for girls who were not identified as potential problem cases (that is, residual cases). In this instance, the change must be attributed to maturation alone. Exposure to social work services would seem, therefore, to have facilitated in the experimental cases an apparently desirable change that occurred in any event among residual cases. Put somewhat differently, the findings may be interpreted to suggest that the absence of social work treatment for potential problem cases inhibited an otherwise expected development.

6. Adventurous Cyclothymia vs. Withdrawn Schizothymia

The manual describes this factor as follows: "The *high* scorer is bold, boisterous; the *low* is shy, quiet, polite, aloof, and lacking in confidence. . . . Children high (on the factor) are rather more frequently in trouble for breaking rules, but also tend to be chosen as leaders. This factor would seem to have potential predictive value in a great variety of performance and adjustment situations." The manifest meaning of the factor is obviously relevant to this particular study.

Nevertheless, the data show no statistically significant differences between potential problem and residual cases, or between "dropouts" and "successes." There is a slight numerical difference found through time, suggesting a possible increase in adventurous behavior for experimental cases and a possible decrease in such behavior (or increase in shyness and aloofness) for control cases.

7. Nervous Tension vs. Autonomic Relaxation

According to the manual, ". . . the *high* scoring person is overwrought, tense, excited, irritable, anxious, despondent, easily upset. . . . In children it is particularly diagnostic of a certain type of high-strung, over-extended child. As far as we know, this factor measure can change rather markedly over the course of time with change of environmental stress, therapy, etc."

With such a characterization, it is of note in our data that no meaningful differences were found in any of the comparisons. Potential problem and residual cases did not differ, nor were time trends observable. Furthermore, no interpretable difference was found in comparisons of experimental and control cases.

8. Neurotic, Fearful Emotionality vs. Stability or Ego Strength

"The high-scoring child," the test manual reports, "is emotionally unstable, discouraged with himself, overwhelmed by his difficulties, prone to anxiety, and lacking in self-confidence."

No difference was found between potential problem and residual cases, between experimental and control cases, between "dropouts" and "successes," or in test scores through time. With respect to the last of these comparisons, however, a very small decrease in score is perceptible from first to fourth testing. Although not statistically significant, the difference is worth noting, since it occurred in parallel for experimental, control, and residual cases. Such a decrease with greater age and experience in high school is consistent with the expectation of increased personality integration and in keeping with the manual's comment that persons high on the factor show ". . . marked need for attention and encouragement directed toward better personality integration and self-realization."

9. Cyclothymia vs. Schizothymia

According to the manual, ". . . The *low* scoring individual dislikes groups, is rather rigid, and sticks to old ways, has sleep disorder, and prefers serious friends to fun-loving ones. The *high* score indicates a cyclothymia, sociable, easy-going, warm-hearted individual." Examination of our data does not reveal any meaningful differences in scores on this factor for any of the possible comparisons between groups or for the time trends. A slight difference (not significant) is found when comparing "dropouts" with "successes," the latter having the higher score among the potential problem cases. If this finding were to be borne out in additional research, it would suggest that persons likely to drop out of high school disproportionately give responses indicating rigidity and lack of sociability.

10. Independent Dominance

The manual describes the high scorer on this factor as one who ". . . is dominant, competitive, sticks to his own opinions, feels that he has difficulty in getting across what he wants to say, and does not appreciate obeying rules." The manual also indicates that this is an experiment factor in the questionnaire and requires research clarification.

No differences between any groups compared and no time trends of any magnitude or consistency were observed in our data.

11. Surgency vs. Desurgency

According to the manual, a high scorer on this factor ". . . is talkative and excitable, likes gay parties, prefers occupations like actor and lawyer, and likes constant variety. The low scorer is serious, prefers mechanical interests, and tends to be quiet and anxious."

No meaningful differences were found in our data between the various groups that could be compared. One possible time trend was observed, although it was not statistically significant and time trends of other groups did not clearly support it: among potential problem cases that are "dropouts" there is a slight increase in score on this factor in contrast with stability or slight downward trend for all other groups.

12. Intelligence

Since there are other performance measures in our data, the JPQ factor of intelligence is not dealt with here extensively. The consistent increase in score on this factor with age is statistically significant but may well have been affected by repeated testing on the same test form. No differences were found between potential problem and residual cases, or between experimental and control cases. There is a slight difference (not statistically significant) showing those remaining in school higher on this factor than "dropouts." The *absence* of difference between potential problem and residual cases when one might have been expected is more impressive than the findings that are essentially consistent with expectations of maturation for the age group involved in the study.

Discussion of Objective Personality Data

We may recapitulate what has been found in the data from objective personality testing. On factors of personality where significant or meaningful differences occurred between potential problem and residual cases, the characteristics that might be expected to be associated with girls headed for trouble were generally found. Thus potential problem girls appear to be more tough and insensitive, less tolerant of others and more quick to anger, express more dislike of education and a more surly reaction to authority and to associates, are less likely to think for themselves and more likely to go along with the group, and show slightly less self-control. Potential problem and residual cases did not differ in interpretable degree with respect to self-confidence, tension and excitability, emotional stability or ego strength, sociability, stubborn adherence to opinions, extraversion, or intelligence. Sufficient evidence was found to justify the conclusion that there are personality characteristics concomitant with the differences in background and attitude already noted between high school girls whose records suggest difficulties and those for whom this is not the case. Further research would be needed to establish a socio-psychological syndrome of potential problem high school girls but our data encourage such research.

With respect to personality characteristics of school "dropouts" as compared to those who stay in school, our data offer very little confirmation that important differences obtain. Those who drop out do show greater dislike of learning and more negative reactions to authority and to their associates, and they possibly exhibit more rigidity. There is little evidence that personality characteristics—at least as detected by the test we used—are very good indicators of potential school "dropouts."

A few maturational trends were found in the data. Emotional sensitivity seems to decline with age; intelligence probably increases. There is the slight suggestion that liking for learning decreases and that being more bold and a good mixer increases. What is most striking about the data on maturation is that the measures of personality we have used show such remarkable stability during the three high school years that were studied. It is often assumed that entrance into high school signals a period of rapid and even dramatic change in adolescents. Perhaps external changes in dress and language, in dating interests and behavior, and in other manifest ways of "growing up" have deceived us into believing that fundamental personality changes were also occurring. Obviously, data from our study alone cannot be accepted as conclusive contrary evidence but certainly there is no support for such a belief in our findings.

We do not wish to anticipate at this time any conclusion with respect to the consequences of social work services for the experimental cases in our study. We may note with respect to the personality characteristics that have been measured, however, that relatively little difference appears in the comparison of experimental and control cases. Only with respect to the factor described as Will Control vs. Relaxed Casualness does a significant effect occur in the data. Experimental cases, in contrast with control cases, shift toward self-control, persistence, orderliness. There is also the suggestion of a slight increase for experimental cases in adventurous, bold behavior and a contrary decrease for control cases in such respects. Clearly no wide-ranging, dramatic effects on the measured components of personality have resulted from the exposure of girls among the experimental cases to social work treatment.

PROJECTIVE TEST DATA

As indicated in Chapter II, the MAST sentence-completion test was administered as a projective test measure of personality in order to detect, if possible, more subtle characteristics than those that might be visible in an objective test such as the JPQ. Although differences between experimental and control cases did not appear, there were minor trends through time in some of the MAST scoring categories as well as some small differences between those girls who dropped out and those who remained in school. Because of practical limitations, MAST protocols were scored only for potential problem cases and not for residual cases.

The demands of verbal performance even on a test like the MAST were such as to reduce the number of subjects completing two usable protocols to 330 cases. A minimally usable protocol was one that had at least one-third of the responses interpretable. The number of omitted items (prorated for statistical analysis) in protocols that were minimally usable decreased significantly between the first and last tests taken by the subjects. This is, of course, in keeping with the expectation that language abilities of the girls should improve through the high school years.

MAST 1, Paranoid

This category—given priority in scoring when responses could also fall into other categories—reflects resentment, untrusting, negativistic orientations. No difference was found between girls who dropped out and those who stayed in school. A time trend for the 330 cases was suggested, however, between first and last test scores with the average number of negativistic responses higher at the last test. The difference does not quite attain our criterion of statistical significance.

MAST 2, Hostile

This scoring category includes responses indicating aggressive, cruel, and directly rivalrous as well as hostile meanings. This category is given priority over *MAST 4, Annoyed*, when there is uncertainty in scoring a response. There is a suggestive (but not statistically significant) difference, indicating more hostility among girls who dropped out than among those remaining in school. Whether such a difference is cause or effect is not determinable without further evidence. The difference is, however, consistent with the finding on JPQ Factor 3—Socialized Morale vs. Dislike of Education.

Through time, the last available test scores clearly show an increase in *MAST 2, Hostile* responses, over first test scores. This statistically significant difference may in a rather harsh environment reflect maturation toward self-assertion and greater autonomy. However, this is a speculative interpretation of the evident trend. It does not seem to be a maturational trend toward a more superficial exhibition of assertiveness because no trend was found in the third scoring category.

MAST 3, Assertive

This category includes boastful, self-assured, "cocky," immodest, self-oriented responses. Dropouts were not distinguished from those remaining in school on this category. There were no meaningful differences between first and fourth test scores.

MAST 4, Annoyed

This category includes responses suggesting boredom, annoyance, laziness, frustration, or situations that cause these responses. The category differs from MAST 2 by reflecting a social situation that makes the response interpretable as more rational, the less rational hostile responses being scored as MAST 2.

Differences appeared on this scoring category between girls who dropped out and those who did not, with the greatest difference—statistically significant despite the small number of cases—between first-year dropouts and those completing school. Girls who dropped out consistently show fewer *MAST 4, Annoyed* responses. Furthermore, the time trend also provided statistically significant results, with the average number of responses in this category decreasing between the first and the last tests taken by the girls.

These somewhat paradoxical findings are difficult to interpret consistently. It is plausible that expressions of annoyance and frustration decrease with maturation but it is not equally plausible that fewer such expressions should be associated with early leaving of school. One possible interpretation might suggest that potential dropouts are less involved emotionally in their present situations, even to the extent that they do not exhibit annoyance and frustration. Those who remain in school might be seen, in such an interpretation, as exhibiting at least some emotional response. This interpretation is speculative at best and it is more appropriate to leave the findings on this category of the sentence-completion test without explanation until further data become available.

MAST 5, Conventional

This category captures responses that reflect the common morality, conventionality, moral indignation, self-righteousness, and similar expressions. Objective rather than personalized responses were directed into this category, responses that in the extreme might be designated in categories 1 and 2. MAST 5 favors banal or commonplace statements and, more than any other scoring category for the test, tends to be a residual one.

No differences were found for this MAST category in comparisons of dropouts and nondropouts, or in time-trend analyses.

MAST 6, Avoidant

Withdrawal, avoidance, shyness, overmodesty, timidity, preference or liking for isolation are the terms that define this scoring category. None of the comparisons yields statistically significant differences. However, girls who dropped out of school show fewer avoidant responses and, in time trends, fewer avoidant responses occur in the later tests. These findings suggest, without the strength of statistical significance, that the less withdrawn girls leave school but that those girls who remain become less shy or isolated through the course of their school years.

MAST 7, Depressive

Responses indicating hopelessness, depressiveness, sad, morbid, resigned, pessimistic feelings are classified in this scoring category. A difference was found between dropouts and nondropouts with the latter having fewer depressive responses, but the difference was not at the accepted level of statistical significance. Such a difference would be compatible with the idea that a feeling of futility is expressed by those without potential for success, if it may be assumed that they are aware of this. On the other hand, the interpretation might be turned around: depressiveness could be seen as a cause of failure. In either view, interpretation can only be speculative and suggestive of hypotheses for further investigation.

MAST 8, Anxious

This scoring category is defined to include responses indicating worry, fear, nervousness, anxiety. Dropouts appear to show fewer anxious responses in their initial test, although the difference between their scores and those of nondropouts is not statistically significant. In time trends, again not statistically significant, the later tests show more anxious responses, perhaps anticipating the time when the girls leave school.

MAST 9, Introspective Mood

Self-doubting, guilty feelings, social sensitivity, and concern with others characterize the responses of this category which emphasizes reflection rather than action. No differences appeared between dropouts and nondropouts in the initial test period.

A substantial and statistically significant time trend did occur in the analysis with the self-analytic responses considerably higher in the last test taken by the girls. This suggests the development of a more introspective mood as the end of schooling approaches, perhaps a reasonable accompaniment to the anticipation of a change in status.

MAST 10, Hypochondriac

This scoring category, developed for the test when it was used in a study of a rehabilitation service, centers on references to sickness, pain, disease, and concern over these. It might also be thought to reflect expressions of neurotic symptoms of a somatic type. For the girls in this high school sample, however, no differences between dropouts and nondropouts and no time trends were found.

MAST 11, Optimistic

Euphoric, manic, optimistic, expressions of good feeling and trust are included in this category. Those not completing even the first year show a somewhat lower number of responses on this variable than those continuing in school, but the difference is not statistically significant. With respect to time trends, however, there is a significant decrease in optimistic responses. Possibly, again, this reflects intrusion of reality in consideration of the future as girls prepare to leave school.

Discussion of Projective Personality Data

The findings reflected in the projective sentence-completion test (MAST) are not impressive and they did not seem to warrant analysis of residual cases so as to compare these with potential problem cases. No differences were found between experimental and control cases, and few meaningful differences appear in the comparisons of dropouts and nondropouts. The dropouts, if they differ, may express more hostility, more depressive, and fewer optimistic responses. On the other hand, they show fewer annoyed, avoidant, and anxious responses. Even these weak findings do not suggest a consistent clinical picture and it is perhaps best not to try to develop one on the evidence available. Clearly the use of the projective test did not add to the potential predictors of school dropout.

If the somewhat stronger but still not impressive time trends are summarized, the maturational development is one of increased reality orientation as the girls proceed toward the end of their schooling. They thus become somewhat more untrusting and aggressive, more anxious and introspective. At the same time, responses of annoyance, avoidance or withdrawal, and optimism decrease. The implication is one of greater autonomy, or more adult realism. But as in the case of the objective measures of personality, the overall impression of lack of change outweighs the slight evidence of maturational trends. It is noteworthy that these adolescent years do not exhibit—on the personality measures used—the dramatic changes sometimes said to be characteristic. Nor is there evidence in these data that personality changes of visible importance accompany exposure to the experimental treatment provided or that personality characteristics anticipate failure or success in continuation in school.

CONCLUSION

This chapter has presented data on social and family background characteristics of the population of high school girls involved in the study, on some of their attitudes, and on their personality characteristics as indicated by a standard personality test and a projective sentence completion test. When differences were observed between potential problem cases and residual cases, they were generally in keeping with the intention of the project to identify for treatment a group of girls for whom future school and personal difficulties could be anticipated. It is clear that this intention was achieved and it is to be noted that potential problem girls dropped out of school in greater proportion than their peers who were not so identified.

Of the limited number of observed variables associated with school dropout, those indicating lower socioeconomic backgrounds were most evident and these were not strongly related. There is very little evidence that attitudinal or personality variables that were measured differentiate "dropouts" and school "successes."

The data also indicate that the random procedure for selecting experimental and control cases among the potential problem population resulted in generally similar groups on which to examine effectiveness of social work intervention.

In the following chapters we may turn to the description of the treatment program offered to the experimental cases and to its effects.

NOTE TO CHAPTER III

1. Cattell, R. B., J. Beloff, D. Flint, and W. Gruen, *IPAT Handbook for the Junior Personality Quiz*. Institute for Personality and Ability Testing, Champaign, Ill., 1953, pp. 1–2.

IV. Treatment Philosophy and Rationale*

A CONSCIOUS ATTEMPT was made by the staff of Youth Consultation Service to integrate the demands of the research design of the project into the general philosophy and rationale of the agency's casework services. These do not differ in important respects from the practices and principles customarily associated with diagnostic casework. The experimental attitude pervading the activities at YCS enabled the agency not only to adjust to the rigorous design of the research, but also to profit from its day-to-day experiences. In the second year, the staff concluded that limitations of the individual treatment plan originally proposed warranted a shift into a new and relatively untried scheme of group referral and treatment. The structure and purpose of these groups were subject to continuous revision in techniques and procedures.

INDIVIDUAL TREATMENT

Research operations were not a new experience for YCS and its staff. However, this project presented a major challenge at both the administrative and the treatment levels. In the original planning, the clients were referred to the agency's central office, which was within walking distance of the school. The casework staff at this office consisted of five caseworkers, one casework supervisor, and the director of casework. The agency's psychiatrist and psychologist served as consultants to this project. During

* Chapters IV and V draw heavily for their organization and almost entirely for their content, observations, and expressions of judgment on extensive reports prepared for this purpose by Elizabeth P. Anderson, director of casework at Youth Consultation Service; Dorothy Headley, senior group therapist; and Hanna Grunwald, group therapy consultant. The experiences described here are not research findings; rather they are observations of the professional persons involved in the treatment programs and represent their viewpoints.

the first year of the project, 53 cases were referred for individual treatment. The first 5 cases came into treatment in September, 1955, 25 more in the spring of 1956, and 20 in October, 1956. Three additional cases were added as replacements for clients who dropped out of school prior to agency contact. The first cases treated were in the nature of a test administered to try out the referral procedures. Referral was completed for 50 cases (93 per cent) for individual casework. The first year constituted a pilot stage for the study and, in view of the drastic changes in the plan for provision of treatment that ensued, may well be viewed in that light.

The administration of the agency was faced with the impact of this increased caseload and it was necessary to adjust its regular intake to meet the new demands on its staff. At the same time, careful attention had to be given to distributing the workload so that the agency could maintain its quality of service to all its clients. Additional hours for psychiatric consultation had to be arranged to enable caseworkers to make full use of such consultation. Extra time for psychological testing also had to be provided. In addition to the caseworkers' regular weekly supervisory conferences, extra staff meetings presided over by the director of casework were held each month for the discussion of diagnostic problems, the formulation of treatment plans, and the exploration of special techniques for handling these cases. Monthly meetings of the research committee afforded a critical review of developments as they evolved and permitted the incorporation of relevant changes into the revised design of the service program.

The major problem confronting the casework staff in dealing with the project referrals was the need to involve them as clients in a meaningful relationship when they were not consciously presenting a problem. This required thoughtful and creative extension of the usual casework approach, especially in the area of stimulating motivation. The basic treatment philosophy, based on the conviction that there is capacity for strength in every human being, varying in degree, remained firm. It is probably fair to describe the general treatment aim, therefore, as helping the individual to develop and realize her own potentialities to the extent of her capacities so that she can use her intelligence, her emotions, her aptitudes—her total self—in taking her place as an adult in our society.

Agency-School Cooperation

Considerable time and thought were also given in the early planning for working out an effective liaison with the referring school. It was necessary for the administrative person in the agency, the director of casework, to be in regular communication with her counterpart at the school, the administrative assistant in charge of guidance. Together they arranged to open channels for frequent communication between the agency's caseworkers and the school's guidance counselors and teachers.

When cases were randomly selected for inclusion in the experimental sample, the school was given only the name of the girl. She, in turn, was told of her selection and was encouraged to accept the opportunity to discuss with a skilled person the problems of growing up. A letter requesting the parents' permission for their daughter to attend sessions during school hours was prepared by the casework staff in consultation with the school's guidance department. It gave the parents a positive interpretation of the reasons for their daughter's referral to the agency, prepared them for a future contact by a caseworker, and informed them how they could establish contact with the agency themselves at any time.

With regard to schedules, the school agreed to allow the girls to keep appointments during school hours. Schedules were arranged to permit the school to exercise discretion as to what particular times would be best for the individual girl to be absent for a little over an hour. In accordance with the philosophy of the project, the school exerted no pressure upon the girls to keep appointments. The plan worked as follows: The individual caseworker informed the dean of students of the client's appointment time. A building pass was issued and the girl was excused from class at that hour. If the client did not wish to keep the appointment, she simply remained in class and nothing was said to her about it. For appointments at the first or last hour of school, permission was granted to report late for school or not to return to school after the appointment. Missed appointments were later checked against the school's attendance records, but the information was used by the agency only to distinguish in its records between missed appointments and absences from school. No instance was reported in which a girl left school at the appointed time and did not go to the agency.

Casework Handling

The casework staff found that a remarkably high percentage of the referred girls kept their first appointment, but often with acute anxiety and great concern manifest as to the real reason they were being sent. This in no way reflected on the school's preparation. It did, however, indicate the kind of emotional response evoked by choosing at random girls of this age for referral to a social agency. It became apparent that regardless of what was said in preparing them for the appointment, the girls feared they had been chosen because they were bad, "crazy," not studying enough, or otherwise inadequate in school performance.

This response from the girls underscored the agency's conviction that it was necessary to have experienced, carefully supervised caseworkers carry these cases, and prompted the immediate setting up of additional supervisory staff meetings and the arrangement for full attendance of the casework staff at all psychiatric consultations on project cases. Each case was carefully worked up by the staff, with psychological testing and psychiatric consultation, even if there were seemingly no problems in setting up the treatment plan in supervision alone. The diagnosis and treatment plan, as well as the explicit techniques for carrying out the plan, were written into the record.

As had been anticipated, the major difficulties that arose in establishing a treatment plan for these cases centered about the problem of involving them in treatment—helping them to understand why they were asked to come. Of 47 of the girls referred for individual treatment for whom caseworkers made ratings at the conclusion of the project, 18 (38 per cent) were described as "negative" or "hostile" in their initial relationship with the caseworkers and 5 others were said to be "indifferent." (See Chapter VI, Table 13.) For this reason there was considerable need for interpretation to clarify that their selection was in no way connected with their having been singled out as a behavior problem, as mentally unsound, or as related to any effort to force them to study harder in school. The girls were told that all young people could benefit by casework help, since adolescence was a period of life in which it was natural to have problems of some kind. The caseworkers indicated that because everyone in school could not be seen, the girls who could be seen were chosen more or less at random. Emphasis was placed on the confidentiality of the contact; the girls knew the agency did not share their material with the school and the school understood this as well.

As tentative diagnoses were made, the caseworkers reached the conclusion that without exception every girl referred to the agency needed casework help. Of the 47 girls who were rated by caseworkers on a 6-point scale, 30 (64 per cent) were felt to need treatment "very much" or "to a considerable extent" and only 2 were deemed "not at all" or "slightly" in need of treatment. The conviction that the girls had serious problems strengthened the agency's motivation to find a way to reach them. The caseworkers involved in the handling of these cases adapted themselves readily to this situation. It was exceptional for them to work with clients who did not manifest some definite problem, so it was necessary for the staff to concentrate on getting to know the clients and forming a relationship that would have some meaning and motivating force.

The skills and insights of the consultation staff were utilized in dealing with the problems encountered in diagnosing and treating these cases. From the point of view of the caseworkers, the consultants helped to enlarge their knowledge of the psychodynamic structures of the girls they were seeing, worked with them to develop new and different techniques, and strengthened their security in attempting the unfamiliar. The techniques used were mainly geared to reaching out in a warm, interested, but not overwhelming way. The fact was emphasized that all adolescents are beset by many problems and confusions about the business of living, such as getting along with parents and peers, being popular, handling the problems of dating, planning for future education and career, and other problems as previously suggested. The caseworkers were encouraged to learn the adolescents' language and truly to be "with it," always to be on their side but at the same time represent reality and provide guidance and control. Some of the girls saw their caseworker as being "in the know" and appeared to accept her as an ego ideal.

The caseworkers consciously sought to avoid the mistake of overresponding to the rebelliousness that is found to varying degrees in all adolescents. They were always aware that these children were members of families and had to be able to live and adjust to that reality even if, as in many instances, the family environment was a very difficult or even pathological one. They realized that they could not make up to these girls for all they lacked or for the many deprivations experienced in their early years.

Techniques for carrying out treatment plans were discussed and worked out on a case-by-case basis related to the diagnostic appraisal and the appropriate treatment goal. All the girls were encouraged to keep regular weekly appointments at the agency but the caseworkers did make numerous school visits to talk with the girls in the early stages of the project. It was soon evident that the clients who became involved in treatment were conscientious about keeping regular appointments at the agency. Indeed, the median number of casework interviews (excluding conferences at school and casual contacts) was 9, and 15 girls (30 per cent of the 50 completed referrals) were seen in 16 or more interviews. Nevertheless, the caseworkers did not feel that many of their clients became seriously involved in a treatment relationship. On a 6-point scale, the caseworkers judged 22 (47 per cent) of the 47 girls for whom ratings are available to have become "hardly" or "not at all" involved in a treatment relationship. On the other hand, 13 girls (27 per cent) were rated "very much" or "quite a bit" involved in treatment. (See Chapter VI, Table 11.) Thus the caseworkers saw themselves as quite successful in reaching approximately one-fourth of the girls referred but, despite great effort, unsuccessful in achieving the involvement deemed necessary with about one-half of the girls.

Aware of this problem, the staff at YCS considered other ways of making meaningful contact with more clients. As indicated earlier, the agency was already using group treatment methods with some other clients. This approach had been discussed but discarded before the project began. With the experience of a year it was reasonable, therefore, to consider whether group methods would be more satisfactory.

From Individual to Group Treatment

A few girls among the first fifty referred had some experience in group therapy. This service was concurrent with individual treatment and the agency's existing activity group therapy program was used. Although the first year's experience with individual treatment in the caseworkers' assessments produced some gratifying success with some of this group of cases, the workers were sensitive to the degree of anxiety evoked in a substantial percentage of these clients. Many of those who came to the agency for treatment described their initial feelings in vivid terms after a period of three to six months. The situation was discussed at length among the caseworkers, supervisors, and director, and in consultation with the psychiatrist. The possibility of a less painful method of involving future clients from the project in a helpful agency contact was thoroughly explored. The "facts" already known about adolescents were carefully considered. Those suggested included anxiety at being singled out of the group, an expression of fear of being considered different, and inhibition in communicating fears and asking questions, many of which they feared would sound fantastic to an adult. These facts, together with the girls' apparent suspiciousness of adults in general and their concern with regard to new and untried experiences, gave the staff cause for serious thought. Their discussion was greatly helped by the school's experience, as described by the administrative assistant in charge of guidance, that handling high school students in groups was more successful and far less anxiety-producing than singling them out individually for any kind of attention.

As a result of all these considerations, the decision was made to attempt a group treatment approach with the girls in this project. Despite the fact that the random selection of the experimental sample was a marked deviation from the usual diagnostic workup of clients prior to assignment for group treatment, it was decided to experiment with referrals from the potential problem pool in a group setting.

GROUP TREATMENT

In preparation for this new approach to the girls, careful planning and evaluation based on knowledge of adolescent behavior, casework principles, and group therapy practices were considered in full staff meetings involving the director of casework, the senior group therapist, and the group therapy consultant. Also, extensive consultations were held with caseworkers who had carried the individual cases.

Group Referrals

This new approach was accomplished by stressing the voluntary nature of the girls' participation in groups and the universality of puzzling questions that young people face in their everyday lives. Agency services were interpreted to emphasize factors that might appeal to the girls on the pleasure principle, for example, planned trips, refreshment periods, and time off from school. The refreshment period was considered to be of particular significance, for it was believed that such a break would provide a social experience for these deprived girls. Thus the idea of stigma or uniqueness in having problems was de-emphasized, and the idea that everyone faces day-to-day questions was introduced. The universality of problems and the provision of pleasurable experiences became the keynotes of this group approach which, it was hoped, would be less threatening to the girls.

A letter written by the agency staff which had been used earlier by the school to explain the purposes of the project to parents was revised in the light of the group counseling program. In order to emphasize the voluntary nature of the program and to minimize the agency involvement in their decision, preference was given to the girls "signing up" for group participation in the school. To this end, a secretary from the agency, whom the girls had not had any contact with previously met with them at the school, received their parents' permission letters, and invited them to the first meeting of their new group. She answered all factual inquiries, but any questions of interpretation she referred to the leader, who was scheduled to meet with them the following week.

Recognizing that more traditional casework methods might be preferred for some girls, it was decided that these should be made available when appropriate. Girls who for one reason or another were thought unsuitable for group treatment, would be referred to the casework department for appropriate handling.

During the course of the project 147 girls were referred for group treatment at the agency and referral was completed for 139 (95 per cent) of them. The need for treatment for the group referrals was considered to be approximately as great as that for individual referrals. However, the group approach to making contact with project clients was judged by the social workers to be more successful than the individual treatment approach. The median number of counseling sessions attended by girls referred to groups was 19, and 31 per cent of them attended 31 or more group sessions. Only 19 per cent of the girls in groups who were rated by the social workers on a 6-point scale were judged to have become "hardly" or "not at all" involved in treatment. (See Chapter VI, Table 11.)

Schedule and Setting

The vocational trade classes at the high school were double periods lasting approximately two hours, which fitted well with the group therapy plans for hour and a half sessions and allowed thirty minutes for travel to and from the school. As already indicated, the central office of the agency was within walking distance of the school. When the agency office moved its quarters, the travel time and cost of transportation precluded regular meetings there. For a short period, space was found in the educational building of a nearby church. This setting seemed to the group therapists to have a somewhat repressive effect on the girls who needed a permissive environment, but it was not considered a serious handicap. As the program expanded, quarters were found at the YMCA, which was nearer the school and could accommodate more groups. The atmosphere of the "Y" was congenial, its equipment was adequate, and its coffee shop was available for refreshments.

The question of holding group meetings during school hours was discussed in staff conference. Did this affect the girls' attitude toward using the group for therapeutic purposes? To what extent were the agency and the group leader successfully distinguishing themselves from the school system as a whole? It was recognized that there were disadvantages to the therapeutic effectiveness of groups scheduled during school hours. But these were balanced by disadvantages in attempting to hold meetings after school hours. The school population was drawn from all sections of the city and travel time and carfare would be serious problems for many of the girls. As the group program progressed, the therapists observed fewer drawbacks to the school schedule. One group, however, became so identified with the agency that they asked to have their meetings at the agency. This was tried for a short time but practical factors of time and money soon forced a return to the "Y" during school hours.

The staff also considered the possibility of holding group meetings in the school building. It was felt that this might work out satisfactorily. The neurotic girls might not be expected to have any difficulty discussing their problems in a school setting. The "acting out" girls might present some difficulty in the beginning, but it was felt that their reaction would not be sufficient to prevent treatment from continuing. No opportunity actually arose to hold a group meeting in the school building, but in general the staff felt that the role of the therapist was more important than the setting.

Role of the Therapist

In all the groups the role of the therapists remained basically the same. They were caseworkers utilizing casework concepts and techniques. Although they were always aware of the group's dynamics, the focus was on the individual member and her adjustment.

In the large unselected groups formed at first, the permissive and passive role of the therapist often seemed to create undue anxiety on the part of the girls. With the benefit of this experience, the therapist changed her technique to a mental health educational approach whenever she felt she did not have sufficient diagnostic understanding of the group for a more intensive approach. In groups that included immature and impulsive girls, the therapist needed to be directive. In groups composed of girls with more ego strength, the members were considered able to assume more responsibility for the course of the discussion. The attitude of acceptance on the part of the therapist was met with a general longing for acceptance on the part of these girls. The degree to which it could be given and the way in which it was communicated differed with the various groups.

It was assumed that the success of the program would depend on the skill of the caseworkers and their experience in group therapy. A project of this size and scope requires a stable and competent staff. In the early stages, groups were formed that could be carried by one full-time therapist. As the program expanded, she became responsible for the administrative aspects of the program, for supervision, and for coordination of the project with the other departments of the agency. During the course of the project, ten therapists were employed on a part-time basis. All of these were caseworkers with extensive experience in group therapy. Some of them had worked previously for YCS and several were working at other agencies under the guidance of the group therapy consultant. One was from Puerto Rico and her knowledge of the Spanish language and Latin American culture was a great help to many of the Spanish-speaking girls in the project. Students from Sarah Lawrence College participated in the Activity Groups, in which a "big-sister" role was appropriate. They led the Activity Group sessions, took the girls on trips, and helped with a variety of adjunct services.

At the end of each six months' period, conferences were held at the agency with the director of casework, the senior group therapist, the group therapy consultant, and the several therapists, as well as the agency's casework staff. The major purpose of these conferences was to discuss the experience with the groups as they developed, evaluate their progress, and chart their direction and focus.

Two group therapy consultants were active at different times during the course of the project; one served during the first year and the other took over during the final years. Each had advisory responsibility for setting up the program and for organizing the groups that operated during these periods. The agency psychiatric consultant was used to review diagnoses and treatment plans for girls referred to the casework department and for clients receiving a combination of individual and group treatment. Many of the girls were tested by one of the three psychologists serving the agency during the period of this study. At first the girls were tested in the school without any obvious connection with the program. When this approach proved cumbersome and ineffective, the clients were tested directly by the agency psychologist. Another important member of the team was a volunteer who had been active in the agency in other capacities for several years. She compiled school records on all the clients and kept up with their academic status. Her excellent rapport with school personnel frequently enabled her to interpret the agency's program to the teachers and guidance personnel in a most effective manner.

Contact with the School

From its inception, the group program was in an advantageous position, in that the agency already had a history of good relations with the school and its personnel. The previous year's experience with individual referrals had familiarized them with agency policies and practices. This contact, however, had been a relatively unstructured one. In view of the large number of students who would be involved in the group program, it became practical to designate a liaison person from the agency and another from the school.

The agency liaison person performed several functions. She abstracted school records, scheduled meetings to conform with class schedules, effected class changes for girls whose class schedules conflicted with their group meetings, followed up on absentees, and checked on the girls' current progress in school. This liaison person was also able to interpret the agency's program to teachers and clear up any misconceptions the school staff might have about the agency's services. Occasionally, she was called upon to talk with a teacher who had a misconception of the agency's purpose, believing that it worked exclusively with "bad" girls and, unfortunately, had made inappropriate remarks to a client. In almost every instance, however, the teacher was cooperative when the program had been explained. The functions of the school liaison person were the counterpart of these: answering questions, making reports and records available, and following through on school routines in regard to referrals, parental permission, passes, absentees, and the like.

Both the school and the girls understood that participation in the program was entirely voluntary. However, well-intentioned teachers occasionally put pressure on girls who were having school problems to attend meetings. At one point, the school wanted attendance records from the agency, believing that a girl had left the school building but had not gone to her scheduled meeting. The school accepted the agency's refusal to comply with this request on the grounds that the therapeutic environment would be disturbed if the clients had reason to think that their material was shared with the school in any way.

By and large, teachers were cooperative in giving full reports on the girls and alerting the staff to acute situations arising at school. They also accepted the workers' recommendations for handling particular problems of girls in the project. For example, one girl of limited abilities had a work assignment that was too advanced for her. The school, recognizing that she had been seen in a group for many months and had received psychological tests, was willing to try her out on another job more in keeping with her limitations.

In this and in many other instances, the cooperative effort worked out satisfactorily, but the level of this cooperation would have been improved if the school personnel and the agency staff could have had time for regular monthly conferences. Nevertheless, the continuous close relationship and effective cooperation between the agency and the school reflected their mutual concern for the success of the program and facilitated the formulation of long-term goals for the program.

Early Group Experience

The first five groups were organized between April, 1957, and June, 1958, with S. L. Slavson as consultant. These differed from orthodox therapy groups in several important respects.

Previous groups at YCS involving other types of clients had been composed of five to eight members who were referred to the group only after careful psychosocial evaluation had been made. Members of a group were chosen because they had a good potential for ready identification with each other. Clients assigned to the same group had common central problems, even though their symptoms and clinical diagnoses might vary. However, group therapists differ in their judgments as to what types of clients profit most from group treatment, the length of time clients should be seen in individual treatment before being assigned to groups, and the degree of importance they attach to differences among group members in temperament and approaches to problems. In the absence of any consensus in philosophy or rationale, of any uniformity in the experience and practice of therapists, and of any rigorous research in these areas, it was decided that a measure of innovation and experimentation was not only justified but might yield significant new results.

Recognizing both the obligation to serve the cases prescribed by the research design and the limited basis for composing groups on known criteria, it was decided to attempt larger groups than are usual for treatment aims. From previous experience with individual cases it was anticipated that a considerable number of cases referred would be lost through school dropouts, extreme resistance, or their elimination as unsuitable for group therapy.

The decision was made to refer girls in groups of thirteen, with the expectation that as many as three or four might be lost to each group. The appeal of this new group approach to the girls was apparent in two important respects. In the first place, a very much lower percentage of cases were lost than had been anticipated; and secondly, the therapists recognized some benefits for the girls, in spite of the shortcomings believed to be associated with the larger size of the groups.

The context of referral, that is, the absence of clear and explicit presenting problems as well as anxiety and suspiciousness on the part of many of the girls at the time of referral, precluded the psychological testing and psychosocial evaluation customarily thought necessary for clinical diagnosis. There was not sufficient time available or the usual situation of agency intake for an individual study of each girl prior to referral to the group, although such study (including contact with the family) would have been useful in view of the sparseness of details available on each girl.

In any group therapy program it is always difficult to determine the appropriate moment for closing contact because of the difficulty of evaluating treatment gains. Usually clients are selected because of their apparent need for help in handling a specific problem. Therefore, the evaluation of their improvement depends largely upon a comparison of the client's present handling of her problem with that at the beginning of contact. However, in this project the definite areas of poor functioning of the group members at the time of their referral were known only in the most general way. It was necessary, therefore, to develop criteria upon which to base a clinical evaluation of improvement. The task of evaluation was further complicated by the lack of frequent contacts on an individual basis either with group members or with members of their families (although such contacts were occasionally made in emergency situations). Objective criteria used by the group therapists were essentially restricted to information gained from the school about the girls' academic performance and their general school conduct. This information at times was used to substantiate the therapists' impressions of progress based upon the girls' behavior within the group.

Later Group Experience

When Dr. Hanna Grunwald was appointed as the new group therapy consultant in June, 1958, the group treatment services of the project to date were evaluated and specific plans were made for serving the last eighty cases needed to fulfill the research sample of two hundred experimental cases.

In reviewing the experiences of the first year with groups, it was noted that the leaders of the five large unselective groups had been successful in creating a permissive atmosphere that was similar to the one created in small, selective treatment groups. This permissive atmosphere was conducive to spontaneity on the part of the girls and several of them brought out emotionally associated material. However, others showed little or no responsiveness to the group contact. Moreover, some members of the group interfered with the involvement of other members, by inappropriate behavior. Their failure to show any understanding of painful material brought by one girl was considered even more disturbing. Also, the large number of members in the group made it difficult for the girls to become well acquainted with each other. Some girls, who might have been able in a smaller group to empathize fully with another member, were restrained from doing so because they could not absorb so many situations appropriately. In spite of these characteristics, most of the members of the group seemed to enjoy attending the sessions. Almost all the girls responded favorably to the permissive atmosphere in the group, which enabled them to have a more realistic understanding of many of the problems typical of adolescence.

Using this assessment of experience with the first five groups, the group therapy consultant and the senior group therapist made a judgment as to each girl's responsiveness to group treatment. In addition, this analysis differentiated the girls according to their common problem areas, their capacity for handling problems, and their ability to use the group experience constructively.

On the basis of this analysis, new groups limited to eight members were formed with more specific focus, and only those girls were included whose previous experience indicated that they could profit from them. Corresponding to the pattern of needs and capacities discerned among the girls to be referred, these newly formed groups were of three basic types: Family Life Education Groups, Interview Treatment Groups, and Protective Groups. Those who apparently did not fit into any of the earlier groups were excluded from these new groups. For some of them, Activity Groups were created. The remaining cases were referred to the agency's casework department for disposition.

Family Life Education Groups

The first of the new groups formed could best be classified as Family Life Education Groups. They followed in structure, method, and process the outline of similar groups formed in social welfare agencies for mothers or parents. The content, of course, differed, since these were for adolescent girls. Through a planned series of discussions, they sought to strengthen family life and prevent personal maladjustment growing out of unhealthy family relations. The approach was basically educational as contrasted with therapy or treatment. It differed from more didactic teaching, in that the group members' feelings and concerns and the sharing of their everyday experiences were the basis for the group's discussions. Group members were given an opportunity to explore their feelings and attitudes, as well as to gain knowledge. Building on the healthy aspects of the egos of the members, the purpose of these groups was preventive rather than ameliorative.

The response of the clients and group leaders to these newly formed Family Life Education Groups was most encouraging. The absence of inappropriate interruptions made possible a much greater evenness in the group discussions and the attention span of the girls was longer. Also, there was a more intensive give and take among the girls. Most of the discussion centered around the common problems of adolescence, with discussion of "individual" problems occurring only occasionally. It was obvious that these groups, however, were different from treatment groups. There was less of a conscious expectation within the group that members would use the group experience constructively. The nature of their involvement remained more uncommitted. The new setup allowed the group leaders to play a more clearly defined role than in the former groups, where they often were obliged to remain vague because an approach that would have been helpful to some members might have been confusing to those operating on a different level.

Interview Treatment Groups

Not all of the girls who seemed to have gained by attending one of the first five groups were referred to the Family Life Education Groups. A second type of group, called Interview Treatment Groups, was set up for the more intelligent and verbal girls who appeared, because of their preoccupation with fears and their reports of severe conflicts with parents and/or siblings, to exhibit neurotic problems. In order to judge their ability to accept help with these problems, the casework department of YCS was asked to secure additional information on each case. In the cases where the neurotic conflict seemed to be severe, they were asked, if possible, to get projective data.

Protective Groups

A third type of group was formed for intelligent, verbal girls who had both enjoyed and profited from their former group attendance, but were forced to cope with severe environmental problems. This type of group was labeled Protective Groups. In general, these girls came from the so-called "hard-core" families, but despite this background seemed to have the ability to function very well and showed surprising potential for growth and development. In most instances, this strength could be traced to the influence in early life of some family member, often an aunt or a grandmother, who had managed to escape the general family pathology.

Many girls who appeared to have gained little or nothing from group attendance were also referred to Protective Groups. However, these girls differed from the girls mentioned above, in that they were less intelligent and less verbal. They resembled those in the first category, in that they also suffered from serious environmental problems and came from extremely disturbed families. However, those in the second category functioned very poorly and showed very little potential for growth. The decision to separate these two categories of girls, who came from similar backgrounds but showed differences of personality makeup, proved to be a significant one.

Activity Groups

Activity Groups were formed for girls who seemed to be fixed in a rather rigid way at a low level of development and who did not show incentive to change. It was hoped that sessions of supervised interaction might provide such girls with healthy, growth-producing experiences that they probably missed in earlier years. Most girls included in these groups came from multi-problem families and lived in the city's worst slum areas. In forming these groups, special care was taken not to select girls who might be likely to regress too rapidly when allowed to feel it was safe to act in an immature way.

Casework Referrals

Before the newly formed groups were started, it was possible to refer some of the cases from earlier groups to the agency's case-work department for closing. The contact was closed for any girl who had left school and had not continued with casework service. Cases were also closed when it was felt that the former group members were relatively mature, were coping adequately with their problems, or were in no immediate need of further help. Sometimes the girls were not very sensitive to the difficulties of co-members who looked for problem solutions that might be in conflict with their parents' values. These girls felt secure in their choice of "right and wrong." Their stable sense of identity seemed to stem from their belonging to closely knit family units with definite sets of values that were never questioned by the girls. Most of the girls in the latter category were Puerto Ricans.

Some girls who showed severe problems—for example, serious psychosomatic symptoms, psychotic trends, or who were "acting out" severely—were referred to the casework department for individual attention. After careful study, some of these cases were carried in individual treatment; a few were later returned to the group that seemed best suited to their present needs; and others were referred to appropriate community agencies for indicated treatment. Cases representing girls who could not be reached at any level were closed or kept inactive awaiting further developments.

Observation Groups

The immediate results of these new types of groups were so encouraging that it was felt advisable to refer the eighty new girls into short-term Observation Groups and repeat this screening process with them. Data obtained were used to determine which type of group seemed most suitable for each girl. The use of short-term groups for screening purposes seemed justified because an analysis of the former groups showed that observations made very early in the life of these groups were seldom contradicted by observations gained in later meetings. After five to eight sessions in the Observation Groups, each member was referred to the specific treatment group of choice. Only very rarely did it become necessary to transfer girls to a different type of group.

The following chapter will discuss in detail treatment experiences and observations made with respect to the total experimental sample, including the girls in individual treatment and those in both phases of the group treatment program.

V. Treatment Experiences and Observations

THE OBJECTIVE EVALUATION of the results of this project and the effectiveness of the treatment intervention was built into the research design as a comparison of the treated sample cases and the untreated control cases. However, among the experimental cases there were variations in the type of service offered, in the efficiency with which contact was established and maintained, in the degree of involvement achieved, and in the amount of time expended on each case. Social workers and group therapists are accustomed to categorizing cases along these as well as more clinical and diagnostic dimensions. In supervision and consultation, varying treatment plans and goals are tailored to meet the specific needs of clients. In the course of treatment, these plans and goals are frequently reevaluated and adjusted in the light of experience. The determination of client involvement and evidence of movement in each case are also subject to frequent review by the professional staff.

These judgments, quite apart from the experimental design, constitute a type of evaluation using such categories as "before and after," "involved vs. uninvolved," "treated vs. relatively untreated." Previous research[1] has indicated that within the necessary limitations of such designs, trained and objective caseworkers can achieve relatively high levels of validity and reliability. While the design of this research is not forced to rely exclusively on such methodologies, the experiences and observations of the caseworkers and group therapists constitute an additional source of data, supply valuable insights into the treatment process, and provide a body of subjective judgments against which the more objective results may be checked.

110

The primary data for these judgments of treatment experiences and observations are the case records of the workers and the group records of the therapists. These individual and group records were reviewed regularly by the supervisors and served as the basis for periodic discussions with the appropriate consultants. The reports of these consultations were also incorporated into the permanent records of each case and group. In preparing summaries of this material for research purposes, a supervisor and the director of casework read the complete records of all individual cases. The senior group therapist and the group therapy consultant read all of the group records. Each of these readers prepared an extensive analysis of the cases involved and these documents, in turn, became the primary source material for this chapter.

INDIVIDUAL TREATMENT[2]

Insofar as the experimental setting would permit, the 53 cases referred for individual treatment in the first phase of the project were handled within the framework of the agency's normal intake processes. When these were not effective in reaching a girl, more intensive efforts were directed toward making contact with her and finding some way to involve her in the agency's program. In six of these cases, such efforts were of no avail and the girls were not seen at all. When the caseload was reviewed by the director of casework, a little more than half of the girls who were seen, 27, were not considered to be involved in treatment to any appreciable degree. The other 20 girls were judged by their caseworkers to have been treated significantly.

Cases Not Seen

Of the six cases not seen, three were discharged from school before casework contact could be attempted. Of the other three, one ran away from home prior to her first interview and could not be located, one girl's grandmother who could not speak English refused to give permission for the girl to attend, and one girl was so fearful that she could not be encouraged to make even the first contact with the caseworker.

Cases Not Involved

The 27 cases considered not appreciably involved in treatment were seen from one to nineteen times by the caseworkers, but little or no progress was reported toward motivating the clients to use the agency's services constructively. Three of the girls were seen once, one was seen twice, four were seen three times, and four were seen four times. In contrast to these 12 short-term cases, 11 girls had from 5 to 8 interviews and 4 girls had from 11 to 19 individual sessions.

These 27 girls ranged in ages from fourteen to seventeen years, with a median age of 15.7 years. Fourteen were Negro, 9 were white, and 4 were Puerto Rican. Thirteen of them were Roman Catholic, 9 were Protestant, 2 were Jewish, and the religion of 3 was unknown. Group intelligence tests from the school's records were not complete, but the scores available ranged from 65 to 100, averaging about 85. Since group test scores are usually lower than individual test scores, the intelligence level of this group of cases should not be considered abnormally low. The clinical diagnoses of the majority of the girls in this category were not precisely known, but severe disturbance was suspected in 16 cases. Of the other cases in this group, the disorders of 7 were classified as character disorders, 2 as schizophrenia, and one each as psychoneurosis and extreme dependency.

Five types of disposition were made of these 27 cases. The following descriptions indicate the number of cases of each type and include a brief case history of a typical example of the girls in each group.

(1) Six cases were either known to other agencies or referral was made for special services. Lola Thomas,* for example, was seen five times by the caseworker. She was an only child, born out of wedlock. She had been a behavior problem in school for some time and had come to the attention of the Juvenile Court for delinquent behavior before being referred to Youth Consultation Service. She had run away from home, been remanded to Youth House, and paroled in the custody of her mother. This example is typical of the cases, such as many Youth Board referrals, that come to the attention of an

* All names and other identifying information about clients have been altered to preserve anonymity.

agency so late that casework is of limited utility. Lola obviously needed help and might have received it from a competent agency if she were available to help. She ran away a second time, was sent back to the Court and placed in a New York State Training School for girls. No progress was reported in the agency's brief contact with Lola, although the decision was made to attempt an authoritative role in an effort to compensate for her mother's limitations.

(2) Five girls were discharged from school early in their contact with YCS. One of these, Louise Chamber, was a shy, passive girl of low average intelligence, considered by the caseworker to have a weak ego, diagnosed as schizoid. She was seen thirteen times in individual treatment. An effort was made to establish a relationship that might help her feel less fearful and become less withdrawn. Individual treatment did not seem able to accomplish this and group therapy was felt to be the treatment of choice. Therefore, Louise was referred to the agency's regular activity group therapy program. However, she went to only one group meeting before she dropped out of school. Efforts were made to help Louise return to school, but school authorities would not permit her to continue after her seventeenth birthday because of her low intelligence and poor performance. Without any connection with the school, the agency was not able to maintain contact and the case was closed.

(3) Four girls moved out of the city early in their contact with YCS. Freda Klein, for example, was seen twice and then transferred to a high school in the Long Island community to which her family moved. These two interviews did not provide enough indication of need for treatment to warrant a referral to an agency near her new home. Both the caseworker and the guidance counselor thought Freda was reasonably well adjusted and would require no further attention from a social agency at this time.

(4) Two girls were judged to be functioning adequately and were not pursued in the face of extreme resistance. Elsie Wharton was seen eight times. She was the foster daughter of a childless couple who had separated the year before Elsie came to the attention of YCS. She was doing fairly well in school, was active in the Glee Club, but seemed to have many problems in her relationships with her estranged parents. According to the caseworker, she was exceedingly resistant to efforts to establish a "real" relationship with her. The conclusion was reached in psychiatric consultation that Elsie was probably a psychopathic personality. A sustained effort was made to maintain contact with her in order to explore this tentative diagnosis and to offer her a supportive relationship. However, this failed and Elsie withdrew from any further contact with the agency.

(5) In ten cases the girls were judged by the caseworkers and supervisor to be too disturbed and fearful for individual casework to be hazarded. Bernice Claussen was seen eight times and her mother twice. She was a very depressed, fearful girl with a poor self-image and was diagnosed as schizophrenic. The record describes a very pathological family history, with the mother having been declared unfit because of heavy drinking and the children removed by the Court when Bernice was nine. The Court had found the mother to be somewhat improved and the children had been returned to her some years before Bernice was referred to YCS. Both mother and daughter were extremely fearful of contact with anyone. If a relationship could be established, the treatment plan was to use a mental hygiene approach with a limited goal focused on clarification with Bernice of some of her extremely unrealistic fears with regard to herself. However, neither Bernice nor her mother became involved in treatment; both withdrew. One year and four months after the case was closed, Mrs. Claussen telephoned to complain that her daughter was misbehaving and engaged in sexual activities. An appointment was offered which was not kept.

In most of these 27 cases the families were reported as not interested in having any contact with the agency, although they had given permission for their daughters to be seen. In one situation, the mother had got in touch with the school about her daughter's problems and in another situation the father had been seen by school personnel. Two mothers made appointments at YCS but failed to keep them. Seven mothers were seen by the caseworker and 16 did not make any contact or respond to any of the agency's efforts to reach them.

Cases Reported to Have Been Treated Significantly

The other 20 cases referred for individual treatment were judged by the caseworkers to have been sufficiently involved in the relationship for it to have had some significant effect upon them. The number of interviews with these clients ranged from one client who was seen only five times, 15 who were seen from ten to fifty times, and four who were seen from sixty to ninety times. The average for this group was about 35 interviews. This figure is approximately one per week for a school year of nine months. These girls ranged in age at the time of referral from fourteen to seventeen years but their median age, 15.4 years, was somewhat lower than that of the group who did not become involved. Eight of these clients were Negro, 8 were white, and 4 were Puerto Rican. Nine were Roman Catholic, 7 were Protestant, 3 were Jewish, and one was Greek Orthodox. Their group IQ scores as reported in school records ranged from 60 to 100, averaging about 87. The differential diagnoses made of the cases in this group were clearer than those in the previous group. The disorders of ten were classified as schizophrenic, seven as character disorders, two as psychoneurotic, and one case was judged normal but living in a severely pathological home situation.

The disposition of these cases was judged by the caseworkers to fall into three categories corresponding to the degree of improvement observed in each girl.

(1) Six of the cases were judged to have shown no appreciable improvement in their behavior and psychological adjustment. Of these, three were diagnosed as character disorders and three schizophrenic. In three situations the mothers were seen one or two times, but no contact was made with the families of the other girls. Three of the girls became pregnant out of wedlock shortly before or just after withdrawing from treatment. All of these girls were said to be severely disturbed and unable to respond to casework methods. The workers were doubtful that they could have been successfully treated by any method. The inability of the workers to reach these girls was not due to lack of time or limited contact; each client was seen an appreciable number of times. The interviews numbered 65, 49, 29, 17, 13, and 10, respectively.

(2) Eight girls were judged by the caseworkers to have improved when the case was closed. The average number of interviews with these girls was about one-half that received by the girls who showed no improvement. One girl in this group, Doris Kramer, was seen only five times. The goal of this contact was to help the mother accept Doris' intellectual limitations and refrain from putting pressure on her to strive for impossible goals in her school work and career plans. The caseworker judged that this limited goal was accomplished. The other seven girls were seen on a weekly basis for three to eight months. They all related well

to the treatment situation and were judged to have improved in their school performance and social functioning. The workers felt that their clients would make adequate work adjustments after graduation and, in all probability, would achieve normal marriages. Two of the girls were said to need further treatment through a family agency but both families refused to involve themselves in another referral. However, it was felt that these girls made a good adjustment to the limitations of their families.

(3) Six cases were discharged by YCS as greatly improved. Three of these girls were seen on a weekly basis for about one year and the other three were seen for more than two years. Three girls in this category were Negro, one was white, and two were Puerto Rican. All of them were said to come from extremely unhappy and deprived home backgrounds, and three of the families were judged pathological by the caseworkers.

> In the case of Jane Spanner, the second oldest of eight siblings, the agency's activity group therapy program and camping services were used in addition to individual casework. Support, environmental manipulation, and help with health problems, including a serious dental condition, were all a part of the treatment plan for Joan Ehrenwald. According to the record, Nora Jones was an extremely fearful girl with marked anxiety in regard to authority figures and a primary problem in her relationship to her mother. At first Nora was unable to relate at all except to ask a few questions designed to test the worker. She thought all adults were against her. As she came to trust the worker, a marked improvement in her social life was reported and her relationship to her mother became more meaningful and satisfying. The caseworker found that Nancy Mann at first had difficulty verbalizing but as she became able to discuss the problems she faced at home, she was better able to handle her relationship with her mother. When the case was closed, she had an excellent job but was considering going back to school to study practical nursing. Early in the course of treatment, Daphne Poteat, the only white girl in this category, was faced with the responsibility of caring for five siblings when her mother deserted the family. She managed to keep up her school work, run the household, and help her father in the small family business.

In spite of these handicaps, all of the clients are said to have responded well to the casework situation, used the opportunity appropriately, and showed great gains in their school performance and personal adjustment. All of them graduated from high school and obtained jobs in line with their vocational training. Two of the girls had married at the time this report by the casework director was prepared. In the course of treatment, both the mother and the fiancé of Rita Tollo, one of the Puerto Rican girls, was seen by the agency. Some time after her case was closed, Joan Ehrenwald returned to the agency to discuss some problems she was encountering in her marriage. She accepted a referral to a family agency for marital counseling.

FROM GROUP TO CASEWORK TREATMENT

In the later years of the project, girls were referred from groups to the casework department for individual treatment when the group therapist and consultant thought this might be the preferred treatment technique, when there were special or unusual problems requiring individual attention and handling, or in order to clear the case for official closing by the agency for whatever reason. In the course of the project, 72 cases were so referred.

The subsequent handling of these cases by the casework department resulted in effective contact being made with one-half of the referred clients. The 36 cases in which no response could be elicited were closed for a variety of reasons, including inability to see the client at all, removal of the client from the school or from the city, extreme resistance on the part of the girl, or a clinical decision that the girl was not suitable for casework treatment in any event. In two instances, the records were insufficient to make a judgment as to what if anything had been done with the case after it was referred.

Of the 36 cases with whom some meaningful contact was made, six were successfully referred to other agencies, clinics, or hospitals where the girls' particular problems could receive the specialized services indicated. Nine of the cases were judged upon workup not to require casework treatment. Of these, six were returned to groups as the treatment of choice and three were successfully closed as requiring no further services from the agency at this time. In the remaining 21 cases, the casework goals were judged to have been successfully met within the limitations of the clients' abilities and the agency's capacities. Marked improvement was reported for all of these cases and the clients were judged to be functioning as well or better than would be expected. Several of these were still active in the agency at the time this report was prepared.

GROUP TREATMENT[3]

As indicated earlier, the decision to try large unselected observation groups as a referral technique was made in the spring of 1957 when one group was activated. Four others were activated early in the next fall term and continued through the school year. With a change in group therapy consultants, the entire group treatment program was reevaluated the following year and the decision was made to continue working with general discussion groups which, however, should be smaller in size—composed of seven or eight members instead of 13 as in earlier groups. The girls already in the program and the new referrals coming from the short-term orientation groups were reassigned to one or another of the specialized treatment groups designed to meet their particular needs.

Group Referral

In group therapy as conceived by the agency, as in individual contact, the levels and goals of treatment should be based upon a psychosocial evaluation of the client. The groups in this project had to proceed without the benefit of what was considered significant diagnostic material since only the more general facts were known. However, the girls were adolescents of the same age range and thus could be assumed to be subject to conflicts characteristic of their age group, such as ambivalence about dependency needs, conflicts about sexual identification, and so forth. All of the girls experienced adolescence in settings that had much in common. They lived in the same cosmopolitan city with rapidly changing neighborhoods. Also, many of them lived in slum areas characterized by such problems as overcrowding, family disorganization, gangs, dope addiction, and the like. Attendance at the same coeducational, vocational high school was another experience common to all the girls.

Clearance of all cases through the Social Service Exchange showed that with a very few exceptions none of the girls had previously been brought to the attention of a private social agency. However, many of their families were known to hospitals, the Welfare Department, and to the courts, particularly with regard to delinquent siblings. The data on their school records, which were used as the basis for including them in the research sample, did not always indicate whether the difficulties were isolated instances due to a specific set of circumstances or were chronic conditions that marked the girls as present or potential behavior problems. The specific nature and etiology of their problems were not known at the time of selection and referral. There was no indication of how the girls felt about their problems or whether they were willing or able to attempt to find new and more constructive ways of coping with them.

In the absence of more specific information, the group therapist proceeded in the same way an intake worker might start with a new client. First, an effort was made to get the girls to feel free to bring their problems to the group for discussion and to express their feelings about important events in their lives. To reach this goal, the worker tried to communicate to the girls that she "understood" adolescent girls, that she liked and respected them, and that each of them was important to her. She was accepting of their feelings and showed by her nonjudgmental, permissive attitude that she was not like the adults they had known outside the group.

As frequently reported in treatment situations, the group members tested the worker's reliability and the limits of her trustworthiness. In the groups, this process of testing was facilitated, in contrast with individual contact, especially in working with adolescents, where it is often said to present a bottleneck to the treatment process. The group therapists found that the girls in the project groups made full use, at times in trying ways, of the group's possibilities to test the worker. However, they were said to come rather quickly to feel that it was safe to trust the worker in spite of a lingering feeling that there might be a concealed line of communication between the group leader and the school, which was understandable in view of the special setting in which these groups operated.

UNSELECTED GROUPS

Work with the first experimental group of 13 members was begun in April, 1957. These girls, randomly selected from the potential problem research pool, were assembled in a lounge at the school. Eleven of them met with the senior group therapist and the two who were absent joined the group for the first meeting at the YCS headquarters. After a brief discussion of the agency's program for adolescent girls, their interest was readily observable in their relaxation and eagerness to ask pertinent questions about the program and their participation in it. Their questions included: "Why were we singled out?" "How many will be in the group?" "How long will the meetings be held?" They seemed to the therapist to be reassured by the answers and all of them indicated an interest in continuing.

This initial group met five times prior to the close of the school term and the beginning of the summer vacation period. The leader reported that from the very first session the girls responded well to the meetings and there were only eight absences at the five meetings of the group held before the summer recess. A sixth meeting was scheduled but it conflicted with the final examination period at the school and was not held. In reviewing the first five meetings, the staff found that considerable aggression had been expressed by the members and that their impulsive remarks had probably created feelings of anxiety. The therapist therefore planned to increase her efforts toward channelizing the group's expressions of aggression.

From the beginning, the meetings seemed stimulating to the girls and the worker was impressed with the response from the group as a whole. She reported that most of the girls had no difficulty in talking freely and openly. At times they seemed somewhat critical of each other, but were able to draw out the less active members and involve them in the discussions. The topics of conversation reflected the whole gamut of adolescent preoccupation. Central themes in this and later groups were: boys (correct behavior on dates), school (reaction to authority), and parents (conflicts between independency-dependency needs). Problems of life in the community were frequently discussed with fear and hostility. These conversations reflected the hardships of living in slums and rapidly declining neighborhoods. However, there was also much discussion of their hopes for the future. Interest was expressed in vocational planning, in gaining employment, and in becoming responsible citizens. In all of these discussions, the worker recognized the girls' intense need for direction and the seriousness with which they were struggling in their desire to be heard, their need to be understood, and their wish to be mature.

The initial impression of the therapist was that the girls saw this experience as different from a student-teacher relationship. This was shown most clearly in their open discussions of topics not generally shared with adults. This freedom of expression was believed to develop as a result of the worker's permissiveness, acceptance, and understanding of the girls as individuals. It was immediately apparent to the worker that they were deeply concerned about their personal inadequacy, their lack of adjustment, and their inability to cope with tensions and problems of their daily lives. According to the therapist, once the group members came to feel that there would be no retaliation for whatever they would say in the group, they freely discussed their more intimate problems. They ventured to express fears, wishes, and fantasies that they had learned, at times the hard way, to suppress on the outside, especially in the presence of adults. However, as the girls frequently admitted, even in the exclusive presence of peers they had retained a social mask more than they did within the group.

Types of Girls Referred

None of the girls referred to the unselective groups had had previous casework or group counseling experience. The groups were all racially mixed, including Negro, white, and Puerto Rican girls. The first group was composed, as the group therappist appraised them, primarily of immature, impulsive, and "acting-out" girls. Their average age was sixteen years and they were tenth-year students. All had low-average intelligence test scores in their school records, except two who were of superior intelligence and planned to attend college. In the four unselective groups that were started in the second year, the average age was fourteen years and most of the girls were in the ninth grade. In these groups, the IQ scores were higher and a greater number of the girls were preparing for entrance into college. At the time of referral, they appeared to the worker to be much the same as girls in the first group, but the manifestations of their problems and the use they made of the groups differed widely. The following is a cursory outline of the types of girls referred to the unselective groups as the leader saw them. There is overlapping in the types mentioned.

(1) *Girls Whose Behavior Was Normal.* These girls were seen as showing good ego strength and they functioned well in school. Although they came from families with varying degrees of apparent disorganization and pathology, they seemed equipped to deal with their problems. They were an asset to the groups, furnishing acceptable peer models for the more disturbed girls and exercising a stabilizing, reality-oriented influence in the discussions.

(2) *Girls Exhibiting Neurotic Symptoms.* The neurotic anxiety of these girls was, in the view of the therapist, reflected in their inability to work up to their intellectual capacity in school and their distortions of themselves, their parents, and peers. Some of these girls suffered from psychosomatic symptoms, such as headaches, allergies, and asthma. For the girls who somatized their problems, the group was not believed by the worker to be of real help in their underlying pathology, but she believed that a few of the neurotic girls used the group to work through some of their reality problems. The nature of the groups and the time limitations under which they operated during school hours precluded the structuring of a therapy group that the worker believed would be of sufficient intensity to answer the needs of neurotic girls. In spite of this shortcoming, however, the workers noted that girls

with problems of a psychosomatic nature showed signs of improvement. Wherever possible, these girls and their families were encouraged to accept referral for treatment in a more appropriate setting, such as a hospital, clinic, or private therapy.

Doris Dailey is an example of a neurotic, nonverbal girl who was reported to make a positive use of the group. She was of average intelligence, but was not working up to capacity in school and was frequently tardy. Doris never missed a session of the group and her attendance in school improved. Initially, she was shy and appeared self-conscious. It took her a long time to verbalize any problems to the group. When she did, it concerned going on a trip; and her interest in the group was shown by helping with the refreshments and planning a Christmas party. Doris is the third oldest in a family of six children. The last two children in the family were born out of wedlock. Doris' father was killed following an argument at a card game. An older brother was known to the courts for possession of marijuana. The mother worked full-time in domestic service. The worker felt that Doris had no real ties at home and was completely uninterested in her family. The group seemed to be one of her few positive experiences. When Doris finally did discuss her problems, she felt this to be a great achievement for her and acknowledged it openly. She later expressed quite well the positive effects that the group had in helping her develop self-confidence. This improvement was also reflected in her better school adjustment. While the worker recognized that the underlying pathology of this depressed, phobic girl was not worked with, it was concluded that the group experience did sustain Doris and enable her to function better in her immediate situation.

(3) *Girls Suffering from Poor Ego Strength.* These girls tended to come from families beset by severe social pathology. The intelligence level of many of them was interpreted to be dull normal and a few were considered even lower. The group leader saw them as immature, restless, depressed, nonverbal, belligerent, and without conscious awareness of their problems or any motivation to seek help. In the early meetings, the immature girls were preoccupied with food and brought candy and potato chips to eat throughout the sessions. For the most part they showed no ability to verbalize or even to recognize their problems. Their families were deemed generally inadequate and openly rejecting. Their

homes tended to be primarily matriarchal, with several siblings. The girls usually had heavy household responsibilities which made their continuation in school quite unlikely. Within this classification, two groups of girls could be differentiated by the therapist, one tending to act out problems, whereas the other seemed, on the surface at least, to function surprisingly well.

Agnes Alanza, a fifteen-year-old Puerto Rican girl in the first group, was chosen by the group leader as representative of this type. In elementary school, Agnes was described as overtalkative, but a willing worker and liked by her peer group. Her grades throughout her school career were borderline and there were notations on her record that indicated she was unhappy at home. Before entering the group, she was described by her junior high school teacher as "downright nasty." She was frequently absent and late for school. In the group, she was a compulsive talker who tended to dominate the sessions. In the beginning, there was some question as to whether she could be tolerated, but she remained in the group for more than a year. She was always a stimulus for the group, although at times it seemed to have a negative effect. She impressed the worker as one of the sickest girls in the group. Agnes presented herself as a highly competitive girl, with very little feeling for or interest in other members. She tended to provoke arguments, attack new members in subtle ways, and consistently to generate tension. She was markedly preoccupied with gory stories. The psychiatric consultant reviewing her case noted that these gory stories indicated how she libidinized everything. She was obsessed with sex in early meetings but, as she continued as a member of the group, this tendency diminished and at the time the cases were reviewed by the supervisor for this report Agnes appeared much less obsessed with sexuality. Overt anxiety was detected by the therapist in her later stories and her fantasy material was considered less bizarre. In this respect, the therapist thought Agnes had shown some improvement as a result of her group participation. Her functioning in school had also become noticeably better. Teachers commented, for example, that whereas previously she had been very disagreeable, she was now pleasanter and responded quickly when asked to help. She could come to her teacher and tell her when things went wrong. By the end of the year, Agnes was coming to school regularly and her tardiness was no longer a problem.

(4) *Girls Showing Psychotic-like Behavior.* These girls were characterized by the group therapist as showing marked depression,

extreme anxiety, and almost total disorganization in their lives. Mental illness and delinquency were frequently noted in their family histories. In groups they responded by being overtalkative and monopolizing the discussions, or by extreme withdrawal and suspicious unrelatedness or self-preoccupation. Some of these girls could not be kept in the groups as constituted and had to be referred to other sources of help.

Caroline Petty is an example of a sixteen-year-old girl whose psychotic-like behavior necessitated her later referral for casework consideration. When referred to the group, her grades were border-line and she was very frequently absent and late for school. On her permanent school record, her ratings on dependability and coopera-tion were extremely poor and there was a drop in her IQ scores from 91 to 64 during the last four years, which indicated, the therapist believed, a marked depression. The worker described her as an at-tractive, slender girl with clean features. During the early sessions of the group, Caroline appeared sullen, dejected, and never smiled. She gave the impression of being unduly critical of the other girls and usually spoke only after there had been considerable interaction among the other group members. In the first meeting, when one of the girls talked about marriage, it was Caroline who hoped that she would consider this seriously, pointing to the heavy household re-sponsibilities. The meaning of this remark became clear in a later session when Caroline discussed her own family situation. She had to cook, clean house, and watch the younger siblings. She complained about her father, who never gave her permission to go out but she went out anyway. She did not give the impression of one who openly defied her family without cause. At school, Caroline seemed to see herself as victimized by her teachers. She was failing for no apparent reason. During the refreshment periods, Caroline seldom socialized with the other members, but directed her conversation to the worker. Through the Social Service Exchange, the worker learned that Caroline's mother had been committed to a state mental hospital since Caroline was six years old, following a suicidal attempt after the birth of the youngest brother. Later, Caroline confided to the group that her mother was in a mental hospital. The father was de-scribed as hostile with paranoic trends. The worker felt that Caroline needed relief from her inner pressures and, in view of the positive re-lationship she had developed with the worker, the subject of referral to the casework department was discussed with her. The experience in the group was believed to have helped her recognize that she could talk to an adult, that at least some adults would listen to her without judgment or reproach, and that such interaction was helpful and meaningful. The worker felt that without the reassurance she received from the other group members it was doubtful that Caroline would ever have been able to take this step toward treatment.

Content of the Group Discussions

In contrast with similar girls in individual casework, the girls in these groups were seen by the social workers as less tense and apprehensive and better able to ventilate their feelings, whether hostile or not, about unhappy and depressing facts in their lives. Whenever they did so, they seemed to gain reassurance by noting that others had similar problems. Each week a different girl emerged, presenting her own particular problems, and most of the girls in the group could relate to the material.

The following are illustrations reported by the group therapist of the ways in which the girls began to bring out their problems and how they helped each other view these problems more constructively.

At the first meeting, Mariann Rubio, a petite, fifteen-year-old Puerto Rican girl, became the center of attention when she announced her plans to marry soon. She presented the details of her plan in logical sequence. To the worker the forthcoming marriage seemed a means of escape from a poor mother-daughter relationship. The girls were forceful in their criticism of her early marriage, giving sound and rational reasons why she should think carefully before acting. They questioned her boy friend's maturity and her own readiness for marriage, and stressed the need for her to complete her high school education so as to be prepared for life. Mariann listened intently and responded by saying how "fed up" she was with school and with her past life, which was beset by frustrations and deprivation and a feeling of being unloved. The girls immediately picked up her tendency to act out and, through their discussion, helped her think what she was getting herself into. This kind of discussion became the stimulus for other girls to bring up their problems with boy friends and their aspirations for the future.

At the fourth meeting of one group, Nola Sanborn said, "Don't let's talk about fighting, let's talk about mean mothers." Beatrice King thought that mothers were not mean; Daphne Rappo said hers was. Beatrice answered by saying that mothers have to do certain things that girls don't agree with. "Mine isn't mean except when she

beats me with a strap, but she doesn't do that much anymore."
Daphne recalled that boys wear belts with wide buckles and sometimes parents take these belts and use them to punish children. When
the worker asked what caused disagreement between their mothers
and themselves, Beatrice explained that her mother was broad-
minded about sex and boys. Nina Quintero picked this up by saying
that her mother would let her boy friends come to the house if her
sister or brother was there. Following this, there was discussion about
mothers' fears of leaving girls alone with their boy friends. Thus even
in the earliest sessions, the girls revealed themselves, complained, and
defined their problems in the group setting.

In order to get a more complete picture of each girl's total environment, the agency decided to employ a skilled caseworker to
explore individual family situations through collateral contacts,
Social Service Exchange clearances, and visits with parents
wherever possible, to consult teachers and school guidance counselors, and to arrange for psychological testing whenever necessary. This effort to gain as clear a picture as possible of each girl
in her total environment—community, home, school, and therapy group—was limited by the personnel and funds available to
the agency. Within these limitations, however, considerable information was collected, especially from interviews with parents
and teachers.

Contact with Parents

The caseworker assigned to the project for this purpose saw the
parents of girls in three of the first five groups. Six parents of girls
in the first group were seen; none of these families was intact. In
each case the father was missing through divorce, death, or deser-
tion, usually when the client was quite young. The fathers, where
known, tended to be delinquent, known to the courts on charges
of rape, dope addiction, or gambling. One girl had lived with a
maternal aunt since infancy and knew very little of her natural
family. Three of the families were self-sufficient and the others
received assistance from the department of welfare.

Of the twelve parents of girls in the later groups who were seen,
seven were separated and nine were self-sustaining. In all the
groups, families tended to be quite large, ranging from one to

eleven siblings with an average of about three. In every case the parent seen was the mother, except in the one instance when the father responded to the invitation to meet the caseworker. Social and environmental pathology was found by the caseworker to permeate all the families seen, and was supposed to be even more pronounced in those that could not be seen directly.

The caseworker felt that one contact was insufficient for gaining an adequate and reliable picture of the family situation. She reported, however, that the parents seemed to be relieved that someone else was handling their adolescent daughters. In general, they seemed to find it hard to cope with the problems that arose; the caseworker believed this to be due to their own rejection or overburdened feelings as parents. They were positive in their attitudes toward the groups.

> The mother of Julia Harris reported that her daughter was taking more interest in reading the newspapers and in talking about and judging people and events. She was much more alert to what was going on around her. Julia's mother was not sure whether this was part of the process of growing up or whether it was the influence of the group. Joanna Light was an anxious, conflicted girl, preoccupied with parental restrictions. Her mother noticed that she was less impetuous and fought less with her sister, which the mother attributed to the group experience. Ann Tomas was frequently absent from school and became increasingly depressed. She revealed to the group that she shared a bed with her younger brother and was afraid to go to sleep. Her mother was interviewed and the sleeping arrangement was changed. Ann's depression was no longer apparent. In only one instance did a mother actively interfere with the group treatment of her daughter. The therapist reported that Beatrice King became able with the group's help to stand up at times to her mother and that, in retaliation, Mrs. King removed Beatrice from the group. The worker thought this step might have been prevented if she had had the opportunity to work with the mother in a parents' group.

The workers felt that, in general, most of the parents would have responded to some form of group participation. For the most part, they were not deemed ready for intensive individual contact. Viewing their feelings of inadequacy as parents, the workers felt that a mothers' guidance group would have been of immeasurable help if the agency had had facilities for such a program. In fact, one parent with serious problems was seen by a YCS caseworker over a period of several months. Another parent, who expressed positive feelings for the agency, was later involved in treatment when her daughter became pregnant out of wedlock.

Contact with the School

The high school emphasized the importance of preparing for work after graduation. Its guidance department tried to be sensitive to the students' incipient problems, taking the initiative in helping them, and following through with appropriate plans and decisions. In the agency's contacts with the school, consultations were held with grade counselors and trade and academic teachers. Generally, the girls involved in the group program were believed to show progress in school. Improvements were especially noted in attendance and grades. In reporting on effects, the senior group therapist selected a few representative cases to show these apparent trends.

Betty Randolph, a compliant, immature girl of average intelligence, seemed to have greater potential than she exhibited, and in the course of the year while in the group she became a leader in school and assumed responsibility with increasing assurance. Birdie Ann Rhea showed improvement in her grades but was still considered a problem in regard to tardiness. Sally Shell's marks improved from C to B in her trade courses and in conduct. There was decided improvement in Gertrude Cresco, who was admittedly very shy and never spoke up. A teacher reported that she "now smiles and even gets up enough nerve to speak in class." She participated more actively and got on the honor roll. There were contradictory reports from the school regarding Doris Dailey. Some teachers found her less shy and making progress in her work habits. However, in other classes no improvement was reported. Caroline Petty had improved, particularly in her response to male teachers. Julia Harris' performance in school was uneven, but she had won a special award in her trade course. Aline Herrero, an ardent Jehovah's Witness from a Catholic background, developed from an anxious, frightened girl into a confident, secure member of the group. She volunteered that the group had helped her greatly. Her appearance was considered better and she seemed to place her religious interests in perspective. Two very depressed and withdrawn girls showed no improvement, either in the group or in their school performance, and they were referred for individual casework treatment.

In general, the teachers and guidance counselors were enthusiastic about the effects of the groups and, in the therapists' view, tended, if anything, to exaggerate the overall effectiveness and impact on the girls' behavior and progress in school. The program seemed to have an effect on the teachers themselves and to orient them toward a new appreciation of the guidance department and the work it was trying to do.

In reviewing the experience after the first year, the staff commented on the girls' attempts to understand themselves and to overcome their inadequacies and low self-esteem. The staff believed that as a result, some potentials were revealed. The girls ventilated their feelings in the group and gained some understanding of how to handle specific situations, whether at home or at school. As these girls felt more confident, they increasingly revealed more about themselves. At times the worker gave individual attention to a girl or her family when a problem indicated the need, such as referral to a clinic, intervention with the housing authority, and the like. That the groups had reached these girls to some degree was evidenced by their regular attendance at meetings, their participation whether active or passive, and the progress they seemed to make, particularly in the area of school achievement.

Observations

In evaluating the experience with the first five, unselective groups, the agency staff felt that the workers had definitely made contact with these girls, although not in great depth or at a sustained level. The staff believed, however, that such girls would not have been referred to an agency if it had not been for the project. The staff felt that the general bases for referral—occasional truancy, not working up to capacity, unreliability, shy withdrawal, immature behavior, and so on—did not indicate the degree of disturbance later observed by the workers. Although the needs of these girls were less apparent and most of them had not been in serious trouble in the community, the workers found the girls just as much in need of help as those who usually come to the attention of social agencies. At the same time, these clients seemed less resistant than adolescents whom the workers had seen in individual treatment; they were more willing to tell how they viewed their problems, both through nonverbal communications and through earlier verbalizations.

Although these first groups were large and unselective, the staff felt that a certain kind of constructive change occurred among the girls. For the most part, the improvements seemed temporary and the workers questioned whether they would be lasting. The clients were viewed as having limited psychological involvement in therapy and as lacking conscious motivation to change. The workers felt that a longer time was needed for gains to be integrated. Nevertheless, they felt that attention given to acute social and psychological problems helped to alleviate anxiety when it did occur. Extreme behavior was readily apparent in the groups and was attended to quickly. The staff felt, however, that the fact that the girls were accepted for referral without the benefit of a diagnostic workup limited what could be accomplished by the staff, and they considered the data obtainable through group observation inadequate to give an accurate picture of intrapsychic problems. The staff concluded that in unstructured groups of that size, many girls who might benefit from more deliberately structured group therapy could not be reached in a meaningful way.

An attempt was made to meet this situation by developing new principles for the formation of groups. The new groups consisted of fewer members and an attempt was made to be selective about their composition. The underlying assumption was that, if the members were better able to identify with each other, the leader of the group would be in a position to give them more constructive help. The basis for the composition of these smaller, selective groups has been discussed in the previous chapter.

SELECTIVE GROUPS

The new series of small, selective groups was introduced by reassigning girls from the earlier unselective groups and adding new members from the current orientation screening groups that were subsequently formed for all new referrals. During the remaining part of the project, 13 selective groups, averaging 7 members each, were formed. These consisted of 5 Observation Groups, 2 Family Life Education Groups, 3 Interview Treatment Groups, 2 Protective Groups, and 1 Activity Group. All of these were not in existence at one time and many of the girls were in more than one group. Generally, girls who were placed first in the Activity Group were later put in other groups or referred for individual treatment.

The group leaders reported that when each group was activated, the girls sought direction as to the topics they might discuss. They did not see how just talking about their problems would solve anything. This led to a discussion between the workers and the girls about the understandings that can come from talking. The workers saw in the discussion a release of suppressed material that was a major ego strengthening device and the group members soon experienced this as helpful. However, the group therapists believed that treatment gains could be sustained only through appropriate handling ("working through") of the material. Much of the "working through" was done by the group members themselves, with the workers shifting discussion only in minor ways, as when it seemed indicated to protect a member against an attack for which she was not ready or to pick up a topic that the members had dropped because it seemed to be too threatening. The attitude of the worker, her manner of "mulling over" problems, her consistent willingness to accept expressions of feelings were believed to influence the members to work with each other in an atmosphere that was characterized by mutual respect and trust. This is in contrast to the larger, unselective groups in which some members, operating on different levels, had interfered with the smooth flow of this process. In the selective groups, the workers observed that the girls were able to focus on problems with more sustained interest and showed more understanding of each other's difficulties. They provided each other with an opportunity to view their common problems in perspectives different from those to which they were accustomed. Often a member was led to reduce her feelings of guilt over "forbidden thoughts" once she realized that "others were in the same boat."

The girls were usually more receptive to suggestions from peers than to those coming from the adult leader. They readily accepted interpretations from each other which, had the worker made them, might have increased their anxiety and caused them to become defensive.

In working with the groups, the therapist's view of the nature of the client's problems was frequently challenged. As the group therapists saw it, they had to acknowledge the full impact of the reality situation upon the client's distress, whereas the worker in individual contact was more likely to assume that the client was magnifying or otherwise distorting the problem. In group experiences, the clients had a greater opportunity to "bring in their world." When all or a majority of the members of the group, in spite of differences in their psychological makeup, almost simultaneously described situations of external stress in similar ways, the worker herself came to view the problem differently.

In work with the selective as well as the unselective groups, the group leaders felt they had an unusual opportunity to gain a new understanding of "the world of the adolescent." This was because the numbers of girls referred were much larger than those usually found in an agency's normal caseload. More unusual than this, however, was the fact that these girls had not yet met failure. Hence the worker was not obligated to focus on problematic areas, and could "listen" before "acting."

Content of Discussion

As the senior group therapist and consultant reviewed the group records, the same central themes recurred in the group discussions. A major theme was the girls' distress over sexual problems: menstruation, intercourse, pregnancy, and childbirth. In general, the workers found that the girls lacked adequate information about sex. Menstruation was viewed as a punishment because Adam and Eve had sinned. The ideas of pregnancy and childbirth were beset by fears. However, this provided the worker with an opportunity to clarify their misconceptions. The decision was made to use the worker as a major source of "information" instead of encouraging the girls to find solutions on their own, as is often the approach in individual casework. The more didactic approach, viewed by the group therapists as essentially mental hygiene education, dictated the formation of the Family Life Education Groups for girls who were particularly in need of information and direction in this area.

Discussions of violent acts—suicide, gang warfare—occurred frequently in the group sessions. However, in the group setting it seemed clear to the leaders that talk about such things was more related to actual happenings than to the girls' inner preoccupations with such events. As far as the workers were able to determine, none of the group members was actually involved in gang activities, although some had marginal connections with the male gangs in their neighborhoods. Some, however, had friends who were active gang members and dope addicts. Once a group member, Sarah Jones, was accused of active involvement in a gang fight. However, detailed exploration of the happenings by the group enabled the worker to discover that Sarah was only marginally involved in it. She was not suspended from school as had been planned because YCS promised to continue working with her in the group.

Another main theme of the discussions in the meetings of each type of group reflected the girls' eager search for a reliable set of values that would be helpful in making the many decisions required of them in this particular period of their lives. "Is it right to date a boy who is five years older?" "Is it right to accept a gift after only one date?" "Is it right to date a boy of another religion, of another race?" "Is it right to have intercourse before marriage?" The girls helped each other explore these problems and gave each other advice. Rebellious attitudes toward parents and their own neurotic drives were seen to play some part in thwarting development of comfortable standards for behavior and the worker handled difficulties in such a light. What impressed the caseworkers who were group leaders was that the girls' individual disturbances were less responsible for their distress than their lack of a workable set of values. They seemed to be searching for an "anchorage of mind," as Suzanne Langer has termed it, which they found at least in part in the group. The group seemed to be a haven that allowed them to find a frame of reference they had not found in the restless world outside. The dynamics of the therapy situation were considered to be particularly helpful in this process. In the group, as indicated earlier, each girl was assured of the worker's acceptance; the worker gave careful attention to details; she was always patient no matter what a girl might do or say; the worker liked and respected the girls and made them feel that they were important to her. They also got support from their peers. A member of the group who became anxious when forced to cope with a problem on the outside felt strengthened by the thought that she could bring it up for discussion in the group. Discussion could flow evenly in the group, where the train of thought was not drowned out by jazz records, where newly born, fragile feelings were nursed instead of becoming a victim to loud television noises. There was no pressure to achieve; one was allowed "to be as you are"; here one was important, one counted. Girls who had the opportunity to note repeatedly that a "nice girl" may also get into trouble, who were exposed to the painful birth of new attitudes, who had the opportunity to come close to persons with whom she had no personal or social ties could be gradually sensitized to the inner world of human beings. There was little room in their culture for this kind of emotional experience, which is vital for the growth of mature attitudes. This type of experience formed the core of the helping process of the group therapy program.

In spite of their best efforts, the girls' search for sound solutions to their problems frequently ended in failure. It seemed obvious to the therapists that the girls were inadequately equipped for the adolescent tasks required of them. What did they see as the cause of these inadequacies? Neurotic symptoms and behavior disorders due to neglect were thought to account for many of their weaknesses. However, the workers were impressed by the fact that almost all of the girls seemed to lack the emotional resources needed for handling the problems that confronted them at this period of their lives. This lack of emotional maturity was found in similar degrees among the "normal," "neurotic," and the "neglected" girls. The exception was a small group of severely disturbed girls whose lack of maturity was "covered" by their more overt illness. The workers were inclined to assume that these deficiencies did not stem only from internalized problems or from stress due to social pathology, rather that they were caused by the inadequate guidance these girls had received from their parents, from the school, and from the community in their earlier years, and were receiving at the present time.

Even so, the workers observed that the emotional experiences in the group enabled the girls to become more mature and that they seemed, in turn, to be able to handle their problems more effectively. The staff were agreed that as social workers they needed to understand these phenomena better and to try to analyze them more scientifically.

It is difficult to probe this type of emotional experience and to test in systematic ways its role in the helping process. In the absence of more objective measures to substantiate or challenge the workers' observations and conclusions, these evaluations represent only abstractions made with a variety of purposes in mind, usually in order to prepare for supervisory conferences or for staff seminars. Often the conclusions are based on hunches alone although, occasionally, supporting data were found in psychological tests and family histories. Even without the benefit of further data, the workers and consultants felt encouraged and entitled to use some of their experiences in their later practical work. Social workers often have to perform a job in an area where theory is still vague or missing. In such instances, they venture to work with hypotheses based on experience, or "practice wisdom," to use Werner Boehm's term. To a certain extent, in the absence of more scientific data, the interpretation of the group therapy program and its consequences for the girls also had to depend on "practice wisdom."

Family Life Education Groups

As indicated earlier, the Family Life Education Groups were modeled after mental hygiene education groups that had seemed to be successful in other settings.

The workers were surprised to learn the extent to which these girls were in need of sexual information. They had assumed that many parents had given their daughters such information, and this was indeed often confirmed during group discussion. Also, New York City schools provide some pertinent instruction relating to sex and reproduction. Many girls had heard rather uninhibited talk about sex in their neighborhoods. Some girls were avid readers of the *True Confession* type of magazine in which there is much discussion of sex. Yet the information the girls had received outside the group did not seem to have been integrated by them either intellectually or emotionally. When the workers gave group instruction on sexual matters, the girls expressed great relief. Frequently they said or implied that the opportunity to get this kind of information as members of a group was perhaps the main reason they valued the experience.

The group leaders knew that at times the information given by the workers might not have been really new to the girls. They also recognized that information which parents give to their children on sexual matters is often coupled with the strongly implied expectation that the daughter will use the information "the right way." In school the instructor "teaches" matters that should be memorized for tests. Such a procedure is not conducive to the assimilation of emotionally charged material.

In contrast with these approaches, the workers gave this information with no accompaniment of expectations or demands. The girls were free "to take it or leave it." Moreover, the worker became for some girls an ego ideal and they genuinely trusted her. "I believe her," a girl exclaimed upon learning from the worker what happens during the "wedding night."

In reporting their experience with Family Life Education Groups, the social workers also included topics about family living other than sex, although the girls themselves were said to make this a central theme. Woven around this theme, other problems, such as getting along with brothers and sisters and with older persons in the household, and realistic problems of marital conflict, were also discussed. What characterized these groups was their tolerance for and encouragement of direct, matter-of-fact discussion of things the girls felt to be important but could not discuss elsewhere without feeling guilty.

Although there were frequent setbacks in helping these girls toward more mature family life experience, the workers felt encouraged by the overall results and considered this type of group extremely effective. They believed that this level of group treatment could have preventive and therapeutic effects with some neurotic girls, even though it omits direct work with the neurotic core. They noted that girls who had resisted earlier approaches became enthusiastic about their group experience, which enabled some of them to become ready for more intensive individual or group therapy in the future.

Special Groups

In contrast with the Family Life Education Groups, the organization and structure of the "special groups"—Interview, Protective, and Activity Groups—were more like such groups in group therapy programs in social work agencies. In these groups, many problems arose, requiring environmental manipulation, that were handled as in regular group work, or by the group therapist herself, or by the individual casework department of YCS. The staff saw some groups as effective in reaching non-verbal, passive, withdrawn girls who, on account of being insecure and suspicious, might not have been accessible to individual casework. In a group, such girls were allowed to "take in by listening" which at times helped them without requiring their active participation. Some of these girls were considered by the workers to be seriously emotionally disturbed, yet their smooth facade prevented parents and teachers from detecting that they were in trouble. This group experience made possible by their chance selection for the project seemed to the workers an exceptional opportunity for them to become involved in a helping process that they very much needed.

As an example of such a case, the senior group therapist named Kate Shriver, a fifteen-year-old girl who was intelligent but seemed to have great fears about sex. She was assigned to an Interview Treatment Group composed of girls of relatively high intelligence with ego strength and who showed some motivation. From the school records, it was believed that she needed encouragement, was easily led and rather shy, and was not working up to capacity in her school work. Kate sat quietly for several weeks, although she seemed aware of what was going on. When another member expressed resentment of her stepfather, this was the impetus for Kate to speak up. With considerable feeling, she told how she also hated her stepfather, who was a strict disciplinarian. Although the girls discussed other problems in the succeeding weeks, Kate invariably returned to the same theme. The members began to ask her direct questions about her home life. They noted that she was permitted to date weekends and that the attention given to doing her homework at a specific time showed interest on her stepfather's part. The worker helped Kate discuss the evolution of this problem. Kate began to describe her past life, how she had been placed in a foster home at an early age because of marital difficulties. She had felt rejected and punitively treated by her foster parents. She looked forward to the day when she would return home to her mother. When this finally occurred at the age of eight, Kate learned that her mother had remarried. She spoke of her resentment toward this "stranger." The other members were sympathetic about Kate's early deprivation, but indicated that her mother needed companionship, too. In many meetings that took place over a one-year period, the members helped Kate view her stepfather in a more realistic light and this seemed to allow her to function with greater ease and effectiveness.

In school, Kate kept to herself and did not cause disciplinary problems; other girls like Kate who are suffering from difficulties are not as likely to be detected as are aggressive girls who are always causing trouble. In the group, such girls were allowed to remain passive, sometimes for many months. No one pushed them into an activity that for them was equated with danger. Even without active participation, however, the girls had an opportunity to be exposed to discussions among group members who freely shared feelings of anger and hate, and to the worker's emotionally neutral response. Gradually these experiences helped them get out of the shell in which they had been hiding. They ventured to speak out once they had learned that showing weakness does not provoke attack, that expressing hate and anger is not the same as committing an act of violence. When at times the discussion focused on a nuclear core of a girl's neurotic problem, the therapeutic effect of the group experience seemed vivid to the therapist and could lead to a dramatic change, a "spontaneous recovery."

The group therapists pointed out that sometimes it took a long time for a situation to arise in which the members could start to help a rather withdrawn member of the group. The experience of Anna Troy, a shy, depressed girl of fifteen who is the oldest of eleven children, is a good example.

> While Anna was attending the Observation Group, she mentioned frequently that she would no longer attend meetings. This seemed to be her way of testing the worker's acceptance of her. In an Interview Treatment Group, for a long time Anna remained withdrawn and mute, although it seemed to the worker that she was quite aware of what was going on in the group. Finally, one day when some of the girls were discussing their difficulties with alcoholic fathers, Anna related to this. Apparently this was one of her greatest problems (at one point she had to take her father to court for a drunken assault upon herself), but she had not dared to bring it out on her own. In a group of girls who also suffered from deprivation, but who were better able than Anna to talk about their situations, the worker could protect her from attacks and encourage her potentialities. Anna was reported as still giving the impression of suffering from severe limitations in certain areas. Although her school marks remained low, she was determined to graduate and expressed the desire to continue, a goal which for many reasons may be beyond her reach, but which expressed her determination to better herself and her life.

A number of these special groups ran concurrently and operated on different levels. One of the Interview Treatment Groups, for example, was composed of six members who met weekly during a full school year for a total of thirty-three sessions. All of the girls selected for this group had been screened in orientation groups and were similar in having average intelligence and some ego strength. They were all juniors in high school, either sixteen or seventeen years old. They all showed some motivation to accomplish in school and none of them presented gross behavior problems that interfered significantly with their school adjustment. The attendance in the group was excellent and this provided a stable membership that seemed to facilitate movement.

The group therapists noted great differences among the girls in this group on every level. Some were emotionally and socially more mature than others; some more aware of their own anxieties and problems; some experienced great difficulty in expressing themselves verbally, while others could communicate readily. There was also a mixture of neurotic and characterological disturbances that naturally resulted in different preoccupations and concerns. The group as a whole discussed the usual adolescent concerns relating to school, social life, curiosity about sexual matters, and ambivalent feelings about growing up. In addition, three of the members used the group to discuss very personal problems centering around traumatic childhood experiences and intense sibling rivalry situations. Sexual guilt and anxiety, related to restrictive parental attitudes at home, were also brought up for consideration. As the group progressed, the discussions of general areas became more personalized and therefore more amenable to clarification and help. There was no monopolization of leadership in the group, although two members tended to alternate in leading the discussions. The rest of the group accepted this, however, and when these girls were absent others who were usually more passive were able to assume responsibility. The group offered different degrees of helpfulness to its members, depending upon the type of problem each brought up and her degree of involvement in the group. The girls who could be most motivated by the worker's direction and were most mature and verbal in the group were the ones who became more involved and therefore seemed to the leader to make the greatest progress.

Throughout the year there was a high degree of interaction among the members and a real feeling of loss was expressed when one member left the group at the end of the year because of being discharged from school. Although the girls were unable to verbalize clearly the meaning of the group for them, they indicated a definite desire to continue the next year. In the last session, they brought up very significant material which was indicative to the therapist of their need for continuing help. In the view of the social work staff, none of these girls could have been reached consistently in an individual casework contact, whereas all of them were particularly accessible in the group counseling situation.

Anita Warren was a member of this group for a year and was selected by the group leader as an example of a girl who seemed to use the experience constructively. She was a fairly attractive Negro girl of medium height who wore her skirts very short and looked as if she were wearing a costume. In school, Anita was described as sullen, hostile, frequently absent, resentful of correction, disagreeable, and lacking self-control. She was known to the Youth Board because her mother had complained that she stayed out all night with a boy and might be pregnant. She had seen a social worker at another agency for a short time, but this contact had apparently not been used constructively.

In the beginning group sessions, Anita behaved as she did on the outside with authority figures and with her peers. She was uncommunicative and detached. She also seemed to make the other girls feel uncomfortable by separating herself from the larger group and talking with two girls on the side. Fairly early in the first meeting, she made comments about having been in trouble and having seen a social worker, but it was difficult to follow her and she did not wish to elaborate. Gradually, Anita began to discuss problems in school and fights in which she had been involved. She expressed a fair amount of hostility toward teachers, but was unwilling to admit that she had done anything to provoke the difficulty. She showed positive feeling toward school, however, and expressed ambivalence about transferring to another school, which had been her initial threat. She was very protective of her parents or her troubles at home. When the other girls were expressing hostility toward parents and describing ways in which their parents punished them, Anita indicated that her mother was attentive to her and did not use physical punishment.

At the end of three months in evaluating Anita, the worker felt that Anita vented hostility in school about situations that initially arose at home, where she felt unable to express herself. She appeared to be afraid of her parents and one got the impression that her mother was quite suspicious and controlling. Occasionally Anita would spend a night away from home and bitterly resented her mother's checking up on her.

As Anita continued in the group, she became more communicative. One interesting difference occurred in her use of verbalizations. In the beginning she would talk in "bop" language, which made it difficult to understand her. Later, she communicated a good deal more about herself and used more appropriate language. She was the most active member of the group, but she did not try to monopolize the sessions or prevent other girls from speaking.

A decided improvement was noted by the worker in Anita's school functioning. Her attendance was good and she passed all of her major subjects at the end of the year. She showed interest in her school work and asked the worker to see her individually a number of times to help her with some school work she had been deficient in. The worker felt that the group had served to channel some of Anita's aggressiveness into learning pursuits. She frequently used characters from stories she had read or movies she had seen as a vehicle for communicating theories about herself. From her discussion of herself in the group, the group therapist sensed that Anita had problems about her sexual identification, seeing herself as quite inadequate and physically unattractive. The therapist attributed this feeling in part to a view that women generally are somewhat provocative, sexually promiscuous, and therefore undesirable. Anita was very active in the group when any subjects relating to this topic came up, such as how girls dress and behave with boys, parents' attitudes toward dating, and so forth.

At a later integration conference assessing group members, the worker reported that Anita had continued to improve. She was performing better in school and acted out less. However, the less she acted out, the more noticeable her neurotic anxiety became. At this point, it was judged appropriate for the worker to contact the family in order to explore the source of her apparent neurosis. At the final session of the year, Anita seemed deeply moved, thanked the worker for her help, and added, "Now I can even like my mother again."

The staff felt that the group control seemed generally to be effective with "acting out" clients, such as Anita. However, they were uncertain as to the long-range effects of such an interview group program with girls of this type.

Activity groups were created by the group therapy staff for those girls who suffered from extreme deprivation, who were nonverbal and seemed grossly immature. At first, casual games were used in such a group as a means of helping the girls relate to each other and to the worker. The girls soon dropped the use of games and relaxed sufficiently in this permissive atmosphere to gain confidence in the worker, who led them in a discussion of problems on a superficial level. They could then be prepared for transfer to a more intensive, interview type of group or to individual contact with a caseworker at the agency. This individual attention was often necessary in view of the need to help the girls and their families with environmental problems.

Some girls, suffering severe social deprivation and psychological consequences, were referred to individual casework. Most of such girls received concurrent individual and group treatment. Several girls became too anxious when in a group, but were able to use individual casework. However, the staff felt that without previous group experience, these clients would not have been able to do so; the group had given them a positive attitude toward the agency and reassured them concerning its policies. Generally, referrals to casework occurred when acute situations came to the attention of the group worker.

A few of the clients were found by the staff to be out of reach of either group therapy or casework treatment because of severe pathology and psychosis, narcissistic personalities, psychopathic behavior, or marked depression. The inaccessibility of such cases was in keeping with the previous experience of the staff. These girls were viewed as having been referred too late. Their home troubles were severe and it was hard to understand why neither the girls nor their families had previously come to the attention of authorities.

> Jane Alfonso was such a girl. For years she had been exposed to cruel handling by her sadistic mother and to abuses from her unscrupulous stepfather. She talked readily in the group about her plight and felt gratified by the members' interest in her. The worker learned in an interview with the mother that the girl's descriptions were not exaggerated. She tried to initiate court action but the situation was already out of hand. During a brief vacation period Jane was again beaten unmercifully and ran away from home, reportedly with a sailor on leave. The worker was unable to discover her whereabouts. Still many months later, the girls in the group frequently asked the worker if she had heard from Jane. They had been deeply moved by the girl's misfortunes.

General Appraisal of the Group Therapy Program

At the conclusion of the project, the group therapy consultant made a general summary that embodies both the rationale for the approach taken and the sense of accomplishment.[4] This summary is a fitting conclusion to the presentation of observations by the staff of their work in the group therapy program.

Adolescence is a critical phase in the growth of every human being. Many important changes occur; bodily changes (pubescence) take place; sex drives emerge. The adolescent is expected to control these drives according to modes determined by the culture in which he lives. Also, the adolescent has to change his social role. He "loses the protection of childhood but does not yet have the strengths and the privileges of the adult."[5] His insecurity is heightened by financial hardships, poor housing, by problems of discrimination, and by the shadow of a possible nuclear war. These difficulties expose the adolescent to conflicts on all levels of emotional experience. Traditional patterns of social work usually try to deal with the personal and social consequences of such conflicts.

In this program, the emphasis began to shift, however, from the correction of unhealthy consequences to a stress upon the need to help adolescents in their healthy but inadequate strivings. As a direct result of this experience with adolescents who were more representative of the "normal" population than clients usually seen in a social agency, the workers began to choose methods conducive to "substitute" experiences in preference to those of a "corrective" nature. Despite the multitude of pressures described above, the workers were impressed with the fact that these girls had a strong desire to "act the right way." This was shown most clearly by their eagerness to find the most appropriate answers to their many questions. However, their resources for such an undertaking were insufficient, probably because of the lack of healthy emotional experiences in human relationships that are so vitally necessary for normal growth. When, through this program, an effort was made to make up for some of these deficiencies, it brought forth an impressively favorable response from the girls. They eagerly absorbed the "emotional vitamins" they must have missed so much in their earlier years.

The workers continually received comments from the girls regarding their attitudes toward the groups. Aldena Wray, after being in a group for six months, credited her new-found confidence directly to the group experience. Other girls were amazed that they were able to talk about their problems in a group and frequently expressed it. After their group experience, several girls mentioned the meaning it had for them. One girl, Edith Casper, had nothing to say while a member of the group, but when she was seen individually much later by a caseworker she gave an unusually good report of many things that had happened in the group and reported on various areas in which she had been helped by the group discussion. Frequently, the girls reported that because of the group experience they had dropped a previously conceived plan that might have had unfortunate consequences. Such reconsideration of unsound decisions is certainly indicative of the possibilities of preventive work.

Even some girls whom the workers thought they had failed to reach later returned to the agency asking for help with concrete problems, such as employment. Lydia Kinney, a schizoid-type girl, came back to the agency on her own a year after she had transferred to another school. She wondered whether groups were still in existence and said that she had found her group very helpful. For a number of girls, Youth Consultation Service remains a possible resource that they will be able to use if the occasion should arise in the future. If they do return, they will be better motivated and will have some understanding of how to cope with problems through discussion with a caseworker.

Needless to say, there were many girls who did not report such successful applications of their group experience. Yet their growing ability to handle in a more mature way the problems that were tossed back and forth during the group sessions supports the assumption that when conflicts do arise they will be better equipped to handle them. One of the benefits the girls gained from the group was learning to mull things over before acting, which, in turn, protected them from unfortunate consequences. This can be considered the core of the program's preventive help, which was supplemented by special attention geared to answer needs emanating from specific problems of an individual nature.

In the most general terms, the program tried to help adolescent girls who face crises "to add significantly to their repertoire of reality-based problem-solving techniques and thus improve their crisis-coping capacity for the future."[6] It is hoped that this intervention helped them emerge relatively undamaged from the critical period of adolescence.

NOTES TO CHAPTER V

1. Hunt, J. McVicker, and Leonard S. Kogan, *Measuring Results in Social Casework: A Manual for Judging Movement*, Family Service Association of America, New York; Hunt, J. McVicker, Margaret Blenkner, and Leonard S. Kogan, *Testing Results in Social Casework: A Field Test of the Movement Scale*, Family Service Association of America, New York, 1950; Ripple, Lillian, "Motivation, Capacity and Opportunity as Related to the Use of Casework Service: Theoretical Base and Plan of Study," *Social Service Review*, vol. 29, June, 1955, pp. 172–193; Shyne, Ann W., editor, *Use of Judgments as Data in Social Work Research*, National Association of Social Workers, New York, 1959.

2. Discussion of individual treatment efforts is based on the report written by Elizabeth P. Anderson, director of casework.

3. Discussion of group treatment is based on a report prepared by Dorothy Headley, senior group therapist, and an additional analysis of the group program made by Hanna Grunwald, group therapy consultant.

4. This summary was written by Dr. Grunwald.

5. Ackerman, Nathan W., *The Psychodynamics of Family Life*. Basic Books, New York, 1958, p. 209.

6. Caplan, Gerald, *Prevention of Mental Disorders in Children: Initial Explorations*. Basic Books, New York, 1961, p. 12.

VI. Staff Ratings of Clients in Individual and Group Treatment

THE TWO PRECEDING CHAPTERS presented the views of those who directed the individual and group treatment programs provided for the girls at Vocational High who were referred to Youth Consultation Service. The judgments expressed, although based on the records as well as on personal participation, represent generalized statements formulated in reference to categories of clients and types of treatment effort. The perspective of the total treatment program, rather than the observation of each treated case, is necessarily adopted. Documentation of observations and evaluations is illustrative rather than quantitative.

To obtain a case-by-case assessment of the sense of accomplishment as seen by the social workers who worked directly with the girls, a rating form was developed for the social worker primarily responsible for casework or group therapy to use for each client. This rating form was completed at the conclusion of the project and is therefore subject to errors of recall and afterthought by the raters, although they referred to case records for information on which to base their judgments. It is also subject to limitations of reliability since, except for explanations to the staff of the meanings of items to be rated, no special training in the use of the rating form was provided. Therefore, unknown variability between social workers in interpretation of what was rated limits conclusions to be drawn from the data provided. However, all the raters were professionally trained social workers who had many months of association with one another at the agency and were directed by the same supervisors and consultants. Hence some common bases for judgments may be assumed.

In this chapter the ratings by social workers of the clients served in individual casework will be compared with those in the group therapy program. Then, ratings for the entire population of experimental cases will be considered.

COMPARISON OF CLIENTS IN INDIVIDUAL AND GROUP PROGRAMS

Involvement in Treatment

The analyses in the preceding chapters strongly suggest that the group approach was considered more successful by the agency staff than the approach to clients through individual casework methods. Such a conclusion is also borne out by the almost exclusive use of group approaches after the first phase of the project. Individual casework was then used only as an adjunct to group therapy where the main thrust of the treatment effort was concentrated. Certain judgments were noted in Chapter IV which indicate that workers rated girls more involved in treatment in the group program than in individual casework, although girls seen individually or in groups were deemed equally in need of treatment. Evidence for this conclusion is presented in Tables 11 and 12. Social workers judged almost half (47 per cent) of the girls in individual casework

TABLE 11. SOCIAL WORKERS' RATINGS ON THE QUESTION: "How Involved Did This Client Become in a Treatment Relationship?"

Rating Category	Individual Treatment	Group Treatment	All Cases
	(Per cent)		
Very much or quite a bit	27	40	36
Some or a little	26	41	37
Hardly or not at all	47	19	27
Total	100	100	100
Number of cases[a]	47	127	174

[a] In this and subsequent tables based on social worker ratings, the numbers reported represent cases for which ratings were available. The total sample consisted of 189 cases of which 50 had been referred to Individual Treatment and 139 to Group Treatment. Subsequent to initial referral, 3 (6 per cent) of the individual cases attended some group sessions, and 45 (32 per cent) of the group cases had at least one casework interview.

treatment to have become "hardly" or "not at all" involved in a treatment relationship, whereas only one-fifth (19 per cent) of girls in group treatment were so rated. (See Table 11.) Ratings of involvement in treatment do not seem to reflect differences between individual and group cases in terms of need of treatment as judged by the social workers. Negligible differences between the two groups in this respect are shown in Table 12.

TABLE 12. SOCIAL WORKERS' RATINGS ON THE QUESTION: "Do You Feel This Client Was Really in Need of Treatment When She Was Referred?"

Rating Category	Individual Treatment	Group Treatment	All Cases
	(Per cent)		
Not at all or slightly	4	6	6
Somewhat or quite a bit	32	38	36
To considerable extent or very much	64	56	58
Total	100	100	100
Number of cases	47	132	179

TABLE 13. SOCIAL WORKERS' RATINGS ON THE QUESTION: "Which of the Following Best Describes Client's Initial Relationship with Caseworker or Group Therapist?"

Rating Category	Individual Treatment	Group Treatment	All Cases
	(Per cent)		
Warm acceptance	4	18	14
Acceptance but guarded	47	37	40
Tolerant but little more, or indifferent	11	28	23
Rather negative, or quite, or very negative, hostile	38	17	23
Total	100	100	100
Number of cases	47	130	177

Girls referred to group treatment were seen as less negative or hostile than those referred to individual treatment in their initial relationship with their social workers. (See Table 13.) Although about one-half of each type of case was judged to show at least some acceptance of the workers, more than one-third of the individual cases, compared to 17 per cent of the group cases, were seen as negative or hostile in their initial relationship.

Such ratings must be accepted in the limited sense that they are expressions of caseworkers' and group leaders' perceptions of their clients. It is possible, of course, that the social workers who were group leaders expected less of their clients in order to consider them involved in treatment. Or the group leaders may simply have been more enthusiastic about their form of treatment than the caseworkers were. We have no way of excluding such explanations of the data based on ratings of the social workers. However, all the group leaders were trained as caseworkers and several actually carried individual cases concurrently with their groups. Moreover, there were in all ten different group leaders over the course of the project and at least six caseworkers who carried project cases on an individual basis. It is plausible that the ratings represent differences, as the workers saw them, in their clients' responses to the two approaches. Nevertheless, these cautions should be kept in mind as the ratings are interpreted.

Assessment by Workers of Effects of Treatment

The social workers were asked to make a number of ratings to express their assessment of changes they perceived in their cases. One of these ratings asked for a general judgment of how much change was felt to have been produced in the course of contact. Table 14 shows that substantially more of the clients in individual treatment than of those in group treatment were felt to have changed "hardly any" or "not at all."

TABLE 14. SOCIAL WORKERS' RATINGS ON THE QUESTION: "How Much Change Do You Feel the Casework or Group Experience Produced in This Client?"

Rating Category	Individual Treatment	Group Treatment	All Cases
	(Per cent)		
Very great deal or quite a bit	10	19	17
Some or a little	30	49	44
Hardly any or not at all	60	32	39
Total	100	100	100
Number of cases	47	126	173

It must be remembered that the group approach was used over a period of three and one-half years, whereas an exclusively individual approach was used only for about a year and a half. It is therefore possible that longer experience with the group approach colors in part the ratings of the workers. Neither the data nor the impressions of the workers encourage this interpretation, however. Girls referred to groups seemed to the workers from the first to respond more to treatment efforts than girls referred to individual casework.

In an attempt to differentiate the meaning of change during contact with the agency, the social workers were asked to rate their clients on the components of the Hunt-Kogan Movement Scale.[1] The workers were given the following definitions of each of these components:

> *Adaptive Efficiency.* Changes in the effectiveness of functioning in any area, e.g., school habits, family relationships, peer relationships, etc.

> *Disabling Habits and Conditions.* Changes in the direction of eliminating inadequate mechanisms (and thus the converse of changes in adaptive efficiency). Changes in attitudes, behavior, etc., inimical to good social relations; improvement in habits which formerly limited her adjustment, etc.

> *Verbalized Attitudes and Understanding.* Changes indicated by what client says about her understanding of herself, other people or her situation, including understanding and accepting counsel on some specific point; development of insight, etc.

> *Environmental Circumstances.* Changes indicated in the manner in which people close to client behave toward her, in her physical environment, in her economic circumstances, or changes in these areas for other members of her family which affect her directly or indirectly.

The ratings obtained for girls in individual and in group treatment are given in Table 15.

In each component of the Movement Scale substantially more of the girls in group treatment than in individual treatment were judged to have shown positive movement, although it should be noted that the caseworkers did not (except with respect to Environmental Circumstances) rate any individual client as getting worse during treatment whereas a few clients in group treatment were so rated.

TABLE 15. SOCIAL WORKERS' RATINGS ON COMPONENTS OF HUNT-KOGAN MOVEMENT SCALE

Rating Category	Individual Treatment	Group Treatment	All Cases
	(Per cent)		
A. *Adaptive Efficiency*			
Great or considerable improvement	11	20	17
Distinct or visible but minor	37	49	45
No movement	52	25	33
Somewhat or distinctly worse	..	6	5
Total	100	100	100
Number of cases	47	124	171
B. *Disabling Habits and Conditions*			
Great or considerable improvement	6	11	10
Distinct or visible but minor	27	55	47
No movement	67	30	39
Somewhat or distinctly worse	..	4	4
Total	100	100	100
Number of cases	47	125	172
C. *Verbalized Attitudes and Understanding*			
Great or considerable improvement	6	19	15
Distinct or visible but minor	34	52	47
No movement	60	25	35
Somewhat or distinctly worse	..	4	3
Total	100	100	100
Number of cases	47	126	173
D. *Environmental Circumstances*			
Great or considerable improvement	6	9	9
Distinct or visible but minor	28	48	43
No movement	56	39	42
Somewhat or distinctly worse	10	4	6
Total	100	100	100
Number of cases	47	125	172

The workers were also asked to make prognoses for their clients, differentiated with respect to salient future roles anticipated for high school girls: relationships to men, marriage, and motherhood, on the one hand, and to work careers, on the other hand. The results of these ratings are given in Table 16.

TABLE 16. SOCIAL WORKERS' RATINGS ON CLIENT'S FUTURE ADJUSTMENTS

Rating Category	Individual Treatment	Group Treatment	All Cases
	(Per cent)		
A. *"What sort of relationship with men would you say this client is likely to have—when 20–22 years old?"*			
Average, normal, or better relationship	18	38	33
Fairly or very difficult relationship	82	62	67
Total	100	100	100
Number of cases	44	126	170
B. *"Do you think client is likely to get married by time she is, say, 25 years old?"*			
Very likely or quite likely	48	65	61
About 50–50 chance	38	29	32
Quite or very unlikely	14	6	7
Total	100	100	100
Number of cases	44	125	169
C. *"How would you estimate client's behavior as a mother?"*			
Very good or pretty good mother	5	19	15
About average mother	38	48	46
Pretty poor or very poor mother	57	33	39
Total	100	100	100
Number of cases	42	125	167
D. *"How would you estimate this client's future work career?"*			
Very or quite successful	16	23	22
About average	45	53	50
Rather or very unsuccessful	39	24	28
Total	100	100	100
Number of cases	44	125	169

The three sets of ratings having to do with relationships to men, marriage, and motherhood show that girls in individual treatment were less favorably rated than those in group treatment. (Sections A, B, and C of Table 16.) There is less difference between these two groups of cases with respect to estimates of future work careers but the difference still favors the group clients. (See Section D of Table 16.)

Finally, workers were asked to make a global prognosis of their clients' chances of achieving a good adjustment in about five years. As Table 17 shows, less than one-third of the group cases compared to more than half of the individual cases were given a poor chance of achieving a good adjustment.

TABLE 17. SOCIAL WORKERS' RATINGS ON THE QUESTION: "WHAT DO YOU FEEL THE CHANCES ARE THAT THIS CLIENT WILL ACHIEVE A GOOD ADJUSTMENT, SAY, ABOUT FIVE YEARS FROM NOW?"

Rating Category	Individual Treatment	Group Treatment	All Cases
	(Per cent)		
Very good or quite good	5	8	7
Pretty good	16	18	18
About 50–50	24	45	39
Pretty poor	23	21	22
Quite poor or very poor	32	8	14
Total	100	100	100
Number of cases	44	126	170

Individual vs. Group Treatment

In summary, the data based on ratings of social workers leave little doubt that the group approach adopted by the staff after its experience with the usual individual casework approach was seen as more appropriate and more successful with the kind of clients served in this project. There is no evidence that different kinds of problems or girls of different characteristics were presented for the two approaches. It must be concluded that the shift from individual to group methods was, at least in the views of the staff, desirable. The rationale for using group methods has been presented in previous chapters and it gains support from the judgments of the social workers who carried the responsibility for treatment in the project.

STAFF ASSESSMENTS OF TOTAL EXPERIMENTAL SAMPLE

When the ratings of the social workers for the total sample of girls seen at the agency in the treatment effort of the project are examined, several observations are noteworthy. In the experimental design of the research, it will be a comparison of the total sample of treated cases with the control cases that interests us.

We note, first, that slightly more than one-fourth (27 per cent; see Table 11) of all the girls were considered by their workers to have become minimally involved in treatment. We note further that approximately one-fifth (see Tables 14 and 15) of all the girls were judged to have changed or moved positively during treatment. In addition, an even greater proportion were given no more than an equal chance of satisfactory future adjustments in their own family and work roles. (See Table 16.) It should be noted that these were clients whose median number of treatment contacts was 17 casework interviews or group therapy sessions attended. This is considerably more than the short-term contact characteristic of so many cases that come to social agencies.

It is evident that the social workers did not allow themselves to express indiscriminate enthusiasm in the appraisal of their own success. Rather, they seem highly sensitive to the shortcomings of their efforts. Or, if their ratings reflect observations of change in their clients that might have occurred without benefit of treatment at all, they have shown a distinct capacity to differentiate among clients who change positively and those who do not.

Critics of the subjective evaluations of success made by those in the helping—or therapeutic—professions often assert that enthusiasm for conscientious effort causes exaggerated beliefs in the efficacy of treatment. To be sure, the apparently restrained estimate of social workers in this project that one-third of their clients were unchanged by their efforts may itself be an unrealistic exaggeration. This can be determined only by comparing the clients with nonclients who were initially similar to them. But it can hardly be asserted that these social workers lack awareness of their failures as well as their successes.

How can one account, therefore, for the strong sense of success of the efforts of the treatment program conveyed in Chapters IV and V when the director of casework services and the senior group therapist and group therapy consultant report their observations? It is unlikely that these experienced professional persons deceive themselves to a greater extent than the casework staff itself. In fact, for approximately 30 cases rated on the same rating form both by supervisors and by individual social workers, agreement on the ratings was quite high. It is more plausible to interpret differences in appraisal as a result of differences in the context of evaluation.

When *each case* is evaluated, its success or lack of success is judged in terms of what has happened to the individual client in all the complexity of her realistic situation. When the *treatment program* is evaluated, the achievement of the purpose of the program becomes the frame of reference and the procedures, techniques, responses of clients, and theoretical plausibility of the program are considered. The sense that the therapeutic intent could be carried out becomes the basis for judging success rather than the outcomes for individual clients. The analogy is to the quip: "The operation was a success but the patient died." This may indeed be true when the criterion is therapeutic performance rather than therapeutic outcome.

It would not be argued that such a position can be maintained indefinitely if therapeutic performance and therapeutic outcome do not finally coincide. The implication is, however, that the therapeutic effort *can* succeed in achieving the therapeutic outcome and the evaluation becomes a statement of conviction, a hypothesis. Thus the professional staff of Youth Consultation Service were convinced that their approach to preventive intervention with potential problem high school girls was a beneficial one even though it might not succeed with many clients. Such a conviction encourages further efforts, more deliberate attempts to specify those clients for whom the treatment is appropriate, and more consideration of refinements in the approach that might improve its therapeutic focus.

The value of a rigorous assessment of effectiveness in terms of criteria of outcome is undeniable and the results of such an evaluation are not to be taken lightly. However, it would seem that progress in developing effective treatment programs and techniques would require reconciliation between these two contexts of evaluation. A theory of practice is not destroyed by its outcome; it is only tested. Discrepancies between a theory of intervention or prevention and its empirical effects should be a challenge both to revise the theory and to perfect the measurement of effects.

It is with such a perspective that we turn in succeeding chapters to the evidence of effectiveness of social work services for interrupting deviant careers of the high school girls served in this project.

NOTE TO CHAPTER VI

1. Hunt, J. McVicker, and Leonard S. Kogan, *Measuring Results in Social Casework: A Manual for Judging Movement.* Family Source Association, New York, 1950.

VII. Effects of Social Work Service: Objective Criteria

IN THE DIRECTLY PRECEDING CHAPTERS we have described the girls who participated in the individual and group treatment programs as seen through the eyes of the social workers who served them and in terms of the treatment program as it developed and was applied. In this chapter and the one following we will compare these experimental cases with their counterpart control cases.

It has been demonstrated in Chapter III that experimental and control cases were, as intended, essentially alike at the beginning of the experimental project. This was to be expected from the random procedure of assigning potential problem cases to experimental and control groups. It was also shown that the potential problem group itself (including both experimental and control cases) differed from the remaining girls in their school classes (residual cases) in the "negative" ways one would expect from the deliberate selection of potential problem girls to constitute the pool from which experimental and control cases were chosen. For example, a significantly smaller proportion of potential problem than of residual cases remained throughout the three high school years. We may be reasonably confident therefore, that the therapeutic program for experimental cases among the potential problem group was offered to girls who were less promising, girls who were, for the most part, "in need of treatment," as the social workers saw them. We have shown (in Chapters II and IV) that almost all of the girls (95 per cent) received some treatment services, and that half of these had 17 or more treatment contacts with social workers. Indeed, only 16 per cent of the 189 girls in the experimental group had fewer than five such contacts, whereas 44 per cent of them had more than 20 treatment contacts. Therefore, the experimental cases as a group were clearly well-exposed to the therapeutic program. In short, the experimental cases consisted of high school girls more likely to get into trouble, recognized by social workers as needing treatment, and actually receiving treatment.

On the other hand, however, we have seen (in Chapters IV and V) that the overall success of the therapeutic effort—as assessed by those responsible for its direction—was cautiously asserted, recognizing that it was necessary to learn as the program proceeded and to adapt the program as experience dictated. Furthermore, the social workers who conducted the program reached an even more cautious conclusion when they assessed change in their clients on a case-by-case basis. They judged that almost three-fifths (59 per cent) of the girls had changed "a little" or less, and more than one-third (39 per cent) had changed "hardly any" or "not at all." We should not, therefore, anticipate dramatic results when we compare experimental cases and control cases on the spectrum of criteria that have been used to detect the effects of the program.

Recognizing the untried nature of the experiment in preventive services, recognizing as well the variety and unspecified nature of the problems presented by a random sample of high school girls for whom a wide range of difficulties was foreseen, we have (as pointed out in Chapter II) sought to observe a great variety of effects. The range includes objective measures related to school success, personality test measures, judgmental ratings and self-assessments on the part of the girls involved as well as their social workers. In this chapter we shall examine the effects of the treatment program on the more objective criteria.

Measures of effect are provided by the periodic testing procedures at the end of each school year and by the collection of terminal data about each potential problem case three years after entrance into high school or as of a cut-off date in the summer of 1960. Four cohorts were subject to the experimental program, beginning with the cohort entering in September, 1955.

Therefore, the normal three-year period of the high school had elapsed for the first three of the cohorts by the terminal date in 1960. For the fourth cohort, only two years had elapsed. In the analysis of effects, where criteria are appropriately applied only to cases with the longer time span (for example, graduation from high school), the first three cohorts taken together will be examined. This group of cases had the longest exposure to the therapeutic program. Where lapse of time is less relevant (school grades or behavior ratings), the fourth cohort will be included and the total potential problem sample examined. For all cohorts the random selection procedure resulted in equivalent duration of time for experimental and control cases when measures of effect were taken.

The samples used in the analysis may be summarized as follows:

Elapsed time from school entrance to terminal date:	Experimental cases	Control cases	Total cases
Cohorts with three years elapsed time	129	132	261
Cohort with two years elapsed time	60	60	120
All cohorts	189	192	381

COMPLETION OF SCHOOL

The most obvious question to ask about a program intended to interrupt careers leading to potential problems for high school girls is whether it succeeded in increasing the likelihood of their staying in school. Although neither a negative nor a positive answer to this question necessarily satisfies all pertinent questions about effects of the therapeutic program, few will deny its relevance. We shall compare experimental and control cases on a number of related, but conceptually distinguishable, measures of staying in school.

School Status at the End of the Project

Identical proportions of all experimental and control cases had graduated from high school by the termination of the project: 29 per cent of each. Equal proportions had left school without graduation or were in school, either in their normal grades or below normal grade. Success in the sense of graduation or achieving normally expected grade was the school status of 53 per cent of both experimental and control cases and lack of success in the sense of dropping out of school or being behind normal grade in school was the school status of 47 per cent. Table 18 shows these findings.

TABLE 18. FINAL SCHOOL STATUS OF ALL EXPERIMENTAL AND CONTROL CASES

Final School Status	Experimental Cases	Control Cases
	(Per cent)	
Graduated from high school	29	29
Not graduated, but in normal grade	24	24
In school, but behind normal grade	8	7
Out of school, but not graduated	39	40
Total	100	100
Number of cases	189	191[a]

[a] Excludes one case for whom information was not available.

When only those girls are considered who could be observed over three full school years, 48 per cent of both the experimental and the control cases had graduated or were in normal grade. By way of contrast, 65 per cent of the residual cases who could have graduated actually did finish high school. This comparison is presented in Table 19.

TABLE 19. FINAL SCHOOL STATUS OF EXPERIMENTAL, CONTROL, AND RESIDUAL CASES WITH THREE YEARS ELAPSED TIME IN PROJECT

Final School Status	Experimental Cases	Control Cases	Residual Cases
	(Per cent)		
Graduated from high school	43	42	65
In school, but in normal grade[a]	5	6	..
In school, but behind normal grade	5	4	7
Out of school, but not graduated	47	48	28
Total	100	100	100
Number of cases	129	132	536[b]

[a] These represent cases that entered in the ninth grade and hence would be in the twelfth (or senior) grade after three years.

[b] Excludes 10 cases for whom information was not available.

Clearly the treatment program had no discernible impact with respect to the criterion of graduation from high school.

Highest School Grade Completed

Graduation is the formal symbol of completion of high school. Nevertheless, girls who complete their senior year of high school, whether they formally graduate or not, represent a higher level of success when compared to those who do not remain in school as long. Each successive grade completed is that much more education. As Table 20 shows, proportionately more of the experimental cases than of the control cases completed higher

TABLE 20. HIGHEST GRADE IN HIGH SCHOOL COMPLETED BY EXPERIMENTAL, CONTROL, AND RESIDUAL CASES WITH THREE YEARS ELAPSED TIME IN PROJECT

High School Grade Completed	Experimental Cases	Control Cases	Residual Cases
	(Per cent)		
Senior	49	42	70
Junior	24	22	13
Sophomore	24	29	10
Freshman	3	3	4
Did not complete freshman grade	..	4	3
Total	100	100	100
Number of cases	128[a]	132	539[b]

[a] Excludes one case for whom information was not available.

[b] Excludes seven cases for whom information was not available.

grades of school, although the differences between the two groups are not statistically significant. Among experimental cases, 49 per cent compared to 42 per cent among control cases completed the senior year whether they graduated or not. Completing at least the junior year were 73 per cent of the experimental cases and 64 per cent of the control cases. None of the experimental cases compared to 4 per cent of the control cases failed to complete at least the freshman year of high school. This is evidence that the treatment program had a slight effect on retention of the experimental cases in school and this suggestion is further strengthened by the evidence of Tables 21 and 22.

Table 21 shows the number of years attended by those girls who might have attended any high school at least four years by the terminal date of the project. We see that 56 per cent of the experimental cases and 49 per cent of the control cases attended four or more years of high school, and 83 per cent compared to 75 per cent attended at least three years. The distribution for residual cases, presented for comparison, shows that significantly more of them than either experimental or control cases attended high school four or more years.

TABLE 21. NUMBER OF YEARS ATTENDED ANY HIGH SCHOOL BY EXPERIMENTAL, CONTROL, AND RESIDUAL CASES WITH THREE YEARS ELAPSED TIME IN PROJECT

Years Attended Any High School	Experimental Cases	Control Cases	Residual Cases
	(Per cent)		
Four years or more	56	49	73
Three years	27	27	11
Two years	15	18	15
One year or less	2	6	1
Total	100	100	100
Number of cases	128[a]	132	531[b]

[a] Excludes one case for whom information was not available.

[b] Excludes 15 cases for whom information was not available.

A smaller percentage of experimental cases (52 per cent) than of control cases (56 per cent) were suspended or discharged from school during the period of the project but, again, the difference is not statistically significant. As Table 22 shows, when the reasons for suspension and discharge are classified into nonpunitive and punitive, slightly more of the control than the experimental cases were removed from school for nonpunitive reasons, such as poor health, employment, transfer, or other circumstances not reflecting misbehavior or poor academic performance. This difference hints at the possibility that the services given to girls by the social agency helped those with circumstantial problems somewhat more than it helped those with behavior problems. This is only the barest of speculations, of course, in view of the minimal difference observed but it may be worth noting when considering benefits of service programs to high school girls with potential problems.

TABLE 22. SUSPENSION OR DISCHARGE FROM HIGH SCHOOL OF EXPERIMENTAL, CONTROL, AND RESIDUAL CASES WITH THREE YEARS ELAPSED TIME IN PROJECT

Ever Suspended or Discharged?	Experimental Cases	Control Cases	Residual Cases
	(Per cent)		
No	48	44	65
Yes, for nonpunitive reasons	18	20	16
Yes, for punitive reasons	34	36	19
Total	100	100	100
Number of cases	128[a]	132	536[b]

[a] Excludes one case for whom information was not available.
[b] Excludes 10 cases for whom information was not available.

Taken together, the findings with respect to completion of school can be said to support only an extremely cautious suggestion that the treatment program had any effect. At most, it can be said that extremely small differences in staying in school favor the experimental cases. Since the differences are not statistically significant, only their consistency permits even this cautious conclusion.

ACADEMIC PERFORMANCE

Beginning with grades earned in their vocational and academic subjects, a number of measures of academic performance of experimental and control cases can be used. It would surely be a desired effect—indirect, perhaps—of the provision of a therapeutic program to potential problem high school girls if they were found to perform better in their school subjects. Other indicators reflecting success both in subject matter courses and in other aspects of the school program, such as honors and awards, service ratings, and normal assignment to the work-study cooperative program, will also be examined.

Grades Earned in Vocational and Academic Subjects

The number of failures can be taken as one indication of academic performance. Table 23 presents data that compare experimental and control cases during their first year and each of the two succeeding years. If the treatment program had any effect, it should be most evident after it had been in operation some time, either because of cumulative influences or because selectively students who perform better stay in school. We know that similar proportions of experimental and control cases drop out. Therefore, unless some factor is operating to differentiate them, similar proportions ought to show failures.

Table 23 shows the trend of failures for both vocational and academic subjects, and they are essentially similar. Decreasing proportions of both experimental and control cases are found to have failures between their first and third years, but the

TABLE 23. NUMBER OF FAILURES IN VOCATIONAL AND ACADEMIC SUBJECTS FOR ALL EXPERIMENTAL AND CONTROL CASES BY YEAR IN HIGH SCHOOL

Number of Failures	Year of Cohort Entry		First Year After Cohort Entry		Second Year After Cohort Entry	
	Experimental	Control	Experimental	Control	Experimental	Control
	(Per cent)		(Per cent)		(Per cent)	
A. *Vocational Subjects*						
None	60	69	68	73	84	80
One or two	23	22	19	18	16	9
Three or more	17	9	13	9	..	11
Total	100	100	100	100	100	100
Number, grades available	189	192	151	157	77	74
Number, grades not available[a]	..	..	38	35	112	118
B. *Academic Subjects*						
None	61	67	67	65	76	76
One or two	22	24	21	24	18	13
Three or more	17	9	12	11	6	11
Total	100	100	100	100	100	100
Number, grades available	189	192	151	160	78	76
Number, grades not available[a]	..	..	38	32	111	116

[a] Includes cases not in school and cases for whom information was not available.

decrease is greater for experimental cases. Thus for vocational subjects 40 per cent of the experimental cases had one or more failures their first year but only 16 per cent their third year, and this difference is statistically significant. On the other hand, for control cases there were 31 per cent with one or more failures the first year and 20 per cent the third year, a substantial decrease to be sure but the difference does not reach statistical significance. The corresponding trend for academic subjects is to be noted: a statistically significant decrease from 39 per per cent to 24 per cent for experimental cases compared to a smaller decrease, not statistically significant, from 31 per cent to 20 per cent for control cases. It is further to be noted that the record of experimental cases is not as good as that of control cases in the initial year (although the difference is not statistically significant), whereas it is better or equal to that of the control cases in the third year.

The finding is not so clear when academic performance is measured by the number of A and B grades recorded, as in Table 24. Such high grades are about equally found for experimental and control cases at each year with slight tendencies for proportionately fewer A's and B's in the later years, except for a minor counter trend among experimental cases in vocational subjects. None of the differences is statistically significant.

If one is to interpret these findings as evidence of an effect of the treatment program, it must be seen as an effect mediated through the selection process. Rather than conclude that academic performance as reflected in grades is directly improved by the program available to experimental cases, it is more exact to say that girls who would earn better grades (especially fail fewer subjects) were helped to remain in school. Such a positive selective effect is nevertheless a constructive, if modest, achievement to be attributed to the treatment program.

Advancement with Class and Assignment to Cooperative Work-Study Program

Associated with performance in subjects but dependent as well on additional evaluations by the teachers, the promotion or de-

TABLE 24. NUMBER OF A AND B GRADES IN VOCATIONAL AND
ACADEMIC SUBJECTS FOR ALL EXPERIMENTAL AND
CONTROL CASES BY YEAR IN HIGH SCHOOL

A and B Grades	Year of Cohort Entry		First Year After Cohort Entry		Second Year After Cohort Entry	
	Experi-mental	Con-trol	Experi-mental	Con-trol	Experi-mental	Con-trol
	(Per cent)		(Per cent)		(Per cent)	
A. *Vocational Subjects*						
None	26	24	25	24	20	28
One to three	46	42	47	48	56	40
Four or more	28	34	28	28	24	32
Total	100	100	100	100	100	100
Number, grades available	189	192	152	159	79	75
Number, grades not available[a]	..	..	37	33	110	117
B. *Academic Subjects*						
None	14	11	17	13	19	21
One to three	52	49	44	40	44	33
Four or more	34	40	39	47	37	46
Total	100	100	100	100	100	100
Number, grades available	189	192	151	159	78	76
Number, grades not available[a]	..	..	38	33	111	116

[a] Includes cases not in school and cases for whom information was not available.

tention of a student at the end of each school year and the decision to assign at the normal time to the cooperative work-
study program are further indications of general academic
performance.

A slightly greater proportion of experimental cases than of
control cases advanced normally with their classes. Thus 74
per cent of all the experimental compared to 70 per cent of the
control cases remained in their normal class, whereas 24 per
cent of the former and 28 per cent of the latter were held back
or reclassified to lower standing vocational programs and the
same proportion of both groups (2 per cent) were advanced
above the normal levels for their classes. None of these differences is statistically significant and can only be taken as a possible suggestion of better performance by experimental cases.

At this high school, students are placed in work-study jobs in the industry for which they are trained when their work is adequate and they are deemed responsible by teachers of vocational subjects and by the guidance counselors. This is a prized assignment since it provides on-the-job experience, apprentice wages, and potential access to the job market after graduation. Assignments are normally made for the second semester of the junior year and continued throughout the last year of high school. Occasionally, students will be assigned for the first time at the beginning of their senior year if they have shown improvement deemed to warrant it, and occasionally they will be dropped from the work-study program if they do not perform adequately in it.

No differences of significance are found between experimental and control cases in the pattern of assignment. For both groups, 48 per cent were never selected. Slightly more of the control than the experimental cases (48 per cent and 45 per cent, respectively) were assigned in their junior year but a few more of the latter were assigned later, so that altogether half of each group (51 per cent of the experimental and 49 per cent of the control cases) participated in the "co-op" training program.

Honors and Awards, and Service Ratings

Recognition of outstanding performance and of "school citizenship" are given by the school in the form of honors and awards and of service ratings which are recorded in the student's record. The latter are used somewhat liberally as assignments to service jobs such as hall and door duty, monitoring, and other types of nonacademic responsibility. There appears to be a mixed attitude on the part of the school as to whether such service duties are assigned as rewards for evidence of responsibility or encouragements to be more responsible but, in any event, they constitute a type of special recognition generally considered favorable.

Slightly greater percentages of control cases than experimental cases had entries in their records of awards and honors, but in both groups the numbers were few. Only 14 per cent of the former and 9 per cent of the latter were so recognized. Similarly, more of the control cases (65 per cent) than the experimental cases (59 per cent) had at least one service rating, but this difference also is not statistically significant.

Such minor differences hardly bear interpretation, but it is worth noting that service ratings—and to a lesser extent honors and awards and assignment to the "co-op" work-study program —may reflect attitudes of school staff toward girls known to be involved in the treatment program. Based on our observations, we concluded that only a small part of the staff knew which individual girls were involved, although many teachers knew one or two who were and almost all of the staff knew of the existence of the experimental project. Attitudes that were expressed were by no means uniform as to whether involvement in the project was to be considered a positive or negative mark for the students selected. Our impression is that the guidance and counseling staff and most of the administrative staff might be favorably biased toward such girls, whereas indifference or negative orientations might characterize the teaching faculty. In any event, the slightly lower recognition of experimental cases than of control cases encourages the conclusion that other findings which might favor the former are not likely to be the result of special favorable consideration.

In recapitulation of the findings with respect to the several measures of academic performance, we note the positive selective effect of the treatment program in reducing failing grades in academic subjects.

SCHOOL-RELATED BEHAVIOR

A number of aspects of behavior are related to school but not so directly to academic performance as the aspects previously considered. In this section we examine such measures of effect as attendance and truancy, conduct marks and officially noted teacher ratings for "character traits," as well as special ratings obtained from those responsible for guidance and discipline.

Attendance

No consistent or significant differences were found between the attendance records of experimental and control cases. Calculation of the unexcused absence rate shows that slightly more than one-third of both groups were absent on the average one day a month or less in their initial year; nearly half the cases in school three years later had this low rate of absences. Experimental cases show a slightly better rate for the latter year (49 per cent compared to 43 per cent with less than ten days, not a statistically significant difference). The decrease in unexcused absences in excess of this rate was more substantial for experimental cases than for control cases, falling from 40 per cent in the first year to 23 per cent in the third year, a statistically significant difference for those with 18 or more days of unexcused absences. As may be noted in Table 25, which presents data on absences, this decrease occurs primarily between the second and third years when a lesser decrease for control cases is also apparent.

As pointed out in the discussion of academic performance, differences through time for such measures as attendance may be taken as a positive selective effect of the treatment program

TABLE 25. UNEXCUSED ABSENCE RATE FOR ALL EXPERIMENTAL AND CONTROL CASES BY YEAR IN HIGH SCHOOL

Absence Rate per School Year	Year of Cohort Entry		First Year After Cohort Entry		Second Year After Cohort Entry	
	Experimental	Control	Experimental	Control	Experimental	Control
	(Per cent)		(Per cent)		(Per cent)	
Less than 10 days	37	37	36	36	49	43
Eleven to seventeen days	23	22	23	22	28	23
Eighteen or more days	40	41	41	42	23	34
Total	100	100	100	100	100	100
Number, absence rate available	189	192	154	158	78	79
Number, absence rate not available[a]	..	..	35	34	111	113

[a] Includes cases not in school and cases for whom information was not available.

provided for experimental cases, but since these cases do not differ significantly from the control cases on these measures one must make no claim for direct effects.

Truancy

There were 107 problem-potential cases who were "truant" during the project; 62, or 58 per cent of these cases, were control cases and 45, or 42 per cent, were experimental cases. The difference between experimental and control cases, as presented in Table 26 shows the former to have the better record and is substantial enough to take note of, although it does not quite reach the criterion of statistical significance adopted in this analysis. Instances of truancy occur for ex-

TABLE 26. TRUANCY FROM SCHOOL OF ALL EXPERI-MENTAL AND CONTROL CASES

Reported Truancy	Experimental Cases	Control Cases
	(Per cent)	
No truancy reported	76	68
Truancy ever reported	24	32
Total	100	100
Number of cases	189	192

perimental cases disproportionately in the year of cohort entry when 42 per cent of them are reported. Truancies in later years are disproportionately greater for control cases, being 74 per cent compared to 58 per cent for experimental cases, but with such small numbers of truancies reported this noticeable difference is not quite statistically significant.

We are probably justified in a cautious conclusion that experimental cases were less truant than control cases as an effect of the social work program. This is an effect that might be expected in view of the weekly schedule of interviews or group sessions, attendance at which was of immediate and constant concern to the social workers. Since these scheduled contacts with the social workers took place during the school day, encouragement to meet the appointment with the caseworker or group leader was tantamount to encouragement to come to school. It is perhaps surprising that more favorable truancy and school attendance records were not found for the experimental cases. Nevertheless, the effect that does appear must be accepted as a positive achievement of the treatment program.

Conduct Marks

Each student's official school record includes for each term a teacher's rating on "conduct," that is, on appropriate behavior or misbehavior that may or may not subject the student to some form of discipline. We might expect such behavior to be affected favorably as a result of the therapeutic attention to which the experimental cases were subjected. Table 27 compares experimental and control cases on the basis of the lowest conduct mark entered for each of the years observed.

TABLE 27. LOWEST SCHOOL CONDUCT MARKS FOR ALL EXPERI-MENTAL AND CONTROL CASES BY YEAR IN HIGH SCHOOL

Conduct Marks	Year of Cohort Entry		First Year After Cohort Entry		Second Year After Cohort Entry	
	Experi-mental	Con-trol	Experi-mental	Con-trol	Experi-mental	Con-trol
	(Per cent)		(Per cent)		(Per cent)	
Unsatisfactory (F, D, or U)	29	28	18	22	16	10
Satisfactory (C, B, or S)	67	68	75	68	77	86
Outstanding (A or O)	4	4	7	10	7	4
Total	100	100	100	100	100	100
Number, conduct marks available	188	191	148	153	77	73
Number, conduct marks not available	1[a]	1[a]	41[b]	39[b]	112[b]	119[b]

[a] Case in school but conduct marks not available.

[b] Includes cases not in school and cases for whom information was not available.

In each year, the difference between experimental and control cases was minimal and there were no consistent trends that change the relationship between the distributions of conduct marks for the two groups of cases. Significant decreases occurred between the first and third years in the proportions of both experimental and control cases that received unsatisfactory marks for conduct. The selective process apparently operated with equal effect whether the girls did or did not participate in the therapeutic program. It is to be noted, however, that the major decrease for experimental cases with unsatisfactory conduct marks occurred between the initial and the second years, whereas for the control cases the decrease between each year was more even.

Using conduct marks as a criterion, no interpretable effect from the treatment program was found for the experimental cases.

Teacher Ratings for Character Traits and Work Traits

For each term the student's homeroom teacher, on the basis of reports from all the student's teachers, rated the student on a number of "character traits" and "work traits" and these ratings became part of the official record of the student. Ratings were on a scale from 1 (very poor) to 5 (excellent). The "character traits" rated were: interest, industry, initiative, courtesy, cooperation, self-control, appearance, dependability, and health habits. The "work traits" were: care of tools and equipment, "follows instructions," neatness, speed, attitude, use of English, safety, and workmanship. The records were not entirely consistent in the extent to which all traits were rated but there were usually four or five of each list that were rated. So far as we were able to determine from discussing the ratings with school staff, the teachers varied not only in the meanings and standards they applied but also in the extent to which students were known well enough for judgments to be made. This accounts in part for incomplete ratings for some students and full ratings for others. It is likely that behavior that was noticeably deviant— either negatively or positively—would call the student sufficiently to the teacher's attention so that traits would be rated for her.

With these reservations, the utility of such ratings is obviously limited. Nevertheless, one may assume that students who made up the experimental and control cases had equal opportunities to be rated in the same manner and hence any differences that they exhibited had equal chances of being reflected in the ratings. We have averaged the ratings for each year and the comparison of experimental and control cases may be examined in Table 28.

TABLE 28. TEACHER RATINGS FROM SCHOOL RECORDS ON "CHARACTER TRAITS" AND "WORK TRAITS" FOR ALL EXPERIMENTAL AND CONTROL CASES BY YEAR IN HIGH SCHOOL

Average of Ratings per Year	Year of Cohort Entry		First Year After Cohort Entry		Second Year After Cohort Entry	
	Experimental	Control	Experimental	Control	Experimental	Control
	(Per cent)		(Per cent)		(Per cent)	
1.0 to 1.9 (Very poor)	37	31	26	22	18	17
2.0 to 2.9 (Poor)	28	28	21	23	21	14
3.0 to 3.9 (Fair)	27	35	31	32	50	49
4.0 to 4.9 (Good)	7	4	16	19	10	12
5.0 (Excellent)	1	2	6	4	1	8
Total	100	100	100	100	100	100
Number, ratings available	175	181	140	145	71	65
Number, ratings not available	14[a]	11[a]	49[b]	47[b]	118[b]	127[b]

[a] Cases in school but teacher ratings not available.

[b] Includes cases not in school and cases for whom information was not available.

Essentially, the findings for teacher ratings parallel those for conduct marks: no significant differences appear between experimental and control cases, but the latter tend to have slightly higher ratings. Average ratings for both experimental and control cases shift significantly upward between the first and third years, but the shift is approximately the same for both groups of cases. There is no evidence, therefore, of an effect of the treatment program so far as this measure is concerned.

General Behavior Ratings by Guidance and Counseling Staff

Within the last few weeks of each school year, a list of all the girls in the school cohorts involved in the research was presented to each of the teachers who served as guidance and counseling staff, as well as to the head of this department, and to the administrative officer responsible for discipline. They were asked to indicate whether the particular girl was "outstanding" as they knew her general behavior in the school, whether she constituted a "moderate problem" or a "serious problem," or whether there was no particular reason for distinguishing the girl from the others. Such general ratings are admittedly crude, probably unreliable (except that we noted considerable agreement among the raters at the extremes), and subject to possible bias because these raters, of all school personnel, were most likely to know which girls on the lists had been referred to the social agency. They did not know which girls constituted the sample of control cases. How much this differential knowledge would bias the ratings— or whether it would at all—was unknown. We did not systematically inquire into the attitudes toward the experimental program held by these school staff members; we did not wish to magnify the sense of differential treatment of the experimental cases who were represented merely as girls selected at random from a large group in the school that might be thought to benefit from help by social workers and referred to the agency when they could be accommodated there. Knowledge of the identity of experimental cases might lead these school staff members to think of them as somewhat serious problems at first but decreasingly so over the years because of a general sense that the "special project" was beneficial.

Whatever the factors that affected the ratings by the guidance and counseling staff, there were relatively small differences found between experimental and control cases, as may be seen in Table 29.

Although not quite statistically significant, most noticeable is the difference in the year of cohort entry between the proportions of experimental and control cases designated "indifferent," that is, not sufficiently deviant in either positive or negative ways to call forth any special reaction from the raters. Fewer of the experimental cases than the control cases (44 per cent and 53 per cent, respectively) are in this category. Proportionately more of the experimental cases were seen as representing moderate or

TABLE 29. RATINGS BY GUIDANCE AND COUNSELING STAFF OF ALL
EXPERIMENTAL AND CONTROL CASES BY YEAR IN HIGH
SCHOOL

Rating	Year of Cohort Entry		First Year After Cohort Entry		Second Year After Cohort Entry	
	Experi-mental	Con-trol	Experi-mental	Con-trol	Experi-mental	Con-trol
	(Per cent)		(Per cent)		(Per cent)	
Outstanding	4	4	5	6	4	8
Indifferent	44	53	39	44	63	67
Moderate problem	21	16	21	18	11	11
Serious problem	31	27	35	32	22	14
Total	100	100	100	100	100	100
Number, ratings available	189	192	171	181	93	92
Number, ratings not available[a]	..	..	18	11	96	100

[a] Includes cases not in school and cases for whom no information was available.

serious problems. The difference is, moreover, approximately maintained for the two groups of cases in the subsequent years. Although there is, on the whole, a decreasing trend among the cases identified as problems through the years, it is not marked enough to achieve statistical significance for either experimental or control cases.

One may suppose that the biases in these ratings operated consistently against the experimental cases but not sufficiently to mark them as very different from the control cases. In any event, the findings on this measure cannot support a conclusion that either the treatment program or selective dropout of school had an appreciable effect.

We may summarize the findings on all the measures that have been grouped together as school-related behavior by noting that none of them supplies conclusive evidence of an effect by the therapeutic program. However, the relatively better showing of experimental cases with respect to truancy suggests that the surveillance that accompanies the rendering of treatment services tends to have some effect, and this possibility is by no means a trivial achievement if further research were to show that it does indeed occur. Other deviant forms of behavior have often been observed to be concomitants of truancy. An additional conclusion is suggested by the findings with respect to trends on the measures here examined through the three years observed: that there is some tendency for a favorable differential to develop for experimental cases through the selective process. It would appear that if girls remain in school, those with the benefit of the treatment program exhibit somewhat less negative school-related behavior. From the point of view of the school a less deviant population remains and, possibly, educational objectives might more readily be achieved for them. Likewise, a student body resulting from such favorable selective processes might constitute a more favorable context for students who are not deviant in the ways exhibited by the problem-potential segment of the school population.

OUT-OF-SCHOOL BEHAVIOR

In the design of the research, no interviews out of the school setting with potential problem cases were planned, since we did not wish to vitiate the experiment by giving special attention to the control cases. School behavior and performance were considered appropriate criteria within the scope of the research. Some information could be obtained, however, that bears on out-of-school behavior.

Entries on Health Record

Matters of health arising from acute circumstances, as well as the results of periodic health examinations by the school nurse and physicians serving the school, are recorded for each student on a health record. Such information covers a broad range of observations, including overweight and underweight, allergies, psychosomatic complaints, and emotional or psychological difficulties. It was considered possible that a treatment program addressed in major part to more positive mental health attitudes and self-understanding might be reflected in such school health records. Believing that the records were not sufficiently detailed for refined diagnostic categories, we have taken the frequency of all entries as a rough index of health status. Experimental and control cases are compared on this basis in Table 30.

TABLE 30. ENTRIES ON HEALTH RECORDS FOR ALL EXPERIMEN-
TAL AND CONTROL CASES BY YEAR IN HIGH SCHOOL

Number of Entries	Year of Cohort Entry		First Year After Cohort Entry		Second Year After Cohort Entry	
	Experimental	Control	Experimental	Control	Experimental	Control
	(Per cent)		(Per cent)		(Per cent)	
None or one	27	19	24	21	36	34
Two to five	50	49	55	59	56	57
Six or more	23	32	21	20	8	9
Total	100	100	100	100	100	100
Number, data available	188	188	148	157	75	74
Number, data not available	1[a]	4[a]	41[b]	35[b]	114	118

[a] Cases in school but information was not available.

[b] Includes cases not in school and cases for whom information was not available.

Somewhat fewer entries on the health records are found to be made for experimental cases but the difference from control cases is not statistically significant. There are significant decreases for both groups of cases between the year of cohort entry and the last year observed. It is likely that, in addition to the effects of selection, the older ages of the girls constituting the latter cases would affect this measure. The school health personnel might be less likely to make note of minor health problems for sixteen- to eighteen-year-old than for thirteen- to fifteen-year-old girls, and the girls themselves might be less likely to bring such problems to the attention of school personnel.

Attention of Authorities and Agencies

To see whether experimental and control cases might differ in the extent to which they had come to the attention of the police, courts, and other agencies of community control, the potential problem cases were cleared through the Social Service Exchange at the terminal date of the project. However, the appearance of any entries, especially those with explicit reference to the girls themselves, was so infrequent that it is meaningless to compare experimental and control cases on this measure.

When a girl became involved in court proceedings for some offense, and it was known to the school, a notation was kept and this was taken as a further indication of deviant out-of-school behavior. We cannot accept the information as accurate under the more or less informal manner it was recorded, but the data available do not differentiate experimental and control cases in any event. Thirteen of the former (7 per cent) and nine of the latter (5 per cent) were noted to have been involved in court cases.

Out-of-Wedlock Pregnancy

Because premarital pregnancy is cause for suspension from school, and a rule made it mandatory that resumption of schooling for unmarried mothers must be in a different school, somewhat more reliable information was available about out-of-wedlock pregnancy than other forms of nonschool deviant behavior. To be sure, some such pregnancies were probably undetected, especially those that occurred so late in the school year that they did not become obvious, and it is quite likely that some girls who did not return after the summer recess dropped out of school for this reason. Some pregnancies probably remained undetected because of abortions. It is also likely that some girls gave birth during the summer and returned to school without the pregnancy ever coming to the school's attention. On the other hand, sex and pregnancy, being sensitive areas of concern for adolescents of high school age, and symptoms of pregnancy, being fairly obvious, the school's effort to identify instances of out-of-wedlock pregnancy was persistent. For all the potential problem cases (except five where data were not available), out-of-wedlock pregnancy was reported for 40 girls, or 11 per cent. Of these 41 girls, 23 (56 per cent) were control cases and 18 (44 per cent) were experimental cases, a difference that favors the latter but is not statistically significant.

On the very limited measures of out-of-school behavior available, we may note, in summary, that only the slightest advantage was found for experimental cases. We find very little evidence, therefore, of effect on these measures of the therapeutic program.

CONCLUSION

The measures of effect that have been examined in this chapter are objective, in the sense that they are observations external to the girls we studied in contrast to self-reports or responses. Such measures constitute, therefore, fairly severe tests of an experimental effect of the treatment program. On these tests no strong indications of effect are found and the conclusion must be stated in the negative when it is asked whether social work intervention with potential problem high school girls was in this instance effective.

However, the evidence is not wholly negative. With due recognition of the very low magnitude of any relationship between experimental or control status of the cases and any of these criteria measures, it may be noted that the direction of many of them tends to favor girls who had the benefit of the treatment program. This may be little basis for enthusiasm in view of the tireless efforts of able social workers and the splendid cooperation of school personnel in an attempt to help the girls with potential problems, but it is not entirely discouraging. It testifies to the difficulty of changing deviant careers, a difficulty that is apparent whenever serious evaluative assessments have been undertaken. This is certainly not surprising to social workers who have struggled to find ways to be helpful. And it should caution those who like to believe that ways are already known, if but tried, to meet the serious problems of adolescents in their high school years.

VIII. Effects of Social Work Service: Self-Reports and Responses

THE OBJECTIVE CRITERIA of effects considered in the preceding chapter are unquestionably among the types of outcomes that the therapeutic program hoped to achieve. Using these criteria, the effects were very limited, being represented by tendencies and consistencies in the data rather than by clear experimental conclusions. Such effects, whatever their magnitude, may be considered secondary, in the sense that the treatment program was only indirectly focused upon them; the caseworkers and group therapists did not define their treatment goals directly in such terms as: "to reduce truancy," "to improve school grades and conduct," "to prevent out-of-wedlock pregnancy," and so on. Rather, in keeping with the ideology of casework practice in which the social workers were trained, more proximate objectives of treatment are described in such terms as: to increase self-understanding, to develop more adequate psychological and social functioning, to facilitate maturation, to supplement emotional resources inadequate for the ordinary and extraordinary stresses of adolescence. If such proximate treatment goals are achieved, it is believed, they will lead to the indirect objectives. Hence we must attempt to observe effects of more subtle character in order to assess the treatment program and to explore the hypothesis that changes at the psychosocial level are related to changes at the more external social-behavioral level. Although the relationship between these levels is commonly assumed in the practice theory of casework and other psychotherapeutic approaches, its general validity is not established and we do not have any detailed understanding of how the levels are related.

181

It is difficult to observe and measure these more subtle effects, particularly when the requirements of an experimental design demand identical measures for both experimental and control cases. Because it is difficult to develop objective measures, some researchers have preferred to depend on judgments by professional caseworkers, as in the Hunt-Kogan Movement Scale.[1] In the present study such judgments could be made for experimental cases but the requirements of the experimental design demand identical measures for control cases as well. Less "professional" judgments by school staff, we have seen, reveal little distinction between experimental and control cases. There are limitations, in any event, in the use of judgments, as has been well recognized.[2] Alternative to the use of judgments, and in some ways more adequate, is the use of direct expressions and responses of the subjects whose changes are to be observed. This, too, is difficult at the present stage of technical development in the science of personality and attitude assessment.[3] We have, however, tried a number of such measures and will report findings from their use in this chapter.

All our measures share the characteristic of being self-reports and responses of the girls who constitute both the experimental and the control cases. The measures include general and specific attitudes expressed in response to questionnaires, scores on standardized personality tests, and reports on certain sociometric relations.

ATTITUDE RESPONSES

Three attitude questionnaires were administered: (1) a brief, five-item questionnaire asking general questions about how the girl felt and about related self-orientations; (2) a general questionnaire intended to detect insight into deviant behavior and how it might be affected by help from sympathetic others; and (3) a questionnaire administered to senior students asking them to reflect on their present and future situations.

General Feelings

In Chapter IV we noted that potential problem and residual cases were similar in their initial responses to this questionnaire,

except that the potential problem cases tended to give somewhat more negative responses. We also noted that experimental
and control cases responded in similar ways initially and that
little differentiation occurred between the first-test distributions of students who remained in school and those who dropped
out. We may now examine the data to compare experimental
and control cases as they are observed in successive testings
through the high school years in which the former have participated in the agency's therapeutic program.

In the analysis of this questionnaire, we have examined distributions of all the experimental and control cases who were
present to respond at each of the four testing periods, a succes-
sively smaller number as the girls dropped out of school. We
have also examined separately the changes through time for
those cases that remained in school through all four test periods,
the cases therefore that can be expected to have the greatest
exposure to the treatment program.

TABLE 31. RESPONSES OF EXPERIMENTAL AND CONTROL CASES AT
EACH TESTING PERIOD TO THE QUESTION: "GENERALLY
SPEAKING, HOW DO YOU FEEL?"

Response Category	First Test		Second Test		Third Test		Fourth Test	
	Experi-mental	Con-trol	Experi-mental	Con-trol	Experi-mental	Con-trol	Experi-mental	Con-trol
A. *All Cases*	(Per cent)		(Per cent)		(Per cent)		(Per cent)	
Excellent or very well	50	50	48	39	37	47	43	44
Quite well or satisfactory	39	37	42	53	51	39	42	41
Not too well or not well at all	11	13	10	8	12	14	15	15
Total	100	100	100	100	100	100	100	100
Number of cases	129	132	114	112	77	82	67	59[a]
B. *Only Cases Remaining for Four Tests*								
Excellent or very well	43	46					43	44
Quite well or satisfactory	43	45					42	41
Not too well or not well at all	14	9					15	15
Total	100	100					100	100
Number of cases	67	60					67	59[a]

[a] Information not available for one case.

No statistically significant trends are found that differentiate experimental and control cases in their responses to the question: "Generally speaking, how do you feel?" as may be noted in Table 31. There are also few interpretable differences for the related question: "Do you feel better than you did about two months ago?" as presented in Table 32.

TABLE 32. RESPONSES OF EXPERIMENTAL AND CONTROL CASES AT EACH TESTING PERIOD TO THE QUESTION: "Do You Feel Better Than You Did About Two Months Ago?"

Response Category	First Test		Second Test		Third Test		Fourth Test	
	Experi- mental	Con- trol	Experi- mental	Con- trol	Experi- mental	Con- trol	Experi- mental	Con- trol
A. *All Cases*	(Per cent)		(Per cent)		(Per cent)		(Per cent)	
Much better	40	41	38	36	35	33	34	34
Better or a little bit better	44	45	51	54	52	47	55	39
A little bit worse, worse, or much worse	16	14	11	10	13	20	11	27
Total	100	100	100	100	100	100	100	100
Number of cases	129	132	114	112	77	82	67	59[a]
B. *Only Cases Remaining for Four Tests*								
Much better	42	40					34	34
Better or a little bit better	44	50					55	39
A little bit worse, worse, or much worse	14	10					11	27
Total	100	100					100	100
Number of cases	67	60					67	59[a]

[a] Information not available for one case.

For the first of these questions, the stability of the distributions for both experimental and control samples is evident and a similar finding can be reported when only those cases that remained for four tests are examined. For the question concerning change in feeling over the past two months (see Table 32), one important difference is noticeable that does not quite attain statistical significance: control cases are more likely than experimental cases to say that they feel worse at the fourth testing period (27 per cent compared to 11 per cent). The trend through time is clearly different for the two groups of cases, whether all cases or only those remaining through four tests are examined (Table 32, part B). Those who participated in the treatment program remained about the same as a group, whereas the control cases disproportionately reported a less positive outlook. Insofar as the question reflects the girls' sense of well-being, a less negative outlook may be attributed to the treatment program.

TABLE 33. RESPONSES OF ALL EXPERIMENTAL AND CONTROL CASES AT EACH TESTING PERIOD TO THE QUESTION: "How Well Are You Getting Along with Your Friends, People You Work or Go to School With, and Your Other Acquaintances?"

Response Category	First Test		Second Test		Third Test		Fourth Test	
	Experimental	Control	Experimental	Control	Experimental	Control	Experimental	Control
A. *All Cases*	(Per cent)		(Per cent)		(Per cent)		(Per cent)	
Very well	67	68	60	62	60	57	49	66
Satisfactory	28	26	34	33	37	38	45	32
Not too well or not well at all	5	6	6	5	3	5	6	2
Total	100	100	100	100	100	100	100	100
Number of cases	129	132	114	112	77	82	67	59[a]
B. *Only Cases Remaining for Four Tests*								
Very well	72	65					49	66
Satisfactory	24	32					45	32
Not too well or not well at all	4	3					6	2
Total	100	100					100	100
Number of cases	67	60					67	59[a]

[a] Information not available for one case.

On two questions concerned with reports on getting along with friends and with family, the findings are similar to those just reported. Table 33 presents data in response to the question: "How well are you getting along with your friends, people you work or go to school with, and your other acquaintances?" Table 34 presents data for the question: "How well are you getting along with your family?"

TABLE 34. RESPONSES OF EXPERIMENTAL AND CONTROL CASES
AT EACH TESTING PERIOD TO THE QUESTION: "How
WELL ARE YOU GETTING ALONG WITH YOUR FAMILY?"

Response Category	First Test		Second Test		Third Test		Fourth Test	
	Experi-mental	Con-trol	Experi-mental	Con-trol	Experi-mental	Con-trol	Experi-mental	Con-trol
A. *All Cases*	(Per cent)		(Per cent)		(Per cent)		(Per cent)	
Very well	60	65	58	51	55	49	45	51
Satisfactory	32	26	29	36	27	38	45	29
Not too well or not well at all	8	9	13	13	18	13	10	20
Total	100	100	100	100	100	100	100	100
Number of cases	129	132	114	112	77	82	67	59[a]
B. *Only Cases Remaining for Four Tests*								
Very well	63	70					45	51
Satisfactory	31	23					45	29
Not too well or not well at all	6	7					10	20
Total	100	100					100	100
Number of cases	67	60					67	59[a]

[a] Information not available for one case.

With respect to the first question (see Table 33), one may
note a substantial decrease in the percentage of experimental
cases reporting that they are getting along "very well" with
their friends, a decrease not apparent for control cases. At the
fourth test period, 49 per cent of the experimental cases and
66 per cent of the control cases gave this response. Neither the
trend nor the latter difference quite achieves statistical significance. If these findings are taken as true reflections of actual
differences, they would be contrary to the expected effect of
the treatment program. The trend on prior tests for this response category is similar, however, for experimental and control cases: a gradual decrease in the proportions responding
"very well" and an increase in responses to the category "satisfactory." Therefore, we must be cautious when interpreting the
differential between experimental and control cases that appears
at the fourth testing period.

This caution is especially necessary in view of the data for
responses to the question which asks how the girls are getting
along with their families. (See Table 34.) The control cases show

a somewhat more negative trend in their distributions than the experimental cases although, again, such an interpretation must be most tentative. Approximately the same proportions are maintained for the most positive response category but control cases show a disproportionate increase in the most negative category. At the fourth testing period, 20 per cent of the control cases, compared to 10 per cent of the experimental cases, indicate that they are getting along with their families "not too well," or "not well at all," but this difference is not statistically significant. As was the case for the previous question, however, the trend is not consistent and we must consider both these questions as reflecting little effect of the therapeutic program.

It is of some interest to note that on these questions the proportions decrease for both groups of cases selecting the most favorable category, "very well." This suggests a possible change in inclination of students as they proceed through high school, or as they grow older, to express attitudes on such matters strongly. Or high school girls with potential problems—whether or not participants in a treatment program—may, indeed, get along less well with their friends and families. Perhaps increasing autonomy of later adolescence is reflected in such an inclination.

We have noted earlier that problem-potential and residual cases differed most in response to the question: "Do you have a lot of problems that are bothering you?" When experimental and control cases are compared, however, no meaningful differences between them or important time trends are to be found. Similarly, no differential findings can be reported for the companion question, "Do you feel you are going to be able to take care of your problems all right in the future?"

The limited findings on this instrument may be said, in summary, to suggest modest effects of the treatment program. These are expressed in the indication that those girls who had the benefit of the program respond to a slight degree less negatively to several questions intended to reflect general self-assessments of their personal situations.

Psychological Insight and Reactions to Help

Increased sensitivity to emotional and other causal factors in misbehavior and acceptance of help as desirable were important aspects of the learning experience offered to the girls in the therapeutic program. We sought to examine effects on these aspects by a general questionnaire administered (in the spring of 1959) when the school population would contain the largest number of experimental cases. The questionnaire was answered by girls at all school-grade levels and a total of 813 students responded. Identified by cohort entry year and by status as experimental, control, or residual cases, the respondents were distributed as follows:

Cohort Entry Year	Experimentals	Controls	Residuals	Total
1955 to 1956	..	1	28	29
1956 to 1957	19	12	181	212
1957 to 1958	36	43	197	276
1958 to 1959	53	55	188	296
Total	108	111	594	813

With this pattern of respondents it has been possible to analyze the questionnaire data to compare experimental cases with varying amounts of exposure to the treatment program to their control counterparts. No trends in this respect appeared, however, in the data. The basic comparison between experimental and control cases will be made, therefore, for the two central cohorts—those for 1956–1957 and 1957–1958. Experimental cases in these cohorts had opportunity for at least two years' exposure to the treatment program.

The questionnaire was in two parts, the first asking questions indicating insight into the behavior of a fictional girl whose behavior was described in a vignette, and the second part asking questions pertaining to the student herself.

The vignette was as follows:

> Mary is an imaginary person, but you probably know some girl like her.
> Mary is a high school student about your age. She is often a little late getting to school. Although she is really pretty smart, she

doesn't work very hard and the teacher usually calls her down in class for some reason or other. Mary is always picking arguments and when you try to be friends you soon find out that she talks about you behind your back. Sometimes she loses her temper and once she had a bad fight with another girl over really nothing at all—just some chair that Mary wanted to sit in.

A series of questions about Mary followed, the first of which was intended as a screening question and as a lead to more indirect analytical responses. Question 1 asked: "Is it important for Mary to change the way she acts or is there no particular reason for her to change?" Almost all the girls—whether experimental, control, or residual cases—said that it was "very important for Mary to change."

The next question sought to tap a sense that some factors other than willful action determined Mary's behavior: "Do you think Mary could really stop acting this way if she just tried?" The responses of experimental and control cases from the two central cohorts (the number for each group was 55) are given in Table 35, part A, together with the distribution for residual cases (378) from the same cohorts. No significant

TABLE 35. RESPONSES OF EXPERIMENTAL, CONTROL, AND RESIDUAL CASES TO THE QUESTION: "Do You Think Mary Could Really Stop Acting This Way If She Just Tried?"

Response Category	Experimental	Control	Residual
A. *Two Central Cohorts*		(Per cent)	
Very sure she could stop	36	44	51
Pretty sure she could stop	55	54	45
Not likely she could, or pretty sure she couldn't stop	9	2	4
Total	100	100	100
Number of cases	55	55	378
B. *Most Recent Cohort*			
Very sure she could stop	57	58	51
Pretty sure she could stop	36	38	43
Not likely she could, or pretty sure she couldn't stop	7	4	6
Total	100	100	100
Number of cases	53	55	188

differences are found between experimental and control cases; the direction of difference shows, however, the experimental less likely than the control cases to be sure that Mary's behavior is a matter of "just trying."

A statistically significant difference does appear when experimental and residual cases are compared; 36 per cent of the former compared to 51 per cent of the latter say they are "very sure she could stop." Control cases differ in the same direction but the percentage giving this reply (44 per cent) is intermediate between the experimental and residual groups. This finding suggests an interesting interpretation, namely, that girls who have problems themselves are less confident that simple advice to "control themselves," "make up their minds to behave," and similar injunctions can be followed. Furthermore, when such girls are exposed to casework orientations toward behavior as exemplified in the vignette, they become increasingly skeptical of such approaches. Put in the context of deterministic theories of behavior generally held by caseworkers, the girls involved in treatment become more sophisticated in psychological diagnosis.

Of course, an alternative interpretation might suggest that girls are likely to get into trouble if they do not believe that behavior such as that described in the vignette can be stopped by "just trying." With our data we cannot compare potential problem and residual cases prior to any exposure of experimental cases to the treatment program. But the most recent cohort at the time when the questionnaire was administered could only have had minimal treatment experience of less than one year. If this interpretation is valid, potential problem cases should show a smaller percentage than residuals on this response. As a matter of fact they do not; no important differences appear for this cohort between experimental, control, and residual cases as may be seen in Table 35, part B. To explain the differences that are found for the later cohort, one must assume some differential experience or differential selective factor. It is reasonable to believe that the treatment experience of the experimental cases was a factor in their response pattern.

In the additional questions about Mary the magnitudes of differences between experimental and control cases vary but in no instance enough, with the small number of cases, to be statistically significant. We will not present tables for each item but, instead, will report the direction of the findings that occur.

Several questions offered further opportunity to see if girls who had participated in discussions with social workers would choose responses indicating somewhat more psychological insight in contrast to "common sense" or stereotyped, explanations based on noncausal assumptions. More experimental cases (38 per cent) than control cases (31 per cent) did not think that Mary "will just outgrow this kind of thing." Slightly more experimental cases (85 per cent) than control cases (80 per cent) are sure "Mary acts this way because something is bothering her." But almost equal proportions of experimental and control cases (40 per cent and 42 per cent, respectively) wonder "fairly often" or "a lot" "why girls like Mary act the way they do." Experimental cases are more likely (65 per cent) than control cases (51 per cent) to agree that "Mary acts this way because she goes with the wrong kind of people." And more experimental cases (66 per cent) than control cases (51 per cent) say that Mary "never" or only "sometimes" "feels ashamed of herself for acting this way."

Taken together, with due respect for the fact that differences are minimal, the responses to the questions about Mary make an interpretable pattern. Experimental cases are more inclined than control cases to say that something is bothering Mary, that she will not just grow out of it and cannot change her behavior by just trying, that she goes with the wrong kind of people and does not feel very much ashamed of how she acts. This psychologically plausible pattern is consistent with the diagnostic approach of casework practice and may be considered at least minimal evidence of somewhat greater psychological insight on the part of the experimental cases. It is to be emphasized again, however, that the differences are small and that our interpretations must be taken only as cautious speculation hinted by the data.

One final question about Mary led the respondents into the second part of the questionnaire concerned with getting help with problems from others. The question was asked: "Do you think talking with a friendly adult would help Mary change for the better or don't you think this would make any difference?" The responses to this question are shown in Table 36.

TABLE 36. RESPONSES OF TWO CENTRAL COHORTS OF EX-
PERIMENTAL, CONTROL AND RESIDUAL CASES
TO THE QUESTION: "Do You Think Talking with a
Friendly Adult Would Help Mary Change for the
Better or Don't You Think This Would Make Any
Difference?"

Response Category	Experimental	Control	Residual
	(Per cent)		
Very sure it would	36	25	32
Probably would	44	67	57
Not likely to	20	4	7
Don't think it would	..	4	4
Total	100	100	100
Number of cases	55	55	378

The most apparent differences in this table—but not statistically significant—are the greater proportions of experimental cases responding "very sure it would" and "not likely to" make any difference, with a much smaller proportion giving the ambiguous response, "probably would," and none saying that they "don't think it would." Observing the whole distribution, the control cases to a greater extent than the experimental cases (92 per cent and 80 per cent, respectively) give positive responses. If the pattern of responses is representative of a real relationship, it would suggest greater crystallization of opinion on the part of the experimental cases with respect to the likelihood that "talking with a friendly adult would help Mary change for the better." The data imply that girls exposed to casework orientations tend to have stronger convictions about talking over behavior problems than those who are not so exposed. This suggestion is speculative, of course; the data cannot support the conclusion that experimental cases clearly reflect a sense of benefit from talking over problems.

In fact, there is only the slightest evidence that experimental cases more than control cases value discussing their own problems with an interested adult. This question was asked directly about the girls themselves in the second part of the questionnaire: "When *you* have a problem, is it helpful to discuss it with an interested adult or is it not very helpful?" 40 per cent of the experimental and 35 per cent of the control cases checked the category "very helpful" and 7 per cent of the former compared to 11 per cent of the latter checked "not so helpful." These differences are not statistically significant.

In the matter of talking with adults about things that bother them, however, the experimental cases clearly show that they have had more opportunity to do so and that fewer of them would want more opportunity. This may be seen in the data presented in Tables 37 and 38.

TABLE 37. RESPONSES OF TWO CENTRAL COHORTS OF EXPERIMENTAL, CONTROL AND RESIDUAL CASES TO THE QUESTION: "Since You Got Out of Junior High, How Much Opportunity Have You Had to Talk with Adults About Things That May Bother You?"

Response Category	Experimental	Control	Residual
		(Per cent)	
A great deal	51	38	38
Some	44	36	40
Not much	..	7	12
Very little	5	19	10
Total	100	100	100
Number of cases	55	55	378

TABLE 38. RESPONSES OF TWO CENTRAL COHORTS OF EXPERIMENTAL, CONTROL AND RESIDUAL CASES TO THE QUESTION: "Would You Want to Have More Opportunity Than You Have Had to Talk Over Things with Adults or Don't You Care to Talk Things Over with Adults?"

Response Category	Experimental	Control	Residual
		(Per cent)	
Like a lot more opportunity	11	31	23
Like some more opportunity	38	38	39
Have as much opportunity as want	40	18	30
Don't care to talk with adults	11	13	8
Total	100	100	100
Number of cases	55	55	378

Significantly more experimental than control cases (95 per cent and 74 per cent, respectively) say they have had "a great deal" or "some" opportunity to talk with adults about problems that bother them and a similar difference (also significant) holds when experimental and residual cases are compared. This may with some confidence be attributed to the participation of experimental cases in the treatment program where talking things over with adults was the main preoccupation. Confirming the recognition by experimental cases of greater opportunity to talk over problems, significantly fewer of them said they would like to have more opportunity to do so. (See Table 38.) It is to be noted, however, that more than one-third of the experimental cases nevertheless indicate that they would "like some more opportunity."

On two questions, little difference was found between experimental and control cases with respect to their belief that it is "helpful" or "a good idea" to discuss and talk over problems with friends. Experimental cases are slightly more inclined (the differences are not statistically significant) to favor talking with friends. Residual cases are somewhat (but not significantly) more inclined than either experimental or control cases to look with favor on discussing problems with friends. If the group sessions attended by experimental cases were seen as especially beneficial discussions with friends, they were so seen only to the slightest extent.

On a series of questions asking whether talking about "yourself, your problems, etc." has changed different relationships with others, the differences are again only minor in every instance. To a small extent, experimental cases were more likely than control cases to say that talking about things changed their feelings about themselves and made them want to get along better with their families. On the other hand, control cases were somewhat more likely to say that talking things over helped them get along better with girl friends and boy friends or helped them want to improve their appearance. No interpretable pattern is suggested by these minor differences and one must conclude that the treatment program did not visibly, on the evidence of the measures used, induce its participants to see themselves as directly affected in such relationships with others by their discussions with social workers.

To a final question asking whether the girls thought they were easier, the same, or harder to get along with now than they used to be, proportionately more of the control than of the experimental cases reported that they were "easier to get along with." If the responses are taken at face value as reports of actual relationships with others, this difference (not statistically significant) would be contrary to expectations. If, on the other hand, the responses are taken as self-perceptions, one might speculate that participation in the treatment program encouraged experimental cases to make more realistic self-appraisals. We do not have direct external evidence of whether the girls were, in fact, easier or harder to get along with than formerly. It is to be noted, however, that in the distribution of responses experimental cases are more like residual cases than control cases. One may cautiously reason that girls who were in the treatment program were more likely to appraise themselves in the same manner as girls who were not potential problems, whereas potential problem cases without benefit of the treatment program tended to make more unrealistic self-estimates. Without additional evidence, this interpretation is, of course, purely speculative but it is in keeping with the suggestion elsewhere in the data that experimental cases might have acquired somewhat more psychological insight than control cases.

Reviewing data from the general questionnaire, we may say that participants in the treatment program clearly recognized the opportunity they had to discuss their problems with an adult and, in contrast to the control cases, did not feel that they had been limited in doing so. Experimental cases did not, however, especially attribute benefits to themselves from this opportunity in proportions significantly greater than the control cases. This finding is not a direct assessment of the treatment program by participating girls, since they were asked only indirect questions that could also be responded to by control cases. Nevertheless, if the treatment program had been very salient for the experimental cases and they had valued it highly, one might have expected the rather obvious questions about help from interested adults to reflect this appraisal. Control cases reported in proportions about equal to experimental cases that talking with adults had been beneficial. It is possible, of course, that the ambiguous term "interested adults" might have been interpreted differently by the two groups of girls. If this were the case, it would still follow that participation in the treatment program did not produce differential responses.

The data tend to suggest that participation in the treatment program was associated with somewhat greater psychological insight when experimental and control cases are compared. The evidence for such a conclusion is weak, however, although responses to a number of questions point in that direction. It is always possible that a superficial attitude questionnaire would fail to reflect so subtle a difference as heightened insight, so that the barest tendency on the present instrument might be encouragement that the treatment program had some effect in this respect. However, we must conclude that experimental effects are no more evident in the attitude responses of this questionnaire than they were on the more behavioral criteria considered earlier.

Assessments by Seniors of Their Present and Future Situations

When each cohort reached the end of its senior year, girls still in the school were asked to complete what was called the "Senior Questionnaire." Since the project terminated before the final cohort (entering 1958–1959) reached this level, the population responding to this instrument consisted only of the first three cohorts. Of these cohorts, 67 experimental cases and 56 control cases completed questionnaires. This represents all the experimental cases that remained in school for four test periods; senior questionnaires were not obtained for four of the 60 control cases with similar school tenure.

After requesting the seniors to write a few lines about their future plans, the questionnaire asked specific, closed-choice questions about their future, about help outside the school during the high school years, and about "trouble" they might have been in during that time. It was thought that responses to such questions might be answered differently by girls who had participated for three years in the treatment program. Reports of more help received, greater confidence about the future, and reports of being in less trouble might be expected of experimental in greater proportions than of control cases.

One part of the questionnaire gave the girls an opportunity to indicate on a four-point scale (from "a great deal" to "not at all") how much help they got while they were in high school from the following: parents, friends, a doctor, a social worker, an employer, a teacher, a minister or priest or rabbi, somebody at a community center or "Y," and a policeman. Clearly the experimental cases reported more help from social workers than the control cases: 48 per cent of the former compared to 21 per cent of the latter said they had "a great deal" or "some" help from a social worker, and the difference is statistically significant. The distributions for this question are shown in Table 39. This is evidence that the girls who participated in the

TABLE 39. RESPONSES OF EXPERIMENTAL AND CONTROL CASES WHO COMPLETED THE SENIOR QUESTIONNAIRE TO THE QUESTION: "WHILE YOU WERE IN SCHOOL, HOW MUCH HELP DID YOU GET OUTSIDE THE SCHOOL FOR SOME OF THE PROBLEMS YOU HAD—PERSONAL PROBLEMS, SOCIAL PROBLEMS, MONEY, ETC. HOW MUCH DID A SOCIAL WORKER HELP YOU?"

Response Category	Experimental	Control
	(Per cent)	
A great deal	24	7
Some	24	14
A little bit	15	5
Not at all	37	74
Total	100	100
Number of cases	67	56[a]

[a] Information not available for 4 cases.

therapeutic program did identify their social workers as helpful, although approximately one-third (37 per cent) answered "not at all" to the question. A substantially greater (but not quite statistically significant) percentage of experimental than control cases also indicated that somebody at a community center or "Y" had helped them: 36 per cent of the former compared to 18 per cent of the latter responded that they were helped "a great deal" or "some." This is not surprising since group sessions were often held in a nearby YMCA building. Thus we may conclude that the efforts of the social workers to help were recognized by their clients.

No other significant differences appear on this set of questions. Somewhat more of the experimental than of the control cases reported that a teacher (33 per cent compared to 25 per cent) helped them "a great deal." Somewhat fewer experimental than control cases reported that their parents had helped them "a great deal" (54 per cent compared to 73 per cent). Responses were essentially similar with respect to the other designated persons who might have helped the girls.

On questions concerned with reported trouble during the past two or three years, similar proportions of experimental and control cases said they had never been in trouble at all (46 per cent compared to 45 per cent). The two groups saw themselves about equally as having been in less trouble than "most of the girls in school" (91 per cent of the experimental and 93 per cent of the control cases). And a somewhat greater percentage of experimental cases than of control cases (37 per cent compared to 27 per cent) reported that at least one of their friends had been in serious trouble during the past two or three years. This is not surprising since the experimental cases were thrown with one another in the treatment groups and hence exposed to deliberate discussions of trouble other girls might have had. From these three questions we must conclude that less self-reported "serious trouble" was not an effect of exposure to the treatment program. It should be remembered, however, that both experimental and control cases responding to these questions were selected populations, excluding girls who had dropped out of school who might actually have been in more trouble.

The series of questions about the future also failed to differentiate experimental and control cases who completed the Senior Questionnaire. Approximately the same proportions (slightly more than two-thirds) said they were "not at all" or "a little" worried about their future; about half of each group were sure about what they were "going to be doing in the next few years"; and a little more than one-third of each group said they thought they would get along "very well" or "well" in the future. Greater proportions of experimental cases than of control cases (25 per cent compared to 13 per cent) said that they thought there was "a very good chance" that "things will work out the way you want them to in the next five years," and that they had "a very good chance" of "having a happy married life" (47 per cent for experimental and 41 per cent for control cases). These differences are not, however, statistically significant. They are the strongest evidence in the data, nevertheless, that girls who had been in the treatment program were more optimistic about their personal future.

On the whole, we find only a minimal effect of the treatment program on the assessments of their situation and their future among girls who remained in school to the end of their senior year, although those who participated in the program did report that they had been helped by social workers.

Conclusion with Respect to Attitude Responses

The scant differences that appear on the measures of attitude used in this study can, in summary, support only the slightest indication of effect of the treatment program. At best we may cautiously suggest that taken together the patterns of response on the several instruments tend to be somewhat less negative if viewed from the objectives of the treatment program. There is clearly no indication that subjectively felt and reported feelings and attitudes were affected more strongly than the more indirect objective criteria considered in the previous chapter.

PERSONALITY TESTS

The Junior Personality Quiz, which was the personality test used throughout the series of test periods in the research, has been described in detail in Chapter III. It was noted there that on only two factors was there the suggestion that experimental and control cases differed significantly or meaningfully.

Compared to control cases, scores on the factor designated as Will Control vs. Relaxed Casualness change toward the higher pole of the dimension for experimental cases. Thus we may conclude that the treatment program promoted personality test responses indicating greater self-control, orderly and persistent behavior. These traits did not increase for the comparable control cases.

Although not statistically significant, slight numerical trends with respect to the factor, Adventurous Cyclothymia vs. Withdrawn Schizothymia, occur in opposite directions for experimental and control cases. The former increase in boldness, whereas the latter increase in shyness, aloofness, lack of confidence. This is a suggestive difference in keeping with the objectives of the treatment program to which the experimental cases were exposed.

On the other ten factors that make up this personality test no interpretable differences appear between experimental and control cases. We must conclude, therefore, that the treatment program had only the barest effect on personality changes insofar as this instrument detects them.

The Make A Sentence Test—a projective sentence-completion test with standardized scoring developed in part for purposes of this research[4]—has been described in Chapter II where its eleven scoring categories are listed. Examination of the scores for experimental and control cases failed to reveal interpretable differences and therefore the data will not be presented.

Thus with the use of two standardized measures of personality —one "objective" and the other "projective"—only the barest evidence of an experimental effect of the treatment program can be found.

SOCIOMETRIC DATA

In the design of the research it was planned to obtain minimal sociometric data to test the hypothesis that experimental cases would be less likely than control cases to associate with other girls who had trouble in the school. It was also intended to examine the data to discover whether participation in the treatment program resulted in greater or less isolation in the sense of choosing or being chosen by classmates as "friends—students you pal around with." Therefore, sociometric choices were analyzed for those students who remained in school throughout the four testing periods and these data will be considered here.

When the study was initiated, the treatment program was conceived as individualized casework but we have noted that it shifted after the first year to group treatment. As a result, the experimental cases were brought into constant association with one another and hence might be expected to name one another to a greater extent than those not in their groups. Since potential problem cases were more likely than residual cases to be rated as "serious problems," it is not surprising that opposite trends occur with respect to experimental cases when compared to control and residual cases in the number of "serious problem" students named. Thus between the first and fourth test periods, the percentages of control and residual cases naming one or more "serious problem" students decreases, whereas a greater proportion of experimental cases named one or more "serious problem" students. Even so, the differences between the three groups of cases is not large enough to be statistically significant. Table 40 presents the data on "serious problem" students who were named by and who chose girls who constitute the experimental, control, and residual cases.

It is of some interest that despite the greater likelihood of naming "serious problem" students, the experimental cases are not, in turn, chosen disproportionately by such students. Statistically significant differences between first and fourth test-period distributions are found for experimental as well as control and residual cases but no significant differences between the three groups of cases at either the first or the fourth test periods.

TABLE 40. NUMBER OF "SERIOUS PROBLEM" STUDENTS NAMED BY
AND CHOOSING EXPERIMENTAL, CONTROL, AND RESID-
UAL CASES WHO WERE PRESENT AT BOTH FIRST AND
FOURTH TEST PERIODS

"Serious Problem" Students	First Test			Fourth Test		
	Experi-mental	Con-trol	Residual	Experi-mental	Con-trol	Residual
	(Per cent)			(Per cent)		
A. *Number of "Serious Problem" Students Named by*						
None	46	31	50	38	42	50
One or more	54	69	50	62	58	50
Total	100	100	100	100	100	100
Number of cases	67	60	334	67	59ª	334
B. *Number of "Serious Problem" Students Choosing*						
None	32	45	51	61	66	67
One or more	68	55	49	39	34	33
Total	100	100	100	100	100	100
Number of cases	67	60	334	67	59ª	334

ª Information not available for one case.

As Table 41 shows, when the sociometric data are considered
with respect to "outstanding" students named by and choosing
experimental, control, and residual cases, the trends are similar
for both of the potential problem samples (experimental and
control cases); no significant differences appear between them.
Whether naming or chosen by "outstanding" students, increased
proportions of such students are found at the fourth test period
when compared to the first period, and these differences are statistically significant. This is merely evidence, of course, that all
students become better known as they remain in school and this
phenomenon does not appear differentially to any meaningful
degree for experimental and control cases. The same trend, however, is sufficiently greater for residual cases than for either of the
potential problem samples that the differences found between the
residual and the experimental and control cases taken together
at the fourth test period are statistically significant. Although not
differentiated from one another, both the experimental and the

TABLE 41. NUMBER OF "OUTSTANDING" STUDENTS NAMED BY
AND CHOOSING EXPERIMENTAL, CONTROL, AND RESID-
UAL CASES WHO WERE PRESENT AT BOTH FIRST AND
FOURTH TEST PERIODS

"Outstanding" Students	First Test			Fourth Test		
	Experi-mental	Con-trol	Residual	Experi-mental	Con-trol	Residual
	(Per cent)			(Per cent)		
A. *Number of "Out-standing" Students Named*						
None	58	56	57	29	22	14
One or more	42	44	43	71	78	86
Total	100	100	100	100	100	100
Number of cases	67	60	334	67	59[a]	334
B. *Number of "Out-standing" Students Choosing*						
None	52	50	55	34	30	16
One or more	48	50	45	66	70	84
Total	100	100	100	100	100	100
Number of cases	67	60	334	67	59[a]	334

[a] Information not available for one case.

control cases are found to be less likely to name or be named by
"outstanding" students than the residual cases. Slightly fewer of
the experimental than the control cases at the fourth testing period are found to name or be chosen by "outstanding" students,
but the differences are small and cannot constitute evidence of
a negative result of the treatment program.

With respect to sociometric volume—that is, the total number
of students named by or choosing girls in the several samples of
the research population—there are no important differences between experimental, control, and residual cases. The trend is for
each of the three groups of cases to name more students at the
fourth than at the first test period. Likewise, they are chosen by
more at the later period, with the residual cases somewhat more
likely to be chosen, but not to a statistically significant degree.

The sociometric data do not show evidence of effect from the
treatment program. Insofar as the hypothesis that the program
would reduce the undesirable associations of the experimental

cases is concerned, there is no evidence to support such a conclusion. Nor has there been an evident effect on the level of general popularity of experimental as compared to control cases.

CONCLUSION

The attitude, personality test, and sociometric data presented in this chapter have failed to detect in any important respect an effect of the experimental treatment program. The findings are not entirely negative, since some of the patterns of responses show slight indications that experimental cases appear somewhat less unfavorable in a number of parallel instances. It is clear, however, that response and self-report measures are not more sensitive criteria of effects of the treatment program than the objective behaviors examined in the previous chapter.

We must conclude that, with respect to all of the measures we have used to examine effects of the treatment program, only a minimal effect can be found.

NOTES TO CHAPTER VIII

1. Shyne, Ann W. editor, *Use of Judgments as Data in Social Work Research.* National Association of Social Workers, New York, 1959, *passim.*

2. *Ibid.,* Hunt, J. McVicker, "On the Judgment of Social Workers as a Source of Information in Social Work Research," pp. 38–54.

3. Borgatta, Edgar F., David Fanshel, and Henry J. Meyer, *Social Workers Perceptions of Clients.* Russell Sage Foundation, New York, 1960, pp. 70–72.

4. Borgatta, Edgar F., in collaboration with Henry J. Meyer, "Make A Sentence Test: An Approach to Objective Scoring of Sentence Completions," *Genetic Psychology Monographs,* vol. 63, 1961, pp. 3–65.

IX. Conclusions and Implications

THE IMPLICATIONS to be drawn from the research and the program of service to high school girls described in the preceding chapters go beyond a summary of findings. It is the purpose of this concluding chapter to comment on the project and its results and also to consider broader issues associated with evaluative research in social welfare.

CONCLUSIONS

Systematic and rigorous evaluative research concerning programs of social welfare is still so uncommon that it is quite appropriate to consider the execution of this project as a demonstration.[1] It has shown that it is possible to carry out a complex research design involving experimental and control cases, requiring the coordinated cooperation of a private social agency and a public school, and calling for sustained and adaptive efforts of professional social workers as well as those of school personnel and researchers. The acceptability of the control-group design, and recognition of its feasibility, should be further encouraged by the experience of this project. A promising trend toward field experiments in social work—a matter of debate and hesitation when the project began—may be accelerated.

Another emerging trend gains support from the experience of casework practitioners over the course of this project. The use of group approaches to treatment emerged clearly as the method of choice in this instance. The caseworkers became convinced that their treatment influences were more strongly conveyed when clients were seen in groups. There is no doubt that *initial contact* was more readily achieved between professional social workers and high school girls with potential problems when group rather than individual approaches were used. Moreover, *continued access* to such clients was greater when they were seen in groups than as individual cases. Although the social workers were initially uncertain about working with groups of clients, they were stimulated to see both diagnostic and treatment possibilities not evident to them in the more traditional caseworker-client relationship. These conclusions do not minimize the potential utility of individual treatment but suggest the value of group methods and encourage consideration of alternatives adapted to variations in types of clients and types of client problems.

The intent of the service program to reach a clientele for whom future problems could be anticipated was demonstrably realized. Those selected as potential problem cases were markedly less successful in subsequent school performance and in other criteria of social or personal adjustment. The procedures for identifying potential problem girls among the entering students of the high school were efficient. They used school records to identify students who had previous school or personal difficulties. A general observation about social behavior is once more confirmed: prior behavior is a good predictor of subsequent behavior. However, the potential problem cases did not exhibit acute states of crisis considered by these social workers to be beyond the point of helpful intervention. The girls who became clients were seen as appropriate for the help proffered. Lack of success in helping them might raise questions about whether the point of intervention was the most appropriate. Younger girls might have been helped more but this can be determined only by further experimentation. It would seem as important to devise strategies of treatment that proceed from more inclusive theories of social behavior.

Such a direction of attention is suggested by another conclusion that the data of the study support. An unexpected degree of stability on measures of personality and attitude was evident over the three years of adolescence that were observed. Three years may be considered a short span but it represents a substantial part of a most significant period in the lives of these girls. If confidence can be placed in our measures, one must conclude that only powerful treatment interventions can be effective. Since the intervention utilized in this project gave more intensive personal attention than is usually provided for such girls, we are led to suggest that attention to interpersonal and status systems, rather than personality systems, might be more promising.

The impact of the program provided for the experimental cases must be acknowledged to be small. Few statistically significant differences between experimental and control cases were found. On the wide range of criteria used to detect impact of the treatment program, the most positive evidence is represented by the small, parallel effects found for a number of objective and self-report measures. This encourages no dramatic claims for this type of service program as a major assault on critical school and personal behavior problems of high school girls. The limited demonstration of effectiveness raises important questions of appropriate goals of service programs as well as issues about social work practice and its evaluation.

DISCUSSION

Disappointment with the results of evaluative studies when they fail to show dramatic success has led some researchers in social welfare and social work to conclude that evaluative research should be postponed until "more basic" research has been undertaken. It is our conclusion, however, that evaluative research is itself a potent strategy for promoting clarity of goals of treatment, conceptualizations of treatment modes, and theories of behavior that "basic" research requires. The requisites of the sort of evaluative research reported here force attention to issues not otherwise readily recognized.

This research occurred after prior experience with evaluative research so that attention was given in advance to most problems that such research implicates. The design represented a degree of rigor not often achieved with social data in the field. Experimental and control subjects were carefully specified and the attempt was made to keep the target population in perspective by placing the selection processes within a source population. Experimental and control cases were judged appropriate for treatment and represented a potential for demonstrating change. They could, in turn, be compared to a larger population not deemed in need of treatment that could represent a base-line of normality.

There are some obvious limitations not overcome in this research that warrant emphasis. It was necessary to work with a single agency and a single school. The devotion of the cooperating parties in order to satisfy the rigor of the research was little short of heroic. To obtain the cooperation of many schools and agencies is a possibility for the future but this will require even greater efforts than those represented by the current enterprise. Our study of the change process has been made within a limited setting that is possibly representative of other agencies and schools, but not demonstrably so. How representative the setting, the agency, and the definition of the change task are can be judged by the reader. We have elsewhere concluded that it may be wasteful for single agencies to attempt evaluative research alone.[2] They generally do not have the resources to devote to research or the organizational capacity to undertake the manipulations required to reach conclusions about the effectiveness of programs. Furthermore, the point bears reemphasizing that evaluation studies "would be of greater usefulness if they were part of a systematic program of evaluation studies of alternative services within a community."[3]

In the evaluation of agency services, it is desirable to develop large samples of experimental and control cases and to assure that those selected to receive the services actually do. In this project sample sizes are exceptionally large in comparison to most of the field studies in social work. Furthermore, a very high proportion of experimental cases made contact with the agency and were seen more often than most clients of private casework agencies. One reason such large samples could be obtained was the good operating arrangement between the school and the agency, implemented by conscientious effort of the personnel involved and by watchful encouragement of the research staff. Another reason was the inclusiveness of the clientele, namely, high school girls classified as potentially deviant rather than actually deviant. The target population is broader than one defined by more specific, limited problems or symptoms. For example, a clientele defined in terms of potential for pregnancy out of wedlock would obviously be more numerous than one defined in terms of actual pregnancy out of wedlock. Approximately one-fifth of the girls who entered this high school were identified as potential problem cases. We estimate that about one-fifteenth of the entering girls would have been selected as clients if they had been identified by taking severe or developed behavior problems as criteria for inclusion.

The breadth of definition that permitted the larger samples made less specific the problems presented by the clients. If it is believed that treatment should be made specific to the expressly diagnosed problem, attempts at early intervention will require diagnostic procedures that can detect specific problems in earlier stages of development. Such diagnostic procedures are not yet available for the types of problems these clients were likely to have. Indeed, it was because early intervention was desired that the experimental cases in this project were drawn from a large pool of "potential problem cases."

The breadth and unspecificity of the definition of clients did not mean that clients were selected who were inappropriate for treatment and not in need of help. Most of them were deemed by the social workers to need professional help even though all might not be viewed as receptive to help or able to profit from contact with the social workers. Almost a fifth of all the girls in school were so judged. What proportion of girls would have been seen at intake as having real and substantial problems if a random sample of the entire class, rather than of a potential problem pool, had been referred to the agency? Is it unfair to suggest that the presumptive bases of the profession for making such an identification might have viewed the vast majority of a randomly selected group as having real and substantial problems? The implication leads to questions about the realism of agencies in thinking that they serve special groups with specific needs for help. It raises doubt about the extent to which social work has developed diagnostic capacities to differentiate clients who need help from those who do not. It suggests that there may be a presumption of the need for help rather than a diagnostic determination. Furthermore, it raises questions about the kinds of changes that might be expected if so broad a population is viewed as the clientele to be helped or to have future problems prevented.

Ambiguity in the definition of appropriate clients is coupled with uncertainty about the treatment or service that should be attempted and what the goals of such treatment or service should be. The social workers in this project were made well aware of these ambiguities by the demands that evaluation research forced them to face. In the early discussions of plans for this project, one of the social workers was led to remark: "But how can you possibly evaluate what we are trying to do when we don't know ourselves?" This is not cited to imply lack of skill or knowledge, but rather to acknowledge the state of diagnostic and treatment uncertainty characteristic of the social-therapeutic professions. When the goals of treatment or of services are themselves so unclear, how can the criteria of success be specified? What should be considered effective results? How shall we speak of "more" or "less" achievement by professional efforts? Obviously these questions are relevant when we consider the results of this project.

Our response to this situation was to consider as wide a range of explicit and implicit outcomes as we could conceive.[4] Our criteria included objective behaviors and changes of status as well as judgments of behavioral functioning and reflections of psychological states. These criteria are, it should be noted, primarily located *in the client* rather than in the social system within which the client is located. This has implications for the meaning and strategy of evaluative research. Here we wish to consider how much change in such criteria can be expected as a result of various magnitudes of invested effort under such conditions of diagnostic inclusiveness and treatment variability as obtained in this and in most evaluation experiments.

As we have noted, our sample sizes are large in comparison with most control-group evaluative research reported in the literature. How large should effected differences be to be considered statistically significant? We are not raising the question of when to place confidence in observed differences between the experimental and control sample but rather the question of what should be meant by "success."[5] Generally, about 10 per cent more of the experimental cases than of the control cases would have to show the criterion condition for the shift to be judged statistically significant at the .05 confidence level for sample-sizes in our data. The concept of statistical significance is associated with notions of hypothesis testing in repeated random sampling, and the judgment that a difference is statistically significant is an arbitrary one that the difference is large enough so that it would recur in repeated random sampling by chance only a small proportion of the time, say in 5 per cent of the samples.

Translating this into practical terms, these questions might well be asked in advance of the research: "Suppose that only 50 per cent of students having various types of problems already showing in their school records at entry to high school actually complete their work? What proportion of those 50 per cent expected to drop out could be helped sufficiently so that they would finish school?" Should the expectation be that one-half would be helped? A third? A quarter? A fifth? A tenth? Optimism based on professional confidence or on ignorance of well-known facts might choose the larger proportions. To answer "a half" would mean to expect a change in the dropout rate to 25 per cent, a rate considered very good in many school systems. To answer "a fifth" would be to expect a shift in dropout rate from a high one to a lower one (of 40 per cent) that may still be considered high but might be taken as a reasonable practical objective.

Our data did not show such a shift. This warrants reexamination of the question of the size of shift that it is reasonable to expect. Since there was essentially no difference between experimental and control samples on this criterion (or on most others), the speculation about such shifts is intended to point up the methodological issues involved. The empirical findings in our study show so little difference that, from a statistical viewpoint, the possibility that larger sample sizes would have led to different conclusions is practically precluded. If the observed difference in shift on a criterion were 4 per cent, samples as large as 1,000 would still not be sufficient to achieve the level of statistical significance commonly accepted in sociological research.

Demonstrations of changes in evaluative research studies require assumptions about the magnitudes of the changes that should occur. The presumption of most evaluation research—including the present study—has been that effects will be substantial and that the number of persons involved in desirable changes will not be trivial. If this is not achieved, we do not suggest that the practicing professions can take the position that evaluative research is pointless. On the contrary, emphasis should be placed on a realistic interpretation of what is meant when a profession states that its objective is amelioration of personal or social conditions, or the prevention of deviant behavior or social problems. Perhaps the point can be better made in reverse: Would not the investment of social agencies be important in a preventive undertaking if only 5 per cent of improvement occurred in high school dropout rate? In the whole population of the United States, would not an improvement of even one per cent be impressive? After all, one per cent of the approximately four million children in each age group in school would represent 40,000 persons affected in an important way in a single year.

For such reasons as the above, we have been as cautious about rejecting differences that are not statistically significant as in accepting such differences as evidence of substantial effects. When we have found differences that go in a favorable direction, as has been the case in this study, they may properly be interpreted as palliative. Such effects should be made known to practitioners, policymakers, and researchers conscious of the problem of magnitude in expectations about effects of treatment and service efforts.

From this perspective, consideration of relative costs become important. Whether by deliberate plan or by historical circumstance, resources in the community are directed to one or another objective. Some may go toward vaguely defined objectives, some to those highly specific. For example, much of the professional effort of some agencies may be directed toward helping to achieve a psychological condition for clients deemed desirable, such as "self-realization," "self-actualization," "mental health," or similar notions of the development of personality or personal values. In contrast, the professional effort of other agencies may be directed toward helping clients change their situations and by achieving different statuses affect their psychological functioning and their personal values. An attitude of self-worth might be instilled in a client, on the one hand, through casework treatment or psychotherapy, or, on the other hand, through assistance and direct help in the accomplishment of some goal or the achievement of some status that might result in a feeling of self-worth. The contrast needs to be made clear: in the former approach something is assumed about the need to work on the psyche of the person; in the latter approach, something is assumed about the need to work for a change in the person's situation. Generally, it would seem that the socialization process favors the latter approach since it appears to reward improved status achievements more than improved feelings about oneself. Obviously cause and effect are not separated here, but it is a reasonable supposition that most people define their self-images through their actual or potential achievement of tangible goals rather than through the direct cultivation of favorable self-images.

It may be true that if a girl's ego strength has been increased, she will at some point in life "come through." However, speculation about this is less convincing than would be a demonstration of immediate changes in behavior. In the present project we are not able to test long-range effects of agency services; it is conceivable that they may not be evident until later when in some way a knowledge of alternatives presented and values discussed with a caseworker or a group therapist might be reflected in broader perspective and greater wisdom. This possibility needs to be balanced against that of producing a more direct change in some immediate, practical situation. For example, assistance in obtaining a job, or help that would lead to a high school diploma, may create a set of situational expectations that can determine many attitudes, including those that bear on the behavior, the aspirations, and the achievements of the girl in the present and the future. We do not ignore the possibility that psychological changes may be necessary before social situational changes can be achieved. But this cannot be assumed to be the case. It seems to us equally plausible to argue that cause and effect occur in the opposite direction. We do note, however, that the change efforts of most social workers, including those in this project, have been primarily—almost exclusively—guided by the former assumption and therefore little effort has been directed toward immediate situational changes.

The design of the present research unquestionably neglects the possibility of long-range effects. But likewise the service program has relatively neglected the practical aspects of this period of adolescence. Is it not possible that explicit attention to the immediate problems of getting through school and receiving a high school diploma, of learning how to apply for and get a job, of practice in social behaviors relevant to adequate marriages, and other immediate conditions might help to achieve statuses that themselves generate socially desirable expectations and behaviors? Rather than concentrate almost entirely on self-understanding and attitudes and feelings, might not professional efforts be directed to the situations of family, peer-group, school, and workplace which form, or at least sustain, the psychological conditions of these clients? Should we expect weekly interviews with caseworkers, or weekly counseling sessions in groups, to have critical effects when situational conditions were hardly touched?

We do not suggest that procedures for manipulating the social situations of clients are readily available or demonstrably effective. Rather, we suggest that a serious professional task for social work is to develop intervention procedures in such systems. The achievement per unit cost of effort and resources invested in the type of treatment represented by this project does not encourage us to believe that it is the most efficacious. Unless we are to abandon hope that more than the barest results can be achieved by professional effort, we must develop other ways of helping. These, in turn, will require different conceptions of how to achieve the desirable goals we seek.

IMPLICATIONS

This line of argument bears on the nature of attempts to change clients such as this present project included. Impact should be considered in terms of behavior and status consequences. Indirect efforts through influences on internal psychological states do not seem to have had such consequences. The results of attempts to effect social conditions directly should be put to the test.

Although the analysis of how changes in persons occur is far from established or elaborated in scientific theory, we may make some pragmatic observations that support an approach through attention to immediate, practical situations. Radical changes are infrequent; small and gradual changes are more common than dramatic ones in learning social behavior. Exposure to successful or desirable social forms would seem to precede learning them. Thus changes tend to reflect the proximate and they tend cumulatively to appear gradual rather than episodic and dramatic. What is proximate for the kinds of girls in this project? Their families, their neighborhoods, their friends, their schoolmates and teachers, their jobs and their employers. Is it not through these— in short, the social systems that contain these girls—that we may achieve changes? Should it not be with reference to these that we determine the proximate goals for change? A girl from a social setting of little education may more realistically be helped if she achieves the immediate goal of educational betterment to which she is exposed by being in school. An attempt to help her achieve a psychological orientation exemplified in a middle-class style of life may not be realistic, since she is unlikely to be exposed to the patterns of behavior that support and reflect this orientation. Helping her to get through school by material or other assistance may seem to be a minimal objective, but failure to achieve this may preclude many other desirable goals. In setting priorities of goals, the achievement of proximate, practical advancements may well be considered the most therapeutic.

The argument for a broader social perspective in the attack on potentially deviant careers does not require the abandonment of interventions at the level of individual psychological states. It implies, rather, the recognition of multiple and interrelated levels of possible intervention. We believe that this project has offered a reasonable assessment of effects that can be achieved by conscientious, skilled, professional counseling directed toward psychological changes. To be sure, more intensive psychotherapeutic treatment procedures are known which have not been tested in our research, but most of them depend on types of relationships for which the high school girls in this project seemed least accessible. Whether individual or group, such treatment procedures do not seem feasible. Although replications of studies to evaluate individual and group treatment approaches are necessary, we are not encouraged to expect very much success for populations of this sort.

We can understand the modest claims for successful treatment made by the caseworkers as an implicit recognition that other levels of intervention are necessary. The more confident assessments of supervisors and consultants may reflect their greater insulation from aspects of client situations not so clearly evident when the therapeutic setting is the primary focus of observation. The minimal effects found in the evaluative data may result from posing multi-level criteria broader than those of either the caseworkers or their supervisors. Although not reported in this study, the caseworkers themselves appear to use objective criteria of successful outcome in their assessments even if these are not explicit in their treatment perspective. Thus clients who were seen to change positively were those whose behavioral statuses—progress through school, good grades, avoiding such difficulties as truancy and pregnancy out of wedlock, and the like—were more positive. It would seem appropriate to point change efforts toward conditions directly affecting situations determining these outcomes as well as toward changes in the clients themselves.

If multi-level attacks are to be utilized, two models of service programs, or some combination of these models, can be suggested. Each social worker might seek to operate at various levels, from psychological influences through manipulations of interpersonal and environmental conditions. Or various agencies might seek to coordinate efforts at various levels on behalf of the clients, constructing a comprehensive plan for achieving change. Neither of these models is foreign to the traditions of social work; indeed they are often espoused. Each of them presents difficulties in execution that require imaginative changes in the present systems of providing services. They implicate conceptions of professional social work practice that include many intervention points and differentiated change strategies. Such conceptions are implicit in the view of casework as concerned with the total situation of the client and in the view of social work as an attempt to achieve social change in order to enhance the effective functioning of clients.

We cannot assert that comprehensive, multi-level programs will necessarily succeed. They have not been widely tried or rigorously evaluated. The broad-gauged programs of delinquency control and prevention now being attempted and the groping efforts to conceive and execute comprehensive "community mental health programs" are developments that should teach us much if they are carefully assessed.

Evaluation of multi-level programs will present many difficulties. Adaptations of experimental designs as well as development of new measures of influences and outcomes will be necessary. These will challenge social researchers as much as the devising of comprehensive programs of service will challenge practitioners. There will need to be extensive collaboration of social scientists and social workers to develop forms of intervention that are theoretically based and testable through valid research.

The implications we have drawn from the project described in this book are not intended to devalue either the conscientious efforts now made by social workers or the utility of the type of evaluative research here reported. Only by exposing both practitioners and researchers to the painful experience of testing their best efforts can they proceed to new approaches and new methods that may promise more success.

NOTES TO CHAPTER IX

1. See Shyne, Ann W., "Evaluation of Results in Social Work," *Social Work*, vol. 8, October, 1963, pp. 26–33.

2. Meyer, Henry J., and Edgar F. Borgatta, *An Experiment in Mental Patient Rehabilitation.* Russell Sage Foundation, New York, 1959, p. 106.

3. *Ibid.*, pp. 105–106.

4. Hyman, Herbert H., Charles R. Wright, and Terence K. Hopkins in *Applications of Methods of Evaluation* (University of California Press, Berkeley, 1962, pp. 12–17) have developed at length the importance of "conceptualizing unanticipated consequences."

5. The viewpoint developed here is also suggested by Howard E. Freeman in "The Strategy of Social Policy Research." *The Social Welfare Forum, 1963,* Columbia University Press, New York, 1963, pp. 153–154.

INDEX

Index

ACADEMIC performance during project, 164–166, *table* 165
Ackerman, Nathan W., 147*n*
Activity Groups, 106, 108, 132, 138, 143–144
Adventurous Cyclothymia vs. Withdrawn Schizothymia. *See* JPQ
Affective cohesion in home situation, 68, *table* 69
Anderson, Elizabeth P., 7, 90*n*, 147*n*
Annoyed category. *See* MAST
Anxious category. *See* MAST
Assertive category. *See* MAST
Attendance records during project, 170–171
Avoidant category. *See* MAST

BEHAVIOR: appropriate criteria of, 42–43; inappropriate in group therapy, 105; normal, of girls in unselected groups, 122; psychotic-like, of girls in unselected groups, 124–126
Behavior ratings by guidance and counseling staff, 174–177, *table* 176
Beloff, H., 50*n*
Beloff, J., 50*n*, 89*n*
Benz, Margaret, 9
Berkowitz, Bernard, 8
Binin, Belle, 9
Blenkner, Margaret, 22*n*, 147*n*
Bockian, Pauline, 8
Borgatta, Edgar F., 22*n*, 50*n*, 204*n*, 217*n*
Brim, Orville G., Jr., 7
Brown, Nathan, 8
Byler, John G., 7

CAPLAN, Gerald, 147*n*
Carmichael, Madeline, 8

Case histories, 112–116, 123–129, 138–144
Casework: 16–18, 19, 90–97, 111–117, *passim;* cases significantly affected by, 114–117; effects of, 151–155, *tables* 151, 153; and group therapy, 96–97, 117–118, 149–155, 205–206, *tables* 149, 150, 151, 153, 154, 155; initial reaction to referred cases, 93–94; involvement in, 95–96, 111–114, 149–151, *table* 149; and parents, 92; prognosticated results of, 153–155, *tables* 154, 155; referral from groups to, 108–109, 117–118, 144; schedule of, 92–93
Casework Interview Checksheet, 39–40, 50*n*
Cattell, R. B., 50*n*, 89*n*
Character traits, teacher ratings for, 173–174, *table* 174
Chasan, Evelyn, 8
Collins, Erline, 8
Conduct marks, 172–173
Control group, 15, 18, 23–24, 25, 33–35, 51, *passim;* compared with experimental group by objective criteria, 160–180, *tables* 161, 162, 163, 164, 165, 167, 170, 171, 172, 174, 176, 178; selection of, 26–33
Conventional category. *See* MAST
Coral, Suzanne, 8
Cottrell, Leonard S., Jr., 5, 7
Cox, William H., 8
Cyclothymia vs. Schizothymia. *See* JPQ

DATA-GATHERING procedures, 34, 35, 40–49
Depressive category. *See* MAST
Dickman, Milton, 8
Diller, Juliette C., 8

221

Values & Ethics in Social Work Practice

3rd Edition

Values & Ethics in Social Work Practice

Lester Parrott

Los Angeles | London | New Delhi
Singapore | Washington DC

Series Editors:
Jonathan Parker and Greta Bradley

Learning Matters
An imprint of SAGE Publications Ltd
1 Oliver's Yard
55 City Road
London EC1Y 1SP

SAGE Publications Inc.
2455 Teller Road
Thousand Oaks, California 91320

SAGE Publications India Pvt Ltd
B 1/I 1 Mohan Cooperative Industrial Area
Mathura Road
New Delhi 110 044

SAGE Publications Asia-Pacific Pte Ltd
3 Church Street
#10-04 Samsung Hub
Singapore 049483

Editor: Kate Wharton
Development editor: Lauren Simpson
Production controller: Chris Marke
Project management: Swales & Willis Ltd, Exeter, Devon
Marketing manager: Tamara Navaratnam
Cover design: Wendy Scott
Typeset by: C&M Digitals (P) Ltd, Chennai, India
Printed in Great Britain by Henry Ling Limited at
The Dorset Press, Dorchester, DT1 1HD

Library of Congress Control Number: 2014947110

British Library Cataloguing in Publication data

A catalogue record for this book is available from the British Library

ISBN: 978-1-4462-9387-4
ISBN: 978-1-4462-9388-1 (pbk)

At SAGE we take sustainability seriously. Most of our products are printed in the UK using FSC papers and boards. When we print overseas we ensure sustainable papers are used as measured by the Egmont grading system. We undertake an annual audit to monitor our sustainability.

This new edition is dedicated to my children: Frances, Zoe and Joseph.

Contents

About the author

Lester Parrott is a Lecturer in Social Work at Keele University. He has written a number of books and articles on ethics and values in social work and has just had published *Poverty and Social Work* by Policy Press.

Introduction

Welcome to this new edition of my book. Since the first edition was published, social work has, as ever, faced a number of challenges to its status as a profession. Firstly, the deaths of children such as Daniel Pelka provoked public concern and, as the subsequent public inquiries and serious case reviews show, social work as part of the patchwork of services wrapped around children has much to do to improve its effectiveness. Secondly, the scandals at Winterbourne View showed that, for some learning-disabled people, the public provision of services contracted out to private firms has resulted in poor standards of care and abuse by some of the staff employed by such firms. Thirdly, the further reduction in social work services to older people and the continuing pressure to care for an increasingly older population without the necessary resources to cope mean that home care services have become increasingly rationed to the most serious cases. Fourthly, mental health services are near collapse as social workers struggle to support people with mental health problems in the community, resulting in the admission of people into hospital. Finally, challenges from the Coalition government, which is intent on further privatising as many aspects of public provision as it can, has led to discussions as to the feasibility of privatising children's services, including child protection.

Social workers must face these challenges and do their best within a climate that is increasingly unsettled. The consequence for social workers is that they have become further regulated by managerial procedures and policies which seek to cover responsibility for actions whilst limiting the scope of social workers to deal flexibly and effectively with the problems they confront. Therefore, the values and principles of human rights and social justice which social workers must uphold become the touchstone by which they can hold on to a sense of mission to create decent lives for the people they serve. To be allowed to work with people when they may not necessarily want you to help them requires social workers to keep a firm grasp upon the reasons why they do the work that they do. It is only the values of human rights and social justice, in my view, that can enable them to do so.

This new edition has some changes which reflect the new environment in which social work finds itself and, therefore, any application of social work ethics and values must take account of the existing social context. To this end, Chapter 1 sets out this context as applied to social work. The following chapters remain faithful to the spirit of the first edition but the material has been updated and amended where I felt it appropriate. Chapter 2 then considers the core of social work – anti-oppressive practice – whilst Chapter 3 considers the different ethical approaches taken to apply social work ethics in practice. Chapter 4 deals with the issue of professional accountability; the recent events at Stafford Hospital and the subsequent Francis Report are included in this chapter to highlight some of the issues raised when professionals decide to blow the whistle on dangerous practice in the organisations that employ them.

Chapter 5 discusses the issue of risk in social work and how risk, which is often managed through the application of models of risk assessment, has become an issue that is almost exclusively discussed in terms of risk avoidance. This has the consequence of producing social work which takes the path of least resistance and in which the notion of a risk as an opportunity as well as a threat is removed from the conversation. The impact of restricting the autonomy of people who use social work services then becomes a serious problem when assessments of the social circumstances of individuals seek to remove all risk from their lives.

Chapter 6 looks at the issue of advocacy and the conflicts and dilemmas faced by social workers if they decide to advocate on behalf of service users. This issue has taken on increased significance with the appointment of advocates within mental health services as a result of the Mental Capacity Act in 2005, in considering the best interests of service users and the decision to deprive individuals of their liberty.

Chapter 7 considers the ethics of working in partnership and suggests that there are particular ethical issues which require serious consideration when working with others. It requires a commitment to be open and transparent when working together which, again, may pose serious ethical conflicts and dilemmas, for example, when to share information about a service user with another professional, which may involve issues of confidentiality.

Chapter 8 deals with the ethical challenges of working within social work organisations and asks you to consider what the proper balance is between following rules of procedure and the exercise of professional discretion. Such guidelines, at their most effective, try, for example, to create fair rules of access to services. However, when a social worker may assess that a person requires a service, even though the individual may not fit the criteria, how should he/she respond?

Finally, Chapter 9 is a new chapter which argues that social work has to understand the process of globalisation. There will be service users who move to the United Kingdom who may have quite diverse cultural requirements which are not necessarily accommodated by social work services or who, in some cases, hold values which may be antithetical to social work's mission to uphold human rights and social justice for all.

In my view, for social work to be effective, it has to reflect upon itself continually to determine how well it is achieving its mission. Individual social workers in turn must engage in this process in order to overcome organisational and professional inertia; to stand still using the same tried and tested approaches is not an option if those approaches are not subject to regular evaluation, reflection and scrutiny. I have planned this new edition as a reflection of such a process. I hope you will enjoy engaging with the issues presented within these pages and I would value any feedback which you might want to give, so please do not hesitate to contact me via my email address at Keele University: l.parrott@keele.ac.uk.

Chapter 1
The context of social work practice

Social work has been subject to much criticism by the media, successive governments and service user groups. In response to a succession of scandals involving the abuse of adults, for example, at Winterbourne View, and a number of child deaths, such as Daniel Pelka, social work and social work education have been perceived as failing to respond appropriately to the needs of service users and failing to prepare social work students adequately for the practical realities of social work. There has been a plethora of government-sponsored reports scanning both the previous Labour and the current Coalition government and commentaries from professional bodies, such as the British Association of Social Workers (BASW), suggesting a range of remedies to solve such seemingly intractable problems. Examples of recent reports include:

- **All Party Parliamentary Group on Social Work** (2013) *Inquiry into the state of social work*. **http://cdn.basw.co.uk/upload/basw_90352-5.pdf**

- **British Association of Social Workers** (2012) *The state of social work survey.* **www.basw.co.uk/resource**

- **British Association of Social Workers** (2012) *Voices from the frontline.* **www.basw.co.uk/resource/?id=499**

- **Croisdale-Appleby, D** (2014) *Re-visioning social work education: An independent review.* **www.gov.uk/government/uploads/system/uploads/attachment_data/file/285788/DCA_Accessible.pdf**

- **Macalister, J** (2012) *Frontline: Improving the children's social work profession*. **www.ippr. org/publication/55/9705/frontline-improving-the-childrens-social-work-profession**

- **Munro, E** (2011) *The Munro review of child protection: Final report, a child-centred system*. London: The Stationery Office.

- **Nairey, M** (2014) *Making the education of social workers consistently effective*. London: Department for Education.

- **Social Work Reform Board** (2010) *Building a safe and confident future: One year on*. London: Department for Education.

This blizzard of reports shows just how concerned government and sections of wider society are about the nature of social work. It also asks us as practitioners and students to think clearly about the role and purpose of social work. In particular, in the light of such criticism it requires us to be very clear as to what principles should inform our practice. It therefore involves a very serious consideration of the ethical principles which underpin the work that we do. In essence, social workers who are very skilled and knowledgeable will not be successful in helping people who use social work services unless they have a clear idea as to what the purpose of their intervention should be. An appreciation of the ethical and values implications of social work intervention will enable us to know why we are intervening in the way that we are and on what basis we are deploying our knowledge to achieve a satisfactory outcome for the people we are employed to help. Michael Gove, former Minister for Education, whilst arguably being 'appreciative' of the role of social workers and what some social workers achieve, is also highly critical of the state of social work practice and education. In a speech to the National Society for the Prevention of Cruelty to Children he had this to say on the subject:

> In too many cases, social work training involves idealistic students being told that the individuals with whom they will work have been disempowered by society. They will be encouraged to see these individuals as victims of social injustice whose fate is overwhelmingly decreed by the economic forces and inherent inequalities which scar our society.

> This analysis is, sadly, as widespread as it is pernicious. It robs individuals of the power of agency and breaks the link between an individual's actions and the consequences. It risks explaining away substance abuse, domestic violence and personal irresponsibility, rather than doing away with them.

> Social workers overly influenced by this analysis not only rob families of a proper sense of responsibility, they also abdicate their own. They see their job as securing the family's access to services provided by others, rather than helping them to change their own approach to life. Instead of working with individuals to get them to recognise harmful patterns of behaviour, and improve their own lives, some social workers acquiesce in or make excuses for these wrong choices.

(Gove, 2013)

A BASW survey (2012) of just over 1000 social workers found that social workers were being stretched to breaking point, with 77 per cent reporting unmanageable caseloads as demand for services escalates. In addition, pressures on services for adults were reflected in 69 per cent of social workers reporting that their local authority had further limited the criteria for receiving services at home, resulting in a revolving door of admission and readmission to NHS care.

The impression given by Gove suggests some social workers are gullible fools operating with too many abstract ideas about the nature of service users' problems which deny any responsibility to service users for the problems they experience. It is one thing to suggest that service users are at the complete mercy of social forces outside their control, which for many (despite Gove's assertions) is the case; to deny that people should take responsibility for their own actions is something completely different. In essence, it would appear that Gove moves in the opposite direction, assuming that social factors should not be accounted for in cases such as drug misuse, child neglect and so on. His approach is informed by an individualistic ethos which, in particular, accepts that the nature of people's problems and the amelioration of such problems rest solely with individuals themselves. An example of this approach comes from Gove's statements regarding the use of foodbanks: he has suggested that the pressures faced by families having recourse to foodbanks were *often the result of decisions that they have taken which mean they are not best able to manage their finances* (House of Commons, 2014).

REFLECTION POINT

How far do you feel people are the authors of their own circumstances?

This is a very complex question and social philosophers have argued constantly about the precise relationship between the choices individuals make and the conditions which may influence the choices they make. In the social sciences this is usually described as the relationship between social structure, that is, the recurrent patterned arrangements which influence or limit the choices and opportunities available, and our agency as human beings, that is, the opportunity and capability of persons to act independently to make their own free choices. As you develop your understanding of social issues you may change your understanding of this relationship. It is interesting to note that research presented to the House of Commons (2014) lists a number of factors outside individual choice that influence foodbank use. Some of these factors are as follows.

Food prices

Food prices in the UK (including non-alcoholic drinks) rose by 11 per cent in real terms between 2007 and 2013.

Reductions in earnings from work

The economic downturn has also had a significant impact on those in work. Average UK weekly earnings increased by 1 per cent in the period December 2012 to February 2013, compared to the same period a year previously. This equates to an earnings cut in real terms as inflation (as measured by the Consumer Prices Index) was 2.8 per cent from February 2012 to February 2013.

Benefit conditionality and sanctions

Benefit claimants deemed not to be satisfying the conditions for entitlement to benefit may find that their benefit payment is temporarily suspended or reduced, or their claim 'disallowed'. Figures published by the Department for Work and Pensions (2014) on 15 May 2013 show that the number of Jobseeker's Allowance sanctions and disallowances increased from 279,840 in 2001 to 684,030 in 2010, with the main increase happening after 2006.

Impact of incorrect sanctioning

Under the current regime, in 2012 as many as 68,000 people on Jobseeker's Allowance had their benefits taken away by mistake and faced unnecessary hardship as a result (House of Commons, 2014). In addition, some examples of how claimants will lose money as a result of reform to the social security system, including the introduction of Universal Credit, are given below.

Parents of disabled children who formerly received Disability Living Allowance get a 'disability element' top-up to their Child Tax Credit of £53.62 per week for each disabled child. This money is used to pay for the additional costs involved in bringing up a disabled child, like wear and tear to clothes and equipment. Within Universal Credit, the equivalent 'disability addition' will fall to £26.75 per week.

Changes to Housing Benefit Bedroom Tax

Working-age claimants who are deemed to have a spare bedroom in their council or housing association home are faced with a reduction in their housing benefit. Those affected persons claiming housing benefit faced these reductions from 1 April 2013. The government hopes this will force tenants to move to a smaller property to free up larger properties for families. The government's own impact assessment describes that affected households will lose between £13 and £14 per week, with some 40,000 households losing all their entitlement to housing benefit.

Impact of Universal Credit

Brewer et al. (2012) have produced a preliminary analysis of the likely winners and losers as a result of the introduction of the Universal Credit scheme. From the analysis not everyone on low incomes will benefit from these changes. The analysis assumes full take-up of benefits under the old regime and under Universal Credit. Overall, out of some 6.4 million families, 1.4 million families will lose out.

(All examples from Parrott, 2014)

Given these examples (and more could be provided), it is clear that, irrespective of individuals' ability to affect their own circumstances, changes in social security policy far beyond the influence of individuals to alter will result in claimants receiving less money to live on than previously. It is not surprising that the leading foodbank charity, the Trussell Trust, in its report for 2014 observed:

> *Trussell Trust foodbanks gave emergency food to 346,992 people nationwide in 2012–13 financial year, 170 per cent more than the previous year – the biggest increase since the charity began. One third of those helped were children – 76 per cent increase in numbers of foodbanks launched in past year. In the last 12 months alone we have launched over 150 foodbanks nationwide. The exceptional need, a growing awareness of foodbanks and our highly effective social franchising model has enabled the Trussell Trust to launch three new foodbanks per week, compared to two per week in the previous year. We currently have almost 350 foodbanks launched nationwide.*
>
> (Trussell Trust, 2014)

The weight of evidence using the example of food poverty suggests that forces beyond the immediate influence of individuals are clearly placing more and more people into food poverty. Nonetheless, an individualistic philosophy argues that society has less responsibility for the problems people face and that we as citizens owe little to one another. This has the effect of weakening the social ties and social support that we all rely upon in certain stages of our lives. Within the welfare sector, services which were previously provided on a social basis through the provision of state and local authority services, social work and social care services are increasingly put out to tender to the private and voluntary sectors. The 'social' element of 'social work' is therefore subject to a concerted assault, which undermines the collective provision of services which individuals in general are unable to provide for themselves. As society is increasingly atomised, then the nature of social problems is seen as emanating from a lack of responsibility of individuals rather than the retreat of the social, understood here as the retreat of the state from protecting citizens against such social harms as unemployment, poor health and homelessness (Kwong Kam, 2012).

These developments present challenges to social workers, whose professional vocation is to work towards social justice for those groups of people who are unable to achieve this of their own volition.

In any consideration of ethics and values in social work then the social, economic and political context in which social work operates is crucial in influencing what is ethically possible or what is ethically desirable. An ethic of individualism will, if not challenged, prove significant in shaping the way social workers understand their duties and responsibilities. This book will consider these issues to be critical in any development of ethical practice for social workers and will challenge such an ethic when it becomes an impediment for effective social work practice. People who use social work services have a right to be treated as individuals with their own history and their own particular understandings of the world in which they live. People who use social work services also have a right to be treated fairly through a consideration of social justice. In other words, how their problems may not be dissimilar to others when, for example, millions experience unemployment as a result of the recent global economic crisis. In the UK this has led governments, for example, to increase sanctions against unemployed and disabled people through the withdrawal of benefit or a reduction in supporting services. A famous sociologist, C. Wright Mills, had this to say about such problems:

> *When, in a city of 100,000, only one man (sic) is unemployed, that is his personal trouble, and for its relief we properly look to the character of the man, his skills, and his immediate opportunities. But when in a nation of 50 million employees, 15 million men are unemployed, that is an issue, and we may not hope to find its solution within the range of opportunities open to any one individual.*

(Mills, 1959, p9)

Social work has been defined in a number of ways by professional groups representing social workers; look at the definition below, adopted by the International Federation of Social Workers (IFSW). This definition has also been accepted by professional associations of social work across the world (including BASW in the UK).

Definition

> *The social work profession promotes social change, problem solving in human relationships and the empowerment and liberation of people to enhance well-being. Utilising theories of human behaviour and social systems, social work intervenes at the points where people interact with their environments. Principles of human rights and social justice are fundamental to social work.*

(http://ifsw.org/policies/definition-of-social-work)

REFLECTION POINT

Does this definition define social work as only concerned with individuals separate from their environment and society?

As you can see from this definition, social workers across the world define social work as both involving human relationships and well-being and also understood within a wider social context. This means that social workers should therefore understand that their intervention focuses upon the interaction between people and their environment. Recent critics other than Gove have sought to undermine this focus and the Nairey Report (2014), which investigated the appropriateness of social work education for children and families, had this to say about the IFSW definition:

It's not that it's an appalling definition. But in terms of describing the work of a Children's Social Worker in England it is, I would argue, thoroughly inadequate. We need a more satisfactory and relevant definition. And we need a definition that concentrates on that work, generally carried out in the statutory sector, which is about protecting children.

(Nairey, p13)

Nairey does not elaborate on why he thinks the IFSW's definition is inadequate and in general provides little evidence of sufficient quality to suggest what should be included in the definition that he is seeking.

This book takes the IFSW definition as one which best encapsulates the profession of social work and will ask you at all times when considering your ethical practice to think about how ethical practice can best be understood within the context of the interaction between individuals' circumstances related to the wider social context in which they find themselves.

Markets and managerialism

In terms of understanding the context of service users' lives, we have argued that social work has to see people as situated in the social environment and look for solutions to the problems in the way that they experience these as involving an interaction between the individual and social level. Increasingly, as has been argued above, social work has to work alongside the private and voluntary sectors. Social work is, on the one hand, increasingly involved in brokering services on behalf of people, for example, around the personalisation of services. In addition, there is a continuing narrowing of its responsibilities towards protection of adults and children in terms of safeguarding.

These two central tasks involve:

1. an understanding of the way services which have been privatised involve the role of markets in delivering social work, creating service users as consumers of services;

2. an understanding of how social work is now controlled by the belief that the close monitoring of individuals to protect them from harm is the only feasible approach to keeping people safe.

Underpinning both of these approaches is the pervasive control of social workers by a burgeoning managerial ideology. This belief in the ultimate efficacy of management is assumed to lead to better outcomes in terms of an increased efficiency and effectiveness in service delivery. Many critics (for example, James, 2004; Rogowski, 2011) see these claims as chimerical, undermining the professional expertise of social workers and diminishing effective contact with service users. Social workers and service users are therefore subject to an increasing commodification of their interactions through the market and a cumulative increase in the procedures which police their face-to-face practice relationships.

Definitions

- Commodification is the transformation of goods and services, as well as ideas or other entities that normally may not be considered goods, into a commodity that is something which is bought and sold in a market. For example, social care in the form of support to live independently is increasingly rationed so that more service users are paying for their own home care.

- A market is the place where buyers and sellers of a specific good or service come together in order to facilitate an exchange. In the context of social work the local authority which employs the social worker will purchase social care services from a range of providers in the area. The social worker, after assessing a person's needs, will then access a particular service for which either the service user will pay or it will be provided by the local authority. Who pays is usually determined by assessing the ability of the service user to pay, usually described as a means test.

- Managerialism gives priority to the managerial and economic concerns of service funders and providers, focusing on service costs and efficiencies. Some social workers believe this is at the cost of direct face-to-face work with clients. With consumerism, managerialism further promotes service provision by non-state agencies. The role of the social worker moves towards assessment of individuals' needs and the regulation of services delivered. Although the service user is seen less as a 'client' whose needs are determined by a professional perspective, there is nevertheless concern that managerialism as it applies to social work attaches more importance to budgets and targets than to meeting the particular needs of individuals. The managerialist approach removes much frontline social work from professionally qualified social workers and allows service provision to be determined by the market (Asquith et al., 2005).

- With consumerism there is a shift towards the client becoming a consumer able to choose services, rather than being merely a recipient of them at the discretion or judgement of the social worker. The market becomes an important and powerful force in the availability of services to meet needs and the balance of the relationship between social worker and consumer begins to look less hierarchical. However, the relationship is still biased in favour of the social worker because of his/her authority to carry out assessments and knowledge of what the market has to offer. Protection for the consumer is very limited (Asquith et al., 2005).

Having defined these terms, it is important to understand that these particular terms have been closely related to the way in which society has been transformed by a particular from of capitalism, known as neo-liberal capitalism (Harvey, 2005).

What is neo-liberal capitalism?
All areas of life dominated by the organisation of the market

This means that we see ourselves as individuals whose role in life is to maximise our self-interest both in the market as consumers as well as in our private and social relationships. Self-interest dominates over other values such as altruism.

The lean state: less state, more private enterprise

This results in the state taking less responsibility for social harms such as unemployment and ill health, and less responsibility for ensuring that children are cared for or that older people can lead a dignified life in old age. The social programmes that remain are residualised, providing a basic low level of support. If individuals require more than basic care then these functions are privatised so that the quality of care that people receives becomes increasingly tied to their capacity to be consumers of, and therefore purchasers of, such services.

Economic globalisation

This relates to the promotion of free trade throughout the world and the removal of duties and tariffs which prevent free trade between countries. It also encompasses the idea that national economies have to compete for inward investment from the major corporations, resulting in a lowering of social protection (e.g. levels and environmental standards to reduce levels of taxation seen as costs to business, which prevent them from investing in states with higher levels of taxation).

Deregulation

Deregulation does not mean the removal of state regulation. It does mean the use of such regulation to support competitive economic performance and profit from capital. Where regulations are seen to hamper the profit motive, for example, hours of work, health and safety or environmental regulations, then they are limited. An example of this is zero-hours contracts, where it is estimated that some 300,000 care workers are employed on such terms.

The problems of free unregulated markets can be explained by the next exercise, which asks you to think of a society which is devoid of any intervention by the state in regulating how markets operate. Individuals are free to make whatever choices they want, to purchase those things which will make them happy. Our example is taken from residential care. Let us assume that some people will choose to purchase residential care for themselves when they can no longer remain living independently in their own homes. The assumption is that people are, therefore, free to purchase residential care for themselves and that there is no regulation to ensure the quality of care in the residential homes in which they reside. The only regulation is with individual purchasers who can, if they find the quality of the care to be deficient, move to another home where they consider the care to be of their liking.

In neo-liberal capitalism, the individual is perceived as someone who has unlimited choice dependent upon his or her economic resources. The theory underpinning such celebration of choice is called rational choice theory, which identifies that all action is fundamentally 'rational' in character and that people calculate the likely costs and benefits of any action before deciding what to do. Ultimately, people's decisions are motivated by self-interest in which they seek to maximise their utility (happiness). This theory has strong links with utilitarianism, as we shall see in Chapter 3.

In choosing residential care, people are required to have all the necessary information as to what residential care facility optimises their preferences. So, what does it mean to make an informed choice in this way?

What does it mean to make an informed choice?

What is required in order to make a choice?

1. Knowledge of what residential care is;

2. Knowledge of alternatives that may be available both in terms of alternative homes and other alternatives like domiciliary care;

3. Time to make the choice;

4. Ability to make the choice:

   (a) intellectual capacity;

   (b) emotional/psychological capacity;

   (c) economic capacity;

   (d) cultural capacity;

   (e) social capacity.

Given the criteria for making an informed choice in relation to residential care, imagine the following. There is no state-organised residential care and there is no outside inspection or control over private residential care homes. The ideology that prevails relies upon the marketplace, where entrepreneurs decide to set up residential care homes and consumers rationally choose which home is best for them and pay accordingly.

ACTIVITY **1.1**

Heathlands is a privately run residential care home for older people with a range of dependency needs. Some residents remain active, whereas others have limited mobility. Some residents have relatives and friends who visit but the older and/or the more physically/mentally impaired tend not to have any contact with family or friends. There has been a recent change in ownership of the home and some family members have

Continued

---

*ACTIVITY **1.1** continued*

seen a lowering in care standards. Examples include some people remaining in urine-soaked beds for a considerable time, poor standards of personal hygiene by the care staff, a lack of choice over diet, fewer social activities being made available and, when activities are presented, extra charges are instituted for them.

- *How might the residents solve this problem from a rational choice point of view?*

- *Can you identify any problems that might arise with this approach using the different criteria required in order to make a choice as outlined above?*

What becomes apparent from this exercise is that the assumptions behind individual choice and the free market are unable to be justified when faced with the barriers that certain consumers of a service may face if they wish to exit from the good they have purchased. In this case, those people with no family or friends to help them and those people who may be physically or mentally disabled will find that they have to continue living in what are, clearly, unsatisfactory circumstances. If we move to our present society and the organisation of residential care, then it is clear that our current position does not reflect an unregulated market. The Care Standards Act (2000) enforces minimum standards in care homes and the Care Quality Commission inspects care homes on a regular basis. However, the process of inspection is not as thorough as it should be and, as Drakeford (2006) has argued, many deficiencies remain. Drakeford cites problems of poor communication between residential care homes and prospective residents whereby, when contracts were agreed, residents did not have the full information regarding what was being offered. For example, residents were unaware that they would have to pay for extras such as leisure outings and entertainment and aspects of personal hygiene such as hair care. So what happens if a care home is deemed to be inadequate or if the owners shut down a home if it is no longer financially viable? Who takes responsibility for the residents? Ultimately, it falls to the local authority to find suitable provision when a home fails.

The White Paper, *Caring for Our Future* (Department of Health, 2012a), identifies that 80 per cent of domiciliary care and 90 per cent of residential care provision is now with the private sector. It is also important to note that the present government wishes to extend the reach of markets even further. The White Paper identifies the Developing Care Markets for Quality and Choice programme, which will enable local authorities to extend their capacity to deliver an expanded market for social care services. In relation to children's services, the government (Department of Education, 2014) is now consulting upon privatising children's services, including child protection, which will radically increase the impetus for privatisation within social work.

> *The quality of privately run care services is generally lower than those run by councils or voluntary organisations, although the costs were often lower as well.*

> (Care Quality Commission, 2011, p58)

The consequences of poor-quality care in the residential care sector means that those who can afford to choose which care home they reside in are able to access better-quality homes. Studies of people living in residential care show that people from poorer backgrounds are more likely to become residents than those with greater financial resources. Indeed, those service users who have little or no saved income are therefore likely to be provided with residential care that meets minimum standards, and will have less choice in determining the care home in which to reside.

Tronto (2010) argues from an ethic of care perspective (see Chapter 3) and argues that institutions which are increasingly developed upon market principles result in the decline of standards of care. Competition between providers may be useful to motivate providers into more cost-effective ways of providing care but does not necessarily enable standards of care to be delivered. The norms of market behaviour mean that competition focuses providers to compete on the basis of cost or quantity as opposed to the quality of care provided. Heffernan (2014), in an extensive consideration of the place of competition in our lives, suggests that it has a deleterious effect upon the kinds of relationships and institutions upon which we rely:

> *our outsize veneration of competition has left us ill equipped to solve the problems it has created. If we are to invent new ways to live and work together, we need high levels of trust and give and take: attributes that competition specifically and subtly corrodes.*

(p xiii)

This process is further exacerbated by the way local authorities are required to fund social care for those unable to pay for it themselves. Thus they are required to contract social care out to private and voluntary providers. Since local authorities are under increasing pressure to cut services as their funding from central government is cut, in turn there is less funding to buy in quality care. In addition, local authorities try to make up some of this shortfall by increasing charges for social care. This has meant, as Age UK has argued, that funding of social care has been progressively reduced.

The financial demands on older people who receive care are increasing. In real terms, charges were £150 per year more in 2010–11 than in 2009–10 for each older person using local authority care services and £360 more than in 2008–09.

The spending decisions taken by the Coalition Government mean that frontline services have not been protected. Councils have reduced their spending on older people's social care by £671 million in real terms in the year between 2010–11 and 2011–12. This is a decrease of over 8 per cent.

Taking into account growing demand as well, the gap is even greater. In order to maintain the care system at the same level as in 2010 (before current spending cuts) expenditure on older people's social care should be £7.8 billion in 2011–12. This year (2012) total spending is only £7.3 billion. Even making allowances for efficiency gains, this has left a total shortfall of £500 million.

(Age UK, 2014)

The political philosopher Sandel (2012) has argued passionately that the reach of markets and market-oriented thinking into areas of life previously governed by non-market norms is one of the most significant and worrying developments of our time. He argues that the development of markets and competition is worrying because of two reasons, one concerning inequality and the second corruption.

Inequality

In the UK, inequality is already high and is expected to rise from 2013 (Cribb et al., 2013) as benefit levels are cut and incomes are set to rise, particularly at the top end of income earners. Those with greater levels of income therefore have the ability to buy such consumer goods that they wish but, in addition, are able to use their buying power to greater advantage when social goods such as health care, housing, a safe neighbourhood and education all become more commodified. Pickett and Wilkinson (2009) highlight the pernicious effect inequality has upon society's general well-being. They document, through a careful analysis, the impact inequality has upon those countries where it is highest, leading to higher levels of a range of social problems, such as poor physical and mental health, crime and obesity, to identify just a few examples.

Corruption

Putting a price on certain goods corrodes their integrity because they reflect certain attitudes towards the good being purchased. For example, by giving incentives to parents to adopt children, are we corroding the idea of parenthood and the value we place upon children (see Activity 1.2 below)?

Social work and social care have come under increasing media and government scrutiny to become more efficient and more effective. Media interest inevitably focuses upon the recurring problems within hard-pressed local authority children and families departments, which have left some children unprotected from serious abuse, as the many inquiries into child deaths in recent years have reported (Rogowski, 2011). This can lead to the 'demonisation' of both social workers (Ayre, 2001) and the service users they work with, as the news media seek to create 'newsworthy' stories and controversy. Ayre analysed some 30 years of media reportage in relation to child deaths and concluded that, between the 1970s and 1990s, the coverage of child abuse scandals in England and Wales led to aggressive, and often inaccurate, reporting in the mass media of those child welfare agencies deemed responsible for the deaths of the children involved. In his view, this has resulted in a climate of fear, which seeks to blame and scapegoat the families and social workers involved rather than find constructive solutions. The sum total of this reporting has led Stanford (2010) to argue that there is now a more reactive response from social work agencies which seek to cover and absolve their practice from risk of blame by instituting more defensive practices within children and families teams, often to the detriment of the children and families they are trying to help.

Governments have, in turn, responded to media criticism and genuine public concern by introducing more complex management systems to try and ensure that children are protected. However, recent government-sponsored reports such as that by Munro (2011) have recognised the dilemma of increasing the complexity of systems, leading to more bureaucracy and paperwork for social workers, which have, in turn, diminished face-to-face contact with service users.

The Munro review's first report in October 2010 described the child protection system in recent times as one that has been shaped by four key driving forces:

1. the importance of the safety and welfare of children and young people and the understandably strong reaction when a child is killed or seriously harmed;

2. a commonly held belief that the complexity and associated uncertainty of child protection work can be eradicated;

3. a readiness, in high-profile public inquiries into the death of a child, to focus on professional error without looking deeply enough into its causes; and

4. the undue importance given to performance indicators and targets which provide only part of the picture of practice, and which have skewed attention to process over the quality and effectiveness of help given.

These forces have come together to create a defensive system that puts so much emphasis on procedures and recording that insufficient attention is given to developing and supporting the expertise to work effectively with children, young people and families.

(Munro, 2011: Executive Summary)

As Munro identifies above, social workers have become less able to use their skills in creative ways but are required to focus on standardised practice, such as unified assessment procedures in the form of assessment frameworks. When social workers are not encouraged to follow narrow assessment protocols they are required to become managers of resources through the reforms introduced in the wake of the National Health Service and Community Care Act 1990. These developments have led many writers to suggest that current social work practice becomes a rational technical activity. This means that social work is becoming an activity which is increasingly subject to managerial direction, working towards strictly determined practice policy and procedure which has as its goal the control of professional judgement and discretion. It defines social work as the rational application of such procedures in which questions of value become less important than what is achieved in terms of managerially determined service outcomes. In this view, social work is not about the quality of the service provided but about the quantity, i.e. the outcome, because outcomes can be measured. This distorts many aspects of social work, for example, the quality of the relationships social workers forge with service users, because managerially they are less important as they are less easily measured.

This process is presented as a natural development to increase the efficiency and effectiveness of social work and therefore appears to be value-free and neutral. But this claim to neutrality has been used to wrest power from social workers to define and control the nature of their work. Managerial ideas and business-like solutions to essentially practical and moral problems faced by social workers marginalise professional and service user contributions to social work, and undermine the value base of social work. Harris (2003) argues that this process is circular in that competition requires monitoring through contract specification that leads to the need for performance measurement to monitor the effectiveness of contracts, which requires increased managerial scrutiny (Figure 1.1).

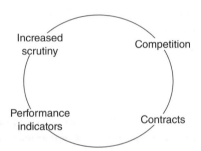

Figure 1.1   Controlling social work: the management and business cycle

- Increased scrutiny. Information technology systems allow detailed specification of social work activities and checks on their completion. Much of this control is expressed in computerised manuals, directions and guidelines that limit discretion.

- Performance indicators. Business-oriented measurable standards and pre-set standardised and repetitive systems with tightly defined criteria for eligibility for services.

- Contracts. The use of contracts ensures that control resides with the purchaser who has the power to make decisions and see them carried through. The provider has to implement the purchaser's decisions, which are often determined in advance from a limited list, which minimises contact time but calls for more throughput.

- Competition. The belief that competition among providers results in more economical, efficient and effective services (adapted from Harris, 2003).

There is a danger that the process of social work can become a series of unrelated activities which prevent practice from being subject to ethical and theoretical scrutiny. As Parton and O'Byrne (2000) state:

even prescriptive assessment and monitoring schedules require interpretation and judgement to be made practical.

(p31)

Social work is better described as a practical–moral activity. This means that social workers hold a privileged position within the public services in working with people who often experience profound problems and significant crises in their lives which require practical solutions but have important moral consequences. This requires social workers to exercise their judgement in informal settings and work in more informal ways. Effective social work is mostly carried out in people's homes and involves negotiation in which problems are jointly identified and then worked through by agreement with service users. Thus social workers are dealing with the practical activities of day-to-day living; for example, how can parents enable their children to thrive? How can older people who may have a disability live a dignified life in old age where they can get the support needed to live independently? These day-to-day activities require social workers to make significant decisions that have a profound ethical consequence. So if, for example, parents are failing to parent their children, what actions ought the social worker to take in order to work in the best interests of the child? Does the social worker remove the child? Does the social worker work with the parents? These problems challenge us to reflect upon our morality and our ethics as social workers.

ACTIVITY 1.2

Below is an example of how business thinking, particularly marketing, is influencing social work practice. The extract below is taken from a government website encouraging more people to become adoptive parents. Do you agree with offering incentives to possible adopters?

The adoption passport: a support guide for adopters

Children adopted from care can have ongoing needs and you and your child may benefit from support. Local authorities provide a range of support services for adopters and their children. Every adopter is entitled to advice about these services, and you are entitled to an assessment of your needs at any time. If you have adopted a child in England you may also be entitled to:

- *free early education for your child from the age of two (from September 2014);*
- *choose which school best meets your child's needs;*
- *priority access to council housing;*
- *Discretionary Housing payments while waiting for your child to be placed with you;*
- *adoption leave and pay when your child is placed with you.*

(First4Adoption, 2013)

On the one hand, you may feel that any initiative which encourages more people to become adoptive parents should be welcome, given that some 4000 children are awaiting suitable adoptive parents at the present time. The Coalition government has voiced similar concerns and has encouraged more private and voluntary-sector adoption agencies to try and overcome what it sees as unnecessary delay. The current adoption process, they argue, emanates from an overcautious and, what they would call, too-stringent approach to matching children in terms of, for example, their ethnicity to prospective adoptive parents. On the other hand, you might question the ethics of providing incentives to potential adopters rather than 'advertising' the benefits of adopting for its own sake and the happiness of the potentially adopted children. We may well question the motives of those who may want to adopt when offered such inducements. Of course, support for adoptive parents is crucial to a successful adoption but the emphasis therefore should be the support provided by the respective agency to help adoptive parents with the potential challenges of parenting an adopted child. Does the end justify the means in this case or is it something about the means chosen (marketing adoption) that can affect the end (quality of the adoptive parent and the happiness of the child)? Higgins and Smith (2002) argue that ultimately marketing children, which includes advertising pictures of children awaiting adoption (Be My Parent, 2013), ultimately turns the children into commodities to be displayed for the consumption of potential adoptive parents.

In highlighting the problems of adoption, what emerges is a conflict between what is considered to be a rational–technical approach to social work and a practical–moral approach (Table 1.1). In particular, there is a conflict in adoption work regarding the appropriate means in enabling more adoptive parents to come forward.

Table 1.1   Rational or practical social work

Rational–technical social work	Practical–moral social work
Management by direction	Management by consultation
Procedurally led services	Focus upon judgement and negotiation between worker and service user to meet need
Danger of early legal/procedural intervention	Legal/procedural intervention as last resort
Resource-focused	Needs-focused
Emphasis on outcomes	Emphasis on process of social work
Limit discretion of social work	Recognises negotiation, flexibility and uncertainty

The challenges which social workers now face in working within an increasingly privatised context of service delivery and increased managerial control over their tasks have developed in some workers what can be called a 'siege mentality'. Social workers feel less valued as professional workers and are treated increasingly as functionaries, called upon to enact the policies and procedures set down for them by their managers. This means in relation to Table 1.1 that the content of their work falls increasingly into a rational–technical mode. There have been a number of surveys looking at how social workers feel about the job they do. A number have been published by *Community Care*, a journal for those working in the social work and social care sector. Surveys of social workers' attitudes to and feelings about their work can be useful barometers to gauge the levels of satisfaction that they feel about the work that they do. A recent survey (McGregor, 2013) carried out involving 650 social workers found the responses shown in Figure 1.2 in relation to what they considered were the barriers preventing them from working effectively.

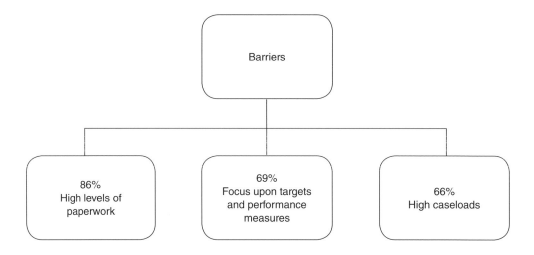

Figure 1.2   Barriers to effective social work practice

Some of the social workers' responses were illuminating as to the impact that the managerial culture had upon them:

> *We are told they know we are overworked but extra staff can't be funded.*

> *You're informed that everyone is in the same position or that others have more cases than you and are not complaining.*

> *I was told I needed to be more organised; it felt like a personal failing and has made me reluctant to raise this again.*

> *It's clear that unmanageable caseloads are endemic in social work and have been for some time. Social workers need to speak out if they cannot cope with their workload and make sure their concerns are clearly documented.*

> *There is a stigma attached to admitting 'I can't cope with this level of work', but it's important for your own wellbeing and that of service users.*

These statements echo the findings of the Munro Report (2011; see the summary in the box above) and as such show the increased dissatisfaction expressed by social workers over the way in which social work has been managed in recent years.

Access at least three social work blogs, including one from a different country to your own. Choose at random any three commentaries from each site and identify both the positive and negative comments in terms of the blogger's experience of social work.

Here are some extracts from a variety of blogs I accessed.

Positives

I loved working with older people, I loved working in mental health – and while I didn't enjoy (you can't ever enjoy) the detention and assessment part of the AMHP [approved mental health professional] role, there was a unique camaraderie with other AMHPs and the access to continued support through forums and legal updates was unrivalled.

I felt I could make a difference to some people's experiences of mental health services by explaining them and guiding them through what was a scary and difficult period of their or their family member's life and if I could take them out the other end, well, there's no better feeling in the world.

(http://fightingmonsters.wordpress.com/2013/09/23/parting-shots-why-i-left-my-social-work-post-and-what-id-change)

On a positive note, however, after six months I feel more confident now in my role and abilities and don't feel like I'm sinking every day. I no longer come home and agonise over whether social work is for me and no longer have quite the same continuous nagging sense of fear. I feel like a valued member of my team and have noticed in recent weeks that I'm no longer the one always asking questions of other colleagues – new staff ask me now and I'm actually able to answer correctly too!

I'm still spinning plates on sticks, but it's getting easier!

(http://sw2be.wordpress.com/2011/08)

While AMHPs may nevertheless feel that there is a conflict between their social care values and the concept of compulsion inherent in Community Treatment Orders (CTOs), there is another way of looking at this. What is better? For someone with a severe and enduring mental illness to have an endless cycle of acute hospital admission, recovery and discharge, followed by refusing treatment, deterioration in functioning and consequent compulsory admission, with the damage it can do to relationships with family, friends, employers and loved ones, or to impose a modest degree of compulsion to ensure that the patient accepts treatment, but can then live happily and with relatively little interference in their own home?

(http://themaskedamhp.blogspot.co.uk)

Negatives

But it got harder. We know there were cuts in the service. Despite the government's mealy-mouthed promises about there not being cuts in frontline services – there were cuts in frontline services and significant cuts. I want to explain why I made the decision to leave – and it wasn't a decision I made lightly.

(http://fightingmonsters.wordpress.com/2013/09/23/
parting-shots-why-i-left-my-social-work-post-and-what-id-change)

The transition from being a student to newly qualified was extremely difficult and traumatic. As a student I only ever held approximately five cases and my hand was held all the way. I was totally protected from any overall responsibility and given supervision every week. I had plenty of time to think and reflect, theory was an everyday concept and time was freely available. Then overnight I had a far bigger and more complex caseload, supervision once every month to six weeks, total responsibility and accountability for decisions that have a huge impact on people's lives, and time to reflect or think theory has become a very rare commodity (if not extinct!).

(http://sw2be.wordpress.com/2011/08)

For those unfamiliar with the game of Jenga, it consists of a tower of wooden blocks. During the game, players take turns to remove a block from this tower and balance it on the top. The structure becomes increasingly unstable as the blocks supporting the structure from lower down are removed. The Coalition Government are currently playing their very own version of this game, which I call Big Society Jenga. They are seeing how many basic elements of the structure that supports British Society can be removed before the entire edifice collapses.

(http://themaskedamhp.blogspot.co.uk)

As you can see from this random selection, there is much you can learn from other social workers. From an ethical stance there are a number of examples of ethical issues which might get you started in thinking about some of the ethical challenges which social workers face. Let us investigate just one example from the blogs – the issue of CTOs. The Masked AMHP outlines the conflict between care and control in relation to mental health and the use of CTOs and argues for the positives in his/her practice experience.

The Mental Health Act 2007 enacted supervised community treatment through the introduction of new sections 17A–17G into the Mental Health Act 1983. The new sections provide for a CTO to be imposed in certain circumstances upon persons who may be in danger of admission into a psychiatric institution. A recent research article in the *Lancet* cast doubt on CTOs and suggested that, for some people, this was an ineffective piece of legislation:

OCTET *[The Oxford Community Treatment Order Evaluation Trial]* has not proved that CTOs are ineffective, the investigators are correct in stating that there is no good evidence to support their use. A major socio-legal intervention has been introduced that might have a greater effect on patients' lives than any drug treatment. Yet this intervention has been introduced without any of the stringent testing that is needed for approval of a new pharmacological agent. I expect that the challenges of obtaining ethical approval might have been one of the reasons that participants in the control group were initially given leave rather than discharged outright, yet we have to ask ourselves what are the ethics of treating patients with an intervention that they will often not desire when we have no evidence of its benefit?

(Burns et al., 2013)

The conflict between social workers' role in upholding their legal responsibilities and their duty to ensure the care of the people they are working with means that there are often difficult decisions to be made as to how social workers should manage this conflict. For the blogger, it was felt that using a CTO, although requiring a service user to accept treatment in the community, was problematic in taking away the service user's autonomy. Nevertheless, the argument was made that this was a better option than requiring the service user to enter hospital for treatment. This argument is one which will be present in many of the examples we will be looking at in this book. Social workers may not always be able to make decisions which they would ideally want to make, but the decision to act in a particular way may be the least harmful option.

CHAPTER SUMMARY

This chapter has described the context of social work practice and how this context will influence the ethical decision making of social workers. It has suggested that the twin imperatives of an increasingly marketised system of social care coupled with an increase in the managerial control of social workers' professional expertise presents significant challenges to social workers wishing to uphold the values of social justice in social work.

FURTHER READING

Pickett, H and Wilkinson, R (2009) *The spirit level: Why more equal societies almost always do better.* London: Allen Lane.

Rogowski, S (2011) Social work with children and families: challenges and possibilities in the neo-liberal world. *British Journal of Social Work* 42, 921–40.

Sandel, M (2012) *What money can't buy: The moral limits of markets.* New York: Farrar, Straus and Giroux.

Chapter 2
Anti-oppressive practice

Anti-oppressive practice: achieving social justice

This chapter begins by exploring the underpinning approach that is adopted by all social work courses and social work practitioners in working with service users – anti-oppressive practice (AOP). On the one hand, AOP represents a general value orientation towards countering oppression experienced by service users on grounds such as race, gender, class and disability (Figure 2.1). On the other hand, it also contains specific practice values; these are the values of empowerment, partnership and minimal intervention.

AOP is, therefore, the means to achieve social justice for service users. It is not adequate merely to analyse a service user's situation and acknowledge his or her social

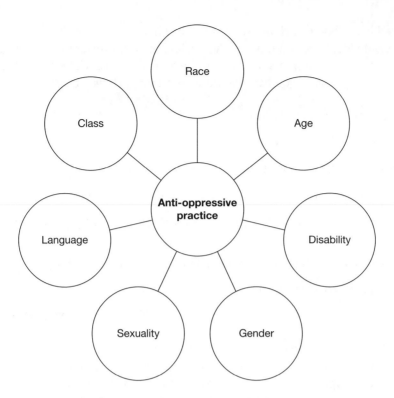

Figure 2.1   Anti-oppressive practice as value orientation

location. It requires us to achieve real change with service users by securing fair treatment from social work services and wider societal resources.

In order to develop our understanding further we must clarify what we mean by AOP. There are two related but distinct approaches which seek to achieve social justice for service users; these are Dalrymple and Burke's (2005) formulation of AOP and Thompson's anti-discriminatory practice (ADP).

Anti-discriminatory practice

An approach to social work practice which seeks to reduce, undermine or eliminate discrimination and oppression, specifically in terms of challenging sexism, racism, ageism, and disabilism . . . and other forms of discrimination encountered in social work. Social workers occupy positions of power and influence, and so there is considerable scope for discrimination and oppression, whether this is intentional or by default. Anti-discriminatory practice is an attempt to eradicate discrimination from our own practice and challenge it in the practice of others and institutional strictures in which we operate.

(Thompson, 2001)

For Dalrymple and Burke, AOP is a much broader term which seeks to challenge the power differences between groups, and understands such power differences as embedded in society to such an extent that they have a pervasive impact in both public and private life. They suggest that ADP is limited in this extent in that it deals with more visible forms of oppression that can be amenable to social reform through, for example, making it illegal to discriminate on grounds such as race or gender.

Anti-oppressive practice requires:

- *personal self-knowledge;*

- *knowledge and an understanding of the majority social systems;*

- *knowledge and understanding of different groups and cultures;*

- *knowledge of how to challenge and confront issues on a personal and structural level;*

- *awareness of the need to be 'research minded' (Everitt et al., 1992);*

- *commitment to action and change.*

(Dalrymple and Burke, 1995, p18)

For Thompson, the difference is in the process, so that discrimination is the process (or set of processes) that leads to oppression (p xii). He recognises the need for a much broader approach that goes beyond reforming the legal system to account for discrimination, and sees differences between AOP and ADP in practice as minimal, becoming semantic problems rather than ones which may require different theoretical explanation. Whichever term you use it is important to understand that there are differences in how the concept can be used and therefore students need to understand if they are adopting a reformist or a radical model (Figure 2.2). A reformist model seeks to make relatively small incremental steps to achieve change within the structure of society. For example, a reformist approach to child care might seek to improve the law relating to how children are treated in the family, which would target the behaviour of parents to prevent physical or sexual abuse. A radical model would focus on the unequal powers that adults have over children in the wider social structure, seeking to empower children by stressing their potential for collective action to counter abusive situations inside the family. It may even

	Reformist	Radical
Changes	Legal powers	Social inequality
Targets	Individuals/organisations	Social structure

Figure 2.2 Competing models of anti-oppressive practice

challenge the concept of the family as the only or most appropriate way of bringing up children, believing that children should be cherished by the wider community as well as their parents.

Since then, Thompson (2012) has modified his definition of ADP specifically to include issues of oppression, so that ADP is:

> *an approach to practice which seeks to reduce, undermine or eliminate discrimination and oppression, specifically in terms of challenging sexism, racism, ageism and disabilism . . .*

(p48)

AOP understands that inequality is a persistent feature of modern capitalist societies. Inequality is experienced in a number of different ways that relate to the manner in which society is divided or differentiated (Giddens, 2006). This process of social differentiation creates inequality when hierarchies of power and influence, including control over key resources, are attached to different positions. This results in some groups achieving a position of dominance and superiority over others. When social divisions such as these arise, they persist over time and become entrenched within a given society. When social divisions occur, they form the social structure of a society. A structure is a set of more or less permanent social relationships which encapsulate the power held by dominant groups to maintain and exercise their power over subordinate groups through every level of society. It is this understanding of social relations which forms a clear difference between reformist and radical approaches. Let us take the example of domestic violence – an example of the way in which aspects of the social relations of gender reflect the domination of (usually) men over women.

REFLECTION POINT

Women's Aid, one of the main charities which support women who suffer from domestic violence, present this information on their website:

- *One in four women will be a victim of domestic violence in their lifetime – many of these on a number of occasions.*

- *One incident of domestic violence is reported to the police every minute.*

- *On average, two women a week are killed by a current or former male partner.*

(www.womensaid.org.uk/domestic_violence_topic.asp?)

Statistics like the above are regularly quoted – but where do they come from? And how accurate are they? Available statistics on domestic violence are likely to understate the extent of abuse, but some sources are more reliable than others.

Continued

> ### REFLECTION POINT *continued*
>
> *One misleading statistic, which is often repeated, is that, while one in four women experience domestic violence, so do one in six men. These figures are, however, based on single incidents, of a criminal nature, and without regard to:*
>
> - *severity of violence;*
>
> - *whether or not it was repeated and if so, how often;*
>
> - *the complex pattern of overlapping abuse of various kinds;*
>
> - *the context in which it took place.*
>
> *They also exclude sexual assaults, which are overwhelmingly perpetrated against women by men, many of whom are partners or former partners of the victims. Finally, emotional abuse – which is often not regarded as a crime, but which survivors often find even more destructive – is excluded from these statistics.*

The scepticism of Women's Aid is borne out by how the Office for National Statistics summarises its key points in relation to violent crime, as this extract makes clear.

> ### *Statistical bulletin: Focus on: Violent Crime and Sexual Offences, 2011/12*
>
> - With regard to sexual and domestic violence, the 2011/12 survey showed there were 536,000 victims of sexual assault in the last year and two million of domestic abuse. Although the estimated levels of domestic abuse experienced in the last year were lower than those in the 2004/05 CSEW [Crime Survey for England and Wales] (the baseline for this measure), there has been no statistically significant change since 2008/09. Sexual assault in the last year has shown no statistically significant change over this time period.
>
> - The CSEW showed that young men were most likely to be the victims of violence. The profile of victims of violence and sexual violence varied according to the type of offence. In 2011/12, as in previous years, more than two-thirds of homicide victims (68 per cent) were male. In contrast, women were more likely to be a victim of domestic abuse. Some seven per cent of women and five per cent of men were estimated to have experienced domestic abuse in the last year, equivalent to an estimated 1.2 million female and 800,000 male victims. Similarly, the survey found that young women were much more likely to be victims of sexual assault in the last year.
>
> - The relationship between victims and perpetrators also differed by gender. For example, homicides against men were most likely to be committed by a friend or acquaintance (39 per cent), whilst homicides against women were most likely to be committed by a partner or ex-partner (51 per cent).
>
> (**www.ons.gov.uk/ons/rel/crime-stats/crime-statistics/focus-on-violent-crime/stb-focus-on-violent-crime-and-sexual-offences-2011-12.html**)

As you can see, this summary does not highlight some of the key 'facts' identified by Women's Aid. For example, the second bullet point, which outlined that *some seven per cent of women and five per cent of men were estimated to have experienced domestic abuse in the last year* makes no mention of the repetition of abuse made upon women. It is important, therefore, to understand how different facts are presented as a result of choices made by the researcher, which can present quite a different picture from that understood by those who work with and experience domestic violence on a daily basis. One of the key questions regarding domestic violence perpetrated upon women is asking why many women suffer repeated assaults but do not leave or seek help. The response by agencies such as the police and social services can often be highly judgemental of such women.

RESEARCH SUMMARY

- *One in four women experience domestic abuse in their lifetime.*

- *In the UK, approximately 100 women a year are killed by a current or ex-partner.*

- *On average, it takes seven years for a woman to leave an abusive relationship.*

- *Women are more at risk in the month after leaving a violent relationship.*

- *A woman is likely to experience physical violence 35 times before reporting it.*

- *One in five young men and one in ten young women think that violence against women is acceptable.*

- *One in five teenage girls have been hit by their boyfriend.*

*(Adapted from **www.idas.org.uk/quiz.pdf**)*

It is not surprising, therefore, that the social relations of gender show how a combination of personal and social factors combines to prevent many women from leaving an abusive relationship.

Personal factors include:

- feelings of shame;

- fear of further violence;

- wanting to protect children or remaining in the relationship for the children's sake;

- social factors;

- homelessness;

- poverty;

- failure of responsible agencies;

- lack of support services.

Stanley et al.'s (2010) study for the National Society for the Prevention of Cruelty to Children showed that many survivors of domestic abuse have a mixed experience of initial contact with the police and social workers, saying that they were often not listened to and the seriousness of the abuse was minimised, particularly if survivors could not provide clear evidence. However, where police and social work responses were appropriate then survivors did feel they were protected, particularly where female professionals were involved.

ACTIVITY 2.1

Look at the list below:

Social division	Category
Gender	Female
Race	Black
Class	Working

If you were a working-class black woman, would you consider yourself as having much power in society at large?

Now identify the opposite for each category in the list above so that the list would look like:

Social division	Category
Gender	Male
Race	White
Class	Middle

If you were a white middle-class male, would you consider yourself to have more or less power than a black working-class woman?

COMMENT

The relative power of groups reflects the control that they have over some of the key resources in society. The experience of advantage or disadvantage structures the way that individuals and groups come into contact with welfare services and their own life chances. The detailed example of domestic violence highlights the way in which women relative to men have less control over the key resources in society. It also highlights the physical and psychological impacts that can be manifested as a result of absence of such

Continued

*control. Women often find themselves trapped in violent situations without the neces-
sary support and resources that would enable them to be safe.*

*How then would an understanding of AOP help to grasp the reality of domestic violence?
In taking Dalrymple and Burke's approach it is clear that focusing upon the more hidden aspects of domestic violence may help us understand more clearly the experiences of
those abused. This means acknowledging how women and men both experience domestic
violence and how they do not come to report it because of fear for themselves or because
of the way agencies may have responded in the past. This understanding uncovers the
nature of domestic abuse in a way that the more visible presentation of statistics and a
singular focus upon legislation do not.*

Understanding difference

From a values perspective, understanding the process by which social groups experience disadvantage and how they cope with the challenges of such discrimination is
essential for AOP. This requires a positive orientation towards those groups in society
and the individuals within them who may have alternative ways of viewing the world
and who therefore may have quite a different understanding of what constitutes a
'good life'.

Valuing 'difference' is, therefore, a complex process that requires social workers
to be open to understanding these different conceptions of the 'good life'. Unless
practitioners follow this path, their reaction to 'difference' is not to value it, but
holds the danger of either dominating it or exterminating it.

An example of this process of domination and extermination can be highlighted
by the film *Rabbit-Proof Fence* (Noyce, 2002). During the first half of the twentieth
century, Australia took children of mixed Aboriginal/white origin from their homes,
trained them in boarding schools and sent them to work in white communities. The
majority of the children never saw their parents again. The purpose was to break up
mixed families, civilise the children and absorb them into white society. *Rabbit-Proof
Fence* is the true story of three young girls who ran away from boarding school at the
Moore River settlement. Living off the land and on hand-outs, they eluded trackers
and the police for months. Two of the girls made it home while one was recaptured.

A.O. Neville, then 'Chief Protector of Aborigines' in 1930s Western Australia, ordered
the round-up (i.e. kidnapping) of all 'half-caste' (known now as dual-heritage) girls
(girls of half Aboriginal and half white descent) from their Aboriginal families for
mandatory education into the ways of white society, leading to eventual low-level
employment as domestic servants. Neville was simply enforcing the Aborigines Act,
a law designed with the intention of 'salvaging' 'half-caste' girls from Aboriginal life
and integrating them into the white Australian world.

ACTIVITY **2.2**

From the brief description of the film above, what comparisons could you draw between the actions of the Australian government at that time and other similar examples you might know about from history?

COMMENT

Comparisons can be drawn between the Australian government's plan to eliminate 'half-caste' Aborigines through the dilution of their so-called Aboriginal genes and the Nazi policies (during the same time period) of eliminating minority populations (Jews, gypsies, etc.) through extermination. Other comparisons can be made between the Australian policies and recent attempted genocides in Rwanda, ethnic cleansing in the Balkans and, in the UK, the policy developed at the turn of the twentieth century of separating people with learning disabilities from the community by placing them in 'special hospitals' as the authorities feared that allowing people with learning disabilities to reproduce would degrade the genetic pool of intelligence in society.

Valuing 'difference' goes against common-sense socialisation, which portrays difference as 'inferior' or deems it in pathological terms as 'deficient', as in the way Aboriginal culture was suppressed. To take a recent example of research into issues of race, there has been increasing interest in the concept of 'whiteness' (Jeyasingham, 2012). This concept is useful because, instead of focusing on the 'black' other in developing AOP, whiteness explicitly requires an understanding of how white privilege and power then construct the debate upon racism. It suggests that white people ignore their own skin colour and its significance, yet define others in terms of their skin colour. As Burton (2009) has argued:

> *The purpose of whiteness theory is to 'race' whiteness and to denaturalize dominant ideologies, discourses and practices that make whiteness almost invisible.*

(p350)

ACTIVITY **2.3**

I am using the terms white/black/mixed race as short-hand, with the realisation that these terms cover a wide range of experiences and backgrounds and different skin colours, but the purpose of this exercise is to ask you to consider, depending upon your skin colour, what it means to be white/black/mixed race. So, bearing in mind the differences of race, reflect upon and answer the following questions.

1. *How important to you is the colour of your skin?*
2. *How would you describe who you are, i.e. focusing upon your identity?*

Continued

ACTIVITY **2.3** *continued*

3. *How do you think others see you?*

4. *How have others' descriptions of who you are influenced you?*

COMMENT

I would guess that if your skin colour is white that you may struggle to explain the importance of your skin colour to you, whereas if you are black or mixed race you will have a well-developed sense of what your skin colour means in everyday society. These are assumptions on my part; however, much research has emerged on how the 'problem' of whiteness is conceived by white people, i.e. as not a problem or one that is ignored. Why should this be? Whiteness is largely imperceptible to white people, yet it is very visible to black people because it is a dominant perspective encapsulating strong normative assumptions of superiority and inferiority. Whiteness assumes a normality against which 'others' are judged and through which advantage accrues that is assumed and rarely examined. White people are often asked about their opinions of 'others' whilst their own sense of race, their 'racialness', is ignored and therefore they are never required to think about the issue. Think about this in relation to question four as, again, the power and privilege accruing to white people often mean their voice and evaluation of 'others' are heard loudest.

This presents problems for researchers, often because of white people's reluctance to talk coherently about their own rather than 'others'' racial identity. Picower (2009), for example, found in a study of student teachers that, when the students were challenged about issues of their power and privilege as white people, the intrinsic advantages were deflected or not talked about. Nonetheless, although white people may not recognise their position within a racialised social structure, it is possible to investigate the consequences of whiteness in terms of the privilege accruing to white people and the effects upon black others. As Lewis (2004) argues, white people's:

> *racial composition is not an accident but is a result of whites' status as members of a passive social collectivity whose lives are shaped at least in part by the racialised social system in which they live and operate.*

(p627)

Relatively little research has focused upon the experiences of black social workers and students in social work (Bartoli, 2013). However, Channer and Doel's (2009) article is an exception and documents the experiences of black social workers on a post-qualifying course in social work and shows that the way the course was organised and delivered often neglected the needs of black students by assuming a sameness in the experiences of the different students involved. Williams and Parrott (2012) investigated the issue of whiteness in relation to social work education in Wales and found many course administrators failing to recognise the importance of race and the needs of black students on the courses they had responsibility for.

Whiteness theory can be used as a template in identifying how other aspects of difference can also focus upon the 'other'. As Akhtar (2013) argues, this approach can have parallels with social workers from different social backgrounds wishing to understand their potential prejudices. For example, in terms of disability, many early writers on disability (Gabel and Peters, 2004) identified how the treatment of disabled people reflected an oppressive understanding of disabled people's lives. Disabled people were often described as being deficient in particular ways if they could not participate in society or had difficulty with daily living tasks. The early social model of disability turned this view on its head. Instead of highlighting the 'inadequacies' of disabled people, the focus shifted to the way society constructed barriers to the inclusion of disabled people into society. The shift meant that 'able-bodied' people had to look at the privilege and advantages they took for granted, for example, easy access to public spaces, and reflect upon how a lack of provision for others (i.e. disabled people) meant they were denied such access.

More recently, writers such as Jones (2013) have asked similar questions about the way in which working-class people and the issues of class in general have become marginalised. The absence of informed research therefore leads to the development of cultural and negative stereotypes, which can lead to the further marginalisation of white working-class communities. One example of research that exists comes from Skeggs (2009), who reflects upon this process in her research on white working-class women, encapsulating the daily indignities experienced through the prism of class:

> *'Being looked down on' was their description of a process to which they were continually subject, a visual assessment by others that repeatedly positioned them as lacking value. For instance, when they entered 'posh shops' they were acutely aware of the way they were being read and judged by others.*

> *We'd all gone up to Manchester the other Saturday, you know for a day out, the three of us . . . We were in Kendals during the day, you know where the really posh food is, and we were laughing about all the chocolates and how many we could eat, if we could afford them, and this woman she just looked at us. If looks could kill. Like we were only standing there.*

> *We weren't doing anything wrong. We weren't scruffy or anything. She just looked. It was like it was her place and we didn't belong there. And you know what? We just all walked away. We should have punched her in the face. We didn't say anything until about half an hour later. Can you imagine? Well and truly put in our place . . .*

> *It's things like that that put you off going. You feel better staying around here. (Wendy, 1986)*

> (Skeggs, 2009, p37)

'It's sad that Woolworth's is closing. Where will all the chavs buy their Christmas presents?'

(Jones, 2013)

How might you react to this joke? Is it funny? Offensive? How might you react to this if the joke was aimed at women, disabled people or black people?

I would suggest, as Jones does, that there is more ambivalence about class oppression than other forms in that the suggestion is that we are all middle class now and, therefore, only those who are unable to rise to the ranks of the middle classes deserve to be derided in this way. Jones makes an interesting parallel between two well-publicised news stories of recent years. You may be familiar with the story of Madeleine McCann, who was abducted whilst on holiday whilst her parents were in a nearby restaurant, and the story of Shannon Matthews, who was hidden by her mother Karen in order to claim any rewards that might be offered when she was found. Greenslade (2008) concurs with Jones's (2013) view and suggests the differences in treatment between the two cases:

So what's the reason for the differences? Here's my admittedly tentative view. Overarching everything is social class. Shannon comes from a council house in a deprived working class area of Dewsbury Moor, West Yorkshire. Her mother, Karen, has what one might call an unsympathetic domestic profile with seven children from five different fathers. In 'respectable' working class eyes, she would be regarded as a member of the underclass and, by implication, the author of her own misfortunes.

Unlike the supposedly middle class McCann family, with their 'respectable' careers in medicine, Karen lacks eloquence. Neither she nor her daughter are photogenic. There are not 'cute' pictures of the girl and no video of her. The absence of moving images is particularly important for TV coverage, of course. The repetition of clips of attractive victims of crime is a common feature of TV news bulletins.

The belief is that the audience must identify with the plight of the people involved. There is a hierarchy involved in choosing who gets most coverage.

There are other factors, of course, stemming from Karen Matthews's background and social conditions. She does not have friends and relatives with media savvy, as the McCanns did. The Matthews family does not have the networking connections nor, of course, the finances. It will be said that they don't have the PR back-up either.

In case commenters get carried away with that fact, and try to see it as significant, let me explain that the reason PRs initially got involved with the McCanns was due to the 'spontaneous' media interest once the story broke. The British embassy supplied them with a PR to help them deal with journalists. The Matthews have not been subjected to anything like as much press interest.

So there we have it. A nine-year-old girl goes missing and relatively little appears in print or on screen. A four-year-old girl goes missing and thousands of pages and hundreds of minutes of airtime are devoted to her in media across the world. Is it really, as I believe, all about social class?

(Adapted from **www.theguardian.com/media/greenslade/2008/ mar/05/whyismissingshannonnotget**)

ACTIVITY **2.4**

Search the internet for the respective stories on Shannon Matthews and Madeleine McCann produced by the newspapers at the time. After consulting these sources, do you think Greenslade's commentary is valid?

The extent to which the working class and in particular the white working class has been described in policy and academic work can be identified through an extensive literature review and study undertaken by Bieder (2011), who observed:

Typically communities are viewed as being problematic, dysfunctional and occupying annexed council estates. Fixed attributes are ascribed rather than recognising individuals residing in different areas with composite identities. Deviance and threat posed by white working-class communities pepper most academic and policy narratives.

(p7)

Sayer (2005) argues, in a way that reflects our previous discussion of whiteness, that the middle classes, in passing judgement over working-class people, see their values as universally valid. He explains that the middle class is reticent when it comes to recognising their privileged social and economic position. They display a denial of their class position, showing embarrassment, and evade any recognition that class differences are replete with moral significance. Class is morally significant precisely because it cannot be divorced from how people's moral worth is valued and their identity derided, which in turn contributes to inequality in life chances and personal suffering.

In using the example of whiteness as a template to encourage social workers to think about their power and privilege in relation to different service users, it is important to recognise that each of the differences considered has its own particular dynamic and therefore the experience of oppression which people in these different groups endure is different. In experiencing these differences, and the way in which these differences create social division between groups, we also need to recognise that people's identity is more complex than only being a member of a distinct social group. Rather, we all occupy a multiple of positions which may combine in different ways. For example, a white disabled woman service user occupies a number of social locations in terms of how her race, gender and disability are assessed by powerful others. Understanding the ways in which different identities interact or intersect with one another is called intersectionality and can be illuminated as in Figure 2.3.

Intersectionality

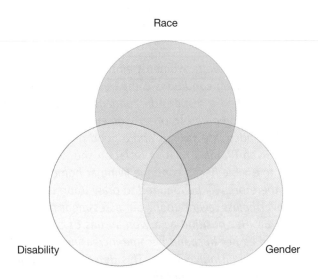

Figure 2.3   How differences intersect and overlap

As you can see from Figure 2.3, these differences overlap and intersect with one another in the centre of the diagram. In order for social workers to understand the complexity of such an identity a careful individual assessment is required to appraise how these differences impact upon the life of the individual service user and the implications in terms of providing an appropriate range of services. To highlight these issues, earlier in the chapter we looked at the issue of domestic violence. Consider Case study 2.1.

CASE STUDY **2.1**

Rhona is a 58-year-old white woman who has onset multiple sclerosis. She has increasingly been subject to violence by her partner, who has now left the family home, leaving Rhona alone. Her two children, who are now adults, live away. Rhona worked as a manager in the NHS for 30 years, but is now reliant on social security benefits. Rhona cannot manage her daily living tasks and therefore requires support at home. She receives home care daily.

In what ways do you think the issues of race, disability and gender intersect in Rhona's situation?

COMMENT

Given the brevity of the case study it is surprising that on consideration the situation is more complex and perhaps beyond what you may have initially thought. Indeed as we look at Rhona's situation, other differences may also come to the fore, which our initial assessment may not have revealed.

In terms of the issues of race, white women's employment reflects a history of relatively low pay and poor working conditions compared to white men. However, Rhona has a good pension as she had a responsible managerial position and therefore her experience is relatively rare compared to other women. Rhona worked for many years and was able to build up adequate savings and a good pension to support her as her disability progressed. Given Rhona's relative isolation she will rely upon the input of domiciliary home care to enable her to continue living at home. She has savings to pay for her own care and therefore will be required to draw upon these to pay for any care she requires. She is nevertheless reliant upon your assessment to enable her to live with dignity in her own home. Her position as a woman has of course left her vulnerable to domestic violence and as her husband became increasingly frustrated with Rhona's disability, so he became increasingly violent. This deteriorating situation outlines the double discrimination here in terms of her disability and her gender. As mentioned earlier, we may assess within this situation Rhona's class position, which is also evident in her previous occupation. As Rhona occupied a position of relative power and is now out of the labour market, she is having to adjust her own identity accordingly, which is likely to prove stressful for her given the position of relative power and responsibility she had within the NHS.

Moving beyond common-sense attitudes about 'difference' requires the social worker to inhabit the world of the 'other'; this exercise of empathy requires a deep understanding of the other person's world and his or her values. It also requires social workers to reflect upon their own values and their own understanding of their identity, what privileges they have had, what struggles they have experienced. In identifying differences, social workers can reflect on their position of power in society and identify ways in which power can be shared with others. In addition, by reflecting upon the struggles they have experienced when they have been in a powerless position, they can see the similarities that they sometimes share with service users. In understanding those similar experiences we are creating service users as a part of 'us'. That is, we all share similar experiences of struggle and stress at times, which enables us to use our empathy in a constructive way to recognise our common humanity. In singularly reflecting upon and identifying our differences we are aware of the potential for creating service users as part of 'them' (Lister, 2004). In constructing service users as others, there is the danger of ignoring the strengths and personal resources that service users bring to their situation and how they manage to maintain their dignity. Krumer-Nevo (2005) argues that service users living in poverty acquire what he calls 'life knowledge'. He argues that this category of knowledge challenges some of the preconceptions about how people cope with hardship and how assistance might be given. People living in poverty are often considered to have only partial knowledge of their situation, yet through their resilience show how they manage their lives on a daily basis. By valuing the capabilities of service users we can develop knowledge that is not alienated from service users or detached from their experiences and therefore help them more effectively.

There are a number of practice values that can contribute to working with service users in an anti-oppressive way:

- empowerment;
- partnership;
- minimal intervention.

These values develop a practice orientation which seeks to place service users at the centre of intervention and therefore work alongside an overall commitment to the value of social justice (Figure 2.4).

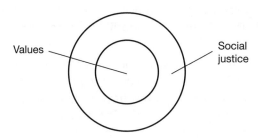

Figure 2.4   Values and social justice

Empowerment

Empowerment requires the recognition that social workers hold considerable power in relation to service users, particularly in their use of statutory power derived from their legal duties. Thus, in any intervention, social workers should encourage the participation of people in the formulation, implementation and evaluation of decisions determining the functioning and well-being of themselves and their wider social environment.

Addressing the ethics of empowerment in your work requires you to consider the power that you can exercise in relation to service users. It requires you to consider ways in which that power can be shared with, and optimally transferred to, the service user. Thus the social and personal barriers which prevent service users from achieving control in their lives is paramount as control implies power to decide on what constitutes a 'good life'.

Empowerment is a contested concept; some writers emphasise the importance of individual empowerment while others focus upon collective and social aspects (Adams, 2003). While individual empowerment is important and necessary, it is the contention here that it is not sufficient. Parker et al. (1999) argue that social workers must be wary of an uncritical approach to the concept. They suggest that empowerment is often done to you by others, or done by you to others. What they mean by this is that professionals have colonised the practice of empowerment so that service users are in passive receipt of empowering practice by professionals which, they suggest, is the opposite of the project of empowerment. As a first step in developing empowering practice, the social worker is required to enter into the world of the service user. This is akin to an empathetic approach but goes beyond this by requiring the social worker to see the commonalities of one service user's experience with others. In this approach service users' interpretation of events and problems in their lives must take centre stage. At this point it requires social workers to view this narrative as legitimate. It requires understanding on the part of the social worker and an acceptance for its validity for the service user. It is not something which requires changing by the social worker as if it may lack a true reflection of a situation or a lack of consciousness on the part of the service user. To take the view that service users' consciousness of their situation needs to be changed at this stage is the complete opposite of empowerment.

> *A person who, for example, has derived most meaning and satisfaction in their life from caring for others is likely to experience being looked after in a nursing home very differently from someone who has been used to having others meet their needs in many ways throughout their life. Someone whose occupational role has been a major part of their identity may interpret the experience of going to a day centre differently from someone whose identity was more closely defined by the quality of their relationships with others. These are factors which will have a profound influence not only on a person's care needs generally, but also on how they can be most meaningfully involved and consulted.*

> (Allan, 2001)

In considering the dynamics of empowerment two aspects are important:

1. control – so that people define their own situation and their needs;

2. self-actualisation – enabling service users to take power for themselves through developing their confidence and self-esteem, their skills and knowledge.

Partnership

Partnership refers to the way social workers should work with service users. This means in effect working with service users in a systematic way but with the service users' consent.

If we look at the basic model of systematic practice, we can highlight how partnership working is integrated in each stage of the process.

- Assessment – investigate and analyse the needs of services user with them, checking the validity of the information gathered at each stage, drawing out the strengths which the service user has as well as those needs which require further development.

- Plan – agree a course of action with the service user but do not impose your own strategy.

- Intervene – draw on service users' strengths, agree on what they can do and what you will do, and review intervention with them on a regular basis. Agree on how much time will be devoted to the task.

- Evaluate – discuss what achievements have been made with the service user, and agree on what has been achieved and what might need to be addressed in the future.

Partnership as a principle is equally valid with involuntary service users. For example, in regard to statutory child care, these principles should continue to be adhered to so that service users have the maximum amount of choice and control over their situation as possible. These principles of partnership working have been validated by families involved in statutory child care who felt that, even though they were subject to intervention in which they had no choice, they were far more positive about this experience where social workers had worked in partnership (Aldgate and Statham, 2001). For an example of this approach using a specific case, see Davies (2009), as the author argues:

> *The awareness that their social worker is loyal to a canon of ethics despite the challenges presented by difficult clients and the temptation in certain cases to adopt a 'them-and-us' position instinctively evokes respect and trust from clients.*

(p327)

We can look at partnership as a pyramid, with the apex being user control and management of services, descending towards participation in planning of services, down to the base of individual consultation via surveys of service users' views to gain feedback on the effectiveness of services (Figure 2.5).

Democratic and consumerist approaches to empowerment

Distinctions have been identified between consumerist/market approaches and citizenship/democratic approaches to empowerment (Crouch, 2003). The extent to

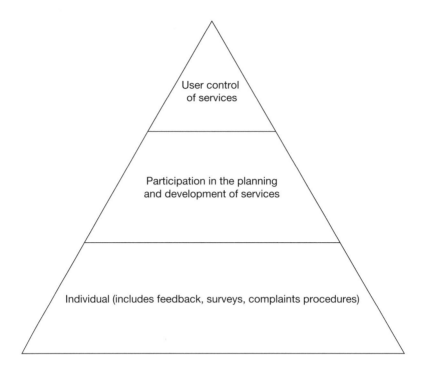

Figure 2.5   Pyramid of participation

which service users are able to exercise their voice depends upon their ability to influence agency-led initiatives to achieve this. Voice becomes more potent where user-led initiatives have been able to control the pace and extent of partnership.

Partnership	Approach	Degree of service user control
Agency-led	Exit	Low
Service user-led	Voice	High

Consumerist – exit

This suggests that service users have power as consumers of the service either to purchase the service directly or have it purchased on their behalf by care managers. This implies that service users will be given a choice over the kinds of service that they want. This is based on a market model in which a person who is unhappy with a particular service can withdraw the purchase of one service and transfer it to another. In terms of consultation, service users as consumers contribute to consumer surveys to voice their satisfaction or otherwise with the service, which is in theory adjusted to meet consumer demand. A recent example of this can be found in the personalisation of social care services. Although there is controversy as to how legitimate this policy is, it does nevertheless imply an increasing role for service users as consumers who manage their own package of care.

Democratic – voice

This suggests that service users should have a voice in the organisation and delivery of services. This means developing processes of consultation and participation in which service users are consulted as to the kinds of service they want and how they ought to be delivered. The more voice, i.e. the more service users have power of decision in planning and organising services, then the more control. This involves membership on planning and management committees as partners with personal social services, or to have control of the planning and organisation of services, with service users in the majority.

At various times social workers and service users may find themselves at different points of this continuum, depending upon how tolerant service users are of being excluded from this process, and how proactive social workers are at actively involving service users in the process.

Partnership is often synonymous with participation, and in the literature is often indistinguishable from it. The extent of participation and partnership by service users in determining the kinds of service that they need depends upon the level of power and the process of empowerment to achieve control over the delivery of services.

Underpinning the concept of partnership is a value that all citizens should be involved in making decisions which affect their lives. The value of partnership has been emphasised in both community care and children's services, and as such has been promoted by the state even within statutory situations such as child protection or mental health work. For example, research into the placement of children away from their parents in the 1980s showed that the outcome for children was much better when parents were involved in the placement process (Aldgate and Statham, 2001).

Minimal intervention

Minimal intervention as a specific value of AOP refers to the need for social workers to be aware of the formal power they have in relation to the lack of formal power of service users. Power used by social workers can be positive as well as negative. The use of social workers' power to advocate and intervene at levels of organisations which have proved inaccessible for service users is one such example. The intervention of social workers to protect service users from the illegitimate actions of others is another. To avoid the disempowering of service users by recourse to early intervention, Payne (2000) highlights a three-stage approach (Figure 2.6).

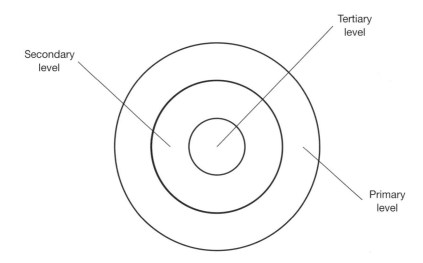

Figure 2.6   Three-stage approach

- The primary level – to prevent problems arising. Services might be adapted to be appropriate and helpful to clients, community resources mobilised to help, and the public and people involved given information and education to enable more control of the process.

- The secondary level – to catch problems and try to deal with them early, before they become serious. This reduces the amount of interference in clients' lives.

- The tertiary level – to reduce the consequences for people when something has gone wrong or action has been forced on the agency.

A good example of how minimal intervention has been compromised is in the area of child support and protection. In the context of the many public inquiries into failures within the child protection system, it is not surprising that social workers take the less risky option and put families through the child protection process rather than providing family support. Broadhurst et al. (2010b) argue that social work practitioners are required to comply with risk-averse approaches to working in child welfare cases. They argue that this has a damaging effect upon social workers' ability to work in a more informal way and impairs the kind of relationship-based work that is often crucial in working successfully with children and families. The way in which social work has become increasingly risk-averse has also been identified by Clapton et al. (2013), who suggest that powerful political forces, for example, in the shape of pressure groups, high-profile individuals and politicians reacting to the moral outrage generated by such groups, have all shaped the direction of child welfare policy. As the argument above outlines, the ability of social workers to work at the primary, secondary and tertiary levels of minimal intervention becomes severely compromised, as all these approaches require a more constructive approach based upon negotiation, relationship building and compromise. What the current system of child protection requires is the focus upon agency policy and procedure, which requires both the social worker and service users to comply within their respective roles.

CHAPTER SUMMARY

AOP requires social workers to focus their understanding on three levels:

1. intellectually – to grasp its central principles and methods of working;

2. emotionally – to feel secure about, and confident in, working in anti-oppressive ways, and to be able to recognise and learn from the mistakes they make when reality falls short of their ambition to work in this way;

3. practically – to be able to implement the principles they have learnt and feel that they are competent in their practice.

FURTHER READING

Thompson, N (2012) *Anti-discriminatory practice.* Basingstoke: Palgrave-Macmillan.

Chapter 3
Principles and consequences

CASE STUDY 3.1

Joyce Phillips, aged 69, cares for her mother Megan Davies, who is 90 years old. She lives just a few streets away from her mother's house and has spent increasing amounts of time with her mother, particularly since her mother was widowed some two years ago. Megan is becoming increasingly forgetful. Joyce's husband, aged 70, suffered a stroke two years ago and relies heavily on Joyce both physically, as he can no longer wash and dress himself, and emotionally, as he sees little of his friends, who find it difficult to visit him.

Joyce gets very tired having to juggle between caring for her husband and her mother. She has never asked for any help from social services. When a social worker did visit her at home she said that she didn't require help. After all, social workers only help people who can't help themselves, and anyway she felt it was her duty to look after her husband and her mother. She added: 'If everybody just dumped their loved ones on to social services then the whole reason for being in a family would just die.'

Continued

CASE STUDY **3.1** *continued*

Whether we agree or disagree with this statement, Joyce has a clear reason why she wishes to continue to care for her husband and mother. What Joyce is expressing here is not only her own justification for her continued care of her family, but also a deep-seated moral stance about the responsibilities, as she sees it, of family members to one another and what that means in practice.

Introduction

In Chapter 1 we looked at different justifications for why people act ethically. Some people had a strong religious belief which they felt inspired them to act; others came from a secular belief system which involved an ethic of social justice, a sense of what was fair. Similarly, Joyce (in the case study above) is expressing her reasons for continuing to care, invoking a principle where she sees care as a duty requiring her to look after her husband and mother.

In this chapter we will examine two underpinning philosophical perspectives that have informed the practice of social workers, i.e. principled and consequentialist perspectives. Having established our understanding of these approaches, we will examine some recent alternatives which have challenged these previously dominant ideas in social work values. These are virtue theory and a feminist ethic of care.

But first it is worth considering more traditional approaches to ethics which have proved significant in helping social workers practise using their discretion to help individual service users. Traditional values typically focused upon the social worker–service user relationship and therefore developed a value base which could develop ethically appropriate principles of action based in the most part upon the individuality of the service user. Thus if service users experienced inequality the solution was understood as developing the same access and the same treatment to all irrespective of any other characteristics such as differences based upon gender or race.

ACTIVITY **3.1**

Three authors stand out as being particularly influential in relation to traditional values: Biestek (1974), Timms (1983) and Butrym (1976). These authors argued that their ethical principles were universal and capable of application within any social work context. See Table 3.1 for the respective lists of ethical principles which these authors developed.

Table 3.1 Ethical principles of Biestek, Timms and Butrym

Biestek	Timms	Butrym
Acceptance	Respect for client	Respect for persons
Non-judgemental attitude	Accept client	Uniqueness of persons

Continued

ACTIVITY **3.1** *continued*

Biestek	Timms	Butrym
Individualisation	Do not condemn client	Persons as social beings
Control emotional involvement	Self-determination	Belief in personal change
Confidentiality	Respect confidence	
Self-determination		
Purposeful expression of feelings		

From the respective lists in Table 3.1, can you identify where at least two of the writers share a common value principle?

COMMENT

The value principles which seem to be shared by at least two of the writers at any one time are:

- *acceptance;*
- *respect for the client;*
- *self-determination;*
- *non-judgementalism/do not condemn client.*

There is much that these authors share in their assessment of which values are important for social work. This has led Horne (1999) to argue that the core of social work values in these traditional approaches focuses upon respect for persons. As he comments, this value is the mainspring from which all other values are derived. It is not the purpose of this book to investigate in depth the meanings of these values, and you are advised to consult Horne's book to explore these further. The purpose here is to contrast traditional approaches with the concerns of this chapter which will focus upon anti-oppressive approaches to social work values.

Social workers, despite the increasing managerial control over their professional discretion, still have significant autonomy in their dealings with service users and have been characterised as *street-level bureaucrats* (Evans and Harris, 2004). This refers to the way social workers are able, through use of their professional discretion, sometimes to subvert accepted policy as laid down by their employers when working alone with service users. In effect they create policy through the decisions they make when working directly with service users, when managerial supervision is at its weakest. Professional autonomy remains important for social work practice as social workers have to apply and interpret policy in relation to individual cases. This puts an even greater emphasis upon ensuring that the decisions which social workers make with service users are supported by sound ethical reasoning. In this chapter we explore the philosophical and ethical approaches upon which social workers can assist service users in making those decisions. There are a number of approaches that can be taken in order to achieve a sounder ethical decision-making process.

These can be summarised as:

1. a principled approach;

2. a consequentialist approach;

3. virtue theory;

4. an ethic of care.

Given the relatively simple definitions in Figure 3.1, how can we apply these principles to Joyce's situation in Case study 3.1 above?

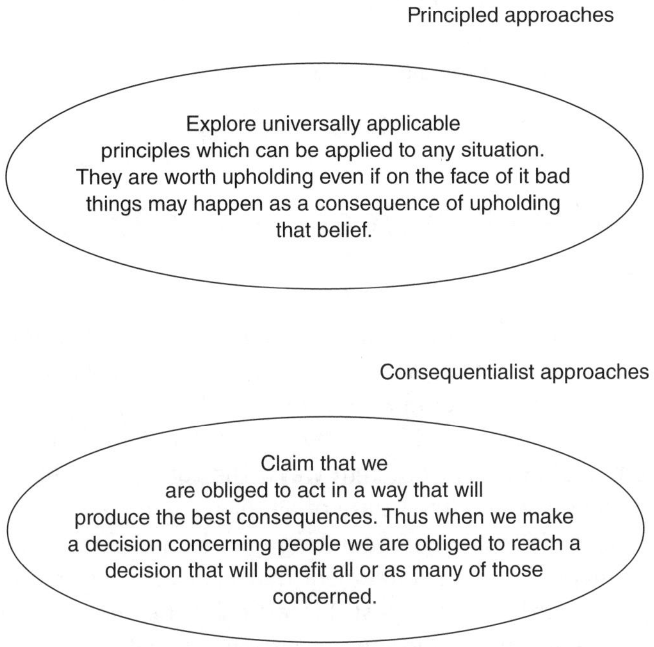

Principled approaches

Explore universally applicable
principles which can be applied to any situation.
They are worth upholding even if on the face of it bad
things may happen as a consequence of upholding
that belief.

Consequentialist approaches

Claim that we
are obliged to act in a way that will
produce the best consequences. Thus when we make
a decision concerning people we are obliged to reach a
decision that will benefit all or as many of those
concerned.

Figure 3.1   Principled and consequentialist approaches

ACTIVITY **3.2**

Make some brief notes on what position you think Joyce is taking in Case study 3.1.

Does she justify her actions based on a particular principle which she believes is important?

or:

Does she justify her decision to care for her mother and husband in terms of its consequences, i.e. that it will have the greatest benefit to the majority of the people involved?

> **COMMENT**
>
> *From the brief description of the two approaches so far, I would hope that you identified that Joyce was employing a principled approach to the care of her husband and mother. Joyce has justified her actions through a principle of responsibility to the other members of her family. Remember that the principled approach is only concerned with the rightness of this principle and that any other reasons should not be considered in justifying the decision. So, even if Joyce is finding the reality of caring very difficult to manage and maintain, these difficulties are of lesser importance than upholding the principle of family responsibility.*
>
> *By contrast, we could analyse this situation in consequentialist terms. Joyce could reduce the amount of time caring for her mother by accessing home care for her mother; in turn this could lead to Joyce feeling less tired and giving more time to her husband, which could improve her relationship with him. In those terms the consequences would benefit two out of the three people involved in this situation, so justifying the reduction in the time spent with Joyce's mother.*

Kant's principled approach – also known as deontology

Emmanuel Kant (1724–1804) was a German philosopher. His moral theory grew out of the Enlightenment, which was the revolutionary intellectual movement that influenced all areas of social life (mostly in Western Europe) by the late eighteenth century, reaching its peak with the French Revolution of 1789. It inspired philosophers and scientists to think in radically different ways. The core of Enlightenment thinking asserted that human beings are the centre of all things, and claimed that human reason should replace traditional ways of thinking and the social institutions supported by it. The goal of many of the Enlightenment thinkers was to use reason as the basis to overturn the superstition of the past. In particular this meant removing God as the source for explaining the world, and replacing this with the power of science. Rational scientific thinking would provide the basis for understanding the natural and social world and lead to human progress. Progress out of the dark ages of tradition could be achieved through the application of scientific knowledge. In Britain, the Enlightenment was primarily the expression of new mental and moral values, new canons of taste, styles of sociability and views of human nature (Porter, 2000, p14).

For Kant, the problem was to develop a moral theory which was informed by rationality. Rationality enables people to understand what their duties are and how their duties enlighten what they do in the world. The issue for Kant was to develop universal principles or guidelines that parallel the way in which religion informs people of their duty, replacing the spiritual tenets of religion with a rational consideration of what one ought to do.

For an action to be moral we must act in accordance with rational principles, which must be true for everyone. In order for us to determine if a principle and the act flowing from it are moral, it must be able to be applied universally, i.e. has the scope to be applied to all situations in which we might need it. A good example of this is the act of lying. If through our reasoning of the universal principle we show that lying can be applied successfully, then we can act on it as a principle worth upholding.

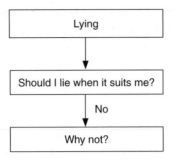

Because if everyone lied (universal principle), then nobody would know what was truthfulness and what was falsity. Universality is the benchmark for testing the decisions we contemplate through the application of reason. A principle is moral only if it can be universalised. If lying was universalised then not knowing what was truth and what was falsity would lead to confusion and social chaos. In this way, then it is an immoral act. Thus we should only act on those principles that can be universalised. So for Kant one of his key principles was always to tell the truth.

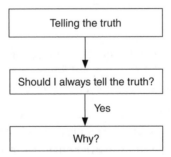

ACTIVITY 3.3

Apply the universalist test to the proposition that it is always moral to tell the truth.

CASE STUDY 3.2

Two years pass and Megan Davies is now in residential care after Joyce has been persuaded that this is the best place for her mother. Megan has now acquired senile dementia; she continually asks when her husband is coming to see her. The care staff

Continued

once told Mrs Davies that her husband had died, which upset her to such an extent that she was crying continually for a number of hours afterwards. This has been repeated on a number of occasions. Mrs Davies's fellow residents also become very distressed at the way that she becomes grief-stricken and they have asked for something to be done. The care staff also feel increasingly uncomfortable telling Mrs Davies the truth and find they have to spend a lot of time with her, which means they are often unable to complete their duties for the rest of the residents. The owner of the home, concerned for her staff and other residents, as well as wishing to do the 'right thing' by Mrs Davies, asks your opinion as to the best course of action to take. She feels it is far better to lie to Mrs Davies, to avoid the repeated distress Mrs Davies experiences when she is told her husband has died.

ACTIVITY **3.4**

What advice would you give if you accepted Kant's categorical imperative regarding truth telling in relation to Megan Davies?

Can you envisage any problems with the advice you have given?

COMMENT

When we have established such a principle (through the universalist test), it becomes for Kant a categorical imperative (a command which must be followed). Act only on that maxim through which you can at the same time will that it should become a universal law.

If we accept that always telling the truth is a categorical imperative, then every time Mrs Davies asks us whether her husband is coming to see her we must, as duty instructs, tell her he has died. There is a problem: explaining that her husband has died many times during the day, given Mrs Davies's poor short-term memory, will cause her great distress. In effect, she continually relives the anguish when hearing her husband has died. It may be very stressful and time consuming for the members of staff to spend time with Mrs Davies and deal with her unhappiness. It may also be stressful for other residents if they witness Mrs Davies's distress.

Kant believes that people's humanity is defined by our ability to think rationally about our position in the world. Thus we can use our reason to determine what the 'right thing to do' is. Morality is the product of our reasoning as humans and this enables us to organise our conduct and live a moral life. The moral life is one that has been arrived at through the reasoning mind formulating rules of behaviour, which tell us what we ought to do, not what our human desires want us to do. The reason why we should act in this way is because by acting rationally we are living up to our status as human beings.

Continued

COMMENT *continued*

Moral considerations therefore have precedence over all other considerations such as personal pleasure; moral considerations are therefore commands that require us to act in a certain way. To do what is right is then our duty and duty comes before all else. For Mrs Davies our duty is to tell her the truth. Focusing upon one's duty has led people to perform both heroic and horrific acts in equal measure. It provides strong motivations that can often blind people to the consequences of their action.

In the book Hitler's Willing Executioners *(Goldhagan, 1996), the author draws on witness testimony of the Nazi murder squads in Eastern Europe during the Second World War. These men were volunteers who justified the brutality of their acts with the comfort that, although what they did was horrifying, it was justified through their duty to the Führer and the Fatherland. The writer Jung Chang, in her autobiography of her family,* Wild Swans *(1991), writes movingly of the way her father, an important civil servant, would always put his duty to the Chinese Communist Party before his family, preferring not to favour his family unfairly above others.*

Before exploring Kant's principled approach further, it is worth considering at this stage some of the assumptions Kant makes here and relate them to social work.

The first assumption to consider is as follows:

- To be human is to be a rational being.

ACTIVITY **3.5**

Make a list of service users who are likely to be unable to act in a rational way.

COMMENT

Social workers often work with people who may have difficulty in thinking and acting in a rational way. A woman seeking refuge from a violent partner and clearly living under periods of extreme stress may require much support to overcome her fear for herself and her children. Do people with severe learning disabilities whose ability to think rationally may be impaired become less human? How should social workers respond ethically to such people if they adopt a Kantian position?

The second assumption to consider is as follows:

- Emotion is illegitimate.

ACTIVITY **3.6**

Think about the reasons you decided to train as a professional social worker and make a list of the most important ones. How far do they relate to issues of duty in the sense that Kant talks about?

COMMENT

Perhaps one of the reasons you chose to become a social worker was that you were motivated by a desire to help others in a constructive way. You may have been moved by a sense of injustice that many people live dangerous and difficult lives with little material and emotional support. These are strong motivations to want to make a difference in the world. To focus upon the rather austere sense of duty and rationality leaves little room for those feelings of compassion that inform our sense of duty and responsibility to change the world in which we live. Without the motivation of our desires and feeling for our fellow human beings, we would not be able to put ourselves in a position to act morally.

For Kant there is a constant struggle taking place between our higher rational selves and what we consider to be our duty, and our lower desires and instincts and how we satisfy them. Fans of *The Simpsons* TV programme will be aware of the battle between Homer, who exhibits a continuing desire to satisfy his basic instincts, particularly in the realm of food and drink, and his wife Marge, who attempts to elevate his thinking and remind him of his duties, often unsuccessfully. Kant argues that rational beings, therefore, are higher because they rise above the so-called baser instincts; as such they are worthy of respect. They are worthy of respect because rational beings set their own goals in life, which also requires us as rational beings not to impose our own goals upon others. We must not treat others as a means to acquire our own goals but as ends in themselves, capable of forming their own goals just as we do.

Rationality is the means by which human beings become free from self-interest and the pursuit of animal pleasure. This must have seemed very liberating at the time of Kant's writing because this not only frees us from our instincts but also from the strictures of the church and the state. Kant calls this freedom 'autonomy', a concept which means that I decide on the principles that inform the way I live my life, free from the external influences of others. This is a highly individualistic approach which has met with much criticism because it fails to look at the consequences for all those involved in a particular situation. Individuals are important, but we must also take into account that individuals live in societies with others and therefore moral decisions do not exist in a vacuum but have inevitable consequences for others.

Utilitarian consequentialism

The best-known moral theory which develops consequentialism is utilitarianism. This philosophy was developed by Jeremy Bentham (1748–1832), one of the most original and extraordinary thinkers of his day. Bentham believed in, among other things, suffrage (votes) for women. He was also a prison reformer and advocated a legal system based on his theory.

Utilitarianism looks at the consequences of actions, balancing the relative advantages and disadvantages of a particular course of action from the standpoint of creating the greatest good for the greatest number of people. Utilitarians hold that it is not the capacity for rational thought which enables human beings to decide on the right course of action; it is a person's basic drives of seeking pleasure and avoiding pain. This is known as 'the principle of utility'. For utilitarians the assessment of how much happiness can be drawn from a particular action as against how much pain is central; if more happiness is gained for more people then that is the right course of action. Each person's happiness in this understanding is the same as anyone else's; in other words, let each person's happiness count as one. This principle was developed further by Bentham's disciple, J.S. Mill, who argued that actions should be judged on the greatest good for the greatest number, which leads us to two principles informing utilitarianism:

- a principle of justice – let everyone count as one and no one's happiness count as more than that;
- a principle of utility – to ensure the greatest good for the greatest number.

For social work there is a constant tension between these two principles.

CASE STUDY **3.3**

A family resource centre has been given an increase in its funding (£50,000) for the next year. After much consultation with the local community, two proposals have emerged:

1. *To renovate the children's play area (which has been closed on health and safety grounds) so that all the children in the community can play safely at the centre.*

2. *To renovate part of the play area for all the children but use the rest of the money for an outreach worker to work with the local Somali community to encourage greater use of the centre for all children in the area.*

ACTIVITY **3.7**

If you were the manager, what course of action would you take? Give reasons.

COMMENT

Is the point of social work to create the greatest amount of happiness in the situations we are faced with, or are other criteria more important, for example creating as much equality as possible, ensuring social justice and fairness for service users? In the case above it seems that proposal 1 does open up the resource to all the children in the community (the justice principle). However, proposal 2 questions how effective this is if some groups in the community do not feel their families can use the centre (the utility principle).

ACTIVITY **3.8**

Let us now apply the utilitarian principle to Mrs Davies's situation, as outlined previously. In considering this situation two of the questions a utilitarian is likely to consider are:

1. What would be the consequences of lying to Mrs Davies?

2. What might be the options to achieve the least harmful or most advantageous outcome overall for all involved with Mrs Davies?

COMMENT

Traditionally, utilitarianism has considered that any decision should account for the balance of pleasure over pain. In looking at the actions of the care staff, we assess in what ways those actions contribute to a balance of pleasure over pain experienced by Mrs Davies and all those involved with her in the home. This can be defined as act utilitarianism. We are evaluating the action or actions of the individual or group of individuals and quantifying the balance of pleasure (benefits) over pain (costs).

Alternatively, we might suggest to the owner that she develop some guidelines/procedures which could increase the balance of pleasure over pain. In this respect, guidelines about the treatment of service users with senile dementia could be developed and then assessed as to how they minimise harm to all concerned. This is known as rule utilitarianism. We are assessing a principle, based here upon guidelines, to see what the relative benefits and costs are when it is enacted.

However, there are a number of problems with the utilitarian approach. Measuring the balance of pleasure over pain tells us nothing about whose pleasure or pain we are accounting for. If we are measuring the total amount of pleasure promoted, whose pleasure do we take into account, for example Mrs Davies, the care staff, the matron, the other residents, Mrs Davies's relatives? To measure the total happiness produced from one course of action, then, we need to measure all those persons whose happiness is affected by lying to Mrs Davies. This is a purely mathematical procedure but is happiness easily quantified? How do we measure the relative happiness of, say, Mrs Davies, who expects her husband to be coming soon against the care staff, who no longer have to deal with the distress of counselling Mrs Davies when she experiences the grief of losing her husband again?

This led some utilitarians, as we identified above, to propose that every person's happiness counts for one, i.e. that it has the same value. This was developed by Mill to suggest that the decisions we make should account for what will achieve the greatest good for the greatest number. However, if this is the case then we can assume that the power of the majority in any situation may well win over the needs of minorities. Would we want to live in such a society?

Recent publicity has focused upon the small minority of young Muslim women wearing the niqab, a veil that covers a woman's face except for her eyes. A college of further education in Birmingham banned the wearing of such veils along with other clothing, which prevented the person be recognised by staff it was alleged for 'security reasons'.

The importance of the principled and consequentialist approaches

Principled approaches provide a set of guidelines which can act as a framework within which social workers can assess when actions should be undertaken. It provides a benchmark in advance of the situations they are likely to face. Social workers who were asked to visit and counsel the parents of learning-disabled children subjected to euthanasia in Nazi Germany may well have felt their role was entirely justified in reducing what was considered to be a malevolent influence that was degrading the quality of the Aryan master race. They may have felt intimidated and feared that they would suffer punishment if they didn't comply. Or they may have taken a principled approach and refused to undertake such work. This is important, as we have seen with the example of the niqab, where principles of justice which extend the rights of a minority could have been denied. The women who wear this covering argued that it was for religious reasons (this is disputed by other Muslims); nonetheless, whatever the reason why a person chooses to wear the niqab, why should a majority deny that person the right to wear what she chooses to wear? Social workers who may be in a situation supporting this right must be able to justify their actions to official bodies like the courts, who may expect a woman to show her face or in meetings related to the woman's care. Social workers who can argue effectively from a sound principled position will therefore be able to advocate for service users much more effectively than those who try and second guess what might be in the interests of the majority.

Consequentialist approaches also have their strengths when policy makers and managers have to make decisions about the appropriate allocation of resources. The case studies outlined above show that decisions have to consider issues of the greatest good for the greatest number when dealing with the allocation of resources across a number of competing groups. This is not to say that this approach is the only or final one, but it can provide the means to understand the problem, and weigh the competing interests of one group against another when scarce resources mean that some groups may lose out.

Both approaches apply formulas to situations. Irrespective of context, you are required either to do your duty whatever the situation might hold, or calculate the consequences of action. Both formulas tend to ignore the overall context in which these decisions are made. Yet social workers have to exercise their judgement in specific contexts, and although principled and consequentialist approaches may provide useful frameworks to inform a possible course of action, they will not fully inform the social worker. Each situation is unique and requires social workers to understand the specific practice situation. For example, requiring a social worker never to lie to a service user may be highly problematic if the service user in question is a violent estranged husband seeking the whereabouts of his partner and children.

Likewise, always to require social workers to uphold the principle of confidentiality when the child you are working with discloses that her father has physically abused her may again require further action and the breaking of that confidentiality.

For these reasons critics of these approaches have looked to the nature of social work and suggested that the exercise of judgement requires social workers to have particular qualities of character which cannot be read off from the maxims of Kantian or utilitarian theory. Social work often operates in an uncertain and unpredictable environment which cannot be tamed by the application of broad ethical maxims. McBeath and Webb (2002: p1018) make such a point when they argue:

> *Kantian and utilitarian ethics to a degree rely, respectively, upon the mechanical application of rights-claims and adherence to duties, or upon the comparison of anticipated outcomes.*

Given the contingent aspect of social work, in exercising their judgement social workers had better do this in the most effective and informed way possible. This often draws upon the special qualities of social workers as human beings who are required to call upon their reserves of character in order to work in ethical ways. One of the key approaches which stresses the importance of character is virtue theory.

Virtue theory

Virtue theory proposes that ethical practice must be cultivated by 'good' social workers; it focuses development upon the character of the individual social worker. For example, social workers who are unable to suppress their feelings of homophobia in their private lives are likely to carry this prejudice into their professional lives. Virtue theory requires individuals to develop themselves as good people as well as good social workers. If social workers are often required to make judgements about service users then they should make sound judgements. The development of sound judgement requires the exercise of qualities such as courage and wisdom; these cannot be taught through the application of rules advocated by deontologists and consequentialists. As Clark (2006) argues, for example, it is important to show respect to service users, but ethical lists do not tell the social worker how to do this within particular practice situations and contexts. This requires the social worker to interpret the meaning of respect within that particular culture and society. These ideas come from the ancient Greeks, in particular the philosopher Aristotle (384–322 BC). Aristotle was concerned with developing the moral qualities of individuals so that they could embody a good life within themselves. Following the good life required the acquisition of character and the qualities which flowed from that, such as kindness and courage. The concept he identified in this regard was that of flourishing (eudemonia). For Aristotle, living the 'good life' meant individuals were required to follow the 'golden mean', a rule of thumb by which the individual avoids excess. This is not to say that the virtuous social worker should avoid being angry but that anger should be evidenced in appropriate ways and at appropriate times. Cohen (2003) provides some useful examples that can be applied to social work, such as the Goldilocks test (from the children's story) where Goldilocks tests which bowl of porridge to eat and chooses the one that is 'not too cold and not too hot' (Figure 3.2).

When developing character, social workers should seek to develop those qualities on the right of Figure 3.2.

Sphere of applicability	Too much	Too little	Just right
Fear	Rash	Cowardly	Courageous
Anger	Irritable	Lacking spirit	Patient
Social skills	Flatterer	Cantankerous	Friendly
Social conduct	Shy	Shameless	Modest

Figure 3.2   Aspects of virtue

Problems with virtue ethics

Houston (2003) has critiqued the development of virtue-based social work. He suggests there are difficulties in establishing virtue. For example, in order to develop virtue we need to define what it actually means. For Houston, this is problematic because if we consider a virtuous person to have such character traits as bravery, courage, justice and truth, where do these come from? As Houston argues:

> to establish virtue we must refer to the virtuous person but in order to identify him or her, we must have some idea of what virtue is in the first place.

(p820)

Social workers seeking virtue are bound to move around in circles. Virtue is what the virtuous person exhibits and the virtuous person exhibits virtue in an endless circular argument. A second criticism concerns suggestions made by virtue theorists that what must be developed is the moral intuition of individuals so that they can decide on what is virtuous. This ignores the dangers of a solitary individual determining what is good without any reference to others. As Houston suggests, all manner of cognitive bias and unconscious self-manipulation can be present — hardly a firm basis for the development of a virtuous social worker.

These are important criticisms, which the social worker wishing to adopt virtue theory would do well to acknowledge. However, virtue theory does point the way to the importance of sound moral judgement in social work. As Banks and Williams (2005) show, many student social workers when faced with an ethical challenge often feel intimidated because of their status as students, as matched against the powerful professionals whom they identify need to be questioned. As Banks suggests, these dilemmas and conflicts relate to professional confidence, competence and commitment. In echoing virtue theory she suggests that merely to develop an understanding of different ethical principles and arguments is necessary but not sufficient to equip student social workers to practise ethically. It is essential to develop:

> qualities in students that enable them to recognise ethical issues and dilemmas (moral sensitivity) and to act on their decisions (courage and strength of will).

(p749)

Clark (2006) supports this view, suggesting that social workers require a sense of vocation involving an ethical commitment in which their identity and their character are inextricably mixed.

ACTIVITY 3.9

To help you think about the virtues of social workers, put yourself in the position of an interviewer selecting students for the degree in social work.

Is it possible for a social work student to hold prejudicial views about people from ethnic minorities in private while working in a non-discriminatory way in public as a social worker?

What qualities would you look for in a prospective student social worker?

What qualities would you judge to be inappropriate for a social worker?

COMMENT

As you may be able to see from the first question, it would be unprofessional to allow a student social worker on to a social work course who evidenced such prejudice while professing to uphold anti-oppressive principles in his or her public role as a social worker. We would expect that the character and motivations of the student would be congruent with those aims of professional social work, including anti-oppressive practice. We could not expect such prejudicial beliefs to be held when faced with many service users from minority ethnic backgrounds.

Drawing on Clark (2006), it is possible to outline those qualities that are appropriate and inappropriate (Table 3.2).

Table 3.2   Qualities of social workers

Appropriate qualities	Inappropriate qualities
Commitment to learn new skills	Technically incompetent or inept
Commitment to social justice	Discriminatory and neglectful
Enabling	Overly controlling
Morally inclusive	Poor moral character
Competent in social situations	Poor social communication/engagement

(Adapted from Clark, 2006).

This is not an endless list but it points to the necessity for social workers to develop qualities of character that can be overlooked by deontological and consequentialist approaches.

Let us now return to Mrs Davies. Let us make some different assumptions and assume that the officer in charge at the residential home has many years of experience in working with people with senile dementia. Let us also assume that your own experience of working in this area as the social worker involved has provided you with insights into what might constitute best practice. Let us also assume that both you and the residential manager have been involved in developing good practice in the area where you work by running training days in which current research upon working with service users with senile dementia is debated. In short, over time you have both built up, consciously – through practice and reflection and through training – a 'practice wisdom' which you can draw upon as any virtuous professional should. For example, see the research summary below.

RESEARCH SUMMARY

- *Dementia patients must be seen as 'active agents' – people with dementia are vulnerable to being 'negatively positioned'.*

- *This negative positioning unfairly undermines the individuals' right to make decisions about aspects of their lives by not taking into account their meaning-making ability and selfhood.*

- *Alzheimer's disease (AD) sufferers have a number of intact social and cognitive abilities, including intact manifestations of selfhood, despite severe loss of cognition.*

- *Due to their inability to use words effectively, they are viewed as being confused, which is mistakenly interpreted as a symptom of AD.*

- *It is not because they cannot communicate, but rather because they are using different means of communication.*

- *Caregiver treatment includes 'labelling', in which the expectations of progressive decline and derangement are set up and a self-fulfilling prophecy comes into play.*

- *Persons with dementia had most periods of lucidity when acting closely with caregivers who did not make demands on them, saw them as human beings with an identity and regarded their behaviour as a meaningful expression of their experiences.*

(Adapted from Alter, 2012)

Rather than thinking in terms of either lying or not lying to Mrs Davies, you may well think about the problem in a different way. Alter (2012) argues that, by agreeing to the consequentialist path, we may very well institute a regime of lying on every occasion that affects not only Mrs Davies but also any other confused resident who asks a question. In essence, lying becomes a technique to manage the behaviour of residents and reduce staff time in interaction with residents. Likewise, a strong Kantian position which introduces the reality of Mrs Davies's loss of her husband may also be inappropriate in this case. However, validating Mrs Davies's feelings of loss is a different matter and by doing so Mrs Davies's sense of self is recognised through the feelings of loss she is experiencing; this approach is called validation therapy. Although there is much to learn about validation therapy, it certainly reflects a strong anti-oppressive approach. A validation worker would not attempt to create a more pleasant but untrue reality for Mrs Davies based upon a falsehood; instead, the validation worker would attempt to address the latent feelings, in this case, sadness and loss: 'You miss your husband. What does he look like? What would you like to say to him?' (adapted from Alter, 2012).

A feminist ethic of care

In addressing virtue ethics we have emphasised the importance given to the moral qualities of the social worker. Virtue ethics then eschews more abstract ethical perspectives and asks social workers and social care workers to look towards themselves and their capacities for empathy, courage and compassion. As Hugman (2005) argues, there is a growing interest in placing emotions at the heart of ethics. The helping relationship is one in which the emotional content is often silent in the discussion of ethics. When we considered Biestek's list approach to ethics we recognised the importance of controlled emotional involvement by the helper. However, this may underestimate the difficulties of achieving such control by social workers in emotionally charged and disturbing situations; for example, when a child may have to be removed from her parents or carers, or when an older person has to relinquish his independence and move into long-term residential care. Professional ethics then must attend to the importance of emotion and in particular those feelings of compassion within the helping relationship, because as Hugman (2005) argues:

> to attend to compassion involves the recognition of the person or situation, in a way that demands a moral response.

> (p66)

Froggett (2002) supports this argument, suggesting that as rational–technical responses in social work become prevalent, so the ability to feel empathy and show concern by social workers through their professional role has been marginalised. In recognition of how abstract principles of ethical practice are unable to attend satisfactorily to these qualitative issues, arguments for an ethics of care attempt to provide a framework that can account for and include these 'softer' aspects of ethical practice.

Banks (2004) calls the development of an 'ethic of care' by feminist writers as being part of a broader range of relationship-based ethics. This means that a moral significance is given to the characteristics of people's relationships. The approach is one which situates ethical decision making in the quality of the relationships people maintain with one another, in particular where people are in vulnerable or dependent relationships that require a specific orientation, such as compassion or care within the relationship. This is similar to virtue ethics in that ethically sensitive practitioners are required to show a quality or attitude towards the ethical problem that confronts them.

Gilligan (1982) proposes what she calls an 'ethic of care'. This work was a response to the work of Kohlberg (1984), who suggested that there were definite stages to moral development. Kohlberg's approach explored the idea that moral judgement is acquired developmentally in tandem with the development of other cognitive and intellectual skills. Kohlberg distinguished six stages of moral development, each stage developing out of the one before (Figure 3.3). These stages move from the basic level of learned obedience and avoidance of punishment, to a middle phase concerned with maintaining and developing social relationships, which he called a conventional morality, through to the most advanced, which is characterised by identifying complex moral issues and developing and applying universal principles.

Level 1 reflects the level of thinking which is dependent on looking to what is socially acceptable – people act in a way which is socially sanctioned by an authority figure. This is reinforced through accepting that punishment may rightly follow any transgression of the rules and therefore deviant behaviours are to be avoided.

Level	Stage	Social orientation
Pre-conventional	1	Obedience and punishment
	2	Individualism, instrumentalism and exchange
Conventional	3	'Good boy/girl'
	4	Law and order
Post-conventional	5	Social contract
	6	Principled conscience

Figure 3.3   Kohlberg's classification

Level 2 has moral thinking developing in response to approval-seeking by others and orients itself in society to doing one's duty through obligations imposed by society, by following existing moral and legal codes.

Level 3 is where moral thinking is relatively rare, in Kohlberg's estimation. This thinking is grounded by the valuing of fraternity and an authentic concern for the welfare of others. This leads into the highest stage for Kohlberg, based on the valuing of independent moral principle, reflected in the developed conscience and respect for universal principles of justice, for example, which may challenge notions of conventional law and morality.

Moral development requires individuals to move through each stage in turn. In order to move to the next stage, individuals first have to appreciate the moral principles informing the previous stage.

Kohlberg's research, although claiming universal applicability, had been conducted upon men only. When Gilligan (1982) conducted her research on young women she found that the 'lower' morality concerned with maintaining relationships predominated in her sample. For Gilligan this reflected not a lower state of moral development in women but a different one. Gilligan called this the 'different voice', an ethic of care based upon maintaining social relationships, rather than an ethic of justice determined to develop the right action from abstract principles of justice. For Gilligan, women's moral voice has been silenced by the male concern for developing abstract principles to inform moral development. The dominance of male philosophers and ethical theorists reinforces this process by insisting on the universal applicability of terms such as rationality and objectivity in the development of ethical theory.

ACTIVITY **3.10**

Ask your male and female friends to solve the problem below.

Joseph is playing with his sisters Frances and Zoe. Joseph wants to play 'firefighters' and suggests they all build a fire engine out of the kitchen chairs. Frances and Zoe want to play 'casualty'. None of the children wants to play the others' game. How could you overcome this impasse?

> COMMENT
>
> *Gilligan's research showed that male and female respondents might solve this problem differently. While most men take the option called 'turn taking' – we play firefighters and then we play casualty – based on a justice model of equal turn taking, most women, by contrast, would seek to resolve the problem by including or merging both games into one, something like 'let's play firefighters who need to go to casualty' (Figure 3.4). This emphasises the essential connected nature of the game, meaning both viewpoints are reconciled through maintaining relationships within the group so that all are included.*

The male voice	
Apply key value	*Solution*
Justice reinforces separation of persons	Play firefighters first, casualty second
The female voice	
Apply key value	*Solution*
Care maintains connectedness between persons	Play firefighters injured in casualty

Figure 3.4   The male and female voice

According to Gilligan, most of our moral concepts have developed from a male perspective and are characterised as abstract principles. They have ignored the particular situations within which people make moral choices. For example, the major approach to moral philosophy over the past several hundred years has been what might be called an 'ethic of justice', which is deeply rooted in a desire for individual autonomy and independence. The concern for an ethic of justice is to balance the competing interests among individuals. Gilligan points out the troubling consequences of an ethic of justice that does not take into account an 'ethic of care'.

Formal concepts such as duty and justice often result in an objectification of human beings or, at least, a distancing of the parties involved in, and affected by, moral decision making. Caring, on the other hand, requires a closer relationship between parties and recognition of the other as a subjective being. Gilligan suggests that the quality of caring is best understood as coming from the feminine, though not exclusively so. Caring considers the needs of both the self and others – it is not just concerned with self-survival. In considering the needs of both self and others, moral decisions should make allowances for differences in the needs of others. Tronto (1993) develops this further, suggesting that the idea of care is a basic and valued premise of human existence. It is founded on the fact that we depend upon others and that we have the capacity to care for others. Care is a process and a practice that has four phases:

1. caring about – recognising the need for care;

2. taking care of – assuming a responsibility to care;

3. care giving;

4. care receiving.

Chapter 3 Principles and consequences

From this, she derives four ethical elements of care:

1. attentiveness;
2. responsibility;
3. competence;
4. responsiveness.

This conception is based on an 'obligation to care'. From this perspective we view ourselves as part of a network of connected individuals whose different needs create a duty in us to respond. By responding, we must attend to the details of the need which is expressed, and to the outcome of our response on others potentially affected by our actions.

This does not mean that every need requires a response. We must also weigh:

- the seriousness of the need;
- the likely benefit derived from our response;
- our ability to respond to this particular need;
- the competing needs of others in our network.

Almost all ethical decisions require us to weigh competing interests. What an 'ethic of care' requires is to relate the need on an emotional level, a consideration lacking in deontology and consequentialism.

ACTIVITY 3.11

1. Look at Figure 3.5 and link the individuals into a network by joining lines between them. For those who you consider are more significant, draw a double line between the respective participants in the network.

2. Look at Figure 3.5 and identify possible conflicts between the partners which have the potential for disrupting the relationships from the point of view of Mrs Davies.

3. Now decide how you can ensure that all the participants in Figure 3.5 can retain those valued relationships so that the network can be sustained.

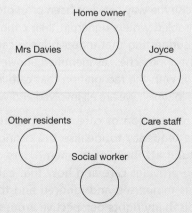

Figure 3.5 How would such an approach relate to Mrs Davies's situation?

63

COMMENT

From Figure 3.5, you can see that the social worker is part of the complex of relationships which have developed around Mrs Davies. To this end, you must take account of your practice within the social network created and the quality of the relationships forged by all the participants. Instead of acting from the outside and judging what your duty might be, or what the most beneficial consequences are, you are ethically required to take account of the lived experience and emotions of all those within this network of relationships. For Mrs Davies the ethic of care requires us to respond to her immediate need, i.e. her despair at continually repeating her feelings of loss for her deceased husband, and to her development as a moral person of worth within the residential home. Within the network of relationships then, the immediate others are also implicated in this, and each of those people's needs must also be weighed in this way. Therefore what becomes the right course of action will nurture the existing social relationships within Mrs Davies's network. To tell Mrs Davies the truth may ultimately destroy her relationship with her daughter as her daughter becomes increasingly wary of talking to her mother if she is being continually asked about her deceased father and then witnessing her mother's grief. This ethical thought process can then be integrated with others in the social network of Mrs Davies. Although you as the social worker may arrive at the same decision as if you were operating, for example, from a consequentialist approach, the importance is derived in the care and attention given in the process of decision making. The quality of the individual's relationships is attended to and given due attention. In this regard the process of arriving at the decision is as important as the decision itself.

Problems of an ethic of care

Criticisms of care ethics have come from writers from the disability movement. These criticisms derive from their concern that care has been used oppressively with disabled people, whose demand for greater independence may be compromised by an uncritical adoption of such an approach. Shakespeare (2000) has argued that two alternative theoretical models for reforming care are available. The first derives from the disabled people's movement and sets out a model of independent living. The second is the feminist ethic of care. Both criticise the way care has been promoted, but they diverge in their vision for an alternative. Disabled writers underpin their critique by emphasising the civil rights of disabled people, suggesting that independence can be achieved via personal assistance schemes. Feminist approaches, as identified above, question the whole notion of care and wish to recast it with the recognition that care is not special but forms the normal part of everyday life in which we are all involved and which we rely on.

While the recasting and recognition of care are important, disability and feminist writers would criticise the tendency to idealise the caring role and the implication that caring may be a natural attribute of women. Users of care services often feel a lack of control over who provides care and how that care is provided. In addition they may feel their voice is minimised and ignored and their very bodies neglected and abused by carers. A disability rights perspective argues for justice in care so that disabled people have the autonomy and independence that some feminists (Silvers et al., 1998) argue is a patriarchal barrier undermining an ethic of care.

CASE STUDY 3.4

Let us assume Mrs Davies does not acquire senile dementia but becomes more physically dependent upon her daughter following a series of falls. Mrs Davies, although preferring her daughter to care for her, realises that she cannot ask her daughter to do more for her as she can see how exhausted her daughter gets. Following an assessment of her needs by her social worker, Mrs Davies is given a significant package of care. Mrs Davies did not like to complain but she felt that the social worker was a little brusque in her attitude and seemed to be rushed.

A support worker will visit three times a day: in the morning to help Mrs Davies get up, at midday to get shopping and at 8 o'clock in the evening to help Mrs Davies into bed. Mrs Davies, although grateful for the care, is unhappy that many of her social needs are not taken into account. She has asked that some of the care hours could be used to enable her to visit her daughter or go to the cinema, which she enjoys, but these do not fit into the carer's rota given that the carers have to organise their time efficiently to meet their commitments to the other people they have to visit.

ACTIVITY 3.12

In what way does the organisation of Mrs Davies's care deny her independence?

In what way does the nature of the care provided limit Mrs Davies's care?

COMMENT

Mrs Davies's independence is compromised by the way that her care is organised. She is unable to maintain her social contacts and her presence in the wider community as the care provided for her is narrowed to her basic care needs. Her independence is compromised further by the way that her assessment was done to her rather than with her.

In respect to care, this provision limits Mrs Davies's options, particularly when the carers are getting her to bed at 8 o'clock.

Feminist writers such as Sevenhuijsen (1998) and Lister (2003) have sought to develop an ethic of care alongside an ethic of justice. They recognise that there is a darker side to care in which frustration, conflict and abuse can be present unless this is tempered by a concern for justice in care. However, there is still considerable tension in these approaches. Disabled people continue to fight for the right of independence and observe that, just as women's dependency is socially constructed, so it is for disabled people. The priority for disabled people is to be able to make choices to exert control over their own lives rather than question independence. As Shakespeare (2000) argues:

> *Rather than challenging the goal of independence, disabled people want to be empowered to become independent. The crucial move is not just to recognise that everyone has needs, but to break the link between physical and social dependency.*

(p80)

The goal of independence as a first step for disabled people is crucial but this should not prevent the ethical social worker from questioning independence. A feminist ethic of care does point towards reconciliation between care and justice and an ethic in which all persons should have the right to care for and be cared for by others. For some disabled people the severity of their impairment may be such that developing the kind of independence argued for above is difficult to achieve but must always be aspired to. This requires an ethic of justice in attending to the validity of those people's needs and ensuring their fair treatment, while at the same time recognising the mutual interests and interdependency that we all share. How care and justice are linked can be evidenced by the claims of some disabled people to be supported to have children. In this regard they have the right to be able to bear and look after children if they so choose. In the achievement of such a right we are attending to the necessary development of disabled people as interdependent as caregivers and care receivers. Research by Tarleton et al. (2006) shows how problematic this issue is, finding that 50 per cent of the parents with learning disabilities researched had had their children removed into care. Trotter and Ward (2013) summarise the key elements of an ethic of care as follows:

1. There is an explicit focus on relationships and the moral requirement to meet the needs of others for whom we take responsibility.

2. Persons are viewed in relational terms rather than construed as self-sufficient autonomous beings.

3. Acts of caring are most reliably motivated by social or moral emotions such as empathic concern, sympathy and compassion; ethical thinking comprises emotional processes such as responsiveness and sensitivity as well as rational principles such as consistency and generalisability.

4. The focus of an ethics of care is on the concrete, specific relationships people are in, often not by choice, rather than the idealised, abstract relationships found in traditional moral theories. More attention is paid to the contexts of moral situations and the details of people's lives and characteristics.

5. There is a rejection of the distinction between public and private spheres of functioning. Relationships in what have been regarded as private domains (e.g. domestic households) have, according to care theorists, been regulated by the wishes of dominant individuals without necessarily revealing any explicit concern for the interests of other persons involved – women and children, for example.

CHAPTER SUMMARY

This chapter has explored the range of philosophical approaches to ethics and related these approaches to social work. It has shown the importance of deontological and consequentialist approaches in social work and has emphasised their significance. We have suggested that any philosophical approach has to be applied in a specific context which requires the social worker to assess the validity of each approach for that particular service user. By contrast we have then considered virtue ethics and suggested that character has importance for social workers in reflecting and living out those principles considered important for ethical social work practice. Finally we have considered a feminist ethic of care and shown how this has been an undervalued approach in social work. The advantages and disadvantages of an ethic of care have been investigated using the critique developed by Shakespeare (2000).

FURTHER READING

Banks, S (2006) *Ethics and values in social work*, 3rd edn. Basingstoke: Palgrave.

Banks's book provides good coverage of all the main philosophical approaches identified in this chapter.

Porter, E (1999) *Feminist perspectives on ethics*. London: Longman.

Porter provides a highly accessible introduction to feminist ethics.

Chapter 4
Being accountable

What do service users value?

RESEARCH SUMMARY

Virtually all our respondents wanted some advice and someone to listen, and when they did get this they were enormously appreciative. It also appeared to work. One couple, for example, where the father had only managed to elicit advice and support over the telephone about their teenage daughter, said it had made all the difference. The young woman (aged 13) herself stated that things were now better because they had all sat down as a family to talk about difficulties. Another mother with two late teenage children felt alone and needed some help and advice: she appreciated the short burst of help and, although critical overall about the provision, liked the fact that the social worker was very clear about her role.

(Leigh and Miller, 2004)

Research undertaken on service users from the 1970s onward shows a remarkable consistency in what service users value from social workers (Mayer and Timms, 1970; Rees, 1978; Winefield and Barlow, 1995). Social workers are valued:

- for their ability to listen;

- for engaging empathically with service users;

- for being clear about what they can and cannot do;

- for providing basic and effective help.

For example, research by Smith et al. (2012) with involuntary service users showed the salience of the list above, as service users who often resented the involvement of social workers commented with approval on the ways in which social workers listened to their views and provided advice of relevance to their situation, even though their relationship with their social worker was often adversarial.

Nevertheless, what service users value from professional social work and what is sometimes provided does not always tally. Social workers can sometimes inhabit a provider ideology which limits service users' options. Ellis (2007) identified how social workers used their discretion to limit the access to direct payments to certain groups they considered would not benefit from them, such as older people. She also identified how social workers felt that direct payments undermined their control over resources, particularly if service users were given more control as to how they should be allocated. She identified how this:

- restricted the rights of people to use services as they wanted to use them;

- emphasised control by social workers;

- limited equal access and opportunities to direct payments.

Such an approach subverts the needs of service users to the requirements of social workers and often the organisations that employ them. This leads to an entrenchment of organisational and professional values which marginalises the rights of service users to a responsive service. Professionalism in this view has for too long limited what was available to service users through what was considered professionally expedient. Professionalism in this sense is closely associated with the concept of 'welfarism' (Froggett, 2002). This reflected a commitment to the provision of universal welfare services defined, administered and delivered by professionals which ignored service users' definitions of need, leading to a 'one size fits all' approach. Delivering welfare services resembled the mass production of consumer goods infamously associated with car manufacturer Henry Ford, who is rumoured to have said: 'Any customer can have a car painted any colour that he wants, so long as it is black.'

Welfarism institutionalises a hierarchical relationship of social worker and client, with power residing with the social worker, using his or her professional expertise to decide upon client need. The evidence remains that service users are rarely involved in key decisions as to how resources are commissioned and allocated. Recent research by Schehrer and Sexton (2010) analysed service users' experiences of consultation over the commissioning of services and found a very patchy response by local authorities. Some authorities were open to ideas of consultation but often service users experienced either hostility to the idea or an ostensible willingness, although the authorities' lack of action led them to identify an unwillingness to engage.

Professional social work is changing fast as local authorities try and manage their dwindling budgets, coupled with the challenges of organisational change. In the health service, social workers are increasingly finding themselves working in a range of environments, from GP surgeries to working from home, which may mitigate against the potential to form a strong professional identity. For example, some 11 per cent of the British Association of Social Workers (BASW) membership now describe themselves as independent social workers (Adetunji, 2012). This process was identified by Asquith et al. (2005), who observed that, in Scotland, pressures upon this identity have come from the move away from direct work with service users and the requirement to fulfil a more limited organisational function within local authority social work departments. This has been reinforced by the requirement to work across agencies, for example, with health and education professionals. They suggest that social work organisations may no longer be necessary in their present form. Similar processes have begun in England, where the requirement for greater partnership, working in adult care with health and child care with education, is leading to new organisational structures such as Children's Trusts, which have been further reformed by the Coalition government. However, as Ellis (2011) argues, the precise nature of how the social work role and in particular the role of professional autonomy has changed varies as to the precise nature of the social work organisation in which social workers find themselves. Her study of social care in this regard identifies a range of different roles adopted by social workers subject to different organisational constraints.

The practitioner

The practitioner is subject to considerable control by the use of new technology which ensures greater managerial control. The practitioner is driven by policies and procedures, particularly in terms of eligibility to services, which encourages social workers to dismiss those who are not eligible. Use of professional autonomy is usually justified by the rules applicable to a particular case, for example, in terms of eligibility to a service rather than arguing for an exemption to the rules.

The bureau-professional

Subject to less procedural control, the bureau-professional is able to negotiate with often specialist workers who operate outside managerial control. Bureau-professionals are more able to negotiate roles and tasks and promote a sense of their own professional expertise and identity.

The street-level bureaucrat

Social workers are required to make informal judgements outside of the normal criteria for accessing services. Because of the pressure of work, where demand for a service exceeds the resources and time available to social workers, social workers bend rules in order to enable them to deal with workload pressures. The rules may then be broken for pragmatic reasons, i.e. getting the job done, rather than to exercise professional autonomy.

The paternalistic professional

Where social workers may work from a therapeutic model, and where they are relatively shielded from the processes of managerial control, then work is defined in terms of what is best for the service user. Service users' needs, defined as emotional rather than practical, can liberate the social worker from processing cases and fitting them into eligibility criteria.

ACTIVITY **4.1**

Make a list of attributes which you would expect a professional social worker to have. Here is my list (not exhaustive). Is yours different?

- *knowledge of social problems – understanding of poverty, discrimination and its effects on different groups;*

- *knowledge of individual problems – child development, mental health;*

- *possession of appropriate skills, e.g. communication skills;*

- *motivation to help people in constructive ways;*

- *sound value base that informs their practice.*

COMMENT

Apart from the attributes that we would expect of a professional social worker there is something more about a profession which takes us beyond the competency of the work that professionals do. Friedson (2001) constructs an ideal list of attributes which encompasses both competence and wider social and political attributes of professions. These are:

- *specialised knowledge;*

- *power to organise and control one's own work;*

- *sole legal power to offer a service;*

- *only fellow professionals can supervise and scrutinise work;*

- *dedicated to service of the public.*

As Friedson (2001) argues, these attributes are only ideals and as such the reality contains positive and negative characteristics. As identified in Chapter 1, the behaviour of some social work professionals does not live up to the ideal. Professionals may collude to protect their status and income from the encroachment of others. Social workers, like other professionals, are increasingly subject to pressure from service users and the state (Figure 4.1). On the one hand, the state has introduced both tighter control through the use of service targets and a greater use of the private sector in the provision of services. On the other hand, service users are demanding a greater voice in the planning, organisation and delivery of services.

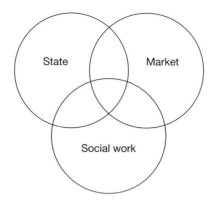

Figure 4.1   Professions, state and market

Compared with other professions, social work is less independent of state control and is therefore more vulnerable when faced with pressure from the state. These differences can be attributed to wider social and political factors which the work of Larson (1977) and Abbott (1988) identifies well.

Larson:

Looks at the historical process by which a limited group of occupations strategically increased their social status as against other occupational groups to gain a monopoly in the marketplace. Thus professions gain economic advantage for themselves by restricting the supply of practitioners and striving for a favoured place in society in terms of the respect and influence afforded to them. Thus a profession gains status or loses it by its ability to control the market for its skill and the extent to which it is then respected by wider society.

Abbott:

Looks at the way occupations gain and maintain control over specific occupational activities. This is viewed through the division of labour in which different occupational groups compete over control of different occupational activities and how they maintain their own social and official boundaries. Thus the ability of a profession to maintain its status relies on maintaining this strict division of labour. He points out that 'professions' (i.e. what members of such professional groups and others normally call professions) develop when jurisdictions become vacant; groups of expert workers convert their work and knowledge into a currency. They present their work as expertise different from other expert work. In turn they can claim an expert status beside other expert groups (occupations, professions).

Social work, therefore, is in a different position from some of the professions analysed by the two writers above as these writers focus mostly upon more traditional professions, for example, medicine and the law. Social work's history is different and is not comparable to those traditional professions. In essence, social work as part of the 'caring professions' is mandated by society to perform certain activities which it is hoped will lead to the general well-being of individuals and the society within which they live (Hugman, 2005). But this social mandate is under increasing pressure, as noted above, from the state and service users. Service user groups have mounted formidable criticism of social workers; for example, the disability movement has successfully criticised the welfarism of social services in reinforcing ideas of dependency on service users. The state, largely as a response to some well-publicised cases which impute neglect on behalf of social workers, has increasingly introduced legislation to require more partnership working with other professionals (Department for Education and Science, 2004). When social workers have tried to develop their own critical practice through anti-oppressive approaches they have been opposed by groups that wish to control and punish those whom social work seeks to empower. Throughout the 1980s and 1990s the tabloid press ran a number of stories which purported to expose the 'political correctness' emanating from so-called left-wing councils and social work departments (Franklin, 1999). In 1987 an unheard-of rise in the diagnosis of child abuse involving some 121 children who were compulsorily separated from their families led to a major inquiry into the methods used to diagnose children suspected of being abused and the subsequent handling of procedures to remove children from their homes. The subsequent report (Butler-Sloss, 1988) criticised the way suspected child abuse was diagnosed and the lack of interagency cooperation.

Such pressure had a significant effect, with the appointment of a lawyer, Jeffrey Greenwood, as chair of Central Council for Education and Training in Social Work in 1993. He declared his commitment to equal opportunities, but also pledged to rid social work training of *politically correct nonsense*. This led to a revision of training policy, where explicit orientation to such politically charged references to race and antiracism was dropped (Mclaughlin, 2005). The focus upon social work and its presumed mistakes at this time highlights the relative weakness of the social work profession to resist efforts to limit its professional discretion, but also reveals the nature of accountability in social work.

Accountability

To be a professional social worker is to be accountable. Accountability means that as social workers we are prepared to be open to the scrutiny of others for our actions, prepared to accept praise and blame in equal measure and prepared to explain our actions. Social workers' accountability is not necessarily transparent. Is social workers' primary accountability to service users, to the wider community which provides the resources for social work or to their employers? To be accountable involves:

- explaining one's actions;
- justifying one's actions;

- admitting one's actions may have been at fault;

- countering unjustified criticism.

On a personal level, accountability requires social workers to be open to criticism, which can be threatening to one's self-esteem, whether criticism is justified or not. But to be a professional requires the worker not to personalise this criticism and understand it as an aspect of the professional role to develop ethical practice. Being accountable not only involves the passive sense; it requires an active engagement in which the social worker may seek to counter unjustified criticism. Practically, being accountable involves social workers keeping case records, attending case conferences, writing case reviews, attending court, giving evidence and writing court reports. All of these actions place the social worker under public scrutiny, and call practitioners to account.

CASE STUDY 4.1

Brian's social worker, Caroline, has written a pre-sentence report for the Youth Court. Because of the pressure to complete the report on time, Caroline did not check the grammar before sending it to the court. Although she made some recommendations on Brian's behalf, this was unsupported by research or other evidence. The magistrates remarked on the poor grammar, which made parts of the report hard to follow. Unfortunately, to compound the situation further, Caroline attended the court in a pair of jeans as she did not have time to change after working with a group of young offenders on a playgroup scheme.

On the face of it, these may seem fairly minor infractions and ones which Caroline would not repeat if she could choose, or could she?

COMMENT

In addressing the practical issues of accountability we need to consider the following:

- *How far did Caroline prepare? Did she read the appropriate research and allow enough time to write a thorough report? Often social workers are pressured by their managers to take on more work than they can cope with. It is essential that Caroline learns to be more assertive with her manager if this happens. If Caroline manages her time and is not overburdened by her caseload, she will be able to be more thorough in her report writing. Likewise Caroline must plan for the day in court. She will then have time to prepare herself for any questions asked and consider what might be the appropriate dress for the occasion.*

- *How far did Caroline practise? Did she go through any information she wanted to present in advance? If there are legal issues involved, she should ensure she is familiar with them and reflect how the court might respond. Researching the practice issues and making sure she is prepared enable her professional persona to flourish in any public forum. When she is on public show it is not only the content of her communication that is scrutinised, but also her general demeanour. How she presents and handles herself in public reflects upon her professionalism and is a part of her professional accountability. Ultimately her practice*

Continued

is designed to provide the service user with the maximum representation through the effective employment of her professional knowledge and her personal engagement in court.

If Caroline presents negatively by being inappropriately dressed, lacking knowledge of the case and being poorly informed, she is signalling her unprofessional approach. If she presents as too casual in her demeanour, can she be trusted, particularly if she appears hesitant and unable to give a clear account of the case? This will therefore reflect on the person, i.e. both Caroline and the service user, and risks any case achieving an unfavourable outcome.

The law and accountability

Social workers are endowed with duties and powers deriving from the authority given to them by law and statute. But what right do social workers have to intervene through the law? What authority do social workers have and where does it come from? Clark (2000) outlines three basic justifications for professional social workers to exercise their legal powers:

1. Professional power is exercised through the law and therefore what constitutes appropriate conduct must relate to how the law defines the rights of citizens and the duties of social workers to intervene.

2. Law should be made through the consent of citizens and it should both promote the general good and not compromise human rights in doing so.

3. Professional power should be informed by professional expertise to promote the general good and protect human rights.

This legitimacy to act becomes complex when confronting the messiness of social work practice and the way in which the law is codified. This requires social workers to interpret what the relevant statutes actually intend. The law by itself is not value-free or objective. It embodies values of its own which reflect the power of dominant groups in society to frame and influence what the law should embody. Social workers need to view the legislative process with some scepticism and constantly scrutinise its operation.

One example can be gleaned from the NHS and Community Care Act 1990: sections 46 and 47 impose a duty on local authorities to provide information to service users about services and a duty to assess need. The problem from a values point of view is that there is no duty to provide the services that the assessment has identified. Yet on the other hand the law does not say the local authority can do nothing as a result of the assessment, so there may be areas for social workers to negotiate and intervene on the service user's behalf to achieve an element of what the assessment identifies in terms of service delivery. In respect of community care legislation, the Act enables local authorities considerable flexibility in deciding which needs are addressed.

Local authorities also have the power to withdraw services. This followed the Gloucester judgement which decided that services could be withdrawn subject to a reassessment of need if a local authority was faced with resource problems requiring resources to be rationed to prevent overspending (*R* v *Gloucestershire County Council, ex parte Barry* [1997] 2 WLR 459). For social workers, then, it is imperative that they understand both the potential to use the law in respect of protecting people from harm, and also its limitations. Our example of community care law shows how limitations affect the rights of service users when their social support is reduced.

Disabled people take care issues to court

In 1995 six disabled people launched a test case in the High Court over the right to community care services. Five pensioners, one of them a Mr Barry, challenged decisions by Gloucestershire County Council to reduce or cut home help and respite care services because of lack of money.

ACTIVITY **4.2**

Let us assume that you are the social worker who originally assessed Mr Barry's needs and you are working with him. You have realised that he, along with many others in the local authority, has had his domiciliary support reduced.

How should you respond when he asks you:

1. to explain the actions of the local authority that you work for?

2. to explain where your accountability lies?

COMMENT

This case identifies the difficulties social workers face when explaining policy which they disagree with. On the one hand, you are accountable as an employee to the local authority which employs you, but you are also accountable to Mr Barry. To use a colloquial expression, you are caught between 'a rock and a hard place'. On reflection, it is appropriate for you to inform Mr Barry that you do not personally agree with the decision. You could also take the case further by suggesting that Mr Barry uses the legal route to appeal against this decision and you could offer to link him with one of the many local and national pressure/service users groups who might take his case further. You could take the issue back to your managers and lobby on Mr Barry's behalf; you might also join with other social workers who have experienced similar problems and put together a case to feed back to your managers. You might take the issue through the local branch of your union (UNISON) to apply pressure through the local joint committees upon which employers and union representatives sit.

As a social worker you are not just an employee, but a professional who has a range of responsibilities which do not begin and end with your responsibility to your employer, although this clearly constitutes one of your responsibilities. As social workers are increasingly involved in

Continued

COMMENT *continued*

rationing resources and prioritising cases, they are caught in a dichotomous accountability in which a concern for individual service users and the service they receive is constantly challenged by the need to ration and control resources. To be accountable, social workers need to balance the corporate responsibility they hold and their duty of service to service users.

The tensions highlighted above draw attention to the ambiguous nature of accountability. Social workers' professional associations have recognised this, as the definition of social work below identifies.

Definition of social work

Social workers will:

(a) strive to carry out the stated aims of their employing organisation, provided that they are consistent with this Code of Ethics;

(b) aim for the best possible standards of service provision and be accountable for their practice;

(c) use the organisation's resources honestly and only for their intended purpose;

(d) appropriately challenge, and work to improve, policies, procedures, practices and service provisions which:

- are not in the best interests of service users;

- are inequitable or unfairly discriminatory; or

- are oppressive, disempowering, or culturally inappropriate;

(e) endeavour, if policies or procedures of employing bodies contravene professional standards, to effect change through consultation, using appropriate organisational channels;

(f) take all reasonable steps to ensure that employers are aware of the Code of Ethics for Social Work, and advocate conditions and policies which reflect its ethical position;

(g) uphold the ethical principles and responsibilities of this Code, even though employers' policies or instructions may not be compatible with its provisions, observing the values and principles of this Code when attempting to resolve conflicts between ethical principles and organisational policies and practices.

(British Association of Social Workers, 2001)

ACTIVITY **4.3**

If we return to the case of Mr Barry, we have already outlined in the comment possible courses of action. From the BASW definition of social work, above, what elements could be used by you to justify challenging your employer's actions?

Clearly paragraph (d) supports an ethical stance to challenge your employer. In particular, the bullet points outlined make it clear your duty is to challenge if you feel an employer's policies run counter to the interests of service users, especially if they operate unfairly or are oppressive and disempowering. Your employers may argue that by cutting domiciliary services across the board they do not discriminate against any one service user. However, you may want to argue that, in respect of Mr Barry, the cut in service may have the consequences of being particularly oppressive and discriminatory if it means he is unable to support himself in the community like others in a similar position.

By advocating for Mr Barry you are operating in a responsive fashion within the constraints of your position as a social worker, paid by the state to enact a particular role. This means as a paid employee you are subsequently accountable to your employer and if you are unable to manage this tension between service users and your employing organisation, then you need to consider if the role of social worker is one that you feel capable of carrying out (Table 4.1).

Table 4.1 Nature of conflicts with service user

Enact social change	Enact social control
Advise	Direct
Enable	Control
Advocate	Manage

Accountability and the law

One of the main reasons for becoming a social worker comes from the desire to help those at risk of exploitation and social exclusion. As a social worker, it is easy to see the law as a hindrance to what you might think of as real social work. The law, as noted above, is imperfect but at any one time it represents what is considered to be the will of the citizens in a democratic process whereby law is legislated through Parliament. The law gives social workers much room for exercising their judgement and discretion but cannot work unless that discretion is used wisely. The law, with all its problems, provides a framework which:

- establishes social work agencies and sets out procedures for helping;

- sets standards for when it is appropriate, and when it is necessary, for action to be taken;

- provides a framework for holding social workers to account.

The law often needs improving, but, for the social worker and others, it cannot be ignored. It is law, and not ideals, which sets out, sometimes with clarity but sometimes with confusion, what social workers are required to do, who they are accountable to, who they have responsibilities towards, and to some extent the overarching principles which govern public services. This is not to say that law is separate from ethics; best practice is both legally and ethically informed, but the imperative for the social worker in deciding how to respond to complex ethical dilemmas is to ensure that their chosen course of action is lawful.

(Brayne and Carr, 2005, p1)

In being accountable, it is clear that when service users' interests conflict with the state's interests, an ethical conflict is presented to the social worker. In certain cases this conflict is less problematic. To override a service user's wishes may result in the protection from harm of that person or protecting others from the harmful effects of that service user's actions. Using force or acting against service users' wishes if they are damaging others may be difficult but has as its justification the prevention of harm. As Clark (2000) argues, social workers are ultimately accountable to the state and their actions must be seen in the light of the purposes which the state has in regulating the behaviour of its citizens. As he observes, the function of social work in society is to *regulate and control* (p106).

Ethics and accountability

In recognising the importance of accountability it is necessary to investigate the role that a code of ethics has in providing guidelines by which social work profession-als can be called to account. Ethics refers to the professional obligations which act as rules of conduct by which social workers should practise. A written code of ethics enables social workers to judge their practice against an ethical standard. Just as importantly, a code of ethics enables service users to understand what they should expect from a social worker in terms of conduct. By definition, then, social work-ers' actions can be judged as ethical or otherwise by reference to a code of practice. As student social workers, you will be required to adhere to the Health and Care Professions Council's (HCPC's) standards and ethical requirements (HCPC, 2014). But there are other codes which you may also adhere to. The BASW operates a code of practice and, as such, if you become a member of the association, you will be required to uphold its code. However, this code is chosen voluntarily. With the HCPC regulations, these are requirements over which you have no choice and you are duty-bound to uphold them.

The HCPC Standards of Conduct, Performance and Ethics were launched in 2012. They are intended to provide a guide for all those who work in social care, setting out the standards of practice and conduct that workers should meet. The code is a cru-cial element in regulating the behaviour of social workers and social care workers. The importance of the standards is clear when social workers who are considered in breach of them can be removed from the HCPC register and prevented from practising.

As research by Banks and Williams (2005) has shown, codes of ethics and codes of practice comprise a range of pronouncements containing rules, principles and general statements, for example, rules of professional practice which workers must comply with. They may also include ethical rules, such as maintaining confidentiality. The list below highlights this further.

General statements

- These may include statements which outline the general mission of a profession, as in social work, which may include the enhancement of human well-being.

- Such statements outline the attributes of a professional social worker, such as: professional social workers should be honest and trustworthy.

General principles

- These describe the general ethical attributes of practice which social workers should adhere to, such as respect for the autonomy of service users or the promotion of their general well-being.

- These are the principles of professional practice which describe the means by which social workers can meet the needs of service users, such as collaboration with colleagues and maintenance of accurate case notes.

Specific rules

- These are rules of professional practice, such as not accepting gifts from service users.

- These are ethical rules such as protecting the confidentiality of service users.

ACTIVITY **4.4**

*To understand the importance of such codes, go to the HCPC website: **www.hcpc-uk.org/assets/documents/performanceand ethics**. Using the general list adapted from Banks and Williams, above, make a list of those statements which contain:*

- *general statements about the nature and purpose of social work;*

- *general principles which social workers should adhere to;*

- *specific rules which social workers must adhere to.*

COMMENT

You should have been able to identify quite a number of answers to fit the specific categories above. To test your answers I have provided a brief, and therefore not exhaustive, list below.

General statements about the nature and purpose of social work

- *It is interesting to note that, because the HCPC document is a generic one and is meant to be applicable to a range of social work and health care professionals, no such statement can be found. This was a slight trick, but important given our discussion above about the changing role and nature of social work and the disappearance of a distinct professional identity.*

Continued

General principles which social workers should adhere to

- *You must respect the confidentiality of service users.*

Specific rules which social workers must adhere to

- *You must effectively supervise tasks that you have asked other people to carry out.*

- *You must get informed consent to provide care or services (so far as possible).*

It is important to recognise that the HCPC, because of its prescriptive nature, tends to focus upon more specific rules and principles rather than making more generalised statements about the nature, and purpose, of social work. It is interesting to note that references to the ethical aspects of the recognition of difference as part of an anti-oppressive practice do not figure as a specific principle, but become part of standard 1, you must act in the best interests of service users. For reference, go back to the HCPC standards and identify those aspects of anti-oppressive practice which are referred to here. As you may recognise, this is instructive of the way in which anti-oppressive practice has been given less prominence by the HCPC. Despite this, its importance is fundamental to ethical practice, as we argued in Chapter 3.

Accountability and practical reason

Professional social workers, by claiming the right to work with service users by dint of their specific knowledge and expertise, must therefore take responsibility for their actions. They have a position of trust in which their knowledge is legitimised by the state and in many respects recognised as of value by service users. Over the past 30 years at least there has been a succession of reports and inquiries which have investigated the various failures of the social work profession in our unsuccessful attempts to care for or protect service users (Stanley and Manthorpe, 2004). However, as Clark (2005) argues, it is almost impossible to highlight in many of the inquiries who is responsible, as many agencies and different people are involved. Nevertheless, from an ethical point of view, social workers must take responsibility for the actions they have control over and must be able to account for their actions if they are to behave in a truly professional manner.

In terms of ethical practice, social workers must draw on their training in which they learn about different ethical responses to practice situations, yet, as we observed in Chapter 1, they must also interpret this knowledge in the light of the context in which the practice problem is situated. This requires the ethical problem to be reconciled within that particular practice context. This reconciliation can be called 'practical reason' and has to be filtered through the way each individual social worker's personal character and ability enables them to respond to a practice problem.

The development of this position is based upon the work of Schön (1987), who argues that professional workers learn from the people they serve in their practice.

Professional workers then reflect back on their practice, using theory both in action with service users and also when later evaluating practice. For Schön, real professionals learn to live with uncertainty, hold the ambiguous moment and are confident to act even when they are not sure what the right answer is. Effective professionals use 'tacit knowledge'. That is, the repertoire of theories and actions which have worked well in the past and can be used to measure and assess the right action in the moment of current practice. The professional social worker therefore acts more at an intuitive level, acting politically and creatively to find solutions as the situation calls. As an ethical practice, reflection is focused upon what service users need rather than what is available from a preset menu of services or standardised managerial responses.

The ethical content of reflection can be outlined by its use in avoiding oppressive practice. To work in an anti-oppressive way requires social workers to be in a mode of constant critical reflection. This means stepping outside one's practice and measuring it against the methods and ethical principles of anti-oppressive social work. Critical reflection means questioning the existing set of social relations as the norm, for example between social worker and service user. It is a critical process, what Schön calls *a*

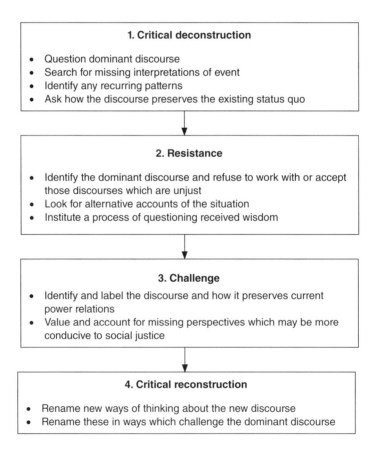

Figure 4.2   Critical reconstructive process

(Adapted from Fook, 2012).

reflective conversation with the situation (see Mullaly, 2002). Critical self-reflection can be broken down into how we reflect upon:

- knowledge about ourselves;
- how our identities are influenced by dominant ideologies and discourses;
- knowledge of our social location;
- our own power to dominate, which may reinforce discriminatory practice;
- our lack of power when we are subordinated to others;
- the sources of our beliefs, values and ethics which may be derived from the dominant ideology and which may itself impose constraints upon our freedom to act.

As Mullaly (2002) argues:

> *Critical self reflection is a form of 'internal criticism', a never-ending questioning of our social, economic, political, and cultural beliefs, assumptions and attitudes.*

> (p207)

Fook (2012), drawing on an analysis of discourse, provides another way to develop critical self-reflection. She argues that discourse shapes the meaning we give to practice through how we describe and label social work intervention, which in turn shapes our experience as social workers. Challenging a dominant discourse requires a four-stage process (Figure 4.2).

CASE STUDY **4.2**

In your case allocation meeting, the team is discussing a new referral about a well-known family which has been referred a number of times over the past four years. This family receives Income Support, and has done so for the past four years following an accident at work which meant that the husband, who was the only member of the family in work, could no longer remain employed. This has led to many financial problems, resulting in much stress in the family. At about the same time as the husband was forced to give up work, both parents experienced problems with their own relationship and their relationships with their children which led to a number of investigations by the social work team into allegations of neglect of the children. One member of the team becomes highly critical of the family, saying they are a classic troubled family whose parents haven't a clue how to parent their kids. Another says: 'Yes, they want us to do everything for them, always asking for money. If I didn't know better I'd call them a bunch of scroungers.'

ACTIVITY **4.5**

Using Fook's approach of critical deconstruction, how would you challenge your colleagues' standpoint in the above scenario?

COMMENT

One strategy may be to pose to the rest of the team how comments that have been made help us to understand the family situation. It may require you to remind the team of the family's history. You could identify words like 'dependent' and 'scrounger' and suggest alternative ways of looking at the family. You could highlight the difficulties any family would experience in living on long-term Income Support. In particular, words like 'dependent' and 'scrounger' legitimise the low and inadequate levels of benefit paid to families with children and place the blame for their poverty on their so-called 'dependency' rather than the inadequacies of means-tested Income Support. You may then ask your fellow team members whether they could exist on the amounts that this family has. You might want to use some evidence which you could get from a number of campaigning groups such as the Child Poverty Action Group. Parrott (2014) showed that the vast majority of users of the personal social services are in receipt of state social security benefits and that their problems are often compounded by social workers' lack of understanding of the realities of living in poverty. A project undertaken by the University of London Royal Holloway (Gupta, 2004) identified the effects of what they call the discourse of 'povertyism' used by some social workers.

Some examples of 'povertyism' were:

- *A lack of knowledge, understanding and appreciation about the impact of poverty on children and families – a poverty-blind approach. Poverty is seen as the 'norm'.*

- *Prejudices and preconceived ideas – you are irresponsible (need vouchers, not cash); you are likely to neglect your children (no food in the cupboard means you are not feeding your children); if you yourself were in care, you must be a bad parent.*

- *Poverty as a risk factor – being blamed for being in poverty and having difficulties – 'It must be your fault because other people cope on benefits'.*

- *'Povertyism' in a system can make people feel they don't matter, their perspectives and needs are not recognised, e.g. having to wait three weeks when in a crisis; social workers not listening to what families feel would help and support them.*

- *'Povertyism' means that workers don't consider the implications of their actions on people's self-esteem – treated without respect, being made to feel grateful for services, 'beggars can't be choosers'.*

*(**www.swap.ac.uk/docs/newsletters/swapnews07.pdf**)*

You might suggest that your team members think about this family's problem from the above perspective, and try to challenge the discourse of 'povertyism'. Your colleagues might think of different ways to describe this family, such as a 'family living in poverty'. Reframing this family's problem in this way opens up the possibility of working with them in a less oppressive manner.

This process of critical self-reflection is an important part of developing accountability to oneself as a professional social worker, but also to service users. Service users have the right to expect that social workers continually reflect upon their practice to ensure that they are knowledgeable of the service user's social location and competent to engage with it in a non-oppressive way.

CHAPTER SUMMARY

This chapter has explored the issue of accountability for social workers and has focused upon the importance of a code of ethics for social workers. It has made a distinction between a code of ethics and the code of practice for social care workers and suggested that both are important. The first is important because a code of ethics provides a set of general statements and principles about the nature and purpose of social work by which social workers can develop sound principles of practice; the second is important because the code of practice provides more direct guidelines which social workers can follow and their behaviour can be assessed and therefore called to account.

There are a number of issues with codes of practice for social workers that need to be addressed and are important to outline as these criticisms can provide the basis for social workers to use their codes in a critical and reflexive way.

One of the key criticisms which has been levelled at codes of practice is the way in which ethics can be reduced to one of individual relationships between service users and social worker. Friedson (2001) argues that the practice ethics based on this one-to-one relationship may not be the most essential part of professional ethics. He argues that the economic, political, social and ideological circumstances create many of the moral problems of professional work. He calls these elements *institutional ethics,* a concern for those defining characteristics of professional practice requiring an ethical critique and a more collective approach to resolve the ethical dilemmas caused by such factors. Dominelli (2002) develops this further for social work practice, arguing that ethical principles, particularly those more traditional values based upon Biestek's approach, ignore the social context by focusing upon the helping relationship. As a result ethics has become a matter of individual professional applicability rather than embedded within wider social contexts. As we have seen above, ethical codes have a number of different features that may provide general guidelines for the profession to follow. They may be more specific in outlining rules of conduct or they may deal with general practice principles. In the code of practice for social care workers we have seen that all three elements are present, and this would be true of BASW's (2002) code of ethics if we subjected that to the same scrutiny. Thus different codes of ethics and practice have different purposes; they are trying to achieve different things either to act as general or more specific guides to practice.

It is important to note the way that ethical codes have changed considerably over time in response to changing circumstances. Thus the code of practice reflects a significant input from service users in terms of ensuring the rights of service users. It may be that as the code is developed further, the room for discretion by professionals would appear to be limited (Banks, 2004). However, no code can be entirely prescriptive, and while professional social workers are given the power to operate and use their professional judgement, there will always be interpretation of even the strictest of codes. By having a separate code of ethics, the special nature of social work is reinforced in which the ethical prescriptions included in codes of ethics will be separate and distinct from ethics of everyday life, as we have noted in Chapter 2. Ethical codes will therefore remain imperfect; they will need continual reappraisal in the light of changing circumstances. The importance of codes of ethics therefore remains, both in terms of providing some basic guidelines which protect service users and of providing some identifiable principles which social workers can reflect upon to enable them to be effective.

FURTHER READING

Banks, S (2004) *Ethics, accountability and the social professions.* London: Palgrave.

Banks provides a challenging but excellent discussion of the key issues surrounding accountability for social workers and other helping professions.

Chapter 5
Managing risk

Risk and social work

Risk refers to the likelihood of an event happening which in contemporary circumstances is seen as undesirable. Risk is often defined as a hazard which must be accounted for, evaluated and then avoided. However, risk in this sense is one-sided and does not fully describe those aspects which confront a person in a 'risky' situation. Risk not only constitutes a hazard but can also be seen as offering an opportunity. As Douglas (1992) has argued, this meant in the past that risk was associated with gain as much as loss. In more traditional societies the notion of risk has been concerned with the vagaries of nature – natural risks beyond the control of human beings. With the rise of scientific and rational thought in the Enlightenment, the promise was that risk in the natural world could be tamed. Science could control the uncertainties of the natural world for the benefit of all. The development of social science extended the possibilities of control to social risks associated with poverty, unemployment and so on through the rational application of planned intervention in society to maintain incomes and limit the impact of unpredictable capitalist economies. Risk in the social world became calculable and therefore controlled by the development of statistical calculation and the idea of a normal distribution of occurrences around the 'bell curve', which provided an element of certainty about how human actions could be predicted against this 'normal' distribution (Hacking, 1990).

The development of the welfare state after the Second World War in the UK was based upon the idea of social insurance in which the social risks of, for example, ill health and unemployment could be removed by universal systems of welfare provision, based on the pooling of risk. In contemporary times, risk has become understood by some sociologists (Beck, 1992; Giddens, 1994) as no longer tameable in the way that the architects of the welfare state hoped. For Beck, the success of a welfare state in limiting social risks to its population has been bought at the expense of an untrammelled materialism which produces technological sophistication but also 'man (sic)-made' risks that have changed the social perception of risk. As Penna and O'Brien (1998) argue,

> the pooling of risk opened up opportunities for marginalised populations to have a limited share in the welfare cake of modern society and wider consumer satisfactions. But what happens if . . . the cake is intrinsically poisonous, its production is the cause of individual and collective sickness?

(p174)

Beck argues that we now live in a 'risk society' which has been created by the very means with which societies attempted to tame the risks of old. Thus the degradation of the food chain by the technological manipulation of agriculture leads to the poisoning of the environment and the risk of serious damage to animal and human life through occurrences such as bovine spongiform encephalopathy (BSE) or the genetic modification of food. Paradoxically, those societies which it is claimed have solved the problem of scarcity and absolute poverty are the very societies most responsible for and most susceptible to these new risks.

However, Beck's position has come under searching criticism, particularly from writers such as Furedi (1997), who see in the development of a risk society a more prosaic problem. It is the nature of the harms and threats which are highlighted by the media and politicians who have a vested interest in illuminating threats to sell newspapers or online web pages or for politicians to position themselves as moral crusaders to attract votes. Other writers such as Culpitt (1998) see the development of neo-liberal capitalism as the progenitor of social risks by reducing the social safety nets in terms of adequate social security benefits, and reductions in local authority services as manufacturing such risk. In addition, risk in this view has a class basis in that some people are therefore more able to manage risk than others. Therefore, as individuals are increasingly expected to provide for their own welfare, those with the least resources suffer the most from the effects of such a 'risk society' (Webb, 2006).

It is with these wider concerns about the nature of risk in modern societies that the current concern with risk within social work can be understood. For Kemshall (2002b) this process has led the welfare state away from attempting to use the collective resources of society and the state to protect its citizens to one that is now concerned with the limiting of social risks and expecting an increase in individual capacity to protect against such risk. Policy directed towards marginalised populations such as troubled families or the long-term unemployed are not couched in how a universal welfare state can meet the needs of such groups. The argument is one in which a risk-averse society can limit the perceived threat of such groups to the social fabric. The individuals caught up in this web of risk avoidance are no longer identified as the accidental products of a rapidly changing industrial society but more individually responsible for their own marginalised position in society.

As we will see, the concern with taming risk within the lives of social workers and the service users they work with may work in the same paradoxical way. The same procedures and guidelines instituted to tame risk may be the very processes by which risks are produced, for social workers and service users alike. This may sound fairly abstract but it is important to move away from seeing such arguments as distant from real life, because they now inhabit much of the terrain in which social workers operate. In order to understand the importance of risk in social work we must define what we mean by risk and why risk needs to be understood in its more traditional sense of a tradeoff between potential hazard and potential opportunity. Let us use an example from Chinese mythology.

A group of eight Chinese merchants have to transport their merchandise across the fast-flowing Yangtse River. They each own a boat which is full of the goods they wish to take to market. At this time of year the river can be very treacherous – last year one merchant lost his entire stock when his boat sank as he tried to traverse the river. It is important that they try and sell their merchandise now, as at this time of year the majority of the farmers from the surrounding countryside descend on the market.

ACTIVITY 5.1

How might the merchants minimise the risk of one of their number losing their entire stock?

What constitutes the hazard here?

What constitutes the opportunity?

COMMENT

For the merchants to minimise the risk, they decide to fill each boat with a part of their merchandise so that all their stock is distributed equally across the eight boats. Thus if one boat sinks in the fast-flowing waters then all will lose just an eighth of their stock. Obviously the hazard presented is that if they do not try and spread their risk then one of the merchants faces the distinct possibility of financial ruin by losing all of his stock to the river. But the nature of this risk could be ignored by them all agreeing to take a chance and hope that they all get to the other side, or they might gamble and hope that it won't be

Continued

---

*their boat that goes down, something more prudent merchants would find an unaccepta-
ble risk to take. The opportunity presented here is that if they do nothing and decide not
to risk their merchandise they may have to wait a considerable time before they can sell
their stock in the market. To manage the risk as they have done means that in the worst-
case scenario they will only lose a part of their stock and in the best they all reach the other
side intact. Nevertheless, they will have taken the opportunity to sell their stock while the
market is at its best.*

Risk management

This scenario of course mirrors much risk management in social work – meetings
around the child in child protection cases in which a group of professionals decides
on the appropriate course of action in a child care case is such a form of risk sharing. Here every member of the panel will bear responsibility for making the decision
and every member has an input into providing and sharing information on the case
to arrive at a considered decision. This in theory minimises the risk of one individual
making a decision in isolation without having the necessary knowledge or support to reach an appropriate outcome. Below is an example taken from *Working
Together to Safeguard Children* (HM Government, 2013) which outlines the processes that should be undertaken in respect of when a child is considered to be at
risk of serious harm.

Strategy discussion

Whenever there is reasonable cause to suspect that a child is suffering, or is likely to suffer,
significant harm there should be a strategy discussion involving local authority children's
social care, the police, health and other bodies such as the referring agency. This might
take the form of a multiagency meeting or phone calls and more than one discussion may
be necessary. A strategy discussion can take place following a referral or at any other time,
including during the assessment process.

Strategy discussion tasks

The discussion should be used to:

• share available information;

• agree the conduct and timing of any criminal investigation;

• decide whether enquiries under section 47 of the Children Act 1989 should be undertaken.

Where there are grounds to initiate a section 47 of the Children Act 1989 enquiry, decisions should be made as to:

Continued

Continued

- what further information is needed if an assessment is already under way and how it will be obtained and recorded;

- what immediate and short-term action is required to support the child, and who will do what by when;

- whether legal action is required.

(Adapted from HM Government, 2013)

So far we have explored the idea of risk management and given an example of a strategy discussion to outline the importance of managing risk in social work. You might be thinking at this stage: what connection does risk have with social work values? When social workers talk of risk they are employing values. When social workers decide that a particular situation is risky, this rests on beliefs about what is good and what is bad in the situation (Brearley, 1982). Let us take an example of working with people with learning disabilities.

ACTIVITY 5.2

Mrs John is a single parent with a daughter, Yvonne, who is 18 years old. Yvonne has been asked to go out dancing in a local nightclub with her friends from college. Yvonne has Down's syndrome and her friends all have different learning disabilities. Mrs John is unhappy that the college has encouraged her daughter and her friends to go out dancing as she is concerned that Yvonne may put herself at risk. As she says, this will be the first time Yvonne has gone out on her own with her friends.

- *What values might be in conflict here?*

COMMENT

The social work value in conflict here is that of autonomy, or the client's right to self-determination, in Biestek's terms. The autonomy of Yvonne to choose what activities she wishes to do conflicts with her mother's concern that her daughter may be putting herself in danger. Problems of risk are particularly poignant here in terms of the rights of people with learning disabilities as citizens to make and act on their own decisions. In the past, of course, people like Yvonne have been seen as socially incompetent and in need of protection from the risks and dangers of life. We should not forget about the safety needs of any young person going into an adult environment for the first time, but we account for Yvonne's right to go out with her friends and her right not to be put in a situation she may not be able to handle. How might Mrs John's position be modified if Yvonne and her friends had, over a period of months, been enabled through different forms of social skills

Continued

and situation training to go out into adult situations? As social workers and care workers, if we value principles of inclusion in society and the autonomy of disabled people to make their own life decisions, then we need to enable people to make positive decisions on their own behalf and have the social skills and support to be able to put them into practice.

Although we have not gone into the detail of risk analysis here, it is clear that values are an inextricable part of such risk analysis, as they form the principles upon which a risk analysis takes place, enabling us to choose what is valuable in determining an acceptable or unacceptable risk.

The increasing focus upon risk in social work and, indeed, wider society has been linked with a tendency to avoid all risk (Stanford, 2010). In a society increasingly worried about threat, governments become less concerned with maintaining levels of material welfare and more concerned with containing risk through the control and compliance of populations. How this emerges in social work is through the increased use of formalised policies and procedures, i.e. technologies to control risk. Broadhurst et al. (2010b) argue that risk management is a complex, often unpredictable and negotiated activity. Social work practitioners are obliged to comply with policies and procedures on risk management, but there are more informal processes at work shaping decisions and actions in this relationship-based profession. The nature of these informal processes is highlighted by Ferguson (2010), who argues that the lived experience of practice enables deeper understandings of risk to emerge as what he defines as practice risk, which deals with:

> *whether professionals meet the requirements of good practice by looking around homes, walking towards children to properly see, touch, hear and walk with them to ensure they are fully engaged with and safe, here and now, on this home visit, or in this clinic or hospital ward.*

> (p1100)

Many social work commentators argue that a preoccupation with risk lies at the heart of child protection practice (Stanford, 2010). It has become a key motif around which the work of the personal social services is organised. With social workers preoccupied by risk, they increasingly make decisions which are defensible, rather than decisions which they consider to be ethically appropriate. This has led to an unacceptable number of families being involved in child protection procedures experiencing considerable distress and trauma, only to be filtered out of the registration process when they are deemed not to warrant further action (Department of Health, 1995). Lymbery (2005) suggests that a similar inflation of risk in assessing older people leads to the overprotection of individuals who are deemed unable to make their own judgements about what kind of life they should lead. This becomes more acute when an older person is assessed as being unable to live independently, for example, with the onset of Alzheimer's disease. Society's failure to adapt itself to the needs of older people leaves older people more open to the dangers of risk. For example, older people not claim-ing their basic pension entitlement leaves an estimated 800,000 older people living in poverty below the minimum considered desirable by the government. In addition, as social work departments become increasingly focused upon risk, then service users who represent the most risky become the prime recipients for social work intervention and resources, rather than those whose needs may be potentially greater. This, in turn, leads to a greater focus upon risky service users as the main beneficiaries of resources, particularly when resources become tighter. Recent figures on the rise in the numbers of children looked after in England may be instructive in this regard.

RESEARCH SUMMARY

Key points

- *There were 68,110 looked-after children at 31 March 2013, an increase of 2 per cent compared to 31 March 2012 and an increase of 12 per cent compared to 31 March 2009.*

- *There were 28,830 children who started to be looked after during the year ending 31 March 2013, an increase of 2 per cent from 2012 and an increase of 12 per cent from 2009.*

- *There were 28,460 children who ceased to be looked after during the year ending 31 March 2013, an increase of 3 per cent from 2012 and an increase of 14 per cent from 2009.*

- *There were 3980 looked-after children adopted during the year ending 31 March 2013, an increase of 15 per cent from 2012 and an increase of 20 per cent from 2009. Although the number of looked-after children adopted fell between both 2009 and 2010, and 2010 and 2011, the number of these adoptions has since increased and is now at its highest point since the start of the current data collection in 1992.*

(Glendinning, 2013)

In a climate of risk aversion, what constitutes risk is dominated by the concerns of pro-fessionals and their fears rather than an assessment of what may constitute a risk for the service user. Faulkner (2012) makes this prescient quote in relation to this argument:

> *In Careland, there are different rules – you are not expected or allowed to do things that might hurt you or might risk your safety even if that 'safety' means risking your own independence and wellbeing.*

(p11)

Ethically, the implication is that the needs of the social worker and his/her employ-ing organisation may outweigh the needs of the service user. Risk increasingly within social work tolerates little uncertainty or ambiguity. Practice must follow that which is certain and which can be accommodated within the set menu of policies, procedures and guidelines, giving the illusion of safety. This expectation of the modern-day social work organisation is inherently unreasonable: life is a risky business and the removal of all risk, even from those seen as dependent, is a life devoid of any real content. Lownsborough and O'Leary (2005) argue that risk is now conceived in a narrow and limited way. They oppose this, suggesting a focus upon a well-being orientation which they differentiate from a risk orientation (Table 5.1).

Table 5.1   Differentation of orientation

Risk orientation	Well-being orientation
• Risk equals danger	• Community governance
• Risk is individualised	• Focus on structure
• Threat, fear and distrust	• Leadership and trust
• Intrusive risk reduction	• Community focus
• Punishment focus	• Strength focus
• Defensiveness	• Supportive
• Vigilance	• Family-sensitive
• Distrust	• Trustful

Source: Lownsborough and O'Leary, 2005.

By emphasising well-being, we are posing different questions about the possibilities inherent within any social work situation. It asks us as social workers to act in an ethically positive and anti-oppressive way. It requires social workers to think of minimum intervention in the sense of avoiding unnecessary use of statutory procedures. Additionally, it requires social workers to look at supportive and life-enhancing aspects of a service user's situation. This asks social workers to focus upon the strengths of communities to manage and support those experiencing problems and by orienting practice around a more trusting orientation as an initial response. Its focus is positive, assessing the strengths of service users and the situations they find themselves in.

The realities of current social work practice in assessing risk were brought into focus by the Baby P case (Laming, 2009). Although Laming identified that some progress has been made in child protection work, he outlines a number of challenges, and the quotation below is significant in reinforcing the importance of a focus upon the family's needs:

> *1.5 . . . ultimately the safety of a child depends on staff having the time, knowledge and skill to understand the child or young person and their family circumstances.*

> (p10)

In their evidence to Laming social workers identified a number of other issues relating to their experience of child protection issues: high caseloads and lack of adequate training for working with at-risk families were the most prominent. UNISON (2009), the trade union which represents social workers, has also entered the debate, providing evidence to Laming and publishing its own research of social workers' views. This report is based upon 369 responses drawn from England and Scotland and provides an interesting snapshot of the pressures which social workers experience. As these social workers' comments drawn from the report express:

> *It is ironic that the Laming enquiry set up procedures to protect children but in some respects these procedures are now harming children because the increased admin and*

paperwork have let crucial events slip by unnoticed or not acted upon due to lack of time out in the community with the families and children we are trying to protect. Less office-based work would mean that we can bring the 'social' back into social work.

(p2)

I have 30 cases – all of which are child protection, I have been working in social work for 22 years, but it has never been as bad as it has in the last year. One third of our qualified posts are vacant and our admin staff have been cut. I have built up over 100 hours of TOIL but I can't take it because of the amount of cases I have been allocated.

(p4)

Given the assessments of the organisation and delivery of social work services from both the main union representing social workers and a government appointee, it is not surprising that risk management has developed in the way that it has, with social workers practising in an environment of increasing workloads with families with higher support needs. The irony is that, as a focus upon risk has become more central, the opportunity for social workers to work directly with families to prevent risky outcomes for them has become more limited by the procedures designed to protect children. White et al. (2009), in their study of the computerised systems used to record and track cases by social workers (Common Assessment Framework), show that the requirements to service this system further limit social workers' ability to respond flexibly to the needs of families. The Common Assessment Framework requires social workers to assess and record work within strict timescales and enter information in a limited form. These requirements do not necessarily fit with the time the social worker has to work with the family that has been entered into the system. Neither does the information entered enable a coherent narrative to be told about the family's needs as they are percolated through language statements that can be best processed through tick boxes into computerised systems of information. This problem is further exacerbated with the increase in workloads and the difficulty in recruiting staff in some areas. UNISON identified that:

Nearly six out of ten of our respondents are working in teams where over 20 per cent of posts are vacant. Over a fifth of all respondents are working with a vacancy rate of over 30 per cent.

(p3)

The consequences of the Baby P case have been wide-ranging and well documented by Jones (2014), who shows how social workers and their managers continue to be harassed by the press. In confronting risk in social work then it is little wonder that social workers themselves may retreat into using in an uncritical way the policies and procedures set for them as they can at least provide some protection from the kinds of media attention described by Jones.

Risk: conflicts and dilemmas

When we investigate the nature of risk it is impossible to remove uncertainty in decision making. As we noted above, social workers, their managers and policy makers can attempt to minimise such situations; for example, as noted above, the *Working Together to Safeguard Children* (HM Government, 2013) guidance outlines the steps to be taken in relation to concerns around the protection and safeguarding of children. Likewise, in the area of adult abuse, the Protection of Vulnerable Adults (POVA) guidelines have been introduced. Potential employees, for example, should be referred to, and included on, the POVA list if they have abused or harmed vulnerable adults in their care or placed them at risk of harm. These examples provide some protection and support to enable social workers and their managers to minimise risk.

Other techniques which can be of help in such situations include the use of risk assessment schedules (see Doel and Shardlow, 2005, for a discussion). Likewise, social workers who assiduously keep up to date with research may also help in identifying risk and opportunity factors in practice situations. But, as we have outlined, social workers will continually face situations where their judgement requires them to chart at times an uncertain journey through potentially hazardous situations. Among the more significant challenges to social workers, especially those new to the profession, are the decisions which involve a conflict or dilemma in values, which inevitably bring with them issues of hazard and opportunity.

A conflict of values occurs when the social worker is faced with competing imperatives which oppose one another. For example, in our final chapter we will look at the possible conflicts identified in relation to female circumcision that entailed the social worker respecting the cultural practices of a particular community as against the rights of the individual to choose whether to undergo this particular practice. A dilemma involves the social worker being presented with two equally unpalatable alternatives; again, a resolution is required which may not leave the worker with the certainty that he or she has made the right decision, but one which is the best in minimising harm, given the prevailing circumstances. Examples of a dilemma may be found in relation to assessing an older person who may be in need of residential care. On the one hand, to assess a person as requiring residential care means that the person is likely to lose much personal freedom and autonomy; on the other hand, to leave a person in his or her own home to face social isolation and to be potentially at risk of physical danger may also be unwelcome. The social worker has to decide which of these two alternatives will produce the least harm. Of course, these decisions can be made easier by the social worker acting positively to assess the relative strengths of the situation and deciding how to build on them in partnership with the person involved.

In cases of conflict and dilemma, then, the element of risk becomes an important factor in making the right decision. In addressing the difficulties posed by such situations it can be helpful for social workers to reflect upon some basic guidelines which may help in resolving such perplexing decisions. Social workers, it is argued, have to act as if they are impartial in their approach to such decisions. This flows, as Reamer (1990) argues, from the ideas of Adam Smith, who argued that individuals are likely to reach agreement about the moral decisions they make only by assuming the position of an impartial observer. Such characteristics would include being knowledgeable and informed about the problem under discussion, and being able to control emotion and act in a dispassionate way. There are two problems with this approach. Firstly, it is expecting too much of any individual to suggest that the characteristics outlined can ever be found in any one individual. Secondly, the actual characteristics of impartiality and dispassionate decision making, for example, are not morally neutral and contain moral judgements in themselves. The implication here is that any decision informed by emotion is, therefore, of less value than that arrived at dispassionately, which of course may not always be the case. For example, coming to a decision regarding the potential dilemmas around our example of residential care assessment may benefit from having an empathic response to the service user. The social worker in this case may very well imagine, on the one hand, engaging with the kinds of emotions and feelings that a service user may be experiencing when confronted with the possibility of losing her home and moving into residential care. On the other hand the social worker may try and understand the social isolation and fear of living on your own when you perhaps feel no longer able to support yourself.

Reamer (1990) draws on the work of Gewirth (1978) to provide some alternatives to this impasse. For social workers, conflicts often occur between the duties they have through their statutory role to uphold the law and/or as employees in terms of their employment contract, against their ethical duties to service users to protect their rights as citizens. Reamer's guidelines will be placed within the context of social work in the UK:

1. Where there is a threat to the physical/mental well-being of a service user (all primary goods), this takes precedence over ethical duties not to lie or reveal confidential information. In addition, welfare which involves physical/mental well-being takes precedence over secondary goods such as wealth, education or leisure if one has to make a choice between them in the provision to service users.

2. Basic well-being must take precedence over another individual's right to freedom. Thus, where an individual's right to freedom prevents or threatens another's basic well-being, then basic well-being must prevail. An individual's right to freedom takes precedence over his or her basic well-being. This involves individuals' right to remain in a risky situation as long as they are able to understand the consequences of the dangers that they place themselves in. This must be qualified by the caveat that their dangerous behaviour does not put others at potential or immediate risk.

3. Social workers are obliged to abide by the rules and regulations by which they are employed and by the wider rule of law. However, this is not to say that they should not campaign against unjust laws or seek to ensure the well-being of service users within their understanding of the particular law where it calls for their professional judgement. Neither should they blindly accept unjust policy and guidelines which limit service users' rights to services that their particular employer may have put in place.

4. The obligation to prevent basic harm, such as poverty and social exclusion, overrides the right to retain property. This refers to the public provision of welfare through taxation and the use of such government money to invest in appropriate welfare services.

These guidelines are general and will need to be applied to the specific cases that you will face as a social worker. You may also wish to think about the usefulness and the truthfulness of the guidelines themselves as a means to help resolve some of the thorny problems you are likely to face. The important thing to note is that, if you do not engage in this debate and have some basic guidelines from which to think through these dilemmas and

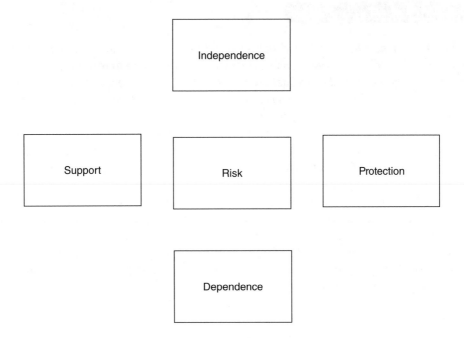

Figure 5.1   Dependence, independence, protection and support

conflicts, you will be leaving yourself open to working in an unethical and ineffective way. By careful consideration of the respective conflicts and dilemmas in any situation, you are engaging in an ethically appropriate and competent practice.

Figure 5.1 highlights some common imperatives often found in competition with each other in social work.

ACTIVITY **5.3**

Using the guidelines outlined above, identify what the likely conflicts and dilemmas might be and identify the hazards and the opportunities present in the case study below.

How might you resolve the dilemmas and conflicts that you have identified here?

CASE STUDY **5.1**

Mr Grey is 85 years old and lives very happily in a supported housing scheme in Wrexham. He values his independence highly. He receives no social service help, refusing any assistance except from his daughter, Mrs Williams, who has increasingly been drawn into providing more care for him, for example, shopping, handling his money and tidying up around the

Continued

home. Over the past few years his daughter, who lives nearby, has noticed a gradual decline in her father's memory. Last weekend she was called by the police to request that she collect her father from the central police station in Birmingham; he had been found in the railway station, lost and confused. This appears to be last straw for the daughter: the previous week she had been called to her father's flat after he had left the cooker on, which caused a small fire in his kitchen. The on-site support workers in the sheltered-housing scheme have also rung social services repeatedly over the last few weeks, requesting a social work assessment. They contend that Mr Grey is surly with his fellow residents, even attacking one of his neighbours with his walking stick. He does not join in any of the social activities and he tells a social worker, quite frankly, that he needs putting into care. Mr Grey tells a social worker that his neighbours are always abusing him, calling him 'ignorant' saying he should speak English when he speaks Welsh to them. To compound the situation, Mrs Williams's general practitioner (GP) has also contacted the office suggesting Mr Grey be considered for residential care. Although wanting to care for her father, Mrs Williams is at the end of her tether and is now being prescribed tranquillisers.

COMMENT

I will identify here one conflict and one dilemma. There are many more which may be suggested.

Conflict

The most striking conflict here is that facing the social worker in assessing Mr Grey's needs. On the one hand, we have an unsatisfactory situation in which the service user is currently coming into conflict with his fellow residents, his care staff and, increasingly, his daughter. This results in some aggression exerted by Mr Grey against his fellow residents and in the exhaustion of his daughter because of his insistence on being cared for by her. On the other hand, Mr Grey is exercising his right to self-determination and autonomy, saying he is happy staying where he is. In relation to Reamer's (1990) guidelines, I would suggest we need to consider point 3, which says:

> *An individual's right to freedom takes precedence over their basic well-being. This involves a person's right to remain in a risky situation as long as they are aware and able to understand the consequences of the dangers that they place themselves in. This must always be tempered by the caveat that their dangerous behaviour does not put others at potential or immediate risk.*

The issue here then becomes: how much harm is Mr Grey doing to his fellow residents, the care workers and his daughter? Does this harm outweigh Mr Grey's right to remain in his own home? In addition, we need to consider if Mr Grey is able to understand some of the presenting problems (which may not all be of his making) in his current situation. We could suggest ways to resolve the situation, firstly, in favour of Mr Grey by seeking some conflict resolution. Clearly, the other residents do not like him speaking Welsh but, as we know, if

Continued

Mr Grey is a first-language Welsh speaker, he may well prefer to try and converse in his own language and seek out other residents who may speak Welsh. We also understand that as people get older they may revert to speaking their first language, particularly if the person's short-term memory becomes a problem. If Mr Grey is suffering more pronounced memory problems and he moves into experiencing Alzheimer's disease, then he may revert to his first language more regularly.

Dilemma

One of the key dilemmas here might revolve around Mr Grey's insistence on his daughter caring for him. From research into the nature of gender and caring we know that approximately seven out of ten carers are women. As people live longer, it is also increasingly the case that older daughters in their late 50s and 60s find themselves caring for their much older parents in their 80s and 90s. We also know the extreme difficulty carers face in tending to their family members, which can result in carers experiencing physical exhaustion and mental and physical health problems. The dilemma concerns, on the one hand, Mrs Williams becoming increasingly exhausted and depressed to the extent that she is now on antidepressants, so that clearly she cannot continue to care for her father in the way that she has. On the other hand is her desire to care for her father. Not to alleviate the caring responsibilities of Mrs Williams is likely to continue her physical and emotional decline, whilst on the other hand to step in immediately to add extra domiciliary care or, if appropriate, remove Mr Grey into residential care is likely to leave Mrs Williams feeling guilty and responsible for failing to keep her father in his own home.

We also need to consider Reamer's second guideline:

> *Basic well-being must take precedence over another individual's right to freedom. Thus, where an individual's right to freedom prevents or threatens another's basic well-being, then basic well-being must prevail.*

In order to assess whether intervention may be required, it is possible to identify three categories of risk (Stevenson and Parsloe, 1993). You may want to apply this typology of risk to Mr Grey's situation to see if your decision might follow a similar path to that which you used under Reamer's guidelines. The three types of risk are physical, social and emotional.

Physical risk

Circumstances causing harm to self or others:

- Caused by Mr Grey:

  o Mr Grey is certainly causing some harm to other residents by his use of his walking stick.

  o Mr Grey is causing harm to his daughter by his insistence that she continues to care for him.

- Perpetrated on Mr Grey:

  o Fellow residents are impatient and abuse him when he converses with them in his first language.

Social risk

Social circumstances where individuals' behaviour isolates and alienates them from others. Others' behaviour in marginalising those considered to be outside the social norm.

- Mr Grey should be encouraged to be more patient with his neighbours regarding the use of his language.

- Residents should be more accepting of Mr Grey's use of his first language and attempt greater inclusion in social activities.

Emotional risk

Physical and emotional health put at risk by the role a person occupies.

- Mrs Williams's poor mental and physical health as carer to her father.

Underpinning the management of these risks are values. The tension inherent in a risky situation puts social work values in opposition to one another as the social worker attempts to wrestle with the problem and chart the best course of action. In terms of managing the risks inherent in Mr Grey's situation we can identify the following conflicts:

- Tension between the individual autonomy exercised by Mr Grey to live in his own home, and protecting Mrs Williams from the burden of care and other residents from Mr Grey's current frustration.

- Tension between overreaction and underreaction in response to the multiple pressures from Mrs Williams, her GP, the other residents and the care team supporting Mr Grey.

- Too much control may lead to an inappropriate reception into care against Mr Grey's wishes and also perhaps against Mrs Williams's wishes if suitable alternatives can be found in terms of additional support for her. On the other hand, an overidentification with Mr Grey's right to live as he wishes and the perceived need to protect him from the pressure of others may leave him vulnerable – unable to continue to live in his own home, with his relationships with others deteriorating and without any other support being put in place could lead to an emergency admission to residential care.

So far, in discussing the ethics of risk assessment, the voice of the service user has been absent. However, if principles of anti-oppressive practice are to be developed then they must be progressed even in the most challenging of situations. An example of involving service users in risk assessment can be taken in respect of those who use mental health services. For many years now there has been much focus upon violence and mental health, particularly in well-publicised cases of some service users who have exhibited violent behaviour and have injured and in some cases killed their fellow citizens. Mental health service users are increasingly stereotyped as being a risk to themselves and the wider community, even though research evidence consistently shows that the exhibition of violent behaviour is negligible. This is what one service user observed:

> *They are always more concerned about the risks to the public than they are about risks to yourself. I'm ten days out of hospital and at discharge they weren't talking about how I would be harmed, they were talking about how the public could be harmed.*

(Faulkner, 2012, p4)

RESEARCH SUMMARY

Evidence shows that there is no significant overall trend in the number of homicides by people with schizophrenia. Between 1997 and 2008, there were 364 homicides committed by people with schizophrenia – 6 per cent of the total sample (which was 6141). In 2007, the latest year for which the figures are available, there were 30 homicides committed by people with schizophrenia. Data-tracking statistics since 2004 suggest a decrease in the number of homicides by people with symptoms of mental illness and psychosis. Some 351 homicides, within the report period, were committed by people suffering from psychosis – 6 per cent of the total sample.

(Mental Health Network/NHS Federation, 2011)

Nevertheless, policy in this area moves towards more control of individuals considered to be a risk to others. As with child protection, assessing and managing risk are now key requirements for mental health professionals. The problem with this construction of service users as dangerous means that people so defined will be excluded from making decisions about their lives by defensive, risk-averse social work professionals.

It is then incumbent upon social workers working towards anti-oppressive practice to involve service users in their own risk assessments, yet this is not always the case. Faulkner (2012) talks movingly about her own experience of risk as a person who self-harmed and the difficulty in understanding risk in relation to the conflicts and dilemmas faced by service users and social workers alike in working in this area. Her research took testimonies from many service users and the quotation below identifies in my view the dilemmas faced by service users when trying to access services which are increasingly focused upon those service users deemed to be a significant risk:

> *When I have a care assessment I have to be careful how I talk about that stuff . . . you don't get any service unless you are deemed at risk and social services put something in to stop you being at risk, that's the only basis on which you get a service. You have to play it carefully. You don't want to be so at risk that you get put in residential care or not allowed out or something but you need to be enough at risk to get a service.*

(Faulkner, 2012, p21)

101

CHAPTER SUMMARY

Values are at the core of social work practice and in the case of risk they become of central importance in enabling practitioners to manage risk. As Kemshall (2002a) argues, risk management cannot guarantee that risk is prevented. It can attempt to limit the chances of risky situations turning into dangerous ones or reduce the consequences of such situations. As she suggests, minimisation rather than reduction is the key (p128). This includes a clear and considered development of procedures to involve service users and carers in risk management. You will experience practice situations where you will be unable to protect service users fully either from the harm of others or the harm they do to themselves. If you are able to justify your practice and show that it was informed by the needs of the service user and the wider community then you may still be criticised for your actions by others, but you will be able to justify your actions in the light of such criticism. What is important here is that you have practised in a way that was informed by your skills, values and knowledge and that you used them in a justifiable, reasonable and principled way.

Social work within the personal social services has always been, despite the best efforts of campaigners, a residualised service to the poor. The risks that we have discussed above fall to a much greater extent upon the shoulders of those who are excluded from the material success of neo-liberal capitalist society that the privileged few now inhabit. To be a service user of the personal social services is, by definition, to be a person living with risks of ill health, poverty and social exclusion. As the social work and social care support for service users have been trimmed, so the language of need has been replaced by an all-embracing language of, and practice of, risk. This results in limiting available social work resources to an ever more prioritised group of service users. Such targeting of services barely alleviates the most pressing need but leaves social workers working with people with more severe problems. This in turn requires more complex decision making, involving riskier and therefore potentially more ethically demanding decisions.

FURTHER READING

Kemshall, H (2002) *Risk, social policy and welfare.* Buckingham: Open University Press.

Kemshall's book discusses both the theoretical and practical implications of risk across the public services as a whole.

Webb, S (2006) *Social work in a risk society: Social and political perspectives.* Basingstoke: Palgrave.

Webb's book is a more challenging read but is worth persevering with, as he delves much deeper into the theoretical issues associated with risk while focusing on social work.

Chapter 6
Advocacy and social work

ACHIEVING A SOCIAL WORK DEGREE

This chapter will help you meet the following capabilities, to the appropriate level, from the Professional Capabilities Framework:

- Professionalism: Identify and behave as a professional social worker, committed to professional development.
- Diversity: Recognise diversity and apply antidiscriminatory and anti-oppressive principles in practice.
- Rights, justice and economic well-being: Advance human rights and promote social justice and economic well-being.

It will also introduce you to the following academic standards as set out in the social work subject benchmark statement:

5.1.5 The nature of social work practice, which includes:

- the characteristics of practice in a range of community-based and organisational settings within statutory, voluntary and private sectors, and the factors influencing changes and developments in practice within these contexts;
- the nature and characteristics of skills associated with effective practice, both direct and indirect, with a range of service-users and in a variety of settings;
- the processes that facilitate and support service user choice and independence.

Advocacy work has taken on an added impetus with changes in legislation in the field of mental health, i.e. Mental Capacity Act 2005, broader developments within adult services around the personalisation of services and the growth of advocacy for children within the care system and families subject to investigation within the child protection system. For example, the White Paper *Putting People First* (Department of Health, 2007) makes an explicit statement of values in relation to the promotion of adult care:

In the future, we want people to have maximum choice, control and power over the support services they receive.

(p20)

In relation to the Mental Capacity Act 2005, independent mental capacity advocates are legally enabled to provide support and represent persons who may be considered for serious medical treatment, or subject to being accommodated by the National Health Service (NHS), or by local authorities in the community or in residential care.

For children and families, the Children Act 1989 outlined a new approach to work in child care and family support. Principles of partnership would enable families to be kept together and, it was argued, lead to greater inclusion within the child care system. Family group conferences were set up as part of this process to enable families and children to have a greater voice within the conferencing process. A key component of this development has been to encourage the introduction of 'independent' coordinators. This has provided an enabler to sit outside of the personal social service culture to run the conferences with the view of promoting an independent and neutral oversight which is impartial and will not prejudicially influence the outcomes of the conference. In terms of the principles of advocacy, this will mean that families and children should have more control over decision-making processes. There are now an increasing number of advocacy services which work with children to enable them to have a voice within the child care process; see Barnardo's (2009) for examples of such schemes.

As advocates, social workers represent the interests of service users when service users are unable to do so. Advocacy work is often the routine of social work, for example, telephoning the local benefits office to find out about a person's benefit entitlement or ringing the housing department or the utility companies. All these activities involve representing service users' interests by negotiating on their behalf. Advocacy only becomes important when and if service users are unable or unwilling to represent themselves. To advocate on behalf of a person is a position of power for the advocate: service users put their trust in advocates to represent them fairly and diligently and it requires social workers to operate in an ethically informed way to ensure their subsequent accountability to service users. Conversely, acting as an advocate is, in a way, also disempowering for service users as they are ceding power to a surrogate who then uses his or her own power and abilities on behalf of the service user. Ethically it is more empowering to enable service users to develop the skills of self-advocacy but in the short term advocacy on behalf of service users may be a necessary expedient which should only be entered into under specific circumstances.

This chapter is concerned with professional advocacy. Other forms of advocacy are just as valid but this book is about social work ethics and how social workers can act in an ethical way for others. Ethical issues are inseparable from the principles of advocacy, particularly when you are required to advocate on behalf of someone who may have acted in ways that you find morally repugnant or dangerous to the wider community. This requires a significant engagement and reflection upon your own personal values and how they may clash with the professional imperative to work in the best interests of the service user. Advocacy is inextricably linked with empowerment and partnership in that social workers engage with powerful organisations that confront service users and use their power to achieve positive outcomes for those service users. Advocacy can also engage with wider political processes when social workers involve their trade union or their professional association to contest government policy or organisational practices which inhibit the welfare of citizens.

Advocacy on behalf of service users is important, yet this chapter will also consider how social workers should advocate for themselves in relation to their employers and the wider political process. Arguably a social worker unable to advocate for his or her own interests may lack the insight and commitment to advocate on behalf of others. For example, to advocate for decent pay and working conditions for oneself as a social worker will be of benefit in the longer run to service users. Well-paid, well-trained and, therefore, competent and settled workers are able to provide a more effective service for others.

A definition of advocacy

- Speaking for someone who has no effective voice of his or her own – this may include enabling individuals to express themselves, to make their own decisions and to contribute and be recognised on equal terms with others.

- Informing and enabling people to make choices about, and remain in control of, their own social and health care.

Forms of advocacy

- Citizen advocacy. This provides a one-to-one partnership between a trained unpaid volunteer and a vulnerable person. This tends to be a long-term relationship.

- Professional or practitioner advocacy. Paid professional staff with expert knowledge (legal, health or social care) act as advocates. They tend to work with people on a shorter-term basis than citizen advocates, supporting the person with a particular issue or issues.

- Collective (or group) self-advocacy. Support is offered to allow vulnerable people to come together and gain strength from a collective voice.

Advocacy in values and ethics therefore speaks to those aspects of individual and collective empowerment which seek to enhance the autonomy and self-determination of those people who are unable to speak for themselves because they are either temporarily or permanently excluded from access to:

- key resources;

- key services;

- social networks;

- political process networks.

Advocacy, then, is concerned with the rights of service users. As Bateman (2000) argues:

> One major advantage of advocacy is that it brings a rights based perspective into individually focused work – work which can otherwise lead to the individual being blamed for the failures of the external world.

(p20)

Thus, advocacy is significant in developing practice which is anti-oppressive. The process takes on a more inclusive and democratic focus, placing service users' demands for appropriate services at the centre of social work. It implies that service users have rights to services. Increasingly, the delivery of services and benefits is being tied to a more conditional approach in which the state requires certain behaviours to be carried out before a service or benefit is delivered. Jobseeker's Allowance is a case in point, where benefit is paid subject to claimants proving their willingness to seek work, rather than being paid because of their status as unemployed. Similarly, approaches to Incapacity Benefit paid to those who are unable to work due to long-standing health problems or disability are taking a similar path, with payment of such benefit tied to a person's willingness to retrain and take up employment. In addressing rights, then, advocacy seeks to enable service users to achieve their full entitlements as citizens (Figure 6.1). However, as noted above, advocacy may need to go further than just enabling the entitlements of persons within the social security system. On a wider political level advocacy may very well require that the actual level of entitlements need scrutiny whereby social workers as part of a wider movement for social change may advocate for increases in the level of entitlement where they are inadequate.

- Political rights are essential to the idea of citizenship and the extension of the franchise in society, in theory demonstrating the liberal-democratic state's commitment to formal equality.

- Civil rights entail in a formal sense 'equality before the law', i.e. equal treatment in law irrespective of income or wealth.

- Social rights involve 'equality of opportunity' to educational, medical and welfare services. For example, the establishment of the NHS in 1948 provided health care for all citizens based upon need.

These rights are, of course, theoretical in the sense that the experience of many user groups shows how these rights have, in effect, been denied. Many disabled people's organisations identify that much service provision for disabled people has been provided by charities. Historically, charities have filled the gaps present in mainstream services provided by the state, thus ensuring that disabled people's social right to appropriate services is not based upon equality of opportunity but on notions of desert. From a rights perspective, the dominance of charity means that service provision is dependent upon the patronage and good will (however misdirected at times) of individuals and philanthropic organisations. This has contemporary resonance with the attempt by the Coalition government to develop the 'Big Society', whereby charities and private organisations are encouraged to play a dominant role in the delivery of service such as social work and social care. Much advertising carried out

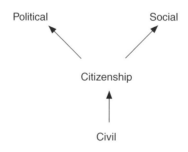

Figure 6.1   Spheres of citizenship

by charitable groups has also reinforced the dependent stereotype of disabled people, portraying disabled people as objects of pity. The issue then is one of rights, not charity (Swain et al., 2003).

The role of social workers and other professionals should be to challenge these crude stereotypes as an ethical practice to ensure that the formal realisation of rights for all marginalised groups is met through a range of empowering strategies and partnerships, including advocacy. For example, in the case of political rights, many service users with a disability are effectively excluded from political participation and even basic voting rights through their lack of access to transport and community networks. Those service users with a mental health problem who require treatment in hospital can be effectively disenfranchised if they are not helped to register to vote or enabled to exercise a vote by proxy or by post. The concern to satisfy the rights of service users is therefore an aspect of the ethical underpinning of social work and its commitment to social justice.

Bateman's principles of advocacy

Bateman (2000) has argued that, in order for advocacy to be both successful and respectful of service users, then the principles outlined in Figure 6.2 need to be employed.

- Best interest. Social workers should act in the best interests of the service user. This is a well-understood but sometimes misrepresented principle. In social work there will be many competing interests which will test your resolve to keep the service user's wishes at the core of your practice.

- Service user's instructions and wishes. Action undertaken on behalf of the service user starts and finishes with the voice of the service user directing the intervention. This requires constant reflection to ensure that the service user's wishes are being met.

- Diligent and competent. In undertaking advocacy, ensure that you have the necessary skills and knowledge to succeed. Preparation means doing your homework to ensure that, if you offer your services, you can carry your promises through.

- Information. To meet service users' wishes, keep them constantly informed so that they can make decisions effectively. Overloading someone with too much information or presenting this in the wrong way by not screening for jargon, for example, is likely to confuse or overwhelm the person.

- Confidentiality. Maintaining trust in the process of advocacy is essential and therefore ensuring that the service user can share information with you in confidence secures a more effective practice. Service users who distrust you may hide information which is crucial to the successful outcome of the process.

- Impartiality. Offer independent advice. This means being able to give service users information they may not want to hear. Likewise, for some workers who may be regularly advocating for a range of people with the same organisation, it is important to keep a professional distance and not become involved in collusive relationships with officials you may be communicating with regularly. You may have to be very assertive with other welfare workers who control resources you need to access in order to advocate effectively for the service user.

Figure 6.2   Bateman's principles

CASE STUDY 6.1

Mr and Mrs Bangara have been contacted by their local housing department to assess the number of bedrooms in their social housing property. If it is deemed that that have surplus bedrooms then they will be required to pay an extra amount in rent for which they will receive no housing benefit. It is now 6 months since the assessment and the couple are struggling to pay their bills as they are paying an extra £15 per week as a result of having a 'surplus' bedroom. They now approach social services as they are concerned that the amount of debt is causing them serious difficulty. They have a letter from their general practitioner (GP) identifying that the couple can no longer share a bedroom as Mrs Bangara's medical condition requires her to make use of oxygen equipment at night and to have access to a commode which will not fit into the couple's existing bedroom. They have repeatedly contacted the local housing department to get a reassessment of their situation but nothing seems to be happening.

CASE STUDY 6.2

A group of local disabled people have been campaigning to keep their local library open as it is subject to closure. In addition, their local library stocks reading materials for the visually impaired which would no longer be available if the library closed. After talking unsuccessfully to the chief librarian, they decide to mount a picket at the next local council meeting when the library closure will be debated and a decision made. They call the local newspaper and local television to get publicity for the story.

Brian Fox is a young ex-homeless man who has just been offered his own bedsit by the local housing association. He comes into the duty office asking you to ring the 'social' (Job Centre Plus) about his Jobseeker's Allowance as the payment has been delayed. You agree to ring on his behalf.

ACTIVITY *6.1*

Identify which of these case studies are examples of:

- *collective self-advocacy;*

- *professional advocacy;*

- *inappropriate advocacy.*

COMMENT

Ethically, it is not appropriate for professionals to handle a person's particular problem immediately without the service user first taking some initiative. Self-determination is a fundamental value that requires us to respect individuals and encourage them to act for themselves. Therefore, in Case study 6.3 we would encourage Brian to make the call himself, though we might want to go through with him what he thinks he should say when he telephones the relevant office, and we may also provide him with access to a telephone and sit with him when he makes the call to provide support. This becomes more empowering if Brian can make a successful call to progress his benefit payment and therefore realises that you as his professional support have confidence in him to deal with his own matters.

In Case study 6.1, professional advocacy would seem an appropriate way forward to progress Mr and Mrs Bangara's problem. Clearly they have tried everything that they can and have come up against the inertia of the housing authority. However, you must be careful not to compromise Bateman's principles (see above) by ensuring that you progress this case with the consent and knowledge of the service users. You need to maintain their confidentiality and work to their instructions and with their best interests in mind. Above all, you must ensure you are competent to deal with this aspect of housing benefit policy, you know on what and how you can negotiate and you are prepared to use appropriate legal pressure to ensure a successful outcome if the housing authority still remains inactive.

Case study 6.2 is an example of collective self-advocacy and can be very effective in providing people who are marginalised by society with the opportunity to experience the power they have as a group. In the case of the library closure it would also bring different groups of people together in order to campaign for the library to remain open.

Government policy

The White Paper *Valuing People* (Department of Health, 2001) is unequivocal in its support for advocacy for people with learning difficulties, highlighting the transformational impact it can have in changing attitudes and services. One of the key objectives of the previous Labour government's Quality Protects programme (now effectively subsumed under *Working Together to Safeguard Children*: HM Government, 2013) for improving children's services was to promote the participation of children, young people and their families in the planning and delivery of services, and in decisions which affect their day-to-day lives. Recent legislation and policy have highlighted the need for participation by service users (see below).

Working Together to Safeguard Children (HM Government, 2013) emphasises two key principles:

1. safeguarding is everyone's responsibility: for services to be effective, each professional and organisation should play its full part.

2. a child-centred approach: for services to be effective, they should be based on a clear understanding of the needs and views of children.

This gives encouragement to social workers and other local authority workers to develop participation of children and their parents/carers but also to advocate on behalf of service users to ensure their wishes are accounted for. The idea of government-sponsored advocacy raises a number of ethical dilemmas for advocates which are worth pursuing. Inevitably, questions arise where a paid employee of an organisation may be advocating on behalf of a service user against his or her employing organisation. Typically this is known as a conflict of interest. Hardwick (2013) argues strongly that statutory social workers are increasingly unable to act as advocates and reach out to the socially excluded, which in turn erodes social work's professional values and principles. Her research shows the way in which statutory social workers' role has been limited in the area of advocacy and concludes with this challenge:

> *Advocacy services are undoubtedly less regulated and less professionally qualified than statutory social workers but, unlike social workers, they promise not only to hold up a torch to people needing advice (a role still believed by many to lie with social workers), but also to shine it on unmet need, failures in service provision and discriminatory practice. Are UK social workers content to accept the limitations on their part in these endeavours, or are they prepared to work towards facilitating change that will enable them, alongside advocates, to help redress social injustice and inequality for the socially excluded in low-income communities?*

(p15)

The more autonomous the advocacy group is, then the more that conflicts of interests in relation to statutory services will be minimised. A recent example of an autonomous advocacy group comes from the experience of relatives of patients who were neglected and/or died as a result of being admitted into Stafford Hospital (**www.curethenhs.co.uk**). As a result of their campaigning activity, they have achieved significant results following the Francis Report (2013), which was set up as a result of their actions to investigate and make recommendations for the future. It will be up to the government to respond in a positive way to ensure that these recommendations are met.

Francis Report (2013) key recommendations

- Nurses are to be held personally and criminally accountable for the care that they provide to their patients. Hospital boards should face dismissal if they fail to ensure minimum standards of safety and quality care.

- GP-led commissioning groups should monitor all hospitals where they send their patients, including carrying out professionally qualified checks on the quality of service offered as well as monitoring outcomes.

- A specialist hospital inspector should be created with the involvement of patients to identify problems early.

- No more top-down reorganisations of the NHS. At all times there should be senior clinical involvement in policy decisions and all staff must spend time on the frontline as well as meeting those who have suffered bad experiences.

Ethical dilemmas

To put the ethical dilemmas of professional advocates into the realm of more direct social work practice, let us consider the following case study.

CASE STUDY 6.4

Janet is a qualified social worker who is employed as an advocate by Parents' Advice, a voluntary organisation set up to advocate on behalf of parents who are being investigated by social services in respect of child protection procedures. Janet sees her role as ensuring that the child's safety is paramount so that she should:

- *empower parents to be informed about the child protection process and to be enabled to speak up for themselves whenever feasible;*

- *keep lines of communication open between the local authority and the parents, and promote a constructive working relationship between the two parties.*

She is currently supporting Mr and Mrs Wolstenholme, who are the subject of an investigation; concerns were raised at their youngest child's school about some unexplained bruises on her legs.

As part of the social work investigation the social workers seek a meeting with Janet in confidence and ask her directly for information upon the parenting skills of Mr and Mrs Wolstenholme and to report any further information she might collect on the parent's behaviour which may affect the investigation. Janet's manager is also very concerned about this case as the local authority provides a significant grant of money each year to support Parents' Advice and asks Janet to 'tread carefully'.

ACTIVITY **6.2**

What ethical challenges should Janet recognise and how should she respond?

COMMENT

It is important that Janet is not directly employed by the local authority and that she is seen by the parents to be independent. The local authority is statutorily responsible for protecting children who are suspected of suffering significant harm. Thus, to avoid any conflicts of interest between the rights of parents and the rights of children, an independent advocate for the parents is vital. How could the parents trust Janet unless her independence is clear? Developing independence as a principle involves a conscious and ongoing effort by Janet to ensure her independence from the local authority social workers. This independence is crucial to developing a trusting working relationship. Janet must therefore:

- *be aware of the reasons why she must maintain her independence and understand the principles informing this;*

- *be aware that her independence could be compromised or be perceived to be compromised, for example if the advocacy organisation she works for receives funding from the local authority.*

Janet must maintain an assertive attitude and vigorously challenge the local authority. She should be prepared to make a complaint on behalf of a parent and recognise that she may experience pressure to keep silent. How should Janet respond to the social workers' request?

Janet should clarify to Mr and Mrs Wolstenholme and the local authority that, where she suspects any significant harm done to the children, she will report any evidence she has.

But she must show her intervention is on behalf of the parent, refuse to express a personal judgement about the level of risk to the child and decline to give an opinion about registration in a child protection conference if invited to do so.

The importance of confidentiality

Janet's work in Case study 6.4 must be informed by confidentiality. This is crucial to maintain parental trust. Parents are more likely to feel secure, enabling them to explore issues of parenting and possible resolutions to the concerns raised by the local authority. However, Janet must inform the parents that there is a limit to her confidentiality. She is under no statutory duty to report information regarding harm to the child but has an ethical duty to communicate information likely to protect the child from harm.

Balancing parents' rights and children's safety

Initially there is no balance to be struck here: Janet is advocating on behalf of the parents and must support them as her first priority. However, she must adhere to the principle of controlled emotional involvement and be aware of any emotional challenges in this case. This means:

- helping the parent to understand any child protection concerns;
- avoiding any false expectations by challenging the parent's wishes if they are likely to compromise the child's safety;
- avoiding collusion with the parents;
- acting on evidence suggesting the child is at risk.

Ethics, the self and others

Writing on ethics has addressed the ethics of the self in social work (Banks, 2004; Beckett and Maynard, 2005; Hugman, 2005). In Chapter 3 we introduced the idea of virtue ethics and in this chapter we will be developing these ideas further. These can be very complex arguments to engage with in an introductory text but it is worthwhile because it asks you to consider the importance of developing the use of self. Professional integrity is central to valuing yourself as a social worker, as it enables you to defend yourself in the light of the increasing pressures on social workers. For example, you may be asked to carry more cases than is appropriate for you to deal with. Thus your professional integrity to provide a valued service will be undermined if you are too overburdened to give each case its due regard.

Supervision

Supervision is an important medium through which your professional self can be developed. There are three kinds of supervision:

1. administrative – the promotion and maintenance of good standards of work, coordination of practice with policies of administration, the assurance of an efficient and smooth-running office;
2. educational – the educational development of each individual worker on the staff in a manner calculated to evoke their maximum potential;
3. supportive – the maintenance of harmonious working relationships, the cultivation of esprit de corps.

(Kadushin, 1992, p293)

For social workers, all three aspects are important in supervision from your immediate line manager. Each element of supervision has important ethical content. The purpose which should inform all aspects of supervision is the interests of the service user and the delivery of the best service possible. Supervision, then, should seek to protect the interests of service users and promote their welfare while at the same time enabling the professional development of the worker.

Administrative supervision

Administrative supervision ensures that you as an employee maintain good standards of work and that your decisions are in accord with the policies and procedures of the organisation you work for, ensuring accountability.

Educational supervision

Educational supervision should be about the development of the skills and attributes of social workers so that as professional workers they can reach the highest standards possible. It is also important in the development of the social worker as a human being in encouraging self-development through identifying the individual strengths and needs of the worker. It should also encourage a reflexive attitude towards the worker's organisation, where encouragement to think critically about the employing organisation can contribute to more progressive policies and procedures.

Supportive supervision

Supportive supervision encourages social workers to see themselves as part of a team with a common purpose. Thus the development of self is also dependent upon the development of other workers in the team to work together. It also contributes to positive and creative practice whereby workers can spark ideas off one another and develop innovative methods of working. Supervision then should be about developing the confidence as well as the competence of workers.

Ingram (2013) adds to this debate by arguing that social work as a relationship-based activity requires social workers to be emotionally intelligent. Emotions are inextricably linked to social work decision making and therefore supervision needs to provide social workers with the opportunity to reflect upon and consider the possibility of any emotional involvement with service users and the issues that this may uncover for the social worker. Hair (2013) researched what social workers themselves identified as important in supervision and found that the overwhelming majority of those interviewed agreed that supervision needed to promote both skill development and emotional support. Interestingly, the majority also recognised that supervision must be conducted by managers who were social workers, which was not the case for some 36 per cent of the respondents.

The importance of supervision was exemplified by the *Victoria Climbié Inquiry* (Laming, 2003). The report argues that, while inadequate supervision was not the only reason for the poor practice that took place, it was one of the contributing factors. Ms Baptiste was one of the managers involved in this case and Ms Arthurworrey was the social worker responsible in Haringey Social Services for Victoria Climbié.

ACTIVITY **6.3**

Read the extract below identifying the problems that the social worker faced in accessing regular supervision. But first read what Lord Laming had to say about the social context within which Haringey Social Services was embedded.

> *Haringey is an outer London borough with many of the characteristics and problems of an inner city area. In its 1998 position statement to the Joint Review of Social Services in Haringey Council, Haringey noted that it is the thirteenth most deprived authority in England. A large proportion of its residents were described*

Continued

as experiencing 'severe poverty, unemployment and deprivation, which manifests itself in all areas of their lives, such as the lack of adequate affordable housing, poor levels of educational attainment, poor health and high numbers of children in need'. I heard evidence that Haringey has one of the most diverse populations in the country, with 160 different languages spoken locally, a long tradition of travellers settling in the borough and a high proportion of asylum-seeking families (nine per cent of the total population). The pressure this places on all departments within the local authority is inevitable – none less so than for the children and families' services.

(Laming, 2003, 6.4–6.5)

The atmosphere within the North Tottenham Initial Assessment Teams (IATs) was hectic in 1999. Shanthi Jacob spoke of the 'bombardment factor' and Mary Richardson, director of social services in Haringey at the time, stated: 'Undoubtedly, North Tottenham was the busiest social work office. As a consequence of that, by definition staff probably held, on average, slightly more cases than their Hornsey counterparts . . . there was regular and fairly unremitting pressure on the North Tottenham office.' It was an issue recognised by the Joint Review team in early 1999, who referred in their report to potential staff 'burn out', which needed to be addressed quickly. Ms Arthurworrey told the Inquiry that, initially, her caseload at Haringey was manageable, but it slowly increased. By the end of August 1999 she was responsible for 19 cases (of which half were child protection). This is seven more cases than the maximum laid out in the Duty Investigation and Assessment Team Procedures devised by Ms Mairs. Mr Duncan argued that it was hard to imagine how a social worker could work on more than 12 cases at a time. Yet Ms Arthurworrey said she was unaware of the guidance, and during 1999 Mr Duncan said he knew, though Ms Wilson said she did not, that staff in the IATs were dealing with a high number of cases and that the average caseload was in excess of the recommended maximum.

(Laming, 2003, 6.13–6.15)

Now read the section on supervision:

The tensions that had featured during Ms Baptiste's time in the children and families' team began to resurface in IAT B. As a result, according to Ms Baptiste, she found it hard to engage some social workers, Ms Arthurworrey included, in the regular supervision so fundamental to good practice. Although Ms Arthurworrey has denied ever refusing supervision when it was offered, there clearly was an issue about the quality and timeliness of the supervision that was provided in Ms Baptiste's team. This was confirmed by the director of social services at the time, Mary Richardson. Ms Arthurworrey understood she would get supervision every two to three weeks, 'but this never happened'. In practice she received supervision about once every seven

Continued

weeks. *'When I asked about drawing up a supervision contract Carole [Baptiste] told me that I was responsible for doing that.'* Ms Arthurworrey said she experienced serious problems in arranging supervision sessions with Ms Baptiste because of her continued unavailability. Often Ms Baptiste would cancel or rearrange sessions or simply not appear without an explanation. Of equal concern, Ms Arthurworrey said she found supervision with Ms Baptiste frustrating because, more often than not, they would start discussing cases and then Ms Baptiste would go off on a tangent. Ms Arthurworrey stated that Ms Baptiste often talked about her experiences as a black woman and her relationship with God. The result was that they would not have time to finish discussing the cases. Ms Arthurworrey said she just tried to manage. Generally it was Ms Baptiste's practice to agree with whatever suggestions Ms Arthurworrey put in front of her. Ms Arthurworrey found this disturbing in the sense that it led her to question Ms Baptiste's knowledge base.

(Laming, 2003, 6.38–6.40)

COMMENT

There are a number of issues here that hindered the supervision process, linked with issues raised in the report:

- *Cancellation of supervision.* Ms Arthurworrey said she experienced serious problems in arranging supervision sessions with Ms Baptiste because of her continued unavailability. Often Ms Baptiste would cancel or rearrange sessions or simply not appear without an explanation.

- *Lack of clarity about the nature of supervision and inappropriate issues raised by the manager unrelated to Ms Arthurworrey's caseload.* Ms Arthurworrey said she found supervision with Ms Baptiste frustrating because, more often than not, they would start discussing cases and then Ms Baptiste would go off on a tangent. Ms Arthurworrey stated that Ms Baptiste often talked about her experiences as a black woman and her relationship with God. The result was that they would not have time to finish discussing the cases.

- *Infrequent supervision.* Ms Arthurworrey understood she would get supervision every two to three weeks, but this never happened. In practice she received supervision about once every seven weeks.

- *Responsibility for supervision placed only on to workers' shoulders.* When I asked about drawing up a supervision contract Carole [Baptiste] told me that I was responsible for doing that.

- *Lack of trust in professional competence of the supervisor.* Generally it was Ms Baptiste's practice to agree with whatever suggestions Ms Arthurworrey put in front of her. Ms Arthurworrey found this disturbing in the sense that it led her to question Ms Baptiste's knowledge base.

It is worth reinforcing the ethical reasons as to why supervision is important and to place this within the wider ethical responsibilities that social workers have towards service users and the wider community.

Social workers not only work with individual problems but when these individual problems are shared by many then they become social problems which require social and individual social work intervention. Social workers have to consider that their work with individuals may then impact upon the wider society. It may very well be the case that sometimes the individual needs of service users clash with the concerns of the wider community. These tensions are reflected in what Banks (2006) argues are the four first-order principles central to social work.

Banks's first-order principles

1. Respect for and promotion of individuals' rights to self-determination;

2. Promotion of welfare or well-being;

3. Equality;

4. Distributive justice.

In supervision, interaction between supervisor and supervisee will circle around these issues. For example, supervisors may have to remind supervisees of the requirement to consider how a course of action they are pursuing leads to promoting the autonomy of service users, or that they are providing services and resources which are distributed according to agreed principles of fairness and need. Supervisees on the other hand may well identify inappropriate and exclusionary procedures within their organisations which may inhibit meeting the needs of service users.

Being part of a professional community

It is necessary for individual social workers to understand that they belong to a wider professional community. Individual actions should fit with the broader professional viewpoint encapsulated in codes of ethics. This is important because the authority to engage in these arguments comes from membership of a professional body (British Association of Social Workers (BASW)) or a statutory body (the Care Council) which requires social workers and their supervisors to account for their decisions in the light of these codes of ethics and of practice (Smith, 1996).

Assertiveness and caring for self

In any advocacy situation the advocate has to show assertiveness in promoting the rights of the service user. This is no different when advocating for oneself, either in supervision or in drawing support from broader political forums such as trade unions. McBride (1998) argues that social workers have been poor in promoting their rights. She argues that believing in your rights is important to giving social workers the confidence to tackle situations likely to create conflicts of interest. Bateman (2000) argues that assertiveness becomes more important where there are fewer structures and procedures to which individuals can refer – what he calls an unbounded problem.

If we refer to the Climbié example, we can see that there were a number of barriers blocking the social worker's access to supervision. This is not to assume that

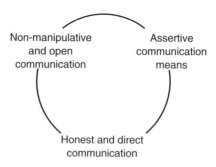

Figure 6.3   Assertiveness

the social worker involved did not try and assert herself or that she was ineffective. What I am suggesting is that social workers, in accessing supervision, need to be very clear why supervision is so crucial for professional development and act assertively to achieve it (Figure 6.3). This is essential in protecting service users as well as social workers' abilities to be effective practitioners. It may require social workers to use the management hierarchy by going above their immediate supervisor if supervision is not happening. It is in supervision that social workers can actively develop their professional capacity to carry out social work.

Assertive behaviour can be developed. Assertive social workers are confident social workers, their confidence coming from their considered use of the knowledge base of social work, their purposeful application of the skills and methods of social work and their reflective application of the values and ethics of social work. The active application of knowledge, skills and values ensures that they will be highly regarded by their colleagues for their professional integrity (Bateman, 2000). In terms of self-advocacy then, social workers must engage with the organisation in which they work, understand the organisational structures and hierarchies, and access relevant information to intervene in an assertive manner when their professional integrity is threatened by poor management practice. In advocating for the self, it can be useful to outline to your immediate supervisor what consequences may follow if your needs as a worker are not accounted for. You could in a clear and factual way suggest that a formal complaint will be made and that this will be put in writing to the relevant manager above the supervisor in the hierarchy. It is important that you can negotiate on some aspects of your position where it is less clear that a formal process has been breached, but where there may be a clear breach of practice then a formal process is much more appropriate. In this regard, putting a complaint in writing is a very good idea in that this creates a record of the event and then requires those in authority to respond.

Trade unions and social work

Joining a trade union is an ethical practice. It is the antithesis of the individualistic approach to society and social problems which we explored in Chapter 1. By joining a trade union you are joining with others to protect and develop pay and conditions for each other, protect and develop the service for service users and promote social justice and human rights for all (Dawkins, 2010). Social workers may find difficulties comprehending this if, as younger professionals, they have been brought up in an atmosphere of distrust for the collective values of trade unionism. As Lawrence (2005) suggests, the image of trade unions is more aligned with blue-collar, i.e. manual, workers who experience problems at work than with white-collar (non-manual) workers who have opportunities for career advancement and relatively comfortable working conditions. Yet trade unions continue to be of relevance for all paid employees, including social workers. The current experience of austerity in North America and across Western Europe has led to a sharp deterioration in the pay and conditions of service of employees, particularly in the public sector (Bach and Stroleny, 2013). A report by the Institute of Fiscal Studies (Cribb et al., 2014) showed that:

> *The public sector workforce stood at around 5.7 million in mid-2013, and made up just under 20 per cent of total employment, lower than at any point in at least the last 40 years. The Office for Budget Responsibility (OBR) forecasts further cuts in general government employment, reaching 1.1 million by 2018–19 compared with 2010–11. This would take the share of the workforce working in general government to just 14.8 per cent, compared with 19–20 per cent during the late 1990s and 2000s. It is thus clear that the nature of the UK labour market will have changed dramatically as a result. These reductions would dwarf the reduction in general government employment of 350,000 that occurred in the 1990s. Public sector employment also fell sharply in the 1980s, but this was largely driven by the privatisation of state owned industries.*

(p1)

From an anti-oppressive practice perspective, trade unions can be an effective voice not only in protecting services but also in progressing equality issues. The Trades Union Congress, which represents the bulk of unions in the UK, campaigns against discrimination at work and in wider society. UNISON, which represents the majority of social workers and social care workers, is a useful case study. Look at the box below, taken from UNISON's website for women workers:

UNISON has almost one million women members – more than two-thirds of our union. Women still earn a lot less than men and face sex discrimination and harassment at work. Our members also juggle work and home commitments. Many have caring responsibilities and almost half work part-time. This is why UNISON takes a lead on negotiating and campaigning on women's rights at work and in the community.

(www.unison.org.uk/women/index.asp)

UNISON runs a series of campaigns focused upon specific groups of people, such as equal rights for part-time workers, equality for black workers, and lesbian and gay rights. Trade unions are currently campaigning in favour of maintaining a woman's right to choose an abortion (UNISON, 2010). Other campaigns involving UNISON include a campaign against domestic violence (**www.unison.org.uk**). These two brief examples show how trade unions are involved in much broader struggles which are of direct relevance for social workers and service users.

CASE STUDY 6.5

For nine months Debbie has been working as a child care social worker. The team in which Debbie works has for the past six months never had more than half its total complement of staff. This has led to some social workers leaving rather than carrying on with the pressurised workload. One of Debbie's colleagues has recently taken extended sick leave because of stress and is likely to be absent from work for the foreseeable future. Her immediate manager has also experienced periodic bouts of stress and she has been off work, leaving the team with little or no appropriate supervision. In her role as the local UNISON steward, Debbie has had repeated discussions with the area manager regarding the problems of staff shortages and the burdens that this is placing on the existing staff, i.e. working above normal contracted hours, increased levels of stress and high sickness rates. The area manager is sympathetic to her argument but he says little can be done at the moment as the local council has frozen any recruitment until the next financial year, which is in three months' time. Debbie decides that the situation is too dangerous to carry on and calls a local meeting of union members to discuss the problem. She will propose taking strike action.

ACTIVITY 6.4

What is your response to this situation?

Do you think Debbie is acting ethically in arguing for strike action?

COMMENT

Debbie argues that both social workers and service users will benefit from strike action. She argues that by calling for more staff to be appointed, the quality of service to service users will be improved and the reduction in stress and extra hours working will benefit the social workers and their families and friends. Alice (one of Debbie's colleagues) recounts her own experience, which is echoed by other members in the meeting in that she repeatedly finds herself in situations where she can provide only a substandard service to the families and children that she is working with because of the pressure of having to juggle so many cases.

Deciding to strike is a serious issue; social workers will feel uncomfortable with this proposal, given their general ethical concern to work for the benefit of service users. In the area of child support and protection, by striking they may potentially cause harm to the very people they are trying to help. Ethically, is it justified to cause distress to service users as a lever to pressurise employers into meeting the strikers' demands?

Continued

COMMENT *continued*

What are the ethical arguments?

Three different ethical approaches will be considered:

1. consequentialist;

2. duty-based;

3. rights-based.

(Benjamin and Curtis, 1992)

Consequentialist

This approach considers whether strike action will on balance lead to a greater number of positive over negative consequences.

One approach to increasing the likelihood of the positive over the negative is:

- not to withdraw services to priority cases (such as those on the child protection register);

- to give advance warning of an impending strike (something which by law must happen, in that a ballot for strike action must be taken if workers wish to operate inside the law under the Trade Union Act 1984).

In arguing for the benefits of strike action, more long-term concerns are of relevance here. Social workers might focus upon the long-term benefits of having qualified social workers who have time to work with service users, rather than having to fill in the gaps made by absent, sick or non-recruited staff. Creating supportive conditions of employment, it can be argued, will lead to the retention of staff and reduce the number of those who are unhappy and who eventually leave. All of these arguments will be of direct benefit to service users in the long term.

From this brief synopsis it can be argued that consequentialist arguments do have some force here. However, although this may be the case, Debbie must also consider the short-term negative consequences, which are immediate and more pressing. Some social workers may feel that they have certain duties which override these utilitarian arguments and they may also consider that service users have rights to a service in the present which may also override any long-term considerations.

Duty-based

In respect of BASW's code of ethics (BASW, 2002) and the Health and Care Professions Council (HCPC) code of practice (HCPC, 2014), it is clear that justifying strike action does pose serious problems. For example, HCPC code of conduct statements could all be interpreted as compromising the idea of strike action.

- You must act in the best interests of service users.

- You must respect the confidentiality of service users.

- You must keep high standards of personal conduct.

- You must provide (to us and any other relevant regulators) any important information about your conduct and competence.

- You must keep your professional knowledge and skills up to date.

- You must act within the limits of your knowledge, skills and experience and, if necessary, refer the matter to another practitioner.

- You must communicate properly and effectively with service users and other practitioners.

- You must effectively supervise tasks you have asked other people to carry out.

- You must get informed consent to provide care or services (so far as possible).

- You must keep accurate records.

- You must deal fairly and safely with the risks of infection.

- You must limit your work or stop practising if your performance or judgement is affected by your health.

- You must behave with honesty and integrity and make sure that your behaviour does not damage the public's confidence in you or your profession.

- You must make sure that any advertising you do is accurate.

In the first bullet point, how could the strike be seen as acting in the best interests of service users? If the point of the strike is to hold out the threat that the interests of service users would be damaged, then the strike would be illegitimate in the HCPC's terms. The fundamental principle here from the code would therefore be violated. Likewise, the BASW's (2002) code of ethics is clear:

4.1.1 Priority of service users' interest

Social workers will:

Give priority to maintaining the best interests of service users, with due regard to the interests of others;

Or:

4.1.3 Self-determination by service users

Social workers will help service users to reach informed decisions about their lives and promote their autonomy, provided that this does not conflict with their safety or with the rights of others. They will endeavour to minimise the use of legal or other compulsion. Any action which diminishes service users' civil or legal rights must be ethically, professionally and legally justifiable.

However, the strength of such arguments depends upon two assumptions which may not necessarily be valid.

The first assumption is that the current service which is being withdrawn does meet service users' interests and enables their rights to be met. Debbie and the managers she has consulted recognise that the current situation does not meet the interests of either service users or social workers, so this first assumption is clearly contestable. Thus, under the existing situation, if children and parents are receiving significantly poorer services which already compromise the safety of children and families, then social workers would not appear to be violating their duties to service users.

The second assumption is that those presently harmed by strike action will not be those who may benefit in the future if the strike was successful. Many children and families are long-term users of the service and as such are more likely to benefit by strike action if it is successful. Thus we can argue here that, on balance, there is not necessarily a current group of service users who would be sacrificed for the future benefit of a different group of service users.

By investigating the two meanings of a duty-based approach it is possible to argue from a duties perspective the validity of engaging in strike action. A recent survey of social workers' views on the social work profession highlights many of the problems which Case study 6.5 is concerned with. Thus the *State of Social Work Survey* (BASW, 2012) found that, of those approached, 1100 social workers responded:

- 88 per cent believe lives could be put at risk by cuts to services;

- 77 per cent say jobs have been cut over the past year, or vacant positions left unfilled;

- 77 per cent of social workers say their caseloads are unmanageable;

- 34 per cent of social workers are considering leaving the profession because of cuts to services.

Rights-based

Social workers and service users have rights. On the one hand social workers, like any other people, have rights and if these are violated by employers then they have the right to protect them. It is surely unacceptable that social workers should be so pressurised in their employment that they suffer from stress and ill health. Therefore in the final instance they have a right to strike. On the other hand, the social workers' right to strike conflicts with service users' right to a social work service. Children's rights to freedom from the dangers of material, physical or emotional abuse are not given a voice in pressing their claims to a service. It would appear that their rights should take precedence over those of the social workers.

Benjamin and Curtis (1992), in assessing the validity of these claims, make a distinction between what they describe as special and general rights, as follows.

Special rights

These are limited in extent and remain conditional; they depend upon a special relationship. A special right occurs when a social worker promises to do something on behalf of a service user, thus the service user has a special right. Such rights are conditional. They are limited to the person who receives the promise; therefore they have a right to it being fulfilled. They are also limited and depend on the special relationship between the promiser and the promisee.

General rights

These are unconditional and have validity purely on the basis of being a human being. They have much in common with human rights and involve such rights as the right to life and the right to freedom. No conditions are therefore set on their fulfilment. They apply without restriction to everyone and therefore require everyone to respect them. We would not wish to place any conditions upon the right of people not to be killed or imprisoned, whereas a social worker who makes a promise does so under the special conditions of his or her relationship with the service user.

If we return to Case study 6.5, we need to identify if the provision of social work services relates to a special or general right. When a social worker assumes care for a service user it is grounded in the special relationship between particular social workers and particular service users. Once work is undertaken, then a service user has a right to expect that service to be fulfilled. If a strike is called then the service user's rights to a service have been violated.

However, once the service has been fulfilled, then the rights of the service user cease and the obligations of the social worker have been fulfilled. If Debbie wins her argument about strike action, as long as the social workers involved meet their existing obligations, give warning about their intention to strike and cover any emergency situations, then the extent to which special rights have been violated has been reduced.

The case of general rights is more problematic and depends upon whether a right to a social work service is a general right. Some commentators argue that general rights occur only in relation to non-interference. These are called negative rights and as such require from others merely not to interfere with another person's life in order for those rights of life and liberty to be fulfilled. This argument has been associated with those who believe in the freedom of individuals to be able to say and do what they choose as long as this does not interfere with others' rights to do the same (Hayek, 1944). From this point of view, then, for a social work service to be met requires a positive action or a positive right to be in place. In order for this to happen it will require others to provide time or money through taxation, for example, to meet that right. This is an infringement, so Hayek would argue, of others' rights, as you are taking their time and money in order to provide this for others. This view has been challenged by those who see positive rights as essential in order to meet those negative rights of life and personal liberty (Marshall, 1950).

Children's services provide an interesting example, as in many cases where social workers work with the most excluded and poorest of children and their families, not to provide such a service would result in loss of liberty and life, for example not engaging in child abuse investigations. However, if, as noted above, emergency measures were put in place to cover such issues of life and liberty, then again the ethical arguments against the strike are reduced.

CHAPTER SUMMARY

This chapter has explored the importance of advocacy for social work. It has highlighted the important role that social workers have in advocating for service users and has shown how this can be justified ethically. It has looked at advocacy from the perspective of professional social work and its use of professional advocacy. It has emphasised that professional advocacy may always be necessary in order to provide some service users with a more effective social work service. Nonetheless, advocacy which enables service users to gain their own confidence and then develop their own advocacy with other service users is the preferable alternative. Collective advocacy truly empowers service users as they take responsibility for and define their own goals. Finally, we have investigated the necessity of social workers advocating for themselves both on an individual basis and from a collective point of view through their engagement with trade unions.

FURTHER READING

Bateman, N (2000) *Advocacy skills for health and social care professionals.* London: Jessica Kingsley.

For those wishing to develop their advocacy skills further, Bateman's book is the key text in this regard.

Laming, Lord (2003) *The Victoria Climbié inquiry.* London: The Stationery Office.

All social workers should read this inquiry and in particular should reflect upon the problems with which the social workers and managers grappled, while striving to deliver effective children's services in an overstretched inner-London social services department.

Todd, M and Taylor, G (eds) (2005) *Democracy and participation.* London: Merlin Press.

These authors provide an interesting discussion in the chapters on the relevance of social and political action in relation to trade unions and wider social movements.

Chapter 7
The ethics of partnership working

Interprofessional working, partnership and social work

Partnership in this chapter is used to describe the ways in which different professionals work together around the needs of service users. This can sometimes be described as interprofessional working or multidisciplinary working but, either way, from an ethical standpoint, professionals have to develop ways of working together which have as their goal the improved delivery of services. Partnership therefore evokes this requirement of collaboration in order to achieve better outcomes for service users.

Social workers in recent years have witnessed a significant transformation in the organisations in which they work. The election of a Labour government in 1997 heralded a distinctive change in the delivery of welfare services to the population. A discourse of partnership became widespread in which terms such as 'joined-up government' gained currency in reflecting ideas of partnership, which Labour argued were essential for their aim of modernising public services (Parrott, 2005). The White Paper *Modernising Social Services* (Department of Health, 1998) outlined this agenda for the personal social services. It criticised previous approaches to delivering social work and health care services. The White Paper argued that:

- the existing configuration of health and social care was contributing to service users failing to access appropriate services;

- service users' needs did not fit into existing organisational frameworks;

- organisations delivering health and social care should consider partnership working to prevent such service failures.

In order to deliver its partnership agenda, the Labour government targeted the reduction in professional and organisational autonomy when it considered that these arrangements frustrated the effective delivery of services to service users (Malin et al., 2002).

Partnership working is now firmly established as one of the core features of social work practice both in children's services, as outlined within the Children Act 2004, and in adult services with the NHS and Social Care Act 2001. This process has been given added impetus with the White Paper *Our Health, Our Care, Our Say* (Department of Health, 2005b).

Joined-up care

All Primary Care Trusts and local authorities should have joint health and social care managed networks and/or teams for people with complex needs. We will also be building modern NHS community hospitals, which will offer integrated health and social services.

(Department of Health, 2005b, p10)

The modernisation agenda, then, gives little room for different professional groups to remain fixed within their own organisational structures. The policy changes instituted require different professional groups to be involved in a wider mission in which they, as the constituent parts, combine to create something of greater benefit to service users. The benefits of partnership can be conceptualised as creating a 'synergy' which is intended to eradicate departmental, organisational and philosophical differences to create 'seamless' services. Unsurprisingly, as different professions come together to deliver services, their different ethical approaches have to be reconciled.

The Coalition government has also placed increasing emphasis upon partnership working in children and families work, with calls for greater coordination between professionals in child protection (HM Government, 2013) and with adults (Care Act 2015).

Current legislation enables partnership working between the National Health Service (NHS) and local authorities in respect of their health and social care functions. In addition, because of the introduction of personal budgets in social care, the Coalition government proposes extending them to cover health care costs in the form of personal health budgets. This will provide further momentum for partnership working when the possibilities for integrating the two are realised. The extension of personal budgets has been further confirmed by the current government in the White Paper

Caring for Our Future: Care and Support, advocating that everyone eligible for social care should have this delivered through a personal budget by 2015 (Department of Health, 2012a). The White Paper also confirmed that the development of personal health budgets pilots would make it easier for people to combine them with personal social care budgets. The Localism Act 2012 also created the opportunity for local communities to access community budgets, which would enable them to develop further more integrated forms of care.

As local authorities begin to outsource more of their social care service to the private and voluntary sectors, so the requirement to work with other professionals from these sectors will increase. This will present significant challenges to those professionals working in the public who embody a public service ethos. Smith (2012) identifies significant challenges when such professionals either work alongside the private sector or are transferred from the public to the private sector. He identifies profound differences in approach whereby private organisations' orientation towards profit undermines the ethos of public service.

The ethics of partnership

As Banks (2010) argues, ethical considerations in partnership working can be understood in two ways:

1. General rules or norms, in the form of protocols and guidance which outline how different professionals should work together. An example of this is explored below in discussing Habermas and principles of communication.

2. A focus upon ethical issues in interprofessional working. This involves studying how different ethical conflicts and dilemmas occur when professionals work together. This would relate to the different ways professionals may understand their respective roles and responsibilities as they work around a particular service user, for example. These conflicts would present themselves in practical terms around issues such as whether to share confidential information or the different ways in which professionals might interpret their roles, or understand different service users' behaviour, an example of which is explored below.

Partnership and professionals

At any one time social workers can find themselves working in partnership with professionals such as police officers, nurses, probation officers, Connections staff and teachers. Given this array of different professions, it is clear that the business of partnership becomes a complex problem. As Bates (2005) argues, partnership working is often misunderstood:

> *Simply assuming that various partners share common aims and that conflict is a matter of a failure to align the aims misunderstands the issues.*

(p52)

Key areas of conflict in partnership working involve different ideologies, values, ethics and cultures of working, all conspiring to make partnership problematic.

In considering the ethical issues involved in partnership working it is important to define what is meant by the term partnership (Figure 7.1). As Carnwell and Carson (2005) argue, discussion in health and social care, for example, is replete with synonyms referring to the need to *work together* more effectively in *partnership* and in *collaboration* (p3). It is important to distinguish the relationship between agencies as a partnership, along with what the protagonists are supposed to do, which is collaborate or work together.

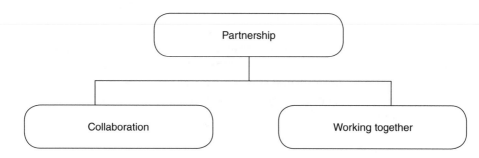

Figure 7.1   Partnership

Whilst the definition of partnership can be a contested term, for the purposes of this chapter partnership can be defined as where two or more independent bodies work together on an outcome that they could not achieve separately (Parrott, 2008).

This relatively simple definition may help clarify, but may also hide, other meanings of partnership, which are also relevant when considering ethical issues. For example, partnership also implies an equal and a willing commitment by those wishing to become partners. It implies notions of shared responsibility for the enterprise which is to be undertaken (see *Collins Free Dictionary,* 2014).

Effective partnerships

Effective partnerships require sustained relationships, shared agendas built over time and a commitment to shared problem solving. Yet difficulties remain because of the complexity that such partnerships involve. For example, Hood (2014) outlines how such complexity involves workers in having to make decisions that require sound professional judgement yet are undermined by the way in which an integrated children's service requires them to focus upon how to manage complex working relationships and work within integrated systems, which hinders their professional judgement in working directly with families. The government's drive to improve public services is not assisted by rapid change, largely imposed from above. This concern with partnership has also been discussed in relation to health and social care: Jones (2005) argues that the frequency and pace of change are causing disruption between health and social care partners.

Partnership, therefore, does not mean merger or takeover of one professional group by another, yet much of the current drive for partnership, particularly within adult care, appears to be moving in this direction. Bailey (2012) argues in relation to changes in the role of the approved mental health worker where the dominance of health has marginalised the role of social workers and reduces the support, particularly in terms of supervision that they can draw on from their local authority, which has seconded them into the new system. In addition, the Health and Care Professions Council (HCPC) taking control over social workers' registration may be seen as a sign that social work is no longer as independent as it once was and that the standards of conduct expected are now the same as in other health professions.

When different professional groupings come together in collaboration, they bring with them their own ways of working, organisational cultures and attitudes, their particular practice experience and their own ethical codes. For professionals who may feel unsure of their own professional standing this can be threatening, as they may feel that their own ethical codes of practice may have to be suspended in order to achieve partnership.

CASE STUDY 7.1

Aileen is a social worker who works in a Child Protection Unit with police colleagues. Aileen receives a referral to visit a family well known to both social services and the police. She feels that a police officer will be needed to accompany her as the allegations are serious and therefore may require police intervention. She tells Bill, her police colleague, that they are visiting the family and he responds with: 'Not those bloody gyppos again'.

ACTIVITY 7.1

How might you respond to such a situation and what do you think is being challenged here?

COMMENT

Social work's ethical commitment to anti-oppressive practice is clearly challenged by the inappropriate comments made by the police officer. Much has been made of the 'canteen culture' which permeates the police force, and evidence suggests that this culture certainly reinforces stereotypical and racist attitudes towards minorities (Macpherson, 1999). The social worker may have met such attitudes before, she may shrug her shoulders and rationalise this as just part of the canteen culture, which may not necessarily be discriminatory once the police officer is working alongside the social worker. However, if she does take that line then there are significant issues which she may feel are being ignored in order to get along with her partner.

Continued

To avoid collusion with this culture, it is clearly in order for the social worker to question her police partner's attitudes and request he refrain from such language. She may wish to engage him in a discussion about the use of such stereotypical language. She may also suggest that if she does not receive an appropriate response then she will take this further and may consult with her line manager, who could make a formal complaint. There is no appropriate way that the social worker can condone such language, and even if it were to be argued that this may undermine partnership working, then the social worker needs to be clear what the point of partnership working is. In other words, it is not to form a workable relationship with fellow professionals which results in the dilution of the social worker's value base and the demeaning of service users. The point of partnership working is not to deliver appropriate services to service users only to have them undermined by some partners exhibiting discriminatory attitudes. However, as the research box below suggests, policing is experiencing change and, as such, social workers may very well find that there is an emergent, although not prevalent, culture which has more in common with some elements of social work.

RESEARCH SUMMARY

McCarthy (2013) outlines subtle changes in the culture of policing, particularly where female officers become involved in partnership working with social workers. However, she concludes:

> *Whilst there may be evidence to suggest that as a general trend the police continue to be a masculine, action-orientated, and largely macho organisation, recent changes to the police organisation place limits on this hegemonic account. In accounting for the marginalisation of women through such accounts, there is an inherent danger of focusing too heavily on the overall outcomes of policing, rather than discovering some of the nuances in what can be considered as 'alternative' policing strategies as this article describes, where the role of female officers is highly active, largely dominant and at times subversive in its operation. This should not lead to a treatment of female officers through a utopic lens which articulates their behaviour as confirmation of a feminist model of direct resistance against their suppression and marginalisation by the police. Rather, the selling of 'soft' policing serves as an interesting example of a counter resistance which reconfigures existing components of police culture to produce support for a model of policing which attempts to be largely progressive in its aims and objectives.*

> *(McCarthy, 2013, p276)*

Lymbery (2005), in addressing collaborative working between social workers and health professionals, suggests there are key knowledge, values and skills that social workers can bring to interprofessional working. These key attributes are not just appropriate for work between social services and health, but may usefully be a starting point from which social workers can develop security within their own professional role. In addition they can play an effective role within collaboration and joint working with other professionals. Lymbery (2005) suggests, with some additional comments:

1. Social workers' values and ethical stance are a key element of an interprofessional team as these highlight the real differences between social workers and other professionals. Of value here is the critical role of challenge and questioning of existing practice that can be developed within a multidisciplinary team.

2. Social workers as 'social' workers bring with them their expertise and knowledge of the social factors which can influence the behaviour of service users and the operation of the team itself. This holistic approach places the individual within a broader community and social context which other professionals may not share to the same extent. This can be particularly strong in professions which have a narrower remit, such as the nursing profession; in the main nurses may operate from a medical model rather than a social model.

3. The administrative role of social workers in coordinating care packages, for example, may give them a strategic position within partnerships with health. They can operate between the different organisations involved to link together various professions into focusing upon the intervention. This connects in many ways to one of the traditional roles of social workers as enablers of service networks, which can be transferred into multidisciplinary teams.

Given social workers' potential to operate at more strategic levels it becomes possible to develop interpersonal relationships with other professionals in a way that other members of the team would be unable to do given their narrower service focus. The more privileged position then of social workers has the potential to provide for an effective enabling role in binding the multiprofessional team together.

Codes of conduct

It is interesting to note that the Nursing and Midwifery Council (NMC) (2014) code of conduct has a specific standard requirement for nurses to work collaboratively:

The NMC code of professional conduct: standards for conduct, performance and ethics

    4. *As a registered nurse, midwife or specialist community public health nurse, you must co-operate with others in the team.*

        4.1. The team includes the patient or client, the patient's or client's family, informal carers and health and social care professionals in the National Health Service, independent and voluntary sectors.

                                          Continued

Continued

For many years nurses have worked alongside different occupational and professional groups within hospitals on a regular basis. Within the HCPC *Standards of Conduct* (HCPC, 2014), social workers now are explicitly required under point 7 of the standards as follows:

> 7. *You must communicate properly and effectively with service users and other practitioners. You must take all reasonable steps to make sure that you can communicate properly and effectively with service users. You must communicate appropriately, cooperate, and share your knowledge and expertise with other practitioners, for the benefit of service users.*

Does this reflect the lessening autonomy of social work, which has until recently had a greater degree of professional freedom to act compared with the more subscribed role of nurses, particularly within the hospital setting?

Although in respect of health workers and social care workers, both codes identify that working with others in partnership is important, they do not specify how professionals should work together. In partnership working some of the more general ethical concepts are also important, i.e. trust, respect, honesty, yet for collaborative work the importance of reciprocity is vital. In studies of partnership working the core of success involves the sense in which partners feel that their professional identity is respected. Where partnership becomes problematic, therefore, is where different professional groupings feel that their particular professional identity is under threat or that it does not receive the same status as others within the team.

RESEARCH SUMMARY

Glendinning (2003) argues that, although management systems have integrated partnership working successfully, at lower organisational levels, professional domains and identities continue to be barriers to successful partnership outcomes. This is echoed by Carpenter et al. (2003), who suggest in relation to partnership within community mental health teams that social workers experienced greater degrees of role conflict than their nurse partners, which requires in their view more support and supervision for social workers.

Codes of ethics

Codes of ethics have a crucial role to play here as they define the principles upon which the professional role is carried forward with service users, and delineate one profession's practice from another. A central concern then for respective partners is that they feel that respect for and trust in their partner's ethical practice is reciprocated. As we noted at the beginning of this chapter, social workers and social care workers do not have any choice in whether they work within multidisciplinary teams. Therefore, it becomes incumbent upon them to derive effective working relationships within these organisational arrangements. In ethical terms there is a problem. As professional values have often been translated into how individual workers can behave ethically with service users, there has been little or no need to develop ethics which require different professionals in a team to come together to provide a service. As Shardlow et al. (2004) have identified in relation to interagency working to safeguard children, there are no specific standards for interagency training used by any of the occupational groups involved. Even where standards exist, few refer specifically to interagency work issues in relation to safeguarding children. It is important therefore to think about how different professionals can operate in ways which enable them to cooperate for the benefit of service users. To date there have been few developments which have considered ethical issues within multiprofessional teams. One such approach, which was influenced by the Climbié inquiry and was given funding to pursue some of these questions, has come from Shardlow et al. (2004). This project, funded by the Department of Health, has set about developing standards for both multiagency education and training and practice. Within its brief it has considered the ethical implications for working in multiprofessional teams.

FIVE – OPERATIONAL STANDARD: ETHICS AND CONFIDENTIALITY

Use and communicate relevant information with due regard for the preservation of the client's confidentiality as is appropriate.

Practitioners should know the ethical position of their own profession/occupation in relation to maintaining the confidentiality of information that is given to them and act accordingly.

However, information should be shared with other practitioners when it is clear that not to do so may place the child or vulnerable adult at risk. In addition, practitioners should have due regard for, and seek to understand the ethical position of other occupational and professional groups which may be different to their own.

(Shardlow et al., 2004, p23)

ACTIVITY 7.2

Look at the statement above. What aspects of the ethics of partnership contained in the box are the most challenging?

COMMENT

As with all attempts to provide ethical statements, those above are qualified and rely upon you as a social work professional to exercise your judgement; for example, when

Continued

to share information. Therefore, those statements which are qualified will provide an element of challenge in that your partner professional may not understand your interpretation of the following ethical statements:

- *preservation of the client's confidentiality as is appropriate;*

- *information should be shared with other practitioners when it is clear that not to do so may place the child or vulnerable adult at risk.*

Both these statements require you to decide what information is appropriate to share and when to share it. In relation to service users, the main justification in breaching confidentiality would be where a child or vulnerable adult is at risk. However, it is likely that different professionals' thresholds of what constitutes risk may vary. For example, a community nurse finding an adult living in relatively unsanitary and unkempt surroundings may interpret this as a risky situation to health, yet from a social worker's perspective it may be tolerable if the person is maintaining independence and not posing any immediate risk to him- or herself. Likewise, a teacher who finds a child's behaviour intolerable and disruptive in class may be more keen to share information about that child's family than a social worker who may see disruption as a lower priority than keeping that child in school, away from his or her disruptive home life.

What needs to be considered here is that both workers are coming from their own ethical codes of practice and, although there are some similarities, it is perhaps difficult to see how different professionals can work in an ethically sensitive way if they do not share some elements of a common ethical base. The importance of values for social workers when faced with the possibility of working in partnership has been highlighted by Peck and Norman (1999), where social workers felt their values could be threatened by a more outcome-oriented culture evident in the NHS. For social workers, outcomes are important, but the process of engaging with service users and the quality of the relationships forged are of equal importance. Thus social work practice is as much concerned with process as with outcome. This focus upon process has been outlined previously in relation to service users and there is ample evidence that process as much as outcome is valued by service users (Aldgate and Statham, 2001). It is relevant here then to think of ethics within multidisciplinary teams as operating on two levels. The first is where individual workers use their particular codes to engage with service users. The second would be to develop shared ethical principles in working with one another. These principles should be the subject of dialogue and discussion in which the different professions come to an agreement on certain basic principles around which they will work together.

Think of some key ethical principles or values that go beyond ideas of individually based ethics that you could develop to enable some first principles of joint working.

As you are thinking of developing relationship-based ethics then those principles based upon individual responsibility may be important but do not encapsulate how partners should work together. Individually based decision making in respect to values assumes that the choices made align with our values as professionals, but those choices which are appropriate in work with service users may not align with other professionals' value choices. Individually based professional ethics therefore ignore the reality of the connectedness between different professionals and their values and code of ethics within multidisciplinary teams.

Communicative reason

One approach which has gained increasing purchase in social work comes from the work of Jürgen Habermas, who has developed ideas on democratic communication between individuals which could be adapted for multiprofessional working. Habermas (see Spratt and Houston, 1999) argues that we need to find new ways of organising the social world in which we live, which should be informed by what he calls 'communicative reason'. This means that how we communicate with one another must involve an ability to be understood and to construct shared meanings. This ought to be ensured by all those involved in joint communication, enabling:

- all to be allowed to speak;

- all to be required to listen;

- all to have the capacity to question.

This process must be democratic, taking place on a fair and equal basis. This is potentially significant for partnership working as it seeks to develop a basis upon which different professional groups can begin to interact and communicate.

In communicative action participants are not primarily oriented to their own individual success; they pursue their own individual goals under the conditions that they can harmonise their plans of action on the basis of common situation definitions. In this respect the negotiation of definitions of the situation is an essential element of the interpretive accomplishments required for communicative action.

(Habermas, 1984, pp285–6)

As this quotation suggests, communicative action invites different parties to negotiate their understanding of their particular goals of action based upon agreed definitions of the situation in which their goals develop. What Habermas is suggesting is that communicative action must be based upon reasoned argument which seeks to construct a valid case upon which mutual understanding can lead to a consensus which is agreed upon by the parties to the communication. Communicative action builds upon those interactions by which people are motivated to understand others so that they can share their lives together. This is the opposite of what Habermas calls strategic action, where interaction is oriented towards 'success', which in his case means getting others to do or to believe what one wants them to, regardless of their subjective needs or experience. The underlying logic of communicative action suggests that mutual understanding is possible. Those engaged in interaction have reached a background consensus with respect to four types of validity claims: comprehensibility, truth, rightness and sincerity. As Outhwaite (1994) suggests, the background consensus between speaker and hearer is concerned to enable a claim that the speaker is making to be justified. Thus the speaker can be questioned on the basis of:

- what do you mean? i.e. comprehensibility;

- is what you say true? i.e. truth;

- are you entitled to say that? i.e. rightness;

- do you really mean it? i.e. sincerity.

A consensus constructed in this way is only valid if, as a matter of principle, we presuppose the possibility of an unrestrained dialogue where all have access to the dialogue and where the logic of the better argument is validated. This process is called an ideal speech situation. As Habermas concedes, the actual ways in which argument occurs is often contrary to this but he is arguing for an ethics by which an open and fair dialogue should and can take place.

As Milley (2002) has argued, this theory can be used to understand that organisations can be moral communities. This can be achieved through a rationally agreed consensus which marginalises individual or small-group preferences or particular traditions and ideologies in order to validate just principles to guide action. From the point of view of partnership working this theory can be utilised to develop the new multiagency teams as moral communities rather than separate interprofessional communities.

Partnership projects

One way to build an underlying consensus can be to develop a shared approach to anti-oppressive practices which seeks to develop social justice. There are many partnership projects which bring different professionals together to work towards social justice or at least to develop social inclusion of marginalised individuals and communities. This was a core approach developed by the Labour government after their election in 1997. Policies towards communities have been developed to tackle the problems of disadvantaged areas through a 'joined-up' approach at national and local levels.

The National Strategy for Neighbourhood Renewal has put in place Local Strategic Partnerships with additional resources through the Neighbourhood Renewal Fund to focus on the 88 most deprived local authority areas. The New Deal for Communities, neighbourhood wardens and Neighbourhood Management Pathfinders are key community-based approaches to deliver the strategy. Working in partnership, the government's new approach to tackling social exclusion emphasised the importance of joined-up working at all levels, together with a more client-centred approach to designing and delivering services. This has been reflected in closer working between central government departments, local government and the voluntary and community sector, and communities (Social Exclusion Unit, 2004, p11).

Thus the experience and expertise designed to tackle social exclusion have focused upon partnership working. This approach is designed to achieve some measure of social justice and, therefore, has the potential to be transferred across to the personal social services such as children's services and adult care. The recognition that oppression is often multiple and, therefore, requires a team with a range of different skills is potentially advantageous. The manifestations of multiple injustice can often overwhelm individually placed professionals working out of their own separate teams. Thus teams could collaborate around the principles of embracing diversity to achieve social justice within and through their partnership arrangements.

CASE STUDY 7.2

The multidisciplinary learning disabilities team in which you are one of the social workers has undergone a rapid reorganisation. The team in which you work is being joined by your partner team from the other half of the city. In essence, the team is now doubling in size. As a result there have been significant problems in developing working relationships between the new team members. Managers have tried to counter these problems by outlining what support each of the respective professionals would get in terms of supervision, and have clarified the management arrangements of the new team. Nevertheless, despite these extensive arrangements, members of the new team have not worked well together. Both teams tend to distrust the other and there have been a number of arguments between individual members regarding the style of work. It appears that this is not necessarily to do with different professional cultures but that in your team, the working relationships were well founded and partnership working tended to develop well. Unfortunately, in merging with the other team their working arrangements were not so well progressed towards partnership, and as such their lack of cooperative working has undermined the new team arrangements. This has affected a number of service users where different members of the team have not communicated effectively over different cases, leaving service users confused about what service they should be receiving and from whom.

ACTIVITY 7.4

Using the approach suggested by Habermas to develop communicative action within the team, what suggestions would you make to develop partnership working?

COMMENT

A useful starting point in developing an ethics of partnership would be to take the principles:

- *comprehensibility;*
- *truth;*

Continued

COMMENT *continued*

- *rightness;*

- *sincerity.*

These can be applied to the idea of partnership, i.e. using comprehensibility as a starting point:

- *How can we speak of partnership?*

- *What do the different professionals understand by the term?*

- *Can they agree on what it means in the newly formed team?*

Secondly, it implies that when we agree to partnership working we are prepared to act truthfully and diligently upon this agreement. Finally, we affirm that our definition of partnership is one on which we can agree, ensuring that it meets what the different professional groupings want from partnership. We may then talk about what the partnership wants to achieve in delivering social justice to the service users it serves. This will require a further exploration using the above principles to agree upon how social justice is then understood, and how it is seen as appropriate for the team to use as its overall objective.

Although Habermas's ideas have been criticised for his belief in the possibility of a shared understanding of truth through democratic dialogue, potentially it can enable different partners to engage in a democratic process designed to provide some basic principles through which 'right actions' can be developed. For Habermas, it is only when everyone in a particular society who has the capacity to make a contribution to what constitutes 'right action' has participated and given their agreement that a particular course of action can be said to be universal. If certain norms have been only partially agreed upon then this represents a sectional interest. For social work this has many implications in relation to partnership working. It means that a democratic dialogue is a prerequisite of partnership. In turn this requires that service users have access to the dialogue, for example in identifying what they require from partnership working. If service users are not given a voice to determine the ethical codes of partnership work then partnership ethics represents a sectional interest (Hugman, 2005).

This approach has been called a discourse ethics approach. What this means is that knowledge is built upon consensus or general agreement. This is achieved through open communication in which knowledge is developed as a public understanding and is not the property of any particular individual or sectional interest (Outhwaite, 1994).

As Milley (2002) shows in relation to organisations, discourse ethics can potentially develop beyond individual or sectional interests to achieve a shared understanding of what the organisation, or in our case the multiagency partnership, is trying to achieve ethically and practically. In relation to partnership working we can distinguish between a partial or subjectivist approach to working together which looks at the implications of actions and ideas from a particular professional or individualistic viewpoint, or we can identify a discourse approach, which takes a more universal and generalised position, looking at the different interests and seeking a consensual view of the actions or ideas under consideration.

RESEARCH SUMMARY

Banks (2004) in her research has identified the following as most challenging to practition-ers wishing to work in partnership:

- *Professional identity. This refers to how professionals integrate themselves into the pro-fessional role and how the professional role influences how they see themselves. This is often developed through initial training in the education process which socialises stu-dents and encourages them to see themselves in a certain way.*

- *Professional values. Used broadly, to refer to general principles which inform the profes-sion to think and act in a particular way. It can refer to those principles within different codes of professional practice. It can also refer to more generalised belief systems or ide-ologies which are said to encompass what certain professionals think, i.e. social workers are seen to work from a social model.*

- *Professional culture. This refers to a professional way of doing and speaking about things, identifying those within the profession from those outside. Cultures often become visi-ble when they conflict with other professional or non-professional cultures. For example, the development of the service users' movement has brought into sharp distinction the conflict between professional culture to construct service users as passive receivers of service in contrast to the proactive and independent culture of service user groups.*

ACTIVITY 7.5

How would a subjectivist approach look at professional identity, values and culture? We will then look at the approach of a discourse ethics.

COMMENT

Professional identity

Identity from a subjectivist approach helps us to understand the importance of individual professional identity and its different manifestations among professional groups. A dis-course ethics will highlight the importance of a shared identity within the team that will accommodate individual identities as a process of the mutual exploration of uncovering those aspects which can be shared within the team.

Professional values

A subjectivist view helps us to understand the particular sets of values and their mean-ings which the different professionals in the multiagency team hold. A discourse ethics

Continued

COMMENT *continued*

provides a means to understand the paradoxes of the particular notions of ethical profes-sional conduct and the importance of identifying commonalities between different codes of conduct for a broader-based ethics within the team.

Professional culture

Subjectivist views will identify the particular differences between professional cultures and how these inform the particular models of practice while a discourse ethics will empha-sise the importance of a shared understanding, which includes different conceptions as a model for a shared understanding to enable the recognition and accommodation of such different professional cultures.

ACTIVITY **7.6**

Look at the following two statements. The first comes from the code of practice for social care workers (HCPC, 2014), the second from the NMC code of professional conduct (NMC, 2014). Identify from each list those statements which nurses and social work and social care workers have in common.

Code of practice for social care workers

- *Protect the rights and promote the interests of service users and carers.*

- *Strive to establish and maintain the trust and confidence of service users and carers.*

- *Promote the independence of service users while protecting them as far as possible from danger or harm.*

- *Respect the rights of service users while seeking to ensure that their behaviour does not harm themselves or other people.*

- *Uphold public trust and confidence in social care services.*

- *Be accountable for the quality of their work and take responsibility for maintaining and improving their knowledge and skills.*

The NMC code of professional conduct

- *Obtain consent before you give any treatment or care.*

- *Protect confidential information.*

- *Cooperate with others in the team.*

- *Maintain your professional knowledge and competence.*

- *Be trustworthy.*

- *Act to identify and minimise risk to patients and clients.*

COMMENT

If we compare the two lists, both professional groups share many value and ethical principles which can provide the foundation for partnership work. From an ethics of discourse perspective in assessing the respective lists, it is important to identify that it is no easy matter to develop partnership working. For example, the principle of confidentiality is a principle shared by both groups. In terms of their partnership working, then it would be necessary for the different professionals to share what they understood confidentiality to mean and to agree under what circumstances they would share information and under what circumstances they would keep confidentiality.

ACTIVITY *7.7*

If you were the nurse in Case study 7.3 below, would you feel it appropriate to share this information? Should Neil share this with the other members of the team who are working on this young man's offending behaviour?

CASE STUDY *7.3*

Neil is a community nurse working within a youth offending team. He is working with a young man who has contracted a sexually transmitted disease and has provided the appropriate initial advice before referring him for treatment.

COMMENT

The rules of confidentiality here are very pertinent. Do we as professionals relax our ethical principles for an imagined belief in partnership work or do we uphold our own professional values while working within the team? Does partnership come with a complete derogation of our own professional ethics or should partnership allow us as professionals to develop those within the context of partnership working?

Within the youth justice team the focus is upon preventing offending behaviour, so the question then needs to be posed: do this young man's problems have anything to do with his offending behaviour? If we can answer that the issue is unrelated, then Neil has a perfect right and duty to maintain confidentiality. If, however, the problem was related to his offending behaviour, then Neil should share the information. Indeed, under section 115 of the Crime and Disorder Act 1998, information pertinent to criminal activity can be shared between agencies (Banks, 2004).

Continued

COMMENT *continued*

Thus, for the team to move forward, some general principles developed from pertinent examples to give context to the ethical problem could be used to reach agreement as to how and if information will be shared.

CHAPTER SUMMARY

This chapter has explored the meaning of partnership working from an ethical standpoint. It has discussed some of the barriers to partnership working and emphasised the importance of culture, identity and value as key concerns for professionals within multiagency teams. These concerns go to the heart of the problems professionals face in working in partnership. This chapter has identified the priority given in partnership working to management and resource systems which provide the structure to partnership. While these are essential, unless the particular professional identities are then addressed by reconciling different professional cultures that flow from this, partnership will be problematic. In addressing these problems, the work of Habermas and the relevance of discourse ethics have been considered as a possible way forward in bringing different professional groupings together to work effectively within a multiagency team.

FURTHER READING

Carnwell, R and Buchanan, J (2005) *Effective practice in health and social care: A partnership approach.* Maidenhead: Open University.

This book provides a wide-ranging discussion of the different aspects of partnership working, drawing upon a range of perspectives to inform the debate.

Quinney, A (2006) *Collaborative social work practice.* Exeter: Learning Matters.

This is an excellent introduction for social workers to the different contexts in which partnership working is now taking place.

Chapter 8
Ethics in social work organisations

This chapter will help you meet the following capabilities, to the appropriate level, from the Professional Capabilities Framework:

- Professionalism: Identify and behave as a professional social worker, committed to professional development.
- Diversity: Recognise diversity and apply antidiscriminatory and anti-oppressive principles in practice.
- Rights, justice and economic well-being: Advance human rights and promote social justice and economic well-being.
- Contexts and organisations: Engage with, inform and adapt to changing contexts that shape practice. Operate effectively within own organisational frameworks and contribute to the development of services and organisations. Operate effectively within multiagency and interprofessional partnerships and settings.

It will also introduce you to the following academic standards, as set out in the social work subject benchmark statement:

5.1.2 The service delivery context, which includes:

- the complex relationships between public, social and political philosophies, policies and priorities and the organisation and practice of social work, including the contested nature of these;
- the issues and trends in modern public and social policy and their relationship to contemporary practice and service delivery in social work;
- the current range and appropriateness of statutory, voluntary and private agencies providing community-based, day care, residential and other services and the organisational systems inherent within these;
- the contribution of different approaches to management, leadership and quality in public and independent human services;
- the implications of modern information and communications technology (ICT) for both the provision and receipt of services.

5.1.5 The nature of social work practice, which includes:

- the characteristics of practice in a range of community-based and organisational settings within statutory, voluntary and private sectors, and the factors influencing changes and developments in practice within these contexts.

Ethics and organisations

Social workers and their employers have an ethical duty to ensure that the organisations they work for operate in a just manner. A just social work organisation must convince those it employs and those whom it serves that social work is something worth upholding as good in itself, and that the operation of social work organisations will lead to good and just outcomes. Social workers and their employers therefore have to act in a way which shows those who contribute through paying taxes and those who require a service from them that their organisation operates in a fair way, treating all with equal respect. It must enable citizens to contribute to how the service is planned, organised and delivered to them. At an organisational level this process enables citizens to give legitimacy to social work organisations and to recognise that social work's aims are to achieve social justice for those it serves (Rothstein, 1998).

Public bodies now have a number of legal duties relating to social justice matters. For example, the Equality Act (2010) requires public bodies like local authority social services departments to operate in a manner which does not discriminate in relation to nine protected characteristics, which are:

1. age;

2. disability;

3. gender reassignment;

4. marriage or civil partnership (in employment only);

5. pregnancy and maternity;

6. race;

7. religion or belief;

8. sex;

9. sexual orientation.

The Race Relations (Amendment) Act 2001 requires all public authorities in carrying out their work not to commit any act constituting discrimination, although some public bodies are excluded, for example the security services and military units. Local authority social services departments must act to eliminate unlawful discrimination and to promote equality of opportunity and good relations between persons of different racial groups.

However, in respect of the treatment of social work and social care employees, the former code for social care employers in England is now defunct but was formerly controlled by the General Social Care Council. Although the Health and Care Professions Council (HCPC) lays down general duties for employers, these involve issues of discipline and registration, but do not require employers to meet even the relatively mild expectations required of them through the former General Social Care Council.

To enable social work institutions to operate in a just way there are two basic assumptions which underpin this principle. Firstly, service users, social work employees and their managers should be able to influence the social work processes and organisational practices in their employing organisations. Secondly, these organisations must take responsibility to ensure that they can respond and reshape those processes and practices in response to all legitimate demands. Nothing within the HCPC expectations of employers meets any of these criteria.

If social workers are to work in an ethical manner then they will have to engage with the ways in which their organisation:

- organises their work;

- resources their work;

- supervises their work;

- enables service users' participation.

This means that social workers need to consider the nature of the managerial and organisational contexts which shape their working lives. In particular, they need to ensure that their professional autonomy is enhanced appropriately and, where it is constrained by policy and procedure, that this is exercised fairly and for the benefit of service users. The problems social workers face in their employing organisation are often translated into issues around professional discretion, in which some antimanagerialist discourses see any imposition of rules and procedures on social workers as necessarily a bad thing. As Evans (2013) argues, the increase in guidance, procedures and rules should not immediately be equated with greater control over professional discretion; excessive rule making may create more discretion, which in itself may not be positive either. This can be the case where a proliferation of rules which may be contradictory or which become overly complex leaves social workers to use their discretion by default creating rules of thumb through the thicket of bureaucratic control. Rules and procedures can operate positively or negatively. In a positive sense, they can clarify and enhance social workers' knowledge of the conditions under which services can be accessed and enable service users' social justice, by ensuring that services are delivered fairly according to agreed criteria which are open and transparent. In a negative sense, poorly conceived rules and procedures can enable managers and professionals to hide behind them, to use them as an excuse for inaction or to create the opportunity for professional abuse of power.

> *Being a professional is associated with having a significant degree of freedom in performing one's work; but social workers, like many professional workers, tend to be employed within organisations in which they are bound by policies and rules. An influential analysis of the relationship between social workers and the organisations within which they work has argued that there has been a proliferation of managerial organisational rules and that these have eliminated social workers' discretion. However, this article argues that, even in rule-saturated organisations, social workers retain significant freedom in their work, and that the ways in which professionals*
>
> *Continued*

> *Continued*
>
> *relate to organisational rules is a key dimension of understanding discretion. This article employs Oakeshott's idea of a dialectic of two attitudes to rules to explore the relationship between organisational rules and professional freedom in adult social work in local authorities. It presents the findings of a qualitative study that explores social workers' attitudes to the formal organisational rules that structure their practice in an English local authority.*
>
> *The study suggests that, while workers split in how they approach organisations in line with Oakeshott's approach, these perspectives are not mutually exclusive, but are adapted and changed for reasons of pragmatism and principled commitments.*
>
> (Evans, 2013, p739)

Social workers, if they work for local authority social services departments, find themselves part of an organisation which is arranged bureaucratically. To work effectively to deliver services to large groups of service users, work has to be delivered in a rational and transparent way. This form of working is often best suited to bureaucratic styles of organisation. Let us define what we mean by an organisation and then what is meant by bureaucracy through an internet search for definitions.

An organisation:

- describes a group of people acting to achieve a common goal (**http://enwikipedia.org/wiki/Organization**);

- deliberate arrangement of people to achieve a particular purpose (**wordnet.princeton.edu**).

The above definitions describe both a way of working together to achieve a common goal and the actual disposition of people into different roles and responsibilities to achieve the most efficient outcome. Roles and responsibilities have been formally organised and managed to achieve a particular purpose.

A bureaucracy:

- is a form of organisation marked by division of labour, hierarchy, rules and regulations and impersonal relationships (**www.crfonline.org**);

- is a system in which people are expected to follow precisely defined rules and procedures rather than to use personal judgement (Camic et al., 2005);

- rules by bureaus of appointed officials. It is a group of agencies marked by a clear hierarchy of authority in charge of implementing collective choices made through political institutions. Bureaucracies are formal organisations that carry out policy through written rules and standardised procedures based on the specialisation of duties and striving for the efficient attainment of organisational goals (**http://socialsciencedictionary.com**);

- is a sociological concept of government and its institutions as an organisational structure characterised by regularised procedure, division of responsibility, hierarchy and impersonal relationships (**http://en.wikipedia.org/wiki/Bureaucracy**).

A bureaucracy such as that found within a social services department divides activities between different people with an identified hierarchy of responsibilities, so that in theory each person in the organisation knows who has which responsibility. Authority for completing activities comes from the top down, so that power is designated down through each level of the hierarchy.

The abuse of professional power in the form of the damage that can be done by a bureaucracy, within which those entwined in its grasp come to inhabit a nightmare world of contradictory and self-defeating rules, has been closely associated with the writing of Franz Kafka and the adjective Kafkaesque. Kafka's book *The Trial* begins with the protagonist Joseph K waking one morning to find himself under arrest. He has not been previously informed that he has done wrong, and no one can tell him what charges have been brought against him. Even the officials who have come to arrest him don't know – they're just doing their jobs. Joseph K spends the rest of the novel trying to discover these charges, attempting to outwit the excessively bureaucratic system that has put him under arrest, while at the same time trying to maintain a hold on his fragmenting personal life. As the forces against Joseph K steadily grow stronger, he slowly comes to the revelation that the entire world may be under the control of the court that is trying to condemn him (Kafka, 2004).

Another associated term which describes some of the essence of bureaucratic thinking comes from the book and film *Catch-22* (Heller, 2005). The story concerns bomber crews in the Second World War, when the chances of survival were slim. We have all come up against certain circumstances where no matter what we try and do to chart a way forward, we are confronted with a Catch-22 situation:

> There was only one catch and that was Catch-22, which specified that a concern for one's own safety in the face of dangers that were real and immediate was the process of a rational mind. Orr was crazy and could be grounded. All he had to do was ask; and as soon as he did, he would no longer be crazy and would have to fly more missions. Orr would be crazy to fly more missions and sane if he didn't, but if he was sane he had to fly them. If he flew them he was crazy and didn't have to; but if he didn't want to he was sane and had to. Yossarian was moved very deeply by the absolute simplicity of this clause of Catch-22 and let out a respectful whistle.

> (Heller, 2005, p55)

This catch keeps the hero of the book, Yossarian, in the war because a concern for his own life proved that he was not really crazy, and to get out of combat you have to be crazy. The catch is used by the superior powers to uphold and increase their power, and yet it is harmful to those who do not have power in the first place.

This frame of thinking describes the way in which an organisation is able to live inside people's heads so that their ability to act is neutralised through the way their thoughts and behaviour are influenced by these organisational and bureaucratic imperatives. A useful analysis of the impact of welfare institutions upon individuals has been provided by Foucault (1977), who investigated the procedures to control and punish criminals in the nineteenth century through the idea of a Panopticon, a prison system designed by the utilitarian Jeremy Bentham. The prisoners were subject to constant surveillance through the architectural design of the prison where all prisoners could be watched from a central point. The surveyed prisoners were induced to be obedient because they did not know when they were being watched. Although prisoners may not be being observed, they must behave if they are and, therefore, control is achieved even when the observation by the guards may be absent. This results in prisoners controlling their own behaviour almost automatically (Prado, 2000). A more commonplace example concerns police speed cameras placed by the roadside which may or may not be switched on; thus motorists do not know if they will be caught speeding by the camera and, therefore, adjust the speed of their car accordingly. Ultimately, motorists respond almost immediately as a speed camera sign is observed and adjust their speed. This deliberate and largely unconscious response can also be evidenced in how some people are socialised into an inflexible bureaucratic mindset. Thus the operation of a bureaucracy which requires the utmost conformity to rules has two effects:

1. It converts deliberate obedience of regulations into habitual compliance with rules and norms. In this way they become 'mores', reflecting a strong moral imperative for workers to feel they 'ought' to comply. A failure to conform to rules will result in a much stronger social response from your colleagues who resent your failure to behave appropriately.

2. The habitual compliance itself converts to adoption or internalisation of these norms.

This rather pessimistic description of bureaucratic forms of organisation has been further reinforced through the work of Bauman (1989, 1994), who suggests that the bureaucratic way of working divorces ethics from the organisation of the work that the bureaucracy processes, so that people become bodies to be processed rather than human beings to be respected.

> *Now this ideal model can work properly only on the condition that all people involved in the work of the organisation follow the commands they receive and are guided only by them (their actions are, as it is said sometimes, 'rule-guided'). And that means that people should not be diverted by their personal beliefs and convictions or by emotions – sympathy or antipathy – to fellow workers or to individual clients or objects of action.*

(Bauman, 1994, p11)

For Bauman (1994), bureaucracies encourage moral ambivalence and ethical blindness, defending themselves and their employees against troublesome ethical criticism in two ways:

1. The phenomenon of 'floating responsibility', which suggests that as long as employees followed the rules faithfully and did what was asked by their superiors, no responsibility can be placed upon workers for the effects of such allegiance that this may have on the objects worked on.

2. Ethical indifference, which neutralises and then exempts members of a bureaucracy from any moral judgement. Thus people are merely following the agreed principles and procedures which are neither good nor bad, but merely requirements to achieve the smooth running of the bureaucracy.

CASE STUDY *8.1*

Mrs Phillipson is a single parent living with her 14-year-old daughter Melanie who is both physically and learning-disabled. Two years ago Melanie was a passenger in her uncle's car when it was involved in an accident, killing her uncle and leaving her with serious body and head injuries. Melanie's behaviour can be very difficult for Mrs Phillipson to handle and the physical demands of caring for Melanie often leave Mrs Phillipson exhausted. In order to give her mother a break, Melanie goes four times a year to a respite care facility. This is a very oversubscribed service and the social services department has limited the use of the facility to four times a year. As you are Mrs Phillipson's social worker, you are now faced with a problem in that Mrs Phillipson is asking for an extra respite care break, even though she has already received her allocated breaks. In supervision, your team manager points out that Mrs Phillipson can be very demanding and that there is no possibility for Mrs Phillipson to receive more than her fair share of respite care, as the resource panel which decides such issues has already refused other carers who have made similar demands.

ACTIVITY *8.1*

What is your response in this case?

COMMENT

You will need to assess the circumstances leading to Mrs Phillipson seeking extra help. If you feel that there are special circumstances which have led her to require a further break and you assess her need is justified, then you may find yourself in conflict with the organisational imperative to ration care breaks in this way. Alternatively, you may agree that the social services department decision to ration services is justified to enable other carers to access some services. Or you may feel sympathy for both positions, in that Mrs Phillipson does have a pressing need which requires some action on your part but you also feel that, imperfect as it is, the social services department does need to ration services in order to spread a limited resource fairly around other carers.

On the face of it there are two initial responses that have been identified by writers such as Banks (2006) and Payne (2000). These can be characterised as a bureaucratic or procedural response in contrast to a flexible or reflective response.

Bureaucratic/procedural approach

This approach encourages the social worker to follow the rules. If procedures are in place and they have been arrived at impartially then ethically nothing else can be done. If Mrs Phillipson feels aggrieved and angry at you because you have reported back that no more care is available, then you do not bear any responsibility and no blame attaches to you. The idea of responsibility means in this case that you have done your duty. You have made a case for extra help but Mrs Phillipson does not meet the criteria.

Flexible/reflective approach

This approach asks you to recognise and critically reflect upon the dilemmas and conflicts which are inherent in social work and social care, rather than taking an 'either/or' approach in which, as a social worker, you argue against the injustice to Mrs Phillipson in having her needs ignored or alternatively follow procedures. If you recognise that Mrs Phillipson has a legitimate need but it is necessary to uphold the impartiality of the procedures to ration services fairly, then you may be able to develop a more flexible approach. You may achieve a solution for Mrs Phillipson and uphold the integrity of the procedures. As Banks (2006) argues, social workers have a duty to make ethical choices where the needs of the agency and individuals are in conflict and develop a practical way forward.

Flexible action

Just because your team manager asserts that other applications have been refused if carers have already had their maximum allocation of respite care, this should not prevent a case being made to the resource panel if it is justified. Thus, all rules and procedures operate from general cases and cannot, by definition, cover all aspects and differences between carers' needs. You might argue that Mrs Phillipson's situation is a special case; you may be successful. More pragmatically, you might inquire if any carers have not used their full complement of care and on this basis query whether you could use the resource so that places do not go to waste.

You may feel that in the long run the only way this problem may be resolved is for carers to take action. Clearly, other carers have been in the same position as Mrs Phillipson and may feel similarly that the overall level of provision is inadequate. Rationing services does not reflect the absolute need of individual carers, but is a relative judgement based upon the numbers of carers with a need and the availability of resources to meet that need. The department's rationing procedure may be necessary in the short run to manage inadequate supply of respite care, but in the long run the problem will remain. Carers may wish to be enabled to pressurise the social services department for a review of the procedure. In this event you may advise them on how to progress this further, while being aware that you are an employee of the organisation.

Social services departments as bureaucracies are concerned therefore to provide services which are delivered in an impartial way and require their employees to reflect this value. But this brings them into conflict with their employees, who are given the duty of administering these procedures, in which they experience the struggles and pains of the service users in trying to meet their welfare needs. The impartiality of the worker is sorely tested, and rightly so. To engage in a soulless assessment of need without recourse to the humanity and context of the situation would be impossible except for a robot. This conflict has been characterised by Clark (2006) as one between the instrumental and the moral.

Instrumental relationship

This limits an employee to a narrow focus upon the business in hand, often to a single transaction or event, for example, buying and selling goods, or when a civil servant processes a passport application. In these examples, neither party to the relationship has any interest or need to be concerned about the character of the other as long as the procedures are adhered to. The quality of the social interaction in the relationship is not intertwined with the transaction. As long as the exchange of goods occurs or the application is processed, then the quality of the relationship between the provider and receiver of the service is incidental to the outcome.

Moral relationship

On the other hand, there are professional–client relationships which are imbued with moral purpose. The social worker–service user relationship is one in which the moral qualities of the persons involved have a significant effect on the quality of the work done. Professional relationships mix both the instrumental and the moral. Social workers may deal with fairly routine assessments for services, which require little beyond a technical competence in assessment and knowledge of the appropriate services. However, on other occasions they may engage with service users over fundamental moral choices relating to a person's autonomy and independence.

The moral elements of the working relationships in social work become more personalised, as Clark (2006) argues, when social workers work alongside service users in more informal ways. As residential social workers find out very swiftly, they are continually compelled to work out what is 'normal' or morally acceptable in respect of the behaviour that they come into contact with when caring for children and young people. In effect, they become surrogate parents who have to provide some moral guidance as to how these children should live their lives. These elements are rarely experienced by the managers and administrators of social services departments (unless they have been social workers themselves), whose concerns take on a more utilitarian mode in deciding what is in the best interests of the many for whom they have responsibility. What social workers are continually required to do, then, is to reconcile the broader policy and guidance statements that form the boundaries of their work with the particular problems which service users face, which do not necessarily fit easily with these general policy statements. It requires social workers to judge the particular situation in the light of the general rules and find an acceptable way through for service users, reconciling their particular needs with the universal rules governing access to services. In reconciling these concerns, ethical codes of practice can provide guides to action, as can a recourse to policy and procedures, but ultimately it requires the judgement of the social worker to assess their relative weight and significance and make a decision accordingly.

The recent critiques of bureaucracy have in part come from the New Right and its restructuring of the welfare state by Conservative governments of the 1980s, carried forward by the present Coalition government. The critique often aimed at state bureaucracies rather than the big and, nonetheless, bureaucratic capitalist multinational corporations, charged government bureaucracies with being inefficient and inflexible with regard to the needs of modern citizens, who increasingly saw themselves as consumers of services rather than beneficiaries of what was argued were paternalistic state services. This analysis also maligned the professionals staffing these bureaucracies as essentially self-interested, with a vested interest in building unwieldy organisations to accrue greater power and personal gain (Frisby, 2013). This critique of bureaucracy was not limited to the political right, but the caricature which it portrays is particularly effective in undermining public organisations in the context of the Coalition government's moves to create what is called the 'Big Society'. David Cameron formulated the concept of the Big Society early on in his government, saying that *the recent growth of the state [under New Labour] has promoted not social solidarity, but selfishness and individualism* (Cameron, 2009). His focus was, he claimed, to empower individuals, families and communities to take control of their lives. Critics have seen this concept as a justification for cutting local authority services and encouraging private and voluntary providers to replace, at a lower level of resource, the services removed from the local authority (Alcock, 2012).

The old-style bureaucratic social services have not been replaced wholesale with supposedly more efficient privatised forms of service but with a hybrid. This hybrid – known as a quasi-market – has introduced market-like competition with a reduction in the provision of local authority social services, replaced in theory by private and voluntary providers competing for contracts to provide services, for example in domiciliary/residential care, family support and children's residential care. Control over the organisation, management, assessment and commissioning of services remains with the local authority social services department. Enthusiasts for such an approach argue this has injected much dynamism and flexibility into social services. For critics such as Bauman (1994), it has brought the worst of both worlds – a bureaucratically managed service with the inequities of competition between providers, leading to a concern with cost efficiency rather than service effectiveness. For some writers, the pressure to develop standardised services within a managed market replicates some of the worst features of the mass consumer market (James, 2004).

An example of such a merger of the rational bureaucratic organisation of services within a fiercely marketised and competitive industry is that of the fast-food chain McDonald's. This has led Ritzer (1993) to suggest that this form of organisation has far-reaching consequences. Rationalisation reaches into all areas of everyday life. Ways of thinking are colonised by self-interested concern with efficiency and formal social control. The supreme manifestation of this is the bureaucracy, representing the process of rationalisation. This has a knock-on effect in which human interaction is controlled and then developed further into a rationalist framework.

Ritzer suggests that the fast-food restaurant and the processes of rationalisation and bureaucratic control encapsulated within it, i.e. McDonaldisation, have become so powerful that their rationalising logic has permeated everyday interaction and individual identity.

> *McDonaldisation is the process by which the principles of the fast food restaurant are coming to dominate more and more sectors of American society as well as of the rest of the world.*

(Ritzer, 1993, p1)

Ritzer outlines five dominant themes within McDonaldisation: efficiency, calculability, predictability, increased control and the replacement of human by non-human technology.

Efficiency

Efficiency develops systems which produce the maximum output for the least cost. In McDonald's this is sold to the consumer as being of benefit to them – fast food delivered quickly and cheaply. Much of the cost for this efficiency is placed on to consumers, for example, in queuing to order their food, and placing their empty food cartons and trays into the waste bin.

Calculability

All actions in the restaurant are calculated and quantified so that the consumer is given the choice of an array of differently sized meals, the bigger the better. Thus, quantity is valued over the quality of the product.

Predictability

Consumers of a 'Big Mac Meal' know exactly what to expect. A Big Mac will be the same whether it is served in Wrexham or Reykjavik – it will be the same size, taste the same and be served in the same environment. Thus, the 'Golden Arches' of the McDonald's logo become the universal sign to attract you from a car driving on a motorway or strolling in a shopping mall. The experience of eating a meal is repeated endlessly across the globe or repetitively each time you buy a Big Mac.

Control through the substitution of non-human for human technology

[T]hese two elements are closely linked. Specifically, replacement of human by non human technology is often oriented towards greater control. The great sources of uncertainty and unpredictability in a rationalising system are people – either the people who work within those systems or the people who are served by them.

(Ritzer, 1993, p148)

Each employee in McDonald's is drilled in what to say and how to say it. The production process which brings the Big Mac on to your tray is pre-packaged, pre-measured, automatically controlled. Both the employee who serves the meal and, to an increasing extent, the consumer are not required to think, just follow the instructions or see what others do in the queue.

This process is, therefore, ethically problematic as our skills and capabilities are diminished and our powers of judgement dulled. Our identities are moulded by our dependence upon and subordination to the rational bureaucratic processes evidenced in the McDonald's experience. Ritzer argues that the process of McDonaldisation shows the ultimate irrationality of a system that does not meet human need but rather does more to damage it.

> *Most specifically, irrationality means that rational systems are unreasonable systems. By that I mean that they deny the basic humanity, the human reason, of the people who work within or are served by them.*

(Ritzer, 1993, p154)

In the USA, this has had a damaging effect, with an increase in diagnoses of type 2 diabetes. Critser (2004) argues that type 2 diabetes has increased dramatically since the early 1990s, quoting figures from paediatric diabetes centres as showing type 2 now making up 45 per cent of new diabetes cases, particularly in the poorer parts of the USA. These figures can be repeated for the UK, where diabetes in general is on the increase.

RESEARCH SUMMARY

As in many countries worldwide, diabetes is increasing in England. Since 1991, the prevalence of diagnosed diabetes has more than doubled in men and increased by 80 per cent in women. It is estimated there will be about three million people with diagnosed diabetes in the UK by the year 2010 (Department of Health, 2005a).

Critser lays the blame for this increase in diabetes mainly at the doors of fast-food chains and government. As fast food has become cheaper, eating out no longer becomes a treat but more the norm. The servings of giant portions are replete with fat, sugar and salt, leading to a huge increase in calorie intake. The US government has not restricted the operations of the fast-food companies, but at the same time has cut back on money available to schools for PE and other organised exercise activities.

ACTIVITY 8.2

When you are on placement, look at how the service in the agency in which you are placed reflects the concerns of:

- *efficiency;*
- *calculability;*
- *predictability;*
- *control through the substitution of non-human for human technology.*

COMMENT

Applying these concepts across the general provision of social services, you may be able to draw interesting parallels with developments in social work. James (2004) argues that the

Continued

processes below have become increasingly important in the organisation of local authority social services departments.

- *Efficiency. The focus on best value requires local authorities to develop and improve services on a continuous basis, informed by the principles of efficiency, effectiveness and economy. However, this has led to an increased concern with efficiency, which predominates in the guidance literature on best value (Boyne, 1999).*

- *Calculability. The Professional Capabilities Framework (College of Social Work, 2014) is used to assess the competence of social work students so that the actions of the students are broken down into discrete areas for assessment. Evidence-based practice is being introduced, which then assesses and calculates the effectiveness of practice based upon outcome rather than process.*

- *Predictability. There is a drive for standardisation through, for example, National Standards for Adoption (Department of Education, 2011) and national assessment frameworks such as Quality Protects in children's services.*

- *Control through the substitution of non-human for human technology. One-stop centres have been developed on the internet, where service users can tap into their local authority website to access different claim forms and information.*

James (2004) suggests that the McDonaldisation of social work will lead to a lack of creativity and innovation, as services and access to them become standardised. From an ethical standpoint, social workers who are required to follow sets of mechanistic procedures will find that their role in engaging in the moral and practical concerns of service users becomes neutered. If values are to remain central to social work practice, then reducing social work to a set of discrete and unrelated actions becomes formulaic and therefore insensitive to the contexts and moral uncertainties of practice.

McDonaldisation represents a powerful critique of modern society but its manifestation is also representative of how neo-liberal capitalism can dominate the moral and ethical debate, as we shall see below when applying this concept to social work. However, this antibureaucratic discourse has been contested by Du Gay (2000), who argues that bureaucracies can embody ethical practices. Du Gay suggests that bureaucracies have their own ethical practices, and should be judged by these standards and not by a generalised ethical perspective which has little relevance to the accomplishments of bureaucracies. In a democratic society, bureaucracies should involve mediation and compromise between conflicting interests. Thus the bureaucrat embodies or should embody ethically an impartial spirit which is crucial for running publicly funded state bureaucracies. For social workers, this means that they ethically embody this form of impartiality and should ensure that services for which they are responsible operate with equity. This requires making tough and difficult decisions between different groups with equal claims to resources. It also requires social workers to act with equity where some groups have been excluded from services, and to work in a positive way to restore equity in an antidiscriminatory framework.

[W]hile we may sometimes experience a sense of personal frustration in our dealings with state bureaux, we might learn to see such frustration as largely the inevitable by-product of the achievement of other objectives that we also value highly: such as the desire to ensure fairness, justice and equality in the treatment of citizens.

(Du Gay, 2000, p2)

Bureaucracy is, therefore, an essential element in the organisation of large-scale public services such as those delivering social work services. What is more problematic is the use of management procedures, which are seen as the solution to the current challenges facing social work. The claim that managerialism in social work leads to greater economy, effectiveness and efficiency has to be evaluated by research.

RESEARCH SUMMARY

McDonald et al. (2008) researched the effectiveness of social workers in applying relevant knowledge to practice and found it has become compromised. They interviewed 20 experienced field workers, each of whom was asked to choose and describe a complex case from their recent practice which had caused them difficulty. They argue that many practitioners display stress when discussing their cases, often using the language of battle and conflict. They found barriers to the retention and use of professional knowledge at three levels:

1. *a structural level, where a rigid hierarchical system did not encourage the use of practitioner knowledge;*

2. *a management level, where practitioners experienced supervision concentrating on workload management rather than professional issues;*

3. *a practitioner level, where staff struggled with gaps in their knowledge and used defensive or procedural practice rather than working proactively and creatively.*

They conclude that, instead of relying upon their knowledge, practitioners were fearful of blame for their actions and had become dependent on a raft of procedures and routines. In effect, they conclude that staff have become institutionally captured by the dominant bureaucratic/rationing regime (adapted from Hudson, 2009).

Research carried out on behalf of the Economic Social Research Council and since disseminated in a number of journals highlights serious concerns with the new managerial systems in child care (Peckover et al., 2008, 2009; Broadhurst et al., 2010a). As White et al. (2009) argue, procedures for entering information into the Common Assessment Framework require social workers to spend more of their time recording their work, with upwards of 80 per cent of social workers' time spent in front of a computer screen entering data rather than in face-to-face contact with families. This shifts the balance of power away from working with families. As White et al. (2009) argue, the use of such managerial procedures produces 'objective assessments' which provide incomplete assessments of need and risk because they can marginalise the service user's own accounts of events. In addition they potentially frustrate social

157

workers who input information, as White's research shows, where social workers' accounts do not always fit the requirements of the assessment form.

RESEARCH SUMMARY

Sullivan (2009) collected data through semistructured indepth interviews with 40 field work staff in two contrasting locations in England. Social workers' ideological position was identified, i.e. collectivist or committed to self-determination, to identify how these ideologies justified and influenced their work with service users.

Findings

Practitioners' principal justifications for their actions originated from a conviction that finite resources had to be allocated equitably – eligibility criteria were seen as the means of ensuring objective assessments, and professional practitioners served as the neutral means of implementation. This attitude was found to be only slightly more apparent among those who had not obtained a full professional qualification.

Sullivan argues that this demonstrates how readily a new form of 'practice wisdom' can become established as part of the worker's repertoire of understandings. This is then introduced to users during initial short assessment visits and can effectively block clients from introducing their own views. In addition, Sullivan found that preferential treatment was accorded to those older clients who showed gratitude (adapted from Hudson, 2009).

The ubiquity of managerial social work has the effect of transforming how social workers practise, think and feel about the work they do. The research material presented above shows how these routinised systems can get 'under the skin' of social workers to such an extent that, despite even long-held beliefs of self-determination and solidarity with service users, it has the consequence of producing defensive and oppressive social work. In order to identify those procedures which enhance social justice, social workers will need to be both individually reflexive in understanding their own practice but also work with colleagues, service users and professional and trade union organisations to challenge the introduction of such managerial systems which are inimical to anti-oppressive practice.

Accountability

For social workers, it is important that their actions are open to public and professional scrutiny, and therefore they are required to keep scrupulous records to ensure that the information upon which accountability depends is made available and accessible to those who wish to ensure that social workers' actions have been undertaken with fairness (Figure 8.1). Payne (2000) argues that professional social workers working within a bureaucracy do have to be accountable, and as such have to explain their actions and justify them, usually on records and files kept by the organisation.

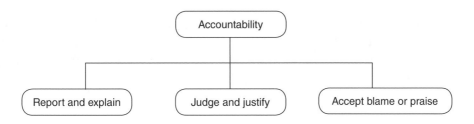

Figure 8.1   Duties of accountability

- Report and explain – involves accounting for one's actions by telling someone what has happened, for example in supervision or writing a report for a case conference. We must also not merely account for but also show why we acted in the way that we did, so explaining our actions.

- Judge and justify – social workers need to judge a situation and make a decision based upon the evidence they have gathered. This is mostly found in social work assessments. Once we have presented the evidence and made our decision, we need to be able to justify that our decision was the right one.

- Accept blame or praise – as a consequence, social workers have a duty to accept blame if they have done something wrong, which may lead to their dismissal. They also have a duty to accept praise, which may lead to promotion if we choose it or extra pay.

In considering the importance of accountability, Banks (2013) argues that there is a tension between the personal engagement with service users by social workers and their wider professional accountability. For Banks, the expectations placed upon social workers, especially aspects of government and employer regulation, can have a negative impact. Yet governments and employers have duties to the wider public to ensure that social workers do not exploit service users or show undue favouritism and that they maintain agreed standards of work. For social workers Banks espouses a virtue-based approach and observes that:

> *Negotiating the balance between personal engagement and professional accountability is one of the main tasks of professional ethics, conceived of as the exercise of professional wisdom in relation to matters of human well-being or flourishing.*

> (Banks, 2013, p601)

CASE STUDY 8.2

This case study concerns Sheila Carpenter, aged 85, who is being assessed for domiciliary care. She qualifies for the full cost of any care provided for her as she is below

Continued

the financial ceiling which would involve her funding some or all of her own care. Your employing local authority announces that in future they will limit directly funded care to those with 'seriously critical personal care needs'; this is higher than the existing Fair Access to Care Services (FACS) critical threshold. You assess that Sheila would have qualified under the previous criteria. You also realise that, if no help is forthcoming for Sheila, she will be at risk if she stays at home. You talk to a colleague, who suggests to you informally that you use your creative abilities to realign Sheila's assessment with the increased level of criteria.

REFLECTION POINT

How do you respond, bearing in mind Banks's argument above?

Thurrock Council consulted on plans to split its substantial threshold into higher and lower levels, and only fund services for those with critical and higher substantial needs. These developments have led some commentators to proclaim the current eligibility banding system to be outdated.

'It's dead,' says Ruth Cartwright, the British Association of Social Workers' joint manager for England. 'When it first came in it was all about supporting people and helping people to be independent and then of course it got turned into a rationing tool.'

'Thurrock's proposals are an inevitable consequence of an under-funded system,' says Richard Humphries, senior fellow for social care at the King's Fund think-tank.

Both Cartwright and Humphries, a former social services director, say FACS puts social workers increasingly in the position of ticking boxes rather than assessing needs and making professional decisions.

(Pitt, 2010)

COMMENT

As the social worker involved, you have been placed in an impossible situation. On the one hand, you can see through the assessment you have made that Sheila will be in danger of moving into residential care if she cannot be supported at home. On the other hand, your local authority has tried to ration its care services according to its budget, which has decreased from last year. This means that fewer service users will be able to access care services and those who can will be significantly requiring intensive support. You will have to decide whether your duty lies with your immediate service user or the

Continued

local authority. If you decide to be creative with your assessment, do you deprive some-one else with greater need from accessing a limited service? Interestingly, you may also need to think about the responsibility of the local authority in denying groups of persons like Sheila with high support needs who would have received a service previously.

There is ample evidence from research which suggests that social workers and their managers often decide to use their discretion in a creative way when they assess that a service user may be severely disadvantaged by following a particular procedure (Ellis, 2003; White et al., 2009; Evans, 2013). This does not necessarily make it ethically appropriate, for example, from a Kantian perspective, as social workers are actually engaged in falsifying their assessment in order to gain an advantage for a particular service user. Yet on an individual basis the consequence of not falsifying this assessment may result in significant harm for the particular service user you are working with. At an individual level social workers will need to reconcile whatever they do with their professional ethics. At a social level social workers may therefore need to engage in the wider political sphere as citizens and advocates for service users to increase current levels of public spending in terms of social care.

Whistle blowing

One of the key developments over the past few years highlighting the negative aspects of public organisations has been the issue of 'whistle blowing'. This has become important, for example, since the events outlined in the North Wales Tribunal (Waterhouse, 2000).

The issue of 'whistle blowing' deals directly with the moral character of social workers. It requires of them, as we shall see below, courage, motivation and commitment to seek justice when, for example, their employing organisation or their superiors act in a dangerous or unjust fashion.

Whistle blowing: a definition

The disclosure by an employee, in a government agency or private enterprise, to the public or to those in authority, of mismanagement, corruption, illegality, or some other wrongdoing.

(http://legal-dictionary.thefreedictionary.com/whistleblowing)

To highlight this an example will be taken from outside social work.

Edward Snowden is a computer professional. He worked for the Central Intelligence Agency (CIA) and later worked for the private intelligence contractor Dell, inside a National Security Agency (NSA) outpost in Japan. He came to international attention after disclosing to several media outlets thousands of classified documents that he

Continued

> *Continued*
>
> acquired while working for Dell. He is now a fugitive living in Russia as the U.S.A. Department of Justice charged Snowden with two counts of violating the Espionage Act and theft of government property. Snowden has been variously called a hero, a whistleblower, a dissident and a traitor. Snowden's reason for leaking documents was to make the public aware of what is done in their name by the security services to 'protect' them.

At the time of writing, Edward Snowden is still living somewhere in Russia.

The provisions introduced by the Public Interest Disclosure Act 1998 protect most workers from being subjected to a detriment by their employer. Detriment may take a number of forms, such as denial of promotion, facilities or training opportunities which the employer would otherwise have offered. Employees who are protected by the provisions may make a claim for unfair dismissal if they are dismissed for making a protected disclosure.

Qualifying disclosures

Certain kinds of disclosure qualify for protection ('qualifying disclosures'). Qualifying disclosures are disclosures of information which the worker reasonably believes tend to show one or more of the following matters is happening now, took place in the past or is likely to happen in the future:

- a criminal offence;
- the breach of a legal obligation;
- a miscarriage of justice;
- a danger to the health or safety of any individual;
- damage to the environment;
- deliberate covering up of information tending to show any of the above five matters.

It should be emphasised that, in making a disclosure, the worker must have reasonable belief that the information disclosed tends to show one or more of the offences or breaches listed above ('a relevant failure'). The belief need not be correct – it might be discovered subsequently that the worker was in fact wrong – but the worker must show that he or she held the belief and that it was a reasonable belief in the circumstances at the time of disclosure.

Making a qualifying disclosure to the employer or via internal procedures

A qualifying disclosure will be a protected disclosure where it is made:

- to the worker's employer, either directly to the employer or by procedures authorised by the employer for that purpose;

- to another person whom the worker reasonably believes to be solely or mainly responsible for the relevant failure.

The only additional requirement on the worker is that he or she should act in good faith. No other requirement is necessary to qualify for protection. Disclosure to the employer will, in most cases, ensure that concerns are dealt with quickly and by the person who is best placed to resolve the problem (see guide from UNISON: **Unison.org.uk/healthcare/dutyofcare/faq/whistleblowing/asp**).

CASE STUDY 8.3

Alison Taylor, a residential care worker in a children's home in North Wales, became concerned in 1989 about the abusive and aggressive behaviour of her manager at the time, Nefyn Dodd, who later had overall responsibility for all the residential child care services in Gwynedd, North Wales. Taylor's allegations were not proved at the time and she was dismissed from her job. She continued to make her claims, and told of other abuses across children's homes in North Wales. When a former child care worker, Stephen Norris, was convicted of the sexual abuse of boys at a community home in Wrexham, Bryn Esten, it was found that Dodd had also worked there. Taylor, with two local politicians and the newly appointed director of social services in Clwyd, joined together and unearthed previous allegations of child abuse in homes across North Wales, which had not been investigated properly. After much pressure from Taylor and her colleagues, a tribunal (Waterhouse, 2000) was eventually set up to look into the allegations, leading to a final report in 2000.

ACTIVITY 8.3

Look at the guidance presented by UNISON on whistle blowing and the Public Interest Disclosure Act 1998 – remember that Alison Taylor's case predates this Act.

Do Alison Taylor's actions make a qualified disclosure?

If Alison Taylor believed this was happening but events prove her wrong, is she still covered by the Act?

What ethical issues in relation to both the employer's code of practice and the code of practice for social care workers are present here?

COMMENT

Under the Public Interest Disclosure Act 1998, Alison Taylor's claims make a qualified disclosure: it involves a criminal offence and a threat to health. As a result of her dismissal,

Continued

there is at least the suspicion that someone was covering up the issue and that removing Alison Taylor might solve the problem.

As the legislation makes clear, as long as Alison Taylor was acting in good faith and felt she had genuinely good grounds for her complaint then she would still be covered by the Act.

What is important is that workers are supported if they are forced to 'whistle blow'. This requires that the process be made easier for workers, and that supportive institutions such as employers, professional bodies and trade unions all provide the assistance needed. To blow the whistle can have a number of consequences for the worker, who can be faced with many challenges which need to be recognised. Alison Taylor (1998) has spoken powerfully about the obstacles she found in addressing her complaint to those in authority:

Often you are blowing the whistle on powerful figures within a local authority who are able if they so choose to mobilise their power to discredit you. Fellow practitioners, through a sense of loyalty to their colleagues, may see you as a troublemaker. Often, the service users on whose behalf action is taken are not listened to and seen as less credible because of their stigmatised status as service users.

(Taylor, 1998, p72)

This requires then a degree of courage and bravery on the part of the whistle blower, which relates to our discussion of virtue ethics (see Chapter 3). For Alison Taylor the costs of her actions were profound.

I made myself unacceptable to employers and colleagues, some of whom shared my disquiet to the extent that they had taken their own concerns to management. However, I was the only one to break out of the institutional edifice, to commit 'professional suicide', while others apparently relegated individual and collective ethics and sidestepped the mess I was creating on behalf of children who were generally regarded as intrinsically worthless.

(Taylor, 1998, pp58–59)

The evidence of the potential costs to whistle blowers has been put into further sharp relief by the Francis Report (2013) into deaths at Stafford Hospital. The report took evidence from Helen Donnelly who, as a nurse, witnessed the unethical practices first-hand and was finally compelled by her own conscience to blow the whistle alongside carers of patients who had died. Here is an extract from the report highlighting the issues from Donnelly's perspective:

23.18 When she did summon up the courage to raise the serious concerns she had, initially the response was positive. However, in the end, the two nursing sisters in the A&E department, against whom she complained, were returned to the department and were publicly described by the Director of Operations, who apparently remained in ignorance of the incomplete investigation and disciplinary process undertaken, as the 'A team'. She was not offered adequate support at that time. She had to endure harassment from colleagues and eventually left for other employment. Clearly, such treatment was likely to deter others from following her example, and she was aware of colleagues on whom her experience had this effect:

> *physical threats were made in terms of people saying that I needed to – again, watch myself while I was walking to my car at the end of a shift. People saying that they know where I live, and basically threats to sort of my physical safety were made, to the point where I had to at the end of a shift . . . at night would have to have either my mum or my dad or my husband come and collect me from work because I was too afraid to walk to my car in the dark on my own.*

(Francis, 2013, p1504)

In material and emotional terms whistle blowing has a cost – the danger of losing your job and income, and the pressure placed on those close to you, i.e. family and friends. However, as recent cases show, such as the Winterbourne scandal (Department of Health, 2012b), where learning-disabled people were routinely abused by staff, the consequences for staff who knew of the issue and did not blow the whistle can be profound. Brian Clarke, a social worker who managed the local Safeguarding Team covering Winterbourne View, was struck off the HCPC register for failing to act on repeated alerts about the treatment of service users at the hospital. As a result of the hearing, the British Association of Social Workers (BASW) responded by cautioning social workers on their duty to blow the whistle on service user abuse or neglect, or to notify their union or professional association.

CHAPTER SUMMARY

This chapter has identified the importance of social workers understanding the organisations that employ them. Organisational policies and procedures are important in defining the boundaries within which social workers practise. Where policies operate in ways which limit service users' fair access to services, this chapter has argued for the ethical necessity for social workers to challenge such injustice. Whistle blowing represents one important response if the social worker's organisation operates in an unethical manner, or if powerful individuals within the hierarchy act illegally. Whistle blowing presents an ethical test to social workers in highlighting dangerous or illegal practices which they believe have been covered up. Because of the powerful consequences that can develop, whistle blowing must not be undertaken lightly or with naivety. Likewise, there are many supportive organisations such as BASW and UNISON who can provide important support and protection to individual workers.

The motivation to become a social worker cannot be divorced from the ethical reasons which inform that motivation. Vague feelings of wanting to help people will not suffice within the challenging environments in which social workers now find themselves. Social workers need to practise a sustained commitment to social justice underpinned by a dedicated application of personal and professional integrity and compassion.

FURTHER READING

Harris, J and White, V (2009) *Modernising social work.* Bristol: Policy Press.

This book discusses the impact of the modernising agenda upon social work services. It focuses upon the interrelationship of modernisation and managerialism, the impact of modernisation upon service users and the effects upon social workers and managers seeking to practise in an environment which limits their professional discretion.

Jones, C, Ferguson, I, Lavalette, M and Penketh, L (2006) *Social work manifesto.* **www.socialwork future.org.**

Read this manifesto and, if you agree with the arguments, sign up!

Payne, M (2000) *Anti-bureaucratic social work.* Birmingham: Venture Press.

This book provides a sound analysis of the ways in which social workers can recognise their duties as social workers and also work within these duties in a creative and non-bureaucratic way.

Chapter 9
Globalisation: Cultures, values and relativism

Social work no longer operates within easily defined national boundaries as the challenge of global migration requires social work to shift its point of reference beyond the nation state. At a minimum, the social changes brought by globalisation require social workers to work increasingly with different groups of service users from diverse cultural backgrounds. Globalisation can be understood as a process and has a number of dimensions:

- political;

- economic;

- social and cultural.

Political

The political impact of globalisation refers to the way that nation states' ability to control their own foreign and domestic policies has been increasingly compromised by wider economic and political forces of globalisation. As a result, a number of organisations of global governance have developed to institute decision making

167

beyond the nation state including, for example, the European Community and the United Nations. How effective these bodies are remains the subject of debate but they reflect attempts to manage globalisation, albeit within a limited framework of capitalist social relations. These bodies are examples of globalisation from above but more locally developed forums, as Yeates (2001) argues, can create new organisational forms of resistance and new ways to organise, such as the antiglobalisation movement or, in terms of social work issues, in the form of global service user movements and the International Federation of Social Workers (IFSW).

Economic

The economic impact of globalisation refers to the increasing global nature of economic processes, such as the worldwide production and exchange of goods and services. In terms of economic policy, governments belong to a number of organisations that govern economic policy, particularly in developing free trade. One of the key organisations in determining economic policy is the General Agreement on Tariffs in Services, part of the World Trade Organization; the commonly referred to term is GATS. GATS covers all service sectors, from energy and banking to predominantly public services such as prisons, water delivery, health care and education. GATS implies that provisions such as welfare services should be increasingly opened up to privatisation. The commitments governments make under GATS are practically irreversible and are known as services agreements. These agreements were originally promoted by a clique of US corporations; American Express and Citicorp were instrumental in promoting GATS in 1994. This agreement began the process of opening up nation states' public services for exploitation by major health corporations, particularly from the USA. These corporations have been instrumental in the buying up of residential care homes in the south of England, as have major European venture capital investment banks (Scourfield, 2007).

Social and cultural

Information technology is seen as a crucial factor in the development of cultural globalisation. With the capability of information technology to process and store information instantaneously, people can communicate across time zones and national borders without being physically present with one another. As a result, the latest branded goods can be bought from across the globe and consumed; the spread of global brands can have an impact upon local cultures, as in the process of McDonaldisation (Dustin, 2007) (see Chapter 8). The spread of powerful brands and other cultural artefacts potentially homogenises, for example, people's consumption of food, clothing and music. The spread of information across the globe means that the most powerful countries have the means to export their culture on an unprecedented scale. For example, in social work and social work education, the International Association of Schools of Social Work and the IFSW have developed global standards for social work education. In turn this has prompted much debate about the desirability of such standards. Some argue that globalised standards reflect a domination of Western approaches to social work whose knowledge base, skills and values are inappropriate for other cultures that have tried to develop more indigenous approaches relevant to their own cultures (Webb, 2003; Sewpaul and Jones, 2004; Williams and Sewpaul, 2004; Sewpaul, 2007).

Think about the following definition of social work that we have encountered previously:

> *The social work profession promotes social change, problem solving in human relationships and the empowerment and liberation of people to enhance well-being. Utilising theories of human behaviour and social systems, social work intervenes at the points where people interact with their environments. Principles of human rights and social justice are fundamental to social work.*

(International Federation of Social Workers, 2012)

As an example, the definition focuses upon concepts of human rights and social justice as being fundamental to social work. Do you think this definition is appropriate irrespective of the culture or sociopolitical context of countries? In thinking about this, read the following extracts which are highly critical of the IFSW definition.

> *The IFSW promotes the universality of human rights; however, Yip convincingly argues that the 'universal' nature of human rights is undermined by its highly Westernised ideologies of 'individualism, democracy and Christianity' (Yip, 2004: 604). Asian cultural values, including Confucianism, Buddhism, Hinduism and/or Islam, tend to emphasise 'collectivity rather than individuality, and responsibility rather than human rights' (Yip, 2004: 604). Confucian values focus on the 'self' as a 'relational being and not an as independent, abstract entity as in the West' (Lam, 1996). Traditional hierarchies in social and family life form an important consideration in an individual's decision making (Tam, 2003). In promoting human rights as a core value, the IFSW is inadvertently asserting the 'universality of western social work values'.*

(Tsang et al., 2000, p150)

> *Like the concept of human rights, the term social justice reflects Western, individualistic and democratic ideals and therefore may not be easily understood or promoted in some cultures. Hare (2004) notes that the concept of social justice has motivated social workers to engage in social action. Again, some governments or dominant groups may deal out harsh treatment to those who challenge prevailing ideologies and beliefs. China's current government has made a greater commitment to vulnerable groups than its predecessors, yet it remains a conservative country and continues to govern social issues by controlling the media and research agendas, and containing individuals who draw attention to marginalised groups (Howell, 2004). If the emerging tradition of social work in China continues to maintain a close relationship with government, social workers are likely to be restricted to those causes they can champion and how they do so.*

(Hutchings and Taylor, 2007, p387)

Discussion

This is a very complex and highly charged subject for those who argue for a universal approach to social work values. The premise of this book is to argue consistently that social workers, as a basis for ethical practice, should adhere to concepts of human rights and social justice. As we shall see below, in considering different 'cultural practices' there is no one single agreement within cultures as to the validity, or otherwise, of universal human rights and social justice. Likewise, it would be difficult for so-called Western social workers to assume naturally that the principles of social justice and human rights represent consistent practices in Europe. For example, the treatment of asylum seekers has been consistently shown to breach principles of human rights and social justice. It has been argued that countries that expound their different cultural practices from the West often do so for political rather than cultural reasons. For example, Iran and Saudi Arabia have consistently argued against promoting human rights and social justice as a means of containing their own disaffected populations. The subjugation of women's rights, for example, is testament to this (Katiuzhinsky and Okech, 2014).

This is not to argue that we ignore different cultural practices but culture, like social justice and human rights, is a contested subject which requires social workers to uphold universalist principles in a critical way which does not assume the dominance of Western approaches to such issues. Neither should social workers sit back and wash their hands when individuals from whatever culture are treated as less than human beings and, therefore, are denied the opportunity to live as human beings and not the slaves of others.

Rights are universal (deontological)

- Actions are inherently wrong regardless of time, place, culture.

- Human rights are universal moral rights.

- All human beings must be treated justly.

- All human beings are born free and equal in dignity and rights.

Rights are dependent upon cultural context (teleological)

- Actions are wrong in particular circumstances and contexts.

- Rights are dependent upon their application in different cultures.

- Rights are socially constructed and should not be imposed on others.

Katiuzhinsky and Okech (2014) identify the implications for this conflict for social workers and suggest that there are good reasons for promoting human rights. Firstly, independently of any social or cultural context, human beings are worthy in and of themselves. Secondly, merely upholding individual rights whilst ignoring social rights such as access to adequate income or basic health care means that social workers could face a paradoxical situation. In some countries, families are forced to require their children to work in order that the family eats. Thus, rights have a limited use if families and individuals are given the freedom to choose how they live irrespective of the culture they inhabit but starve because their basic needs are not being met. Thirdly, rather than having recourse to compulsion to require individuals to reject cultural practices they view as valuable, social workers should engage in dialogue to develop more appropriate practices (see the case of female genital mutilation (FGM), discussed below). Finally, social workers can act as advocates not only to enhance individual rights and social justice but also to promote the recognition of different cultural practices which do not physically harm individuals within them or promote oppressive attitudes which deny choice and/or social justice to individuals within them.

Having identified the conflict inherent between applying universal moral principles which may conflict with a particular society's cultural practices, let us explore these issues in greater detail. Are social workers, therefore, justified in making decisions which may challenge the different cultural practices of the service users they work with? In referring to cultural practices we are recognising the centrality of culture to the way in which different groups live their lives, understand the world they live in and conduct themselves. Culture refers to the everyday habits, attitudes and beliefs of people that influence their general behaviour and way of life.

The importance of being sensitive to different cultures is a crucial element of anti-oppressive practice, for effective social work needs to counter monocultural practice. White culture in the UK is often reflected in the content of social work services. This means not just those practically oriented services such as domiciliary care or family support, but also the whole process of social work, from assessment through to the evaluation of practice. If social workers assess service users using a 'culturally blind' approach, this will result in poor or inappropriate services being offered or no services being offered at all for those who do not fit into a white cultural norm. It is also important to realise that, within the social work profession, different people will come from different cultures, which is likely to influence how they assess a particular situation. Likewise, with interprofessional practice different professionals will also bring experience of their own cultural background.

CASE STUDY 9.1

Indira Sharma, aged 50, is an experienced community nurse who has worked in the National Health Service for the past 15 years. She moved to the UK in the early 1970s from Uganda from a process of 'Africanisation' by the then government, under military dictator Idi Amin, who expelled Ugandan Asians. Her parents are still alive and she lives with her husband near to her parents so that she can provide as much care for them as possible, given that they now require more help around the home. Alan Griffiths is an experienced social worker nearing retirement who has worked with older people for the past 20 years. Indira and Alan are involved in a joint assessment of Mrs Jones, who is 78 years old and profoundly disabled, both physically and mentally.

Mrs Jones's daughter Iris, her only surviving relative, tries to care for her mother but this is becoming impossible. Iris requests a residential care assessment, although she feels

Continued

particularly guilty about this as she feels she has let her mother down; she just feels so exhausted by having to care for her mother. In addition, Iris recognises that having to care for her mother is affecting her employment as she has to take increasing amounts of time off work to attend to her mother's needs. Her manager has already voiced her concern at the way Iris has had to leave work, sometimes without warning, to deal with a domestic problem her mother is experiencing. The situation is complex as Mrs Jones wishes to remain in her own home, where she has lived for the past 50 years.

Following the assessment, Alan and Indira agree that they should focus upon the needs of Mrs Jones and Iris. However, as they discuss the case further it is clear that Indira feels more sympathetic to Iris' feelings of guilt and of obligation towards her mother. She argues that there should not be a hasty recourse to enabling Mrs Jones to move into residential care. Alan, on the other hand, feels that Mrs Jones's needs should not impose such a moral bind upon Iris and that she should also consider her own needs. He argues that this is what social work services are for – to take the pressure off carers when they face difficulties. Alan and Iris recognise their different value positions yet agree to focus upon trying to keep Mrs Jones in her own home as long as this can be facilitated without placing extra demands upon Iris.

(Adapted from Hugman, 2013)

COMMENT

It would be tempting, as Hugman (2013) suggests, to look at this case from a stereotypical viewpoint of an Asian value system emphasising family responsibility conflicting with a Western view of state responsibility for persons. As the case study shows, this is a complex case, not only for the service users but for the workers involved. It is clear that Iris, in order to maintain her employment, requires some decisive intervention which can enable her to keep her job and avoid the consequences of likely poverty following unemployment. It is increasingly the case that traditional cultural beliefs regarding family responsibility are being eroded across all cultures as the demands on family members to remain in employment increase. It is clear, as Hugman (2013) argues, that across cultures people still feel that involving state services is still the option of last resort. Yet the social and economic pressures to remain in employment and in the UK, for example, the diminution of social security support for unemployed people (Parrott, 2014) mean that the sense of family responsibility is increasingly compromised. Across all cultures the conflict between economic development and social solidarity means that the pace of breakdown of family ties is uneven but is nevertheless a reality. As part of this process it is also important to note the changing status and opportunities for women as a result of economic development, education and other social developments. Thus, in examining the respective response of Indira and Alan we may need to look beyond crude cultural stereotypes. Both professionals agree on what should be done and yet exhibit differences in how they initially assess the values implications for Iris. Yet ultimately they are treading a fine line between recognising

Continued

the needs of both Mrs Jones and Iris in order to effect an ethically sensitive outcome. The essential element is that both Indira and Alan can engage in a dialogue which can account for their respective positions and also enable an effective practical solution to the case.

Parekh (2000) argues that there are four principles which are generally employed to evaluate different cultural practices.

1. Human rights principle. An appeal to universal human rights (see Chapter 1) has been one approach by which to make evaluations of other cultural practices.

2. Core values. Every society has acquired over time a character or identity embodied in its core values. These core values form the basis of its way of life and therefore it is both right and proper to suppress practices which offend core values.

3. No harm principle. Given that moral values are cemented into the foundations of society, offending cultural practices should only be disallowed if they cause harm to others.

4. Dialogue principle. Since there are no universally valid moral principles, the concept of core values by which to judge others is problematic. Since harm can be equally defined as being differently evaluated, then what is required is to engage in an open dialogue. This requires an open-minded and serious conversation which seeks as its outcome a consensus.

Parekh favours the last approach, as he argues that core values in any society should not be sacrosanct but should be negotiable. Dialogue would entail a tradeoff between groups where this kind of interaction would help us decide on a generally acceptable resolution to cultural disputes. He calls this intercultural dialogue. This is a useful idea for social workers to adopt as it entails responding to cultural difference through cultural dialogue with service users they work with. It shares an approach associated with Habermas (1984), who contends that it is the act of participating in open and democratic communication with others that can achieve an agreeable resolution of the acceptability of a particular cultural practice. However, there may be occasions when dialogue is unsuccessful. Social workers may then have to assess the relevance of a cultural practice from the point of view of the no harm principle. This may be the case where statutory responsibilities placed on social workers may not allow for an open-ended dialogue, for example where a person may be put in danger through a particular cultural practice.

The 'no harm' principle may also be tied in with a human rights perspective where basic human rights, if they are violated, constitute harm. However, human rights legislation does not seek to impose specific moral standards but, rather, seeks to encapsulate general or universal principles which can be applied cross-culturally. Thus the problem is not easily resolved. For example, when the Human Rights Act 2000 refers to the right to family life, it provides no guidance as to what family life constitutes since there are different forms of family life across different cultures. It leaves us to explore the specific case and then make a judgement. To explore these issues further, consider Activity 9.1.

ACTIVITY 9.1

You are working with a Somali family. The father, Mr Abdullahi 'Issa Mohamud, has been concerned about his daughter Mariam not coming home at night and being disrespectful to him and his wife. He is concerned she is mixing with a local group of Somali youngsters who have been involved in street violence. Sometimes, in his frustration with Mariam, he has locked her in her room and kept her a virtual prisoner, particularly at weekends, when he fears Mariam may go out and mix with the street gang. There are six children in the family, of which the eldest is Mariam. She is 14 years old.

Mariam confides in you that she is about to go on holiday, returning to her parents' village for 2 weeks. She suspects that she will be required to undergo female circumcision, as is the custom in her culture; she suspects this because her father is saying that when she returns she will be a woman and will no longer need to go out with her friends. She asks for your advice as she wants to respect her father but is fearful of the procedure involved in this ritual.

Some information

Female circumcision is a practice common in equatorial Africa that is unfamiliar to many Westerners. Included under the term 'female circumcision' are several different procedures in which varying amounts of genital tissue are removed. This ranges from the removal of the clitoral hood, leaving the rest of the genitalia intact (known as 'sunna' circumcision), to removal of the clitoris and anterior labia minora, to removal of the clitoris, the entire labia minora, part of the labia majora and suturing of the labia majora, leaving a posterior opening for the passage of urine and menstrual flow. This latter procedure is known as infibulation, and is the most common form of female circumcision in Somalia. In Somalia, the procedure is usually performed by female family members but is also available in some hospitals. It is usually performed between birth and five years of age.

In the last 20 years, much attention has been focused on the medical and psychosocial complications of female circumcision. However, most Somali women view circumcision as normal, expected and desirable. It has become the centre of a debate about potentially harmful traditional cultural practices and, as such, has become a complex and emotionally charged subject.

(Reproduced from **www.ethnomed.org/culture/somali/somali-culture-profile***)*

Immediate complications

This depends upon the kind of circumcision carried out, with the sunna method being relatively less physically harmful and akin to a male circumcision. Complications can include severe pain, shock, haemorrhage, tetanus or sepsis, urine retention, ulceration of the genital region and injury to adjacent tissue, wound infection, urinary infection, fever and septicaemia. Haemorrhage and infection can be of such magnitude as to cause death.

Continued

Long-term consequences

These include anaemia, the formation of cysts and abscesses, keloid scar formation, damage to the urethra resulting in urinary incontinence, dyspareunia (painful sexual inter-course) and sexual dysfunction, and hypersensitivity of the genital area. Infibulation can cause severe scar formation, difficulty in urinating, menstrual disorders, recurrent bladder and urinary tract infection, fistulae, prolonged and obstructed labour (sometimes result-ing in fetal death and vesicovaginal fistulae and/or vesicorectal fistulae) and infertility (as a consequence of earlier infections). Cutting of the scar tissue is sometimes necessary to facilitate sexual intercourse and/or childbirth. Almost complete vaginal obstruction may occur, resulting in accumulation of menstrual flow in the vagina and uterus. During child-birth the risk of haemorrhage and infection is greatly increased.

(www.unfpa.org/gender/practices2.htm#15)

In the light of the information presented above, how would you approach advising Mariam?

COMMENT

This case study is problematic and very difficult as it presents you with a clear dilemma in relation to Somalian cultural practices. If you advise Mariam to comply with the wishes of her family, then what are the consequences for her?

Arguments in favour

On the positive side, she will be seen as undergoing a vital rite of passage in Somali culture which will enhance her status as a woman. If she values the idea of marriage to another Somali then, as the information suggests, she will find it easier to marry as she will not be seen as 'unclean'. She will be honouring her father's wishes, which may improve the treat-ment she receives from him.

Against this view

If she is to undergo this ritual, Mariam will certainly be physically and maybe psychologically damaged, whether she agrees to the practice or not. As a social worker, does this constitute a child protection problem in which you have a duty to protect Mariam?

In deciding which course of action may be the best, it is important to take into account choice:

- *Does Mariam have a real choice here? What options are available to her? Although options are present, does this constitute a real choice if she is being forced into having the procedure?*

- *Does your decision require you to give control of the situation back to Mariam?*

Continued

COMMENT *continued*

- *What criteria should you employ in deciding to overrule the wishes of Mariam's father and the cultural practices which are included in this, if Mariam does not wish to proceed (Figure 9.1)?*

```
                        ┌──────────────────┐
                        │  What criteria?  │
                        └──────────────────┘
                         ╱                ╲
            ┌────────────────────┐   ┌────────────────────┐
            │  Danger to others  │   │  Danger to oneself │
            └────────────────────┘   └────────────────────┘
```

Figure 9.1   Criteria for intervention

In this case, Mariam's situation does not directly involve danger to others. In relation to the second criterion then we can see that this action may very well involve some considerable harm. If Mariam does not want to go ahead with this procedure then we may have a duty to act. However, what if Mariam decides in the end that she will go ahead with the procedure? Do we have a right then to intervene against her wishes, given that she is still a minor? We have to take into account the level of understanding of a 14-year-old. All things being equal, we would have to conclude that she is capable of making her own decisions and that she is aware of – or we would ensure she is aware of – the likely physical harms that could develop. Even with that proviso in mind, do we still have a duty to go against her wishes? After all, legally she is still a child and this procedure constitutes harm. Given the knowledge we have of this procedure in Somalia, this practice is usually done when a girl is first born and most certainly done before the child is five years old, so the possible trauma and damage that could be caused to a young person are likely to be considerable. What does the Children Act 1989 have to say about the duties of a social worker in this situation?

Section 31 requires that social workers should take action if the child experiences 'significant harm' and this must be of a severity that the child experiences or is likely to experience an impediment to health or physical or emotional development.

In this instance, the procedure is a very dangerous one for a 14-year-old girl and this is verified by the information provided above. If we decide to act, then what action should we take? If we remove Mariam from the family home, what would be the likely consequences for her? Inevitably she would be separated from her brothers and sisters and her parents. How could we ensure that she could maintain her own cultural lifestyle? This may be very difficult if her father, as would be likely, disowns her.

She may be seen as a highly unworthy person by the majority of people in her own community. What cultural supports could be put in place for her?

Any decision that we make in this case is, therefore, fraught with ethical dilemmas. In making a decision to intervene against particular cultural practices we must be very clear as to the purpose of this intervention and the likely consequences for Mariam. We would need to ensure that Mariam was able to access as much cultural support as possible in allowing her to make her decision, which in this case is to go against her father's wishes. It is important to realise that cultural practices are not set in stone and that the process of acculturation, the description of how cultures change over time, is a significant concept when considering the importance of specific cultural practices. Many women's groups across the UK, in Africa and indeed in Somalia continue to campaign against this procedure. Indeed, such groups no longer term this procedure 'female circumcision' but rather 'female genital mutilation'. Thus, in considering any foregoing or specific cultural practices we need to understand that cultures change and are open to influences which render the whole nature of culture a living social phenomenon. To assume that specific cultures contain within them any particular views, in this case in favour of female circumcision, would be to deny the very defining characteristics of all cultures which are living, evolving and sometimes changing quite rapidly. As Clarke (2004) argues in relation to UK culture, we cannot reduce this culture to any essential notion of 'Britishness'. National cultures are differentiated, as we have already analysed in relation to social divisions, and undergo continual contestation which renders any culture more dynamic and open to change. We may well be falling into the trap of seeing our own culture as necessarily dynamic and open to change while not recognising similar processes in other cultures.

As social workers engage with service users from different cultures it is important to realise that an intercultural dialogue, as Parekh (2000) called it, holds the promise of further development. As the different parties engage openly with one another the possibility of creating a 'third culture' presents itself. Evanoff (2006) argues that the process of dialogue can create a *third culture*. This refers to cultural patterns inherited, created and shared by two or more members of different cultures who are personally (and professionally) involved in relating their cultural practices to each other (Parrott, 2009).

For student social workers, this requires engagement in a process of 'constructive marginality', a process whereby one's own culture and the cultures of others are subject to creative scrutiny in which a high degree of self-differentiation and integration are achieved. This leads to the potential for student social workers to become 'constructive marginals' who act as 'envoys' between cultures; they have the training and commitment to understand the world views of different cultures but seek the integration of different perspectives which may appear to be in conflict. Social workers may need to think of themselves as influenced but not determined by their own cultural values and in turn recognising this possibility for service users from other cultures. Members of different cultures do not necessarily all agree upon every aspect of their own culture and, therefore, social workers can enable a voice for all members of a cultural community to be heard in the way they feel is appropriate for them without compromising social justice. Social workers may, therefore, seek 'cultural allies', i.e. those members of a service user's culture who do recognise the possible harms and breaches to human rights that some contested cultural practices entail.

Hugman (2008), in recalling his own practice as a social worker in England, is interesting in this regard. He recalls his own white British culture whereby domestic violence against women was deemed a cultural norm for men as a means to assert their 'authority' within the family. However, the campaigning and lobbying of the political process by the feminist movement, trade unions and professional groups working in the area of domestic violence have made significant advances in combating this oppressive culture. In turn, there are many organisations such as the Southall Sisters, or less well-known ones such as the Karma Nirvana Asian Men and Women's Project, who campaign and offer support against domestic violence and forced marriage. Sanghera's (2007) personal testimony is also valuable here in identifying differences in how some women in 'Asian cultures' oppose the practice of arranged and forced marriage and the efforts some women have to go through in order to escape from such arrangements. Ultimately the cloak of culture can be used by those who have power to justify inhuman treatment, often perpetrated by men over women in both Western and Eastern cultures. It is difficult to find much agreement across cultures to condone violence upon a defenceless other and therefore there are many points of commonality through which social workers can seek to develop their practice in dialogue with other cultural communities.

FGM is not uncommon. It is estimated that 74,000 women in the UK have undergone the procedure, and about 7000 girls under 16 are at risk. This estimate is based upon the number of women and girls living in the UK who originate from countries where FGM is traditionally practised.

FGM has been illegal in the UK since the Prohibition of Female Circumcision Act 1985. This legislation has been strengthened by the Female Genital Mutilation Act 2003 which prohibits FGM and in addition makes it illegal to take girls abroad for FGM. Guidance issued to local authorities is useful in this regard:

> *Where a family has been identified as at risk, it may not be appropriate to take steps to remove the girl from an otherwise loving family environment. Experience has shown that often the parents themselves are under pressure to agree to FGM for their daughters from older relatives. It might be helpful, therefore, to talk to the family outside the home environment to encourage them to acknowledge the impact FGM would have on their daughter/s. It might also be necessary to ask the police to get a prohibited steps order, making it clear to the family that they will be breaking the law if they arrange for any of their daughters to have the procedure.*
>
> *In areas where there are large practising communities, social services departments should consider incorporating more detailed guidance on responding to concerns*

about FGM to their existing child protection procedures, in partnership with other local agencies and community groups.

(Department for Education and Skills, 2004)

The sensitivity of such cases and the complexity of intervening can be gauged in that at the time of writing no cases of FGM have been prosecuted in the UK, although the Crown Prosecution Service is looking into a number of cases to see if a prosecution can be made. Torjesen (2013) identifies three possible reasons:

1. Prosecutions for female mutilation are difficult because they could require a girl to implicate her own parents in a crime.

2. There are also cultural taboos, and communities may stay silent or close ranks.

3. It is also hard to obtain reliable evidence if the crime was carried out abroad.

In highlighting the tensions inherent in social work practice between the values of social work and the duties of social workers in respect to the law, the following is informative. What follows is an exchange of emails between Jenny Brooks, a social work team leader, and myself on the publication of the first edition of this book. This correspondence has been edited but the content has been agreed between Jenny and myself.

18 January 2008

Dear Sir/Madam,

I have recently been reading the above book, purchased to support social work students in our workplace. On pages 35–37 there is posed an ethical dilemma regarding female genital mutilation; I cannot find any reference in the text to the fact that this practice is illegal in the UK and according to the 2003 Female Genital Mutilation Act it is an offence for UK nationals, or permanent residents, to aid, abet, or procure the carrying out of FGM in this country or abroad, whether or not the practice is legal in that country. Reference to this act and the duties of Local Safeguarding Boards in relation to the prevention of FGM is made in *Working Together to Safeguard Children* (2006), page 150. To my mind this is an omission that completely changes the nature of the ethical dilemma posed in the book.

I look forward to your response.

Jenny Brooks

23 January 2008

Dear Jenny Brooks

Thank you very much for your considered response to the issue identified in my book *Values and Ethics in Social Work Practice*. Please find as an attachment my response.

Best Wishes

Lester Parrott

Email attachment

The issue you identify was a real problem for me in trying to open up the debate as an issue of values with which readers would engage. My initial thoughts were to include the act and guidance into the material but I thought this would prevent readers engaging with the issue, particularly from the perspective of cultural relativism. What I hoped to do was to enable readers to think about the issue in a way that would challenge the absolute value of culture as against other relevant criteria such as human rights or protection from harm. I guess by presenting the legislation it would or could encourage students to say it's against the law so I don't necessarily have to engage with the issue in a deeper way. It is also interesting to read the Female Genital Mutilation Act 2003 and the accompanying guidance *Working Together* (Department of Education, 2003). [Note: Since this email correspondence was undertaken, new guidance has been published; see HM Government, 2014.]

As the guidance makes clear, this is clearly against the law and in effect constitutes a severe form of abuse. The guidance is less clear about how to proceed, i.e. recourse to a more severe approach to remove the child or seek to deal with the issue within the family and community in a less intrusive fashion. Hopefully, this is where I think the book deals with the issue of 'what should be my response to this issue?' Clearly this will be down to the exercise of the social worker's judgement, working from a clear value base and a considered assessment of the issue. How a social worker views this problem from a values perspective will therefore influence how he or she perceives the issue and how to proceed.

I would accept that making the students aware of the law in this regard is important but not as important as getting the students to think about the issues first of all. If this book gets to a second edition (hopefully) I will include some more information with regard to the law and the guidance to respond to your valid concerns.

Best wishes

Lester Parrott

25 January

Dear Lester Parrott

Thank you for your very prompt response. I can see why you would want to engage the reader in consideration of the ethics and values around this issue, but my concern is that social workers, even students, have to consider the whole complexity around any sensitive issue. In a sense we cannot just think about this as an ethical issue, because there is a legal aspect and any social worker will have to take due regard of the law and local safeguarding procedure, whether or not the *Working Together* guidance is vague about what should be done.

Regards,

Jenny Brooks

ACTIVITY **9.2**

Having read the exchange of emails how would you, as a social worker, reconcile the issues presented above?

How far does the existence of the Female Genital Mutilation Act 2003 alter, as Jenny Brooks argues, the nature of the ethical dilemma here?

RESEARCH SUMMARY

A recent report (Options, 2013) sponsored by a number of public bodies outlined both the progress made and the challenges which remain in tackling FGM. Some of the findings I present suggest some progress has been made:

- *Where community-based preventive work is taking place, rejection of FGM has increased.*

- *Working with younger women to empower them to speak out and make decisions has been more effective than trying to change the often deeply entrenched opinions of older people.*

- *The arguments used by funded groups against FGM are maturing and becoming more sophisticated. This has resulted from funded projects sparking necessary discussions and debate about FGM, in a culturally sensitive and grounded way. Projects recognise the risk of legal messages sounding punitive and threatening, and have worked to develop understanding of FGM as a form of child abuse.*

- *Projects have brought together male and female religious leaders and scholars of different faiths to confront misconceptions about links between religion and FGM. There are now clear examples of religious leaders dismissing the perceived religious basis for certain forms of FGM.*

- *There is mounting support within affected communities for a more interventionist stance to be taken by the UK authorities against FGM.*

- *Community groups have a valuable role in comprehensive responses to FGM. They have supported women's access to specialist care, acted as intermediaries with social care professionals in cases of girls at risk, disseminated information in schools and provided training to health and other professionals.*

However the report also identifies that many challenges remain. Again, I present some of those discussed in the report:

- *There is no effective national policy on the role of local authorities in tackling FGM. Without this, funded groups find it difficult to advocate for a comprehensive response to FGM, if the issue is not already on their local authority's agenda.*

- *Some people within affected communities continue to support FGM, which they link to their cultural heritage and/or control of female sexuality. Support for less severe forms of FGM is still also reported.*

Continued

RESEARCH SUMMARY *continued*

- *'Speaking out' within communities still carries risks, and requires sensitivity, safeguards and a long-term approach.*

- *Although there are examples of promising practice (e.g. Bristol), local statutory responses to FGM prevention are largely patchy and inadequate, and do not reflect local levels of need. Although most project areas had policies in place, they were not always translated into concrete actions, e.g. training social care/health professionals in issues relating to FGM.*

- *Government cutbacks, decentralisation and reorganisation have all impacted on projects' strategic relationships. Although the new commissioning landscape may provide opportunities for projects, there is likely to be increased competition for scarce resources in future, which may make relationship building harder still.*

- *Although there have been some successes, most projects faced resistance when trying to work in schools. Many schools said that they did not want to address the issue for fear of stigmatising certain groups.*

- *Some frontline staff, including teaching, social work and health professionals, lack the confidence and/or skills to respond adequately, or to act proactively, in relation to FGM. Some are afraid to raise the issue for fear of appearing discriminatory.*

CHAPTER SUMMARY

This chapter has explored the concept of globalisation and the challenges it presents social workers to practise in an ethically appropriate way. As international borders become more porous, social workers will be required to think about how they respond to different peoples with different cultures seeking a better life for themselves in what they consider to be the affluent West. Social workers' practice must therefore respond to the needs of different peoples not through a culturally relativist framework but seek to enable those groups within different communities to achieve a life which they experience as socially just and that respects their human rights.

FURTHER READING

Dalrymple, J and Burke, B (2006) *Anti-oppressive practice: Social care and the law*, 2nd edn. Maidenhead: Open University Press.

This book looks at the issue of anti-oppressive practice and engages in an interesting critique of Thompson's approach.

Laird, S (2008) *Anti-oppressive social work: A guide for developing cultural competence.* London: Sage.

This book focuses upon the importance of understanding cultural diversity within an anti-oppressive framework. It includes a wealth of information on different communities in the UK and argues for cultural competence as an essential feature in social work to achieve social justice for all service users in the UK.

Parekh, B (2000) *Rethinking multiculturalism: Cultural diversity and political theory.* London: Macmillan.

A challenging read and one that argues for cultural dialogue around issues of multiculturalism. Chapter 10 is valuable in discussing cultural relativism.

Thompson, N (2012) *Anti-discriminatory practice: Equality, diversity and social justice.* Basingstoke: Palgrave.

This book is still the classic text on antidiscriminatory practice and is well written and highly accessible.

Appendix 1

Professional Capabilities Framework

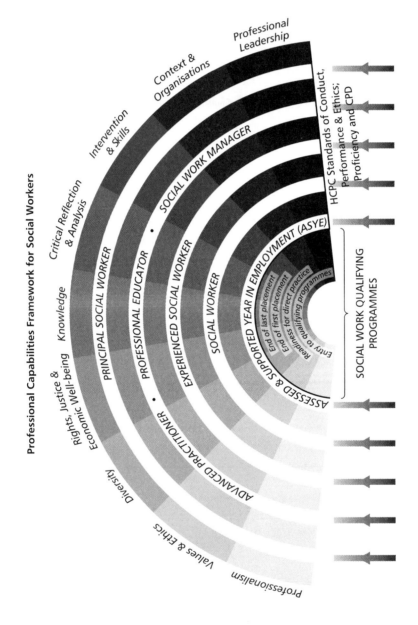

Professional Capabilities Framework diagram reproduced with permission of The College of Social Work.

References

Abbott, A (1998) *The system of professionals: An essay on the division of expert labor.* Chicago, IL: University of Chicago Press.

Adams, R (2003) *Social work and empowerment.* Basingstoke: Palgrave.

Adetunji, J (2012) Should you set up as an independent social worker? *The Guardian,* 19 January.

Age UK (2014) *Care in crisis.* **http://www.ageuk.org.uk/Documents/EN-GB/Campaigns/CIC/PDF**

Akhtar, F (2013) *Mastering social work values and ethics.* London: Jessica Kingsley.

Alcock, P (2012) Pete Alcock replies to Sullivan, 'A Big Society needs an active state'. Big Society – contradiction or con trick? *Policy & Politics,* 40(1), 149–50.

Aldgate, J and Statham, D (2001) *The Children Act now.* London: The Stationery Office, Department of Health.

Allan, K (2001) *Communication and consultation: Exploring ways for staff to involve people with dementia in developing services.* Bristol: Policy Press and the Joseph Rowntree Foundation.

Alter, T (2012) The growth of institutional deception in the treatment of Alzheimer's disease: The case study of Sadie Cohen. *Journal of Social Work Practice: Psychotherapeutic Approaches in Health, Welfare and the Community,* 26(1), 93–107.

Asquith, S, Clark, S and Waterhouse, L (2005) The role of the social worker in the 21st century: A literature review. *Insight 25.* Edinburgh: Scottish Executive Education Department.

Ayre, P (2001) Child protection and the media: Lessons from the last three decades. *British Journal of Social Work,* 31(6), 887–901.

Bach, S and Stroleny, A (2013) Public service employment restructuring in the crisis in the UK and Ireland: Social partnership in retreat. *European Journal of Industrial Relations,* 19, 341–57.

Bailey, L (2012) The role of the mental health social worker: Political pawns in the reconfiguration of adult health and social care. *British Journal of Social Work,* 42(6), 1113–31.

Banks, S (2004) *Ethics, accountabilty and the social profession.* London: Palgrave.

Banks, S (2006) *Ethics and values in social work,* 3rd edn. Basingstoke: Palgrave.

Banks, S (2010) Interprofessional ethics: A developing field? Notes from the Ethics & Social Welfare Conference, Sheffield, UK, May 2010. *Ethics and Social Welfare,* 4(3), 280–94.

Banks, S (2013) Negotiating personal engagement and professional accountability: Professional wisdom and ethics work. *European Journal of Social Work,* 16(5), 587–604.

Banks, S and Williams, R (2005) Accounting for ethical difficulties in social welfare work. *British Journal of Social Work,* 35(7), 1005–22.

Barnardo's (2009) *Advocacy.* **www.barnardos.org.uk/what_we_do/our_projects/advocacy**

Bartoli, A (ed.) (2013) *Anti-racism in social work practice.* St Albans: Critical Publishing.

Bateman, N (2000) *Advocacy skills for health and social care professionals.* London: Jessica Kingsley.

Bates, J (2005) Embracing diversity and working in partnership, in Carnwell R and Buchanan, J (eds) *Effective practice in health and social care: A partnership approach.* Maidenhead: Open University.

Bauman, Z (1989) *Modernity and the Holocaust.* Cambridge: Polity.

Bauman, Z (1994) *Alone again: Ethics after certainty.* London: Demos.

Be My Parent (2013) *Be My Parent* newspaper. **www.bemyparent.org.uk/about-us/be-my-parent-newspaper,32,AR.html**

Beck, U (1992) *Risk society: Towards a new modernity.* London: Sage.

Beckett, C and Maynard, A (2005) *Values and ethics in social work: An introduction.* London: Sage.

Benjamin, M and Curtis, J (1992) *Ethics in nursing,* 3rd edn. Oxford: Oxford University Press.

Bieder, H (2011) *White working class views of neighbourhood, cohesion and change.* York: Joseph Rowntree Trust.

Biestek, F P (1974) *The casework relationship.* London: Allen Unwin.

Boyne, G (1999) *Managing local services: From CCT to best value.* Ilford: Frank Cass.

Brayne, H and Carr, H (2005) *Law for social workers,* 9th edn. Oxford: Oxford University Press.

Brearley, C (1982) *Risk and social work.* London: Routledge, Kegan & Paul.

Brewer, M, Browne, J and Jin, W (2012) Universal credit: A preliminary analysis of its impact on incomes and work incentives. *Fiscal Studies,* 33, 39–71.

British Association of Social Workers (2001) *Code of practice for social workers.* Birmingham: BASW.

British Association of Social Workers (2002) *Code of ethics for social work.* Birmingham: BASW.

British Association of Social Workers (2012) *The state of social work survey.* **http://cdn.basw.co.uk/ upload/basw_23651-3.pdf**

Broadhurst, K, Wastell, D, White, S, Hall, C, Peckover, S, Thompson, K, Pithouse, A and Davey, D (2010a) Performing 'initial assessment': Identifying the latent conditions for error at the front-door of local authority children's services. *British Journal of Social Work,* 40(2), 352–70.

Broadhurst, K, Hall, C, Wastell, D, White, S and Pithouse, A (2010b) Risk, instrumentalism and the humane project in social work: Identifying the informal logics of risk management in children's statutory services. *British Journal of Social Work,* 40, 1046–64.

Burns, T, Rugkåsa, J and Molodynski, A (2013) Community treatment orders for patients with psychosis (OCTET): A randomised controlled trial. *Lancet,* 381, 1627–33.

Burton, D (2009) Non-white readings of whiteness. *Consumption Markets and Culture,* 12(4), 349–72.

Butler-Sloss, Baroness E (1988) *Report of the inquiry into child abuse in Cleveland.* London: HMSO.

Butrym, Z (1976) *The nature of social work.* London: Macmillan.

Cameron, D (2009) Big society can fight poverty. Big government just fuels it. *The Guardian,* 10 November.

Camic, C, Gorski, P and Trubek, D (eds) (2005) *Max Weber's economy and society: A critical companion.* Stanford, CA: Stanford University Press.

Care Quality Commission (2011) *The state of social care in England 2009–10.* London: Care Quality Commission.

Carnwell, R and Carson, A (2005) Understanding partnerships and collaboration, in Carnwell, R and Buchanan, J (eds) *Effective practice in health and social care: A partnership approach.* Maidenhead: Open University.

Carpenter, J, Schneider, J, Brandon, T and Wooff, D (2003) Working in multi-disciplinary community health teams: The impact on social workers and health professionals of integrated mental health care. *British Journal of Social Work,* 3, 1081–103.

Chang, J (1991) *Wild swans: Three daughters of China.* London: Flamingo.

Channer, Y and Doel, M (2009) Beyond qualification: Experiences of black social workers on a post-qualifying course. *Social Work Education,* 28(4), 396–412.

Clapton, G, Cree, V and Smith, M (2013) Critical commentary moral panics, claims-making and child protection in the UK. *British Journal of Social Work,* 43, 803–12.

Clark, C (2000) *Social work ethics: Politics, principles and practice.* Palgrave: Basingstoke.

Clark, C (2005) The deprofessionalisation thesis. *Social Work and Society,* 3(2), 182–90.

Clark, C (2006) Moral character in social work. *British Journal of Social Work,* 36(1), 75–89.

Clarke, J (2004) *Changing welfare, changing states: New directions in social policy.* London: Sage.

Cohen, M (2003) *101 ethical dilemmas.* London: Routledge.

College of Social Work (2014) Professional capabilities framework. **http://www.tcsw.org.uk/pcf. aspx**

Collins Free Dictionary (2014) **http://thefreedictionary.com/_/misc/Harpercollinsproducts. aspx?English**

Cribb, J, Hood, A, Joyce, R and Phillips, D (2013) *Living standards, poverty and inequality in the UK: 2013.* London: Institute for Fiscal Studies.

Cribb, J, Disney, R and Sibieta, L (2014) *The public sector workforce: Past, present and future.* London: Institute of Fiscal Studies.

Critser, G (2004) *Fatland: How Americans became the fattest people in the world.* London: Penguin.

Crouch, C (2003) *Commercialisation or citizenship education policy and the future of public services.* Fabian Ideas no. 606. London: Fabian Society.

Culpitt, I (1998) *Social policy and risk.* London: Sage Publications.

Dalrymple, J and Burke, B (1995) *Anti-oppressive practice.* Buckingham: Open University Press.

Davies, H (2009) Ethics and practice in child protection. *Ethics and Social Welfare,* 3(3), 322–8.

Dawkins, C (2010) Beyond wages and working conditions: A conceptualization of labor union social responsibility. *Journal of Business Ethics,* 95, 129–43.

Department of Education (2003) *Working together.* London: The Stationery Office.

Department of Education (2011) Adoption: national minimum standards. **http://www.gov.uk/ government/uploads/system/uploads/attachment_data/file/192674/Adoption-NMS**

Department of Education (2014) *Powers to delegate children's social care functions.* e-consultation. **https://www.gov.uk/government/uploads/system/uploads/attachment_data/file/321863/ Extension_regs_consultation_response200614_for_web.pdf**

Department for Education and Science (2004) *Local Authority Social Services letter* LASSL (2004) 4. **www.dh.gov.uk/prod_consum_dh/groups/dh_digitalassets/@dh/@en/documents/digitalasset/ dh_4074784.pdf**

Department for Education and Skills (2004) *Every child matters: Change for children in social care.* London: DfES.

Department of Health (1995) *Messages from research.* London: HMSO.

Department of Health (1998) *Modernising social services.* London: HMSO.

Department of Health (2001) *Valuing people: A new strategy for learning disability for the 21st century.* London: The Stationery Office.

Department of Health (2005a) *Health survey for England.* London: The Stationery Office.

Department of Health (2005b) *Our health, our care, our say.* London: The Stationery Office.

Department of Health (2007) *Putting people first.* London: The Stationery Office.

Department of Health (2012a) *Caring for our future.* London: The Stationery Office.

Department of Health (2012b) *Transforming care: A national response to Winterbourne View Hospital.* Department of Health review: final report. **https://www.gov.uk/government/uploads/system/ uploads/attachment_data/file/213215/final-report.pdf**

Department of Work and Pensions (2014) Jobseeker's allowance and employment and support allowance sanctions: Decisions made to March 2014. **https://www.gov.uk/government/statistics/ jobseekers-allowance-and-employment-and-support-allowance-sanctions-decisions-made-to- march-2014**

Doel, M and Shardlow, SM (2005) *Modern social work practice: Teaching and learning in practice settings.* Aldershot: Ashgate.

Dominelli, L (2002) *Anti-oppressive social work theory and practice*. London: Palgrave Macmillan.

Douglas, M (1992) *Risk and blame: Essays in cultural theory*. London: Routledge.

Drakeford, M (2006) Ownership, regulation and the public interest: The case of residential care for older people. *Critical Social Policy*, 26(4), 932–44.

Du Gay, P (2000) *In praise of bureaucracy: Weber – organisation – ethics*. London: Sage.

Dustin, D (2007) *The McDonaldisation of social work*. Aldershot: Ashgate.

Ellis, K (2007) Direct payments and social work practice: The significance of 'street-level bureaucracy' in determining eligibility. *British Journal of Social Work*, 37, 405–22.

Ellis, K (2011) 'Street-level bureaucracy' revisited: The changing face of frontline discretion in adult social care in England. *Social Policy and Administration*, 45(3), 221–44.

Evanoff, R (2006) Integration in intercultural ethics. *Journal of Intercultural Relations*, 30(4), 421–37.

Evans, T (2013) Organisational rules and discretion in adult social work. *British Journal of Social Work*, 43(4), 739–58.

Evans, T and Harris, J (2004) Street-level bureaucracy, social work and the (exaggerated) death of discretion. *British Journal of Social Work*, 34, 871–96.

Everitt, A, Hardiker, P, Littlewood, J and Mullender, A (1992) *Applied research for better practice*. London: Macmillian/BASW.

Faulkner, A (2012) *The right to take risks: Views of risk in adult social care*. York: Joseph Rowntree Trust.

Ferguson, H (2010) Walks, home visits and atmospheres: Risk and the everyday practices and mobilities of social work and child protection. *British Journal of Social Work*, 40(4), 1100–17.

First4Adoption (2013) First year impact report. **http://www.first4adoption.org.uk/wp-content/uploads/2014/03/First4Adoption-First-Year-Impact-Report.pdf**

Fook, J (2012) *Social work: A critical approach to practice*, 2nd edn. London: Sage.

Foucault, M (1977) *Discipline and punish: The birth of the prison*. Harmondsworth: Allen Lane.

Francis, R (2013) *Report of the Mid Staffordshire NHS Foundation Trust public inquiry*. London: The Stationery Office.

Franklin, B (ed.) (1999) *Social policy, the media and misrepresentation*. London: Routledge.

Friedson, E (2001) *Professionalism: The third logic*. Cambridge: Polity.

Frisby, D (2013) Life after the state. London: Unbound.

Froggett, L (2002) *Love, hate and welfare: Psychosocial approaches to policy and practice*. Bristol: Policy Press.

Furedi, F (1997) *Culture of fear: Risk taking and the morality of low expectation*. London: Cassell.

Gabel, S and Peters, S (2004) Presage of a paradigm shift? Beyond the social model of disability toward a resistance theory of disability. *Disability and Society*, 19(6), 571–96.

Gewirth, A (1978) *Reason and morality*. Chicago, IL: Chicago University Press.

Giddens, A (1994) *Beyond left and right: The future of radical politics*. Cambridge: Polity.

Giddens, A (2006) *Sociology*, 5th edn. Cambridge: Polity.

Gilligan, C (1982) *In a different voice: Psychological theory and women's development*. Cambridge, MA: Harvard University Press.

Glendinning, C (2003) Breaking down barriers: Integrating health and care services for older people in England. *Health Policy*, 65, 139–54.

Glendinning, J (2013) *Department of Education statistical release: Children looked after in England (including adoption and care leavers) year ending 31 March 2013*. **www.gov.uk/government/uploads/system/uploads/attachment_data/file/244872/SFR36_2013.pdf**

Goldhagan, DJ (1996) *Hitler's willing executioners: Ordinary Germans and the Holocaust.* New York: Knopf.

Gove, M (2013) *Speech to the NSPCC: Getting it right for children in need.* NSPCC headquarters, Department of Education. **www.gov.uk/government/speeches/getting-it-right-for-children-in-need-speech-to-the-nspcc**

Greenslade, R (2008) Why is missing Shannon not getting the same coverage as Madeleine? *The Guardian,* 5 March.

Gupta, A (2004) *Involving families living in poverty in the training of social workers.* London: Royal Holloway, University of London.

Habermas, J (1984) *The theory of communicative action,* vol. 1. Cambridge: Polity.

Hacking, I (1990) *The taming of chance.* Cambridge: Cambridge University Press.

Hair, H (2013) The purpose and duration of supervision, and the training and discipline of supervisors: What social workers say they need to provide effective services. *British Journal of Social Work,* 43, 1562–88.

Hardwick, L (2013) Advocacy versus social work: What the setting-up of an advocacy rights hub reveals about social work's ability to promote social inclusion. *British Journal of Social Work,* advanced access, 4 April 2014.

Hare, I (2004) Defining social work for the 21st century: The International Federation of Social Workers' revised definition of social work. *International Social Work,* 47(3), 407–24.

Harris, J (2003) Let's talk business. *Community Care,* 21 August, 211–13.

Harvey, D (2005) *A brief history of neoliberalism.* Oxford: Oxford University Press.

Hayek, F (1944) *The road to serfdom.* London: Routledge & Kegan Paul.

Health and Care Professions Council (HCPC) (2014) *Standards of conduct, performance and ethics.* **http://www.hcpc-uk.org.uk/assets/documents/10003B6EStandardsofconduct,performanceandethics.pdf**

Heffernan, J (2014) *A bigger prize: How we can do better than the competition.* New York: Simon & Schuster.

Heller, J (2005) *Catch-22.* London: Vintage.

Higgins, M and Smith, W (2002) Babies cost less at Tescos. *Journal of Marketing Management,* 18, 833–56.

HM Government (2013) *Working together to safeguard children.* **www.gov.uk/government/uploads/system/uploads/attachment_data/file/281368/Working_together_to_safeguard_children.pdf**

HM Government (2014) Multi-agency practice guidelines: Female genital mutilation. **https://www.gov.uk/government/uploads/system/uploads/attachment_data/file/333067/FGMmulti-agencyPracticeGuidelines.pdf**

Hood, R (2014) Complexity and integrated working in children's services. *British Journal of Social Work,* 44(1), 27–43.

Horne, M (1999) *Values in social work,* 2nd edn. Aldershot: Ashgate.

House of Commons (2014) Food banks and food poverty. House of Commons briefing paper. Standard note SN06657. **www.parliament.uk/briefing-papers/sn06657.pdf**

Houston, S (2003) Establishing virtue in social work: A response to McBeath and Webb. *British Journal of Social Work,* 33, 819–24.

Howell, J (2004) New dimensions in civil society: Organising around marginalised interests, in Howell, J (ed.) *Governance in China.* London: Roman and Littlefield.

Hudson, B (2009) Captives of bureaucracy. *Community Care,* 2nd April, p31.

Hugman, R (2005) *New approaches in ethics for the caring professions.* London: Palgrave.

Hugman, R (2008) Ethics in a world of difference. *Ethics and Social Welfare,* 2(2), 118–32.

Hugman, R (2013) *Culture, values and ethics in social work: Embracing diversity.* London: Routledge.

Hutchings, A and Taylor, I (2007) Defining the profession? Exploring an international definition of social work in the China context. *International Journal of Social Welfare,* 16(4), 382–90,

Ingram, R (2013) Emotions, social work practice and supervision: An uneasy alliance? *Journal of Social Work Practice: Psychotherapeutic Approaches in Health, Welfare and the Community*, 27(1), 5–19.

International Federation of Social Workers (2012) *Definition of social work*. **http://ifsw.org/policies/definition-of-social-work/**

James, D (2004) The McDonaldization of social work – or come back Florence Hollis, all is (or should be) forgiven, in Lovelock, R, Lyons, K and Powell, J (eds) *Reflecting on social work: Discipline and profession*. Dartford: Ashgate.

Jeyasingham, D (2012) White noise: A critical evaluation of social work education's engagement with whiteness studies. *British Journal of Social Work*, 42, 669–86.

Jones, R (2005) Disruptive change. *The Guardian*, 17 October.

Jones, R (2013) The best of times, the worst of times: Social work and its moment. *British Journal of Social Work*, 44(3), 485–502.

Jones, R (2014) *The story of Baby P*. Bristol: The Policy Press.

Kadushin, A (1992) *Supervision in social work*, 3rd edn. New York: Columbia University Press.

Kafka, F (2004) *The trial*. London: Vintage.

Katiuzhinsky, A and Okech, D (2014) Human rights, cultural practices, and state policies: Implications for global social work practice and policy. *International Journal of Social Welfare*, 23(1), 80–8.

Kemshall, H (2002a) Risk assessment and management, in Davies, M (ed.) *The Blackwell companion of social work*. Oxford: Blackwell.

Kemshall, H (2002b) *Risk, social policy and welfare*. Buckingham: Open University Press.

Kohlberg, L (1984) *The psychology of moral development*. New York: Harper & Row.

Krumer-Nevo, M (2005) Listening to life knowledge: A new research direction in poverty studies. *International Journal of Social Welfare*, 14(2), 99–106.

Kwong Kam, P (2012) Back to the 'social' of social work: Reviving the social work profession's contribution to the promotion of social justice. *International Social Work*, published online, 1–25.

Lam, CW (1996) Indigenization of social work values in Hong Kong: A brief review. *Hong Kong Journal of Social Work*, 30(1), 10–21.

Laming, Lord (2003) *The Victoria Climbié inquiry*. London: The Stationery Office.

Laming, Lord (2009) *The protection of children in England: A progress report*. London: The Stationery Office.

Larson, M (1977) *The rise of professionalism*. Berkeley, CA: University of California Press.

Lawrence, E (2005) Trade unions, in Todd, M and Taylor, G (eds) *Democracy and participation*. London: Merlin Press.

Leigh, S and Miller, L (2004) Is the third way the best way? Social work intervention with children and families. *Journal of Social Work*, 4(3), 245–67.

Lewis, AE (2004) 'What group?' Studying whites and whiteness in the era of 'color blindness'. *Sociological Theory*, 22(4), 623–46.

Lister, R (2003) *Citizenship: Feminist perspectives*, 2nd edn. Basingstoke: Palgrave.

Lister, R (2004) *Poverty*. Cambridge: Blackwell/Polity Press.

Lownsborough, H and O'Leary, D (2005) *The leadership imperative: Reforming children's services from the ground up*. London: Demos.

Lymbery, M (2005) *Social work with older people*. London: Sage.

McBeath, G and Webb, SA (2002) Virtue ethics and social work: Being lucky, realistic and not doing one's duty. *British Journal of Social Work*, 32, 1015–36.

McBride, P (1998) *The assertive social worker*. Aldershot: Ashgate.

McCarthy, D (2013) Gendering 'soft' policing: Multi-agency working, female cops, and the fluidities of police culture/s, policing and society. *International Journal of Research and Policy*, 23(2), 261–78.

McDonald, A, Postle, K and Dawson, C (2008) Barriers to retaining and using professional knowledge in local authority social work practice with adults in the UK. *British Journal of Social Work*, 38, 1370–87.

McGregor, K (2013) Social workers' caseload concerns often fall on deaf ears, survey shows. *Community Care Magazine*, 3 September.

McLaughlin, K (2005) From ridicule to institutionalisation: Anti-oppression, the state and social work. *Critical Social Policy*, 25(3), 283–305.

Macpherson, W (1999) *The Stephen Lawrence inquiry*. Cmd 4262–1. London: The Stationery Office.

Malin, N, Wilmott, S and Manthorpe, J (2002) *Key concepts and debates in health and social care*. Birmingham: Open University.

Marshall, TH (1950) *Citizenship and social class*. Cambridge: Cambridge University Press.

Mayer, J and Timms, N (1970) *The client speaks*. London: Routledge.

Mental Health Network/NHS Federation (2011) *Key facts and trends in mental health*. http://www.baat.org/Key_facts_mental_health_080911.pdf

Milley, P (2002) Imagining good organizations: Moral orders or moral communities? *Educational Management & Administration*, 30(1), 47–64.

Mills, CW (1959) *The sociological imagination*. Oxford: Oxford University Press.

Mullaly, B (2002) *Challenging oppression: A critical social work approach*. Oxford: Oxford University Press.

Munro, E (2011) *Munro review of child protection: Final report – a child-centred system*. Department of Education, Cm 8062. London: The Stationery Office.

Nairey, M (2014) *Making the education of social workers consistently effective*. London: Department of Education.

National Midwifery Council (NMC) (2014) Code of conduct. http://www.nmc-uk.org/Publications/Standards/The-code/Introduction

Noyce, P (2002) *Rabbit-proof fence* (film). Buena Vista Home Entertainment.

Options (2013) *Tackling female genital mutilation in the UK: What works in community-based prevention work*. http://trustforlondon.org.uk/wp-content/uploads/2013/07/FGM-summary.pdf

Outhwaite, W (1994) *Habermas: A critical introduction*. Cambridge: Polity Press.

Parekh, B (2000) *Rethinking multiculturalism: Cultural diversity and political theory*. London: Macmillan.

Parker, S, Fook, J and Pease, B (1999) Empowerment: The modernist social work concept par excellence, in Pease, B and Fook, J (eds) *Transforming social work practice: Postmodern critical perspectives*. London: Routledge.

Parrott, L (2005) The political drivers of partnership in Carnwell, R and Buchanan, J (eds) *Effective practice in health and social care: A partnership approach*. Maidenhead: Open University Press.

Parrott, L (2008) The ethics of partnership. *Ethics and Social Welfare*, 2(1), 24–37.

Parrott, L (2009) Constructive marginality: Conflicts and dilemmas in cultural competence and anti-oppressive practice. *Social Work Education*, 28(6), 617–31.

Parrott, L (2014) *Social work and poverty*. Bristol: Policy Press.

Parton, N and O'Byrne, P (2000) *Constructive social work: Towards a new practice*. Basingstoke: Macmillan.

Payne, M (2000) *Anti-bureaucratic social work*. Birmingham: Venture Press.

Peck, E and Norman, I (1999) Working together in adult community mental health services: Exploring inter-professional role relations. *Journal of Mental Health*, 8(3), 231–42.

Peckover, S, White, S and Hall, C (2008) Making and managing electronic children: e-Assessment in child welfare. *Information, Communication and Society*, 11(3), 375–94.

Peckover, S, Hall, C and White, S (2009) From policy to practice: The implementation and negotiation of technologies in everyday child welfare. *Children and Society*, 23(2), 136–48.

Penna, S and O'Brien, M (1998) *Theorising welfare: Enlightenment and modern society*. London: Sage.

Pickett, H and Wilkinson, R (2009) *The spirit level: Why more equal societies almost always do better.* London: Allen Lane.

Picower, B (2009) The unexamined whiteness of teaching: How white teachers maintain and enact dominant racial ideologies. *Race Ethnicity and Education*, 12(2), 197–215.

Pitt, V (2010) Is fair access to care services dying? *Community Care Magazine*, 17 December.

Porter, R (2000) *Enlightenment: Britain and the creation of the modern world.* London: Allen Lane.

Prado, CG (2000) *Starting with Foucault: An introduction to genealogy.* New York: Westview.

Reamer, F (1990) *Ethical dilemmas in social services: A guide for social workers.* New York: Columbia University Press.

Rees, S (1978) *Social work face to face.* London: Edward Arnold.

Ritzer, G (1993) *The McDonaldization of society.* New York: Pine Forge Press.

Rogowski, S (2011) Social work with children and families: Challenges and possibilities in the neo-liberal world. *British Journal of Social Work*, 42(5), 921–40.

Rothstein, B (1998) *Just institutions matter: The moral and political logic of the universal welfare state.* Cambridge: Cambridge University Press.

Sandel, M (2012) *What money can't buy: The moral limits of markets.* New York: Farrar, Straus and Giroux.

Sanghera, R (2007) *Shame.* Hodder and Stoughton: London.

Sayer, A (2005) *The moral significance of class.* Cambridge: Cambridge University Press.

Schehrer, S and Sexton, S (2010) *Involving users in commissioning local services.* York: Joseph Rowntree.

Schön, D (1987) *Educating the reflective practitioner.* San Francisco, CA: Jossey-Bass.

Scourfield, P (2007) Are there reasons to be worried about the 'caretelization' of residential care? *Critical Social Policy*, 27(2), 155–80.

Sevenhuijsen, S (1998) *Citizenship and the ethics of care: Feminist considerations on justice, morality and politics.* London: Routledge.

Sewpaul, V (2007) Challenging East–West value dichotomies and essentialising discourse on culture and social work. *International Journal of Social Welfare*, 16(4), 398–407.

Sewpaul, V and Jones, D (2004) Global standards for social work education and training. *Social Work Education*, 23(5), 493–513.

Shakespeare, T (2000) *Help.* Birmingham: Venture Press.

Shardlow, S, Davis, C, Johnson, M, Long, T, Murphy, M and Race, D (2004) *Education and training for inter-agency working: New standards.* Salford: Salford Centre for Social Work Research, University of Salford.

Silvers, A, Wasserman, D and Mahowald, M (afterword by L Becker) (1998) *Disability, difference, discrimination: Perspectives on justice in bioethics and public policy.* Lanham, MD: Rowman & Littlefield.

Skeggs, B (2009) Haunted by the spectre of judgement: Respectability, value and affect in class relations, in Sveinson, K (ed.) *Who cares about the white working class?* **http://www.runnymedetrust.org/uploads/publications/pdfs/WhoCaresAboutTheWhiteWorkingClass-2009.pdf**

Smith, A (2012) 'Monday will never be the same again': The transformation of employment and work in a public–private partnership. *Work Employment and Society*, 26(1), 95–110.

Smith, MK (1996) *The functions of supervision: Encyclopedia of informal education.* Last update 28 January 2005. **www.infed.org/biblio/functions_of_supervision.htm**

Smith, M, Gallagher, M, Wosu, H, Stewart, J, Cree, V, Hunter, S and Evans, S (2012) Engaging with involuntary service users in social work: Findings from a knowledge exchange project. *British Journal of Social Work*, 42, 1460–77.

Social Exclusion Unit (2004) *Tackling social exclusion: Taking stock and looking to the future: Emerging findings.* London: Office of the Deputy Prime Minster: The Stationery Office.

Spratt, T and Houston, S (1999) Developing critical social work in theory and in practice: Child protection and communicative reason. *European Journal of Social Work*, 4(4), 315–24.

Stanford, S (2010) 'Speaking back' to fear: Responding to the moral dilemmas of risk in social work practice. *British Journal of Social Work*, 40(4), 1065–80.

Stanley, N and Manthorpe, J (2004) *The age of the inquiry: Learning and blaming in health and social care.* London: Routledge.

Stanley, N, Miller, P, Richardson-Foster, H and Thomson, G (2010) *Children and families experiencing domestic violence: Police and children's social services' responses.* NSPCC. **www.nspcc.org.uk/inform**

Stevenson, O and Parsloe, P (1993) *Community care and empowerment.* York: Rowntree Foundation with Community Care.

Sullivan, MP (2009) Social workers in community care practice: Ideologies and interactions with older people. *British Journal of Social Work*, 39(7), 1306–25.

Swain, J, French, S and Cameron, C (2003) *Controversial issues in a disabling society.* Buckingham: Open University.

Tam, TSK (2003) Humanitarian attitudes and support of government responsibility for social welfare: A study of perceptions of social work graduates in Hong Kong and the People's Republic of China. *International Social Work*, 46(4), 449–67.

Tarleton, B, Ward, L and Howarth, J (2006) *Finding the right support?* Bristol: Norah Fry Research Centre, Bristol University.

Taylor, A (1998) Hostages to fortune: The abuse of children in care, in Hunt, G (ed.) *Whistle blowing in the social services.* London: Arnold.

Thompson, N (2001) *Anti-discriminatory practice.* Basingstoke: Palgrave Macmillan.

Thompson, N (2012) *Anti-discriminatory practice: Equality, diversity and social justice.* Basingstoke: Palgrave/Macmillan.

Timms, N (1983) *Social work values: An enquiry.* London: Routledge & Kegan Paul.

Torjesen, I (2013) First UK prosecution for female genital mutilation moves a step closer. *British Medical Journal*, **doi: http://dx.doi.org/10.1136/bmj.f2981**

Tronto, J (1993) *Moral boundaries: A political argument for an ethic of care.* New York: Routledge.

Tronto, J (2010) Creating caring institutions: Politics, plurality, and purpose. *Ethics and Social Welfare*, 4(2), 158–71.

Trotter, C and Ward, T (2013) Involuntary clients, pro-social modelling and ethics. *Ethics and Social Welfare*, 7(1), 74–90.

Trussell Trust (2014) *Foodbank report 2014.* **www.trusselltrust.org/foodbank-projects**

Tsang, A, Yan, M and Shera, W (2000) Negotiating multiple agendas in international social work: The case of the China–Canada collaborative project. *Social Work and Globalization. Canadian Social Work Special Issue*, 2(1), 147–61.

UNISON (2009) *Still slipping through the net? Front-line staff assess children's safeguarding progress.* London: UNISON.

UNISON (2010) UNISON briefing on abortion: Women's right to choose – a trade union issue. **http://www.docstoc.com/docs/28700201/UNISON-BRIEFING-ON-ABORTION-Womens-right-to-choose**

Waterhouse, R (2000) *Lost in care: Report of the tribunal of inquiry into the abuse of children in care in the former county council areas of Gwynedd and Clwyd since 1974.* London: The Stationery Office.

Webb, S (2003) Local orders and global chaos in social work. *European Journal of Social Work*, 6(2), 191–204.

193

Webb, S (2006) *Social work in a risk: Society social and political perspectives.* Basingstoke: Palgrave.

White, S, Hall, C and Peckover, S (2009) The descriptive tyranny of the common assessment framework: Technologies of categorization and professional practice in child welfare. *British Journal of Social Work,* 39, 1197–217.

Williams, C and Parrott, L (2014) Anti-racism and predominantly 'white areas': Local and national referents in the search for race equality in social work education. *British Journal of Social Work,* 44, 290–309.

Williams, L and Sewpaul, V (2004) Modernism, postmodernism and global standards setting. *Social Work Education,* 23(5), 555–65.

Winefield, H and Barlow, J (1995) Client and worker satisfaction in a child protection agency. *Child Abuse and Neglect,* 19(8), 897–905.

Yeates, N (2001) *Globalization and social policy.* London: Sage.

Yip, KS (2004) A Chinese cultural critique of the global qualifying standards for social work education. *Social Work Education,* 23(5), 597–612.

Internet

Social Policy and Social Work (SWAP), subject centre of the Higher Education Academy:

- **www.swap.ac.uk**

- **www.swap.ac.uk/docs/newsletters/swapnews07.pdf** (SWAP report: Gupta, A (2004) *Involving families living in poverty in the training of social workers.* Royal Holloway: University of London.)

UNISON on whistle blowing and the Public Interest Disclosure Act 1998

- **www.unison.org.uk/knowledge/issues-at-work/whistleblowing/overview**

Index